East Asian Economic and Socio-cultural Studies
東亞經濟與社會文化論叢

Edited by Angela Schottenhammer (蕭婷)

East Asian Maritime History 8

2010
Harrassowitz Verlag · Wiesbaden

Li Kangying 李康英

The Ming Maritime Trade Policy in Transition, 1368 to 1567

2010
Harrassowitz Verlag · Wiesbaden

Publication of this book was supported by a grant of the Volkswagenstiftung.

Cover illustration: *Ming shi* 明史 (1739) by Zhang Tingyu 張廷玉 (1672–1755), *j.* 205, p. 1a–b, in *Ershiwu shi* 二十五史, vol. 48. (Taibei: Yiwen yinshuguan, no date; copy of a *qianlong*-edition, 1746), p. 2218.

Bibliografische Information der Deutschen Nationalbibliothek
Die Deutsche Nationalbibliothek verzeichnet diese Publikation in der Deutschen Nationalbibliografie; detaillierte bibliografische Daten sind im Internet über http://dnb.d-nb.de abrufbar.

Bibliographic information published by the Deutsche Nationalbibliothek
The Deutsche Nationalbibliothek lists this publication in the Deutsche Nationalbibliografie; detailed bibliographic data are available in the internet at http://dnb.d-nb.de.

For further information about our publishing program consult our website http://www.harrassowitz-verlag.de

Printed on permanent/durable paper.
Printing and binding: Memminger MedienCentrum AG
Printed in Germany

ISSN 1860-1812
ISBN 978-3-447-06172-8

CONTENTS

Acknowledgments vii
Abbreviations ix
Map x

CHAPTER I

INTRODUCTION 3

CHAPTER II

Socio-economic Institutions and Foreign Trade Policy

Confucianism and the Prohibition of Foreign Trade 24
The Redistribution of Social Wealth 27
The Suppression of Commerce 33
The Politicised Culture of Consumption 38
Currency Control 42
Self-Sufficiency 45
The Wider World 48

CHAPTER III

The Collapse of the Early Ming Institutions and Foreign Trade

Land Centralization 57
Commercialisation of the Economy 62
The Silver-Based Tax Reform 67
Paralysis of the State-run Manufacturing Industries 73
The Weakening of Conventional Values 75
The Pursuit of Politics and Social Influence by Merchants 80

CHAPTER VI

The Grand Policy Debate –
Part One: The Problem

External Pressure, the Trade Prohibition and the Wars 97
Internal Pressure, the Two Camps and the Memorial System 100
Trade Prohibition and Prejudice about 'Barbarians' 105
The Foreign Tribute Missions 110
Legitimate Grievances? 119
Social Injustice and Insurgency 123

The Military's Involvement in the Illicit Trade 127
Inability to Maintain the Policy 131

CHAPTER V

The Grand Policy Debate –
Part Two: The Solution

The Power of Trade 140
Trade Diminishes Conflict 141
Trade as a Source of Strength vis-à-vis Foreign Powers 146
Trade as a Means to Restore a China-Centred World Order 150
The Debate on How to Relievc the Financial Crisis 158
Funding the Defence Systems 164
Trade as a Means to Import the Silver 171

CHAPTER VI

Conclusion 177

BIBLIOGRAPHIE 185
INDEX 203

ACKNOWLEDGEMENTS

As it has taken ten years to research and bring to completion this book, I owe a great deal to a number of people. First of all, my gratitude goes to Professor Angela Schottenhammer, who involved me in her East Asian Maritime History project and has given me a lot of valuable suggestions on new research areas to explore for this book. Her encouragement and patience has always been an inspiration for my further efforts while her standard in minute exactitude has always generated an enhancing impact. I wish to take this occasion to thank my supervisor, Professor Brian Moloughney, for without his initial direction, his timely and valuable advice and his constant supervision my thesis would not have been possible nor would the completion of this book. I also wish to thank my doctorate thesis examiners, Professor Billy So Kee Long of Hong Kong Chinese University and Dr Duncan Campbell of Australia National University, who provided me with many expert insights to contribute to the improvement of this book. Finally, I wish to pay tribute to my university teacher, the late Professor S.A.M Adshead. His outstanding scholarship in Chinese history and great personality drew me to study under his tutelage at the University of Canterbury, and his teaching guided me towards a more comprehensive and scientific approach to the past. Unfortunately, he died earlier this year, too soon for me to be able to present him with a copy of this book as a small token of thanks for his friendship and encouragement.

My appreciation also goes to Professor Fang Baochuan 方寶川, librarian at Fujian Normal University, who provided me much assistance during two years of research at the library. He allowed me access to the 200,000 tomes of the ancient book collection in the library, which was a great privilege and was invaluable for my research. Professor Zheng Hui 鄭煇, Director of the Ancient Books department of the library, Ms Chen Biru 陳碧茹, and Dr Zheng Zhenqing 鄭振清 from the then History Department also gave me much support on a daily basis. Particularly, I am grateful to Professor Xie Bizhen 謝必震 and Professor Li Xiangmin 李湘敏 from the History Department of the University, who kindly provided me with a free apartment during my research work there.

I am grateful to Professor Lin Renchuan 林仁川 of Xiamen University for providing me with a great deal of help, not only in hunting down materials but also liaising with libraries during my research work there from 1999–2000. My thanks also go to the staff of the Ancient Book department of the Shanghai Central Library for their timely assistance during my research odyssey there from 2003–2009, especially to Liang Ying 梁穎, Zou Xiaoyan 鄒小燕, Jiang Li 蔣藜, Wu Jianwei 吳建偉, Wu Fangli 吳芳荔 Huang Yanwan 黃燕婉 and Wu Min 武敏. I wish to thank the staff at the National Library in Beijing, who allowed me to copy a great deal of useful material. In addition, I owe gratitude to the assistance from staff at the Hong Kong University library, Huadong Normal University library, the National Library in Taiwan, the Library at Taiwan National University, at Beijing University, Shandong University and also the Shandong Provincial Library. I am also grateful to my assistant Liang Fang 梁芳, for her many years of supporting work.

All of the translations in the thesis are my own, except where indicated. I owe gratitude to all the authors whose work I consulted. All the errors are mine.

I dedicate this book to my father Li Changjiu 李長久 and my mother Wang Xiuhe 汪秀荷 for their devoted parental love.

ABBREVIATIONS

MJSWB	Chen Zilong 陳子龍 (1608–1647) (ed.), *Ming jingshi wenbian* 明經世文編 (*A Collection of Ming Writings on State Affairs*). (Beijing: Zhonghua shuju, 1997).
Siku cunmu	*Siku quanshu cunmu congshu* 四庫全書存目叢書 (*The Collected Corpus of the Complete Library of the Four Treasuries*) complied by the Siku quanshu cunmu congshu bianzhuan weiyuanhui 四庫全書存目編纂委員會 (Jinan: Qilu shushe, 1997).
Siku quanshu	*Wenyuange siku quanshu* 文淵閣四庫全書 (*Wenyuange: the Complete Library of the Four Treasuries*) complied by Ji Yun 紀昀 (1724–1805) *et. al.* (Taibei: Taiwan Shangwu yinshu guan, 1986).
Siku jinhui	*Siku quanshu jinhui shu congkan* 四庫禁燬書叢刊 (*Forbidden Books from the Complete Library of the Four Treasuries*). (Beijing: Beijing chubanshe, 1998).
Siku xuxiu	*Xuxiu siku quanshu* 續修四庫全書 (*The Complete Library of the Four Treasuries: Continued and Revised*). (Shanghai: Shanghai guji chubanshe, 2002).

Map 1, p. x: Segment of coastal map; region between Changle 長樂 and Quanzhou 泉州 in Fujian; some offshore islands and military installations. (Source: Zhang Huang 章潢, *Tushu bian* 圖書編 (printed 1613), *Siku quanshu zhenben* 四庫全書珍本, *wu ji* 五集, vol. 12, *j.* 57, p. 5a).

CHAPTER I

Introduction

On a cold December night in Quedlinburg, Germany, in 1589, thirty-two women were burnt at the stake, accused of possessing mysterious powers that enabled them to perform evil deeds. Thousands of people were similarly persecuted between the fifteenth and the seventeenth centuries.[1] However, this event was not unique, as fifty years earlier on a rainy night in August, 1549, ninety-seven maritime merchants were beheaded on the coast of Zhejiang 浙江 province for violation of the Ming maritime prohibition. In addition, 117,000 coastal people were immediately banished from their homes to prevent them from going to sea. Thousands of Chinese and foreign merchants lost their lives in the subsequent military campaigns in support of the maritime interdiction.[2] If historians were asked to list the early modern phenomena that have most 'disturbed' their academic rationale, the two centuries-long witch-hunt in early modern Europe (1500–1700) and the 200 year term of the maritime prohibition, or "*haijin* 海禁" (1372–1568), during the Ming dynasty (1368–1644) would probably be near the top of the list. For the past few centuries, scholars have debated vigorously the two phenomena and tried to identify the factors that led to their formation, maintenance and eventual change. While the study of the witch-hunt has generated a degree of consensus, there are still many questions surrounding the Ming maritime prohibition.

The maritime prohibition policy, introduced in 1371 by the newly enthroned Ming founder, the Hongwu Emperor 洪武 (r. 1368–1398), was institutionalised to maintain systematic control over foreign contact and foreign trade relations. Chinese people were prevented from leaving the empire and foreigners from entering it. The regulations stated: "Coastal people are prohibited from going to sea",[3] and "Coastal people are forbidden from contacting all foreigners."[4] It was decreed: "Those who have trade dealings with 'barbarians' deserve the death penalty and their family members will be sent into exile. Their neighbours, if found to have failed to report them to the authorities, will be declared guilty and receive the same punishment."[5] Facilities for ocean-going voyages were purposefully destroyed. Regulations stipulated that "no ships with two masts are allowed to be built, and

1 H. C. Erik Midelfort, "Heartland of the Witch Craze: Central and Northern Europe", *History Today* 31 (1981), p. 28.

2 *Huang Ming Jia-Long liangchao wenjian ji shi'erjuan* 皇明嘉隆兩朝聞見纪十二卷 (*Minutes of the Imperial Jiajing and Longqing Administrations in twenty volumes*) edited by Shen Yue 沈越 (*jinshi* Jiajing era – 1522–66), in *Siku quanshu cunmu congshu* 四庫全書存目叢書 (*Complete Corpus of the Four Treasuries*) complied by Siku quanshu cunmu congshu bianzhuan weiyuanhui 四庫全書存目編纂委員會. (Jinan: Qilu shushe, 1997), 史, fasc. 7, *j.* 8, p. 14b [hereafter *Siku cunmu*].

3 *Ming Taizu shilu* 明太祖實錄 (*The Veritable Records of Ming Taizu*), in *Ming shilu* 明實錄 by Yao Guangxiao 姚廣孝 (1334–1418), Xia Yuanji 夏元吉 (1366–1430) *et. al.* (Nanjing: Jiangsu Chinese Studies Library printed copy 江蘇國學圖書館傳抄本影印, 1940), *j.* 70, p. 4a.

4 *Ming Taizu shilu*, *j.* 139, p. 8a.

5 *Piyu zaji* 甓餘雜集 (*Ritual of Brick-carrying to Sharpen my will, Miscellaneous Writings to Demonstrate my Zeal*) by Zhu Wan 朱紈 (1494–1550), in *Siku cunmu* 集, fasc. 78, *j.* 4, p. 27a.

those already made have to be dismantled without exception."[6] Trading ports were deliberately paralysed with stone, rocks and pine stakes. The export of Chinese commodities and the import of foreign goods were forbidden. "Foreign goods, if possessed, must be destroyed within three months."[7] The coast was heavily guarded: "Seventy-four military garrisons were established from Guangdong 廣東 to Shandong 山東. One in every four peasants was drafted to patrol the coast."[8] The grand ideal of the policy was to maintain an imagined situation where "not a single piece of wood was allowed to float in the sea."[9] The *haijin* was not only a policy of the Hongwu administration but was instituted as a part of the *Ancestral Injunctions* (*Huang Ming zuxun* 皇明祖訓) to be upheld by all following administrations. For nearly 200 years, from its establishment in 1371 until its abolition in 1568, the policy remained an important part of the 'established practices of the ancestors' (*zuzong chengfa* 祖宗成法).

During the two centuries in which the maritime prohibition was enforced Chinese and foreign traders tried all ways possible to break the interdiction by smuggling and "piracy". The wars with 'pirates' constituted a major part of the Ming defence. The threat from the "*beilu nanwo* 北盧南倭" (Mongols in the north and Japanese pirates in the south) dominated the Ming political, financial and defence agendas as long as the maritime prohibition policy stood.[10]

It is difficult to understand the logic behind this policy. From the political perspective, why did the Ming administration devote such effort to waging war on merchants who were not enemies of the state but rather people who sought to benefit China through their trading activities? The policy weakened the dynasty's political strength by exhausting its resources in an effort to maintain this continual conflict, which could well have been avoided. Similarly, from an economic perspective, it is hard to fathom why the Ming government deliberately blocked a channel that would have enabled it to gain a considerable amount of revenue, especially when international trade was so lucrative and Chinese products were in such high demand throughout the world. And where was the logic in an administration shutting itself off from the opportunity to enhance its economy by importing what the

6 *Mingshi jishi benmo* 明史記事本末 (*A Complete Record of Important Events in Ming History*) by Gu Yingtai 穀應泰 (*jinshi* 1647), in *Wenyuange Siku quanshu* 文淵閣四庫全書 (*Wenyuange: Complete Library of the Four Treasuries*) complied by Ji Yun 紀昀 (1724–1805) *et. al.* (Taibei: Taiwan Shangwu yinshu guan 臺灣商務印書館, 1986), fasc. 364, *j.* 55, p. 10b [hereafter *Sisku quanshu*].

7 *Ming Taizu shilu*, *j.* 231, p. 2b. See also *Ming Yingzong shilu* 明英宗實錄 (*The Veritable Records of Ming Yingzong*), in *Ming shilu* 明實錄 by Yao Guangxiao 姚廣孝 (1334–1418), Xia Yuanji 夏元吉 (1366–1430) *et.al.* (Nanjing: Jiangsu Chinese Studies Library printed copy 江蘇國學圖書館傳抄本影印, 1940), *j.* 179, p. 15a.

8 *Zheng Duanjian gong nianpu* 鄭端簡公年譜 (*A Chronological Biography of Zheng Xiao, Posthumous Title Duanjian*) by Zheng Lüchun 鄭履淳 (*jinshi* 1562), in *Siku cunmu* 史, fasc. 83, *j.* 3, p. 25b.

9 *Ming shi* 明史 (*The Official History of the Ming Dynasty*) by Zhang Tingyu 張廷玉 (1672–1755) *et. al.*, in *Siku quanshu*, fasc. 300, *j.* 205, p. 1b.

10 *Yanzhou shiliao qianji* 弇州史料前集 (*Wang Shizhen's Collection of Historical Materials; First Part*) by Wang Shizhen 王世貞 (1526–1590), *Siku cunmu* 史 112, *j.* 18, p. 37a.

empire most needed? Such questions as these provide an agenda for the historian to explore. Why was such an apparently nonsensical institution created? What was the mechanism by which it was maintained for so long? And why was such a supposedly unchallengeable constitutional charter eventually challenged and abolished? But perhaps the most important question of all relates to the dynamic that was driving forward the change. What social and economic forces underlay this transformation? Who was it that wanted to see this apparently well-entrenched institutional structure removed and how were they able to succeed in this task?

We are often told that the Chinese emperors would make decisions with a strong regard to precedents and that "the literati officials always looked to the past for guidance in dealing with the present."[11] But there is no evidence that the early Ming administration was following precedent in imposing the maritime prohibitions. International trade had been a major source of revenue in former dynasties. As early as the Tang dynasty (618–907), "the state treasury relied heavily on the income from maritime trade."[12] During the Huangchao uprising (*huangchao qiyi* 黄巢起義, 875–883), when the rebels were marching on Guangzhou 廣州 in 878, Yu Cong 於琮 (?–881), Prime Minister at the court of Tang Xizong 唐僖宗 (r. 874–888), warned the emperor: "If the rebels take over the Guangzhou Maritime Trade Office our state coffers may soon dry up."[13] This was no exaggeration. The income from maritime trade was never less than the total income from the summer and autumn land taxes (*xiaqiu liangshui* 夏秋兩稅).[14] Once the Maritime Trade Office fell into rebel hands the administration soon encountered financial difficulties.[15] The emperor "had no option but to borrow half of the government expenditure from wealthy families and even barbarian merchants from the steppe."[16]

During the Northern and Southern Song dynasties (北宋 907–1127, 南宋 1128–1279), income from maritime trade rose to even higher levels. During the Southern Song in particular, "state revenue from maritime trade reached as much as 20 per cent of the Gross Domestic Product (GDP) in 1128."[17] Customs duties from

11 Raymond Dawson, *The Chinese Experience.* (London: Weidenfeld and Nicholson, 1978), p. 22. See also L. S. Stavrianos, *A Global History: from Prehistory to the Present.* (Eaglewood Cliffs, N. J.: Prentice-Hall, 1991), p. 149.

12 Yu Siwei 于思偉, "Guangzhou shibo si de lishi yange jiqi zai duiwai maoyi zhong de zuoyong he yingxiang 廣州市舶司的歷史沿革及其在對外貿易中的作用和影響" (The Evolution of the Maritime Trade Office at Guangzhou and its Role and Impact in Foreign Trade), *Haijiao shi yanjiu* 海交史研究 5 (1983), pp. 72–73.

13 *Jiu Tang shu* 舊唐書 (*The Old Tang History*) by Liu Xu 劉昫 (888–947) *et. al.*, in *Siku quanshu*, fasc. 271, *j.* 178, p. 16a.

14 *Jiu Tang shu*, *j.* 151, p. 12a.

15 *Jiu Tang shu*, *j.* 178, p. 16a.

16 *Zizhi tongjian* 資治通鑒 (*Comprehensive Mirror for Aid in Government*) by Sima Guang 司馬光 (1019–1086), in *Siku quanshu*, fasc. 309, *j.* 253, pp. 16a–b, 20b, 36b.

17 Chen Yan 陳炎, "Lun haishang sichou zhi lu yu zhongwai wenhua jiaoliu 論海上絲綢之路與中外文化交流" (The Maritime Silk Route and Cultural Exchanges between China and the Outside World), in *Zhongguo yu haishang sichou zhi lu* 中國與海上絲綢之路 (*China and the Maritime Silk Route*). (Quanzhou: Fujian Publishing House, 1991), p. 3.

the three maritime trade offices of Fujian 福建, Guangdong 廣東 and Zhejiang 浙江 alone reached 2,000,000 *min* 緡 in 1159, at a time when the Gross National Product (GNP) was about forty million *min*.[18] The Shenzong emperor 神宗 (r. 1068–1085) proudly declared: "Maritime trade was the number one source of revenue from the southeast of the empire."[19] After the Mongol conquest of China, maritime trade became an important source of revenue that underlay both extensive government expenditure and aggressive military campaigns. In 1272, facing significant financial pressure in order to build a new capital in Dadu 大都 (now Beijing), Qubilai Qan (1215–1294; reigning as Yuan Shizong 元世祖, r. 1260–1294) budgeted the revenue from commerce at a new high of around 45,000 *ding* 錠 (silver ingot) per year. Remarkably, in 1289 revenue reached 450,000 *ding*, largely as a result of administrative support for maritime trade and government protection for merchants. [20] During the Mongol Yuan dynasty (1279–1367) commercial activity reached a new high as the government put everything for sale into the 'global market'. Along with the traditional Chinese goods of silk and porcelain, copper coinage and silver bullion were also significant export items. On account of trade policies that were conducive to maritime activity, the Yuan witnessed so great an outflow and inflow of goods that its paper currency, the *Zhongtong baochao* 中統寶鈔, was said to have become valid in all regions and for an unlimited time period.[21] Indeed, Marco Polo noted that "the Yuan paper notes were as good and pure as gold. All his [the Qan's] subjects receive it without hesitation … because the holder can use it to purchase gold and silver or jewels."[22]

Whereas maritime trade was an important source of revenue during the Tang, Song and Yuan dynasties, it was disregarded and feared by the early Ming administration. Private trade was outlawed. Tribute trade (*gongbo* 貢舶) was the only legal form of trade and it was unilaterally arranged and monopolised by the Ming court.

18 *Jianyan yilai xinian yaolu* 建炎以來繫年要錄 (*Important Files Arranged by Year Since the Reign Period Jianyan*) by Li Xinchuan 李心傳 (1167–1244), in *Siku quanshu*, fasc. 327, *j.* 183, p. 20a. See also Lu Wei 盧葦, "Song Dai haiwai maoyi he dongnanya geguo guanxi 宋代海外貿易和東南亞各國關係" (Maritime Trade and Relations with Southeast Asia during the Song), *Haijiao shi yanjiu* 海交史研究 1 (1985), p. 14.

19 *Song shi* 宋史 (*The Official History of the Song Dynasty*) by Tuo Tuo 脫脫 (1314–1355) *et. al.*, in *Siku quanshu*, fasc. 283, *j.* 186, pp. 24a–b.

20 *Yuan shi* 元史 (*The Official History of the Yuan Dynasty*) by Song Lian 宋濂 (1310–1381), in *Siku quanshu*, fasc. 293, *j.* 94, pp. 26a–b.

21 *Qinding xu wenxian tongkao* 欽定續文獻通考 (*Imperially Commissioned Encyclopeadia of Historical Works, Continued*) by Cao Renhu 曹仁虎 (1730–1786), in *Siku quanshu*, fasc. 626, *j.* 9, pp. 2a–5a. See also "Caiji yi 財計一", in *Mingyi daifang lu* 明夷待訪錄 (A *Plan for a Prince*) by Huang Zongxi 黃宗羲 (1610–1695). (Sichuan cungu shuju edition, 1767–1849), in *Xuxiu siku quanshu* 續修四庫全書 (*The Complete Library of the Four Treasuries: Continued and Revised*). (Shanghai: Shanghai guji chubanshe, 2002), fasc. 945, pp. 42b–43a (no *juan*) [hereafter *Siku xuxiu*]. See also Jacques Gernet, *A History of Chinese Civilization*, translated by J. R. Foster. (Cambridge: Cambridge University Press, 1982), pp. 371–372.

22 Marco Polo, *The Travels of Marco Polo.* Edited and Introduced by Manuel Komroff. (New York: Liveright Publication Corporation, 1953), Book II, pp. 159–160.

The items that could be traded and their prices were fixed and controlled by the Ming administration.[23] Finance ministers issued the following directions to those involved in administering the trade: "Any foreign goods imported with the tributary mission, whatever, are tax-free"[24]; "pay them a few times higher than the price offered in order not to lose their affection"[25]; "always give more than we take."[26] Qiu Jun 丘濬 (1418–1495), Senior Grand Secretary during the first part of the Hongzhi reign 弘治 (r. 1488–1505), claimed that the government did not make any money at all from the tributary trade.[27] In other words, during the early Ming dynasty foreign trade lost its economic identity and became primarily an aspect of the administration's political activities. Even the Yongle emperor 永樂 (r. 1403–1424), notwithstanding his support for the famous maritime explorations led by Zheng He 鄭和 (1375–1435), still regarded profit from trade as shameful. When advised by his officials to levy duty on the goods brought in by the foreign merchants he was annoyed:

> It is not for profit that the government should tax foreign merchants … they are attracted by our morality and righteousness, not by profit! How shameful for us to make profit out of them. Even if we do levy duty on them, how little will that be? We lose more dignity than profit![28]

The early Ming approach to foreign trade presents a dramatic contrast to the approach undertaken by its predecessors, the Tang, Song and Yuan administrations, all of which did their utmost to facilitate and promote maritime trade. As early as the ninth century, the Tang Wenzong emperor 唐文宗 (r. 827–835) instigated a liberal framework for the Tang trade policy. In 834 he decreed: "Foreign goods in whatever quantity are to be free for sale throughout the empire so long as merchants have paid their ten per cent duty and completed *guanmai* 官買 (government purchase)."[29] Earlier still, Tang Taizong 唐太宗 (r. 627–650) made a great effort to protect the interests of merchants from being infringed by local officials. He out-

23 The court demanded that its neighbouring countries show their political obedience ceremonially by paying tribute to the Ming court, and as a reward the court allowed them to trade some of their local products along with the tribute mission. The government was usually the main trade partner. The granting of permission to participate in such tributary trade arrangements became a form of political leverage that the early Ming administration used over its tribute states.

24 *Ming Taizu shilu*, *j.* 45, p. 17a.

25 *Shuyu zhouzi lu* 殊域周咨錄 (*A Comprehensive Record on Foreign Countries*) by Yan Congjian 嚴從簡 (*jinshi* 1535), Wanli-edition, in *Siku xuxiu*, fasc. 735, *j.* 8, p. 18a (467).

26 *Ming Taizu shilu*, *j.* 71, p. 1b.

27 *Daxue yanyi bu* 大學衍義補 (*Supplement to the "Elucidation on the Great Learning"*) by Qiu Jin (1420–1495), in Cao Renhu, *Qinding xu wenxian tongkao*, *j.* 26, p. 26b.

28 *Ming shi*, in *Siku quanshu*, fasc. 298, *j.* 81, p. 27b.

29 *Tianxia junguo libing shu* 天下郡國利病書 (*Strengths and Weaknesses of the Various Regions of the Realm*) by Gu Yanwu 顧炎武 (1613–1682). (Erlin zhaizang edition 二霖齋藏, 1901), *j.* 120, p. 3b.

lawed the imposition of a surcharge on foreign merchants.[30] To enhance the confidence of foreign merchants doing business in China, the Taizong administration granted permits for them to reside in China for as long as they wished: "Foreign merchants were allowed to buy and own property so long as this was purchased with income derived from their trade in China."[31] As a consequence of this, "some foreign traders lived in China for eight generations and became great property owners."[32] Furthermore, the government also provided them with a favourable insurance policy: "If a merchant died in China his property would be looked after by the government for three months pending claim by family or relatives."[33] During the reign of the Daizong emperor 代宗 (r. 763–799), the combination of supportive business conditions and a free-trade atmosphere attracted around 4,000 merchant ships to Guangzhou each year.[34]

The Song emperors went even further than the Tang in promoting international trade. For instance, ignoring his status as 'Son of Heaven', Emperor Taizong (r. 976–997), became personally involved in promoting trade abroad. During the Yongxi 雍熙 (984–987) era, he dispatched eight officials along four different routes to deliver his invitation to merchants overseas, a handwritten message on a piece of silk.[35] The Taizong administration encouraged its officials and merchants to engage in maritime trade by rewarding them with offices and promotion. A decree from the court states: "A higher office will be rewarded to any official who can generate one million *min* annually in tariff revenue from maritime trade in Fujian and Guangdong."[36] As a result of this, Cai Jing 蔡景 (1046–1126) was promoted from the position of "*gangshou* 綱首" (leader of a transport mission) to that of "*chengxinlang* 承信郎" (Master of Ceremonies for Foreign Trade), as he managed to generate 980,000 *min* in revenue from business loan arrangements in trade with foreign maritime merchants. Over and above that, the emperor even awarded official tittles to foreigners who made contributions to promoting trade. A "*Dashi fanke* 大食番客" (a guest from an Arab country) named Louxin 儸辛, was given the official title of *chengxinlang* owing to his business with China being worth some 300,000 *min*.[37] The Song government did not hesitate to spend hard-earned revenue in order to please foreign merchants and make them feel needed and respected. "The Song Zhenzong Emperor (r. 998–1021) in 1009 sent his special envoy to ride a thousand miles trip from

30 *Quan Tang wen* 全唐文 (*Complete Documents of the Tang*) by Dong Gao 董誥 (1740–1818). (Shanghai: Shanghai guji chubanshe, 1990), *j.* 75, p. 342.

31 *Zizhi tongjian* 資治通鑒 (*Comprehensive Mirror for Aid in Government*) by Sima Guang 司馬光 (1019–1086), annotated by Hu Sanxing 胡三省 (1230–1302). (Shanghai: Shanghai guji chubanshe, 1986), p. 1547.

32 Ibid.

33 *Xin Tang shu* 新唐書 (*The New Tang History*) by Ouyang Xiu 歐陽修 (1007–1072), in *Siku quanshu*, fasc. 275, *j.* 163 p. 4a.

34 *Jiu Tang shu*, *j.* 131, p. 3b. See also see Yu Siwei, "Guangzhou shibo si de lishi," p. 73.

35 *Song shi*, fasc. 283, *j.* 186, p. 23b.

36 *Song shi*, fasc. 283, *j.* 185, p. 32a.

37 Ibid.

the capital to Guangzhou, where a large number of foreign guests gathered, to pay visit to them, reward them and entertain them on behalf of the court."[38] Millions of *guan* 貫 had to be disbursed from the Treasury to pay the costs associated with this (strings of cash, in paper currency) 'etiquette' (i.e. visits, rewards, and entertainment).[39]

The Yuan (1206–1368) surpassed both the Tang and Song administrations in implementing policies designed to encourage maritime trade. Duties on foreign goods were reduced to 1/25th and 1/30th of the value of the transaction, whereas during the Tang and Song dynasties they were set at around at 10 per cent.[40] However, this favourable duty was not the real 'magic wand' which generated the vitality of maritime trade under the Yuan. It was the trading partnership between the government and merchants that made the real difference. Qubilai Qan made maritime trade a state monopoly in the 21st year of the Zhiyuan reign (1284): under this system, the "Government provided both capital and ships to merchants; with 30 per cent of the profit going to the merchants and 70 per cent to the government."[41] Such partnerships were compulsory, and wealthy families were not allowed to engage in maritime trade independently. This policy has two implications. On the one hand, the problem of limited finance that had restrained some merchants from expanding the scope of their businesses no longer existed, while on the other hand, it was the government rather than merchants that took most of the risk. As a result, merchants under the Yuan became more competitive and more ambitious. Foreign trade became so indispensable to Qubilai Qan that, in the fifteenth year of his reign (1278), he personally invited the Japanese to come to China for trade, in spite of the hostile bilateral relations at the time.[42] Similarly, in very first year of his reign, the Wenzong emperor 元文宗 (r. 1328–1329) invited Japanese traders to Fujian for trade and selected officials to work out a favourable tariff for them.[43]

This history of encouragement of maritime trade during the 750 odd years from the Tang to the Yuan seemed to have little effect on the early Ming government. The Hongwu Emperor deliberately reversed the general trend of maritime trade history in what seems like an irrational way. Instead of encouraging his subjects to engage in maritime trade, like his predecessors Tang Taizong and Song Taizong had done, the Hongwu Emperor deterred them: "If I do not prohibit you, you could be lured by profit in trade and eventually be punished by law."[44] He believed that "the

38 *Xu zizhi tongjian changbian* 續資治通鑒長編 (*Comprehensive Mirror for Aid in Government, Continued*) by Li Tao 李燾 (1115–1184), in *Siku quanshu*, fasc. 315, *j.* 72, p. 27a; also *Lingwai daida* 嶺外代答 (*Instead of Answers to What is Beyond the Mountain Passes*) by Zhou Qufei 周去非 (*jinshi* 1163, ?–after 1178), in *Siku quanshu*, fasc. 589, *j.* 3, pp. 11b–12a.

39 Lu Wei 蘆葦, *Zhongwei guanxi shi* 中外關係史 (*A history of China's foreign relations*). (Lanzhou: Lanzhou University Press, 1996), p. 224.

40 *Yuan shi xinbian* 元史新編 (*The New Edition of the Official History of the Yuan Dynasty*) by Wei Yuan 魏源 (1794–1857), in *Siku xuxiu*, fasc. 315, *j.* 88, pp. 20a–b.

41 Ibid., *j.* 88, p. 20a.

42 Cao Renhu, *Qinding xu wenxian tongkao*, *j.* 26, p. 15a.

43 Ibid., *j.* 25, p. 25a.

44 *Ming Taizu shilu*, *j.* 70, p. 8b.

ignorant coastal people were so benighted that they contacted barbarians for trade."[45] He branded those people who went in for trade rather than toiled in paddy fields 'vagabonds', and decreed "Vagabonds are to be arrested."[46] Even the legal tributary trade, the "*shibo* 市舶", was constrained by harsh conditions. Japan was restricted to pay tribute only once every 10 years, with missions to comprise no more than 200 people and the port of entry limited to Ningbo 寧波. The state of Jiaozhi 交趾 (in present-day Vietnam) was allowed to pay tribute once every three years via a port in Guangdong. The Ryūkyū Kingdom 琉球 was permitted to send tribute missions twice a year but with no more than 50 emissaries each time and only through the port of Minxian 閩縣 in Fujian province.[47]

Whereas Tang Taizong had issued 'permanent residence' to the foreign traders, and Song Xiaozong (r. 1163–1189) spent millions entertaining overseas merchants, the Ming Jaijing Emperor 嘉靖 (r. 1521–1567) organized 200,000 soldiers to attack and pursue foreign merchants.[48] Similarly, whereas the Yuan government had built numerous inns and business centres along trading routes for merchants' convenience and had stationed government-dispatched military archers to guard their hotels and protect their lives and goods,[49] the Hongwu Emperor ordered the construction of fifty-nine heavily-manned fortresses along the Zhejiang coast and sixteen along the Fujian coast to prevent foreign merchants from getting ashore.[50] The Duke of Tangguo 湯國公 (1326–1395) ordered a 300-roomed Grand Buddhist temple on Putuoshan Island 普陀山 burnt to the ground in 1387, suspecting it housed illicit traders passing themselves off as pilgrims.[51] Anyone found to be trading with foreigners was to be evacuated from their hometown for good.[52] Whereas during preceding dynasties the income from maritime trade had been an indispensable part of government income, the early Ming administration had no hesitation in spending

45 *Ming Taizu shilu*, *j.* 23, p. 2b.

46 "Dagao xubian 大誥續編" (Imperial Pronoucement, Continued) by Zhu Yuanzhang 朱元璋 (r. 1368–1397), in *Zhaodai wangzhang* 昭代王章 (*The Great Law Code of a Venerated Dynasty*) by Xiong Mingqi 熊鳴岐 (*jinshi* 1607), in *Xuanlantang congshu* 玄覽堂叢書 (*Collection from the Xuanlan Ancestry Hall*). (Nanjing: Guoli zhongyan tushuguan, 1947), *j.* 1, pp. 57b–58a.

47 *Da Ming huidian* 大明會典 (*The Collected Statutes of the Ming Dynasty*) by Shen Shixing 申時行 (1535–1614), in *Siku xuxiu*, fasc. 791, *j.* 105, 4b–8a.

48 *Wobian shiluo* 倭變事略 (*A Record of Japanese Piracy*) by Cai Jiude 采九德 (Ming), in *Congshu jicheng chubian* 叢書集成初編 (*First Edition of a Comprehensive Collection of Documents*). (Beijing: Zhonghua shuju, 1985), *j.* 3, p. 61.

49 Tian Changwu 田昌五, *Zhongguo fengjian shehui jingji shi* 中國封建社會經濟史 (*A Social and Economic History of Feudal China*). (Jinan: Qilu Wenjin Publication, 1994), vol. 3, p. 728.

50 Gu Yingtai, *Mingshi jishi benmo*, in *Siku quanshu*, fasc. 364, *j.* 55, pp. 3a–b.

51 *Putoushan zhi* 普陀山志 (*Annals of Putoushan*) by Xu Yan 許琰 (Qing), in *Siku xuxiu*, fasc. 723, *j.* 2, p. 2a.

52 (*Guangxu*) *Dinghai ting zhi* 定海廳誌 (*The Gazetteer of Dinghai Prefecture*) by Huang Yizhou 黄以周 (1828–1899) and Chen Zhongwei 陳重威, in *Zhongguo difangzhi jicheng* 中國地方誌集成 (*The Collected Chinese Gazetteers*). (Nanjing: Jiangsu guji chubanshe, 1991), vol. 38, *j.* 20, p. 6a.

two million *taels* of silver, the total annual cash revenue the government received, on blocking maritime trade.[53]

What motivated the early Ming administration to go against the traditional current of maritime trade? What was the rationale for maintaining such a costly system? And why was the maritime trade prohibition lifted after being maintained so strictly for 200 years? It has been generally agreed by scholars that the fundamental reason for this policy, one that explains such a reversal of past practice, was the need to defend the Chinese coast against Japanese piracy. No alternate arguments have been put forward that seem more convincing than this.

John Wills directly related Japanese piracy to the policy of maritime prohibition. He argued: "It is clear that a very important determinant of early Ming policies toward maritime foreign relations was the court's reaction to the menace of the 'Japanese pirates,' many of whom were actually Chinese. Private maritime trade by Chinese was entirely prohibited."[54] Along the same lines, James Geiss argues that the eventual military victory over these pirates explains the lifting of the prohibition policy. The prohibition policy was lifted only after "much of the land and many people who had formerly been in the hands of brigands returned to imperial control" in 1567 (a year before the prohibition was lifted) and piracy was obviously no longer a serious problem along the southeast coast.[55] Similarly, John K. Fairbank emphasized the political and social disorder caused by Japanese piracy. He argued that the prohibition on maritime trade came from the government's response to this growing problem.[56] Wang Gungwu approaches the issue from the perspective of resources, suggesting that the maritime prohibition was a necessary part of a larger policy aimed at controlling the Mongols. He argues that the maritime prohibition was an expedient measure because the Hongwu Emperor could not afford to carry out the same aggressive foreign policy as the Yuan had enjoyed. He faced a considerable threat from the north, where the Mongols remained powerful, and needed to secure his southern and south-eastern coast so that he could concentrate on pacifying the great Mongolian-Turkish confederation that occupied the region between western Manchuria and eastern Tibet. Consequently, the Hongwu Emperor sought to nullify any threat from the coast through the implementation of the maritime

53 *Chongkan jingchuan xiansheng wenji* 重刊荊川先生文集 (*Reprinted Collected Works of Mr Tang Shunzhi, Hao Jingchuan*), by Tang Shunzhi 唐順之 (1507–1560). (Shanghai: Shanghai hanfenlou cang, Wanli keben 上海涵芬樓藏明萬歷刻本, 1574–1619), in *Sibu congkan*, *j.* 8, p. 57b.

54 John E. Wills Jnr., "Relations with Maritime Europeans, 1514–1662," in Frederick W. Mote & Denis Twitchett (eds.), *The Cambridge History of China*, Volume 8, *The Ming Dynasty*, 1368–1644, Part 2. (Cambridge: Cambridge University Press, 1998), p. 334.

55 James Geiss, "The Chia-ching reign, 1522–1566", in Frederick W. Mote & Denis Twitchett (eds.), *The Cambridge History of China*, Volume 7, *The Ming Dynasty*, 1368–1644, Part 1. (Cambridge: Cambridge University Press, 1988), p. 504.

56 John K. Fairbank & Edwin, O. Reischauer, *China: Tradition and Transformation*. (London: Allen & Unwin, 1989), p. 203.

prohibition.[57] Chen Xuewen 陳學文 argues that the main reasons for maritime prohibition were, on the one had, the political fragmentation in Japan during the sixteenth century and the consequent loss of control by Japanese pirates, and on the other, the weakness of the Chinese coastal defences.[58]

The defence policy approach seems convincing. No sooner had the new dynasty been established than the Hongwu Emperor realised the vulnerability in national security. The threat from the Mongols remained a reality. Although driven out of China, the Mongols still claimed to "have an army of one million archers on horseback."[59] They still occupied a large territory, stretching across the north from Liaodong 遼東 to the east of Shaanxi 陝西. In the three military confrontations after the Yuan court had fled Dadu, the Ming armies were defeated twice. A stalemate situation had lasted ten years until 1382.[60] The Hongwu Emperor told his government: "We must carefully prepare for war, we must choose capable generals and train soldiers in the north because the "*hu* 胡" (Mongols from the north) and *rong* 戎 (peoples from the west) are dangerous on the border."[61] When the Ming released Maidiribala 買的里八剌, son of the former Zhaozong emperor 元昭宗 (r. 1371–1378), and then recognized the legitimacy of Mongol rule in the northern regions, the former Yuan court showed little appreciation.[62] No one grasped the implication of this better than the emperor himself, who recognized that the Mongols were "roving along the border intending to restore the Yuan."[63] Here we see the cogency of Wang Gungwu's argument. Priority was given to defence against the aggressive Mongols in the northern border region and this gave rise to a passive attitude towards coastal defence. The inability to afford a more comprehensive policy along the coast was one of the vital factors behind the introduction of the maritime prohibition. As Wang Gungwu argues, the first Ming emperor could not afford to fight the Mongols in the north and "his southern neighbors at the same time."[64] The human and material scarcity in the early Ming years was devastating. The late Yuan crisis and years of war exhausted the national resources. "The society and economy in the early years was in a destitute situation. In the ten counties of

57 Wang Gungwu, "Ming Foreign Relations: Southeast Asia", in Denis Twitchett & Frederick W. Mote (eds.) *The Cambridge History of China*, Volume 8 (1998), p. 308.

57 Gu Yingtai, *Mingshi jishi benmo*, *j.* 10, pp. 30b–31a.

58 Chen Xuewen 陳學文, "Mingdai haijin yu wokou 明代海禁與倭寇" (The Maritime Prohibition and Japanese Pirates in the Ming Dynasty), in Yang Guozhen 楊國禎 (ed.), *Zhongguo shehui jingjishi yanjiu* 中國社會經濟史研究 (*Studies in the Socio-economic History of China*). (Xiamen: Xiamen daxue chubanshe, 1983), pp. 33–36.

59 Gu Yingtai, *Mingshi jishi benmo*, *j.* 10, p. 31a.

60 Cai Meibiao 蔡美彪, *Zhonguuo tongshi* 中國通史 (*A General History of China*). (Hongkong: Sanlian shuju, 1995), *j.* 7, p. 6.

61 *Huang Ming zuxun* 皇明祖訓 (*Emperor Taizu's Ancestral Injunctions*) by Zhu Yuanzhang 朱元璋 (1368–1396), in *Siku cunmu* 史, fasc. 264, pp. 5b–6a.

62 Cai Meibiao 蔡美彪, Li Xun 李洵, Nan Bingwen 南炳文 and Tang Gang 湯綱, *Zhonguuo tongshi* 中國通史 (*A General History of China*). (Beijing: Renmin chubanshe, 1993), pp. 6–7.

63 Ibid., p. 7.

64 Wang Gungwu, "Ming Foreign Relations: Southeast Asia" (1998), p. 303.

Changde prefecture 常德 in Hunan province 湖南, nobody was found working in the fields. Most people had fled and their lands were unattended."[65] In Yangzhou 揚州, once a thriving commercial city, there were said to be only 18 households that remained occupied.[66] The crisis of human and material resources and the continued tension along the northern border meant that maritime policy was given little attention; it was sacrificed to greater needs.

As a defence policy, the maritime prohibition was seen as a relatively effective way to deal with the Japanese, the so-called "*dongyi* 東夷" (eastern barbarians). The new dynasty hoped to use trade as leverage for political manipulation. The huge demand for Chinese products in Japan, many of which were objects commonly used in Japanese daily life, such as cotton, sewing needles, porcelain and iron woks, made the early Ming administrations believe that it could use trade as a way to enforce its political interests. After the disruption to trade caused by the Mongol-Japanese wars, the Ming administration wanted to use the 'carrot' of trade access to restore the tribute relationship.[67] The ten-year restriction on tribute missions from Japan was devised as a means to strengthen Ming political control in the East Asian region. In practice, however, the restricted tribute trade resulted in continued instability along the coastal regions. The Japanese dependence on Chinese products meant that it was simply impossible to meet the demand for Chinese goods through a single tribute mission once every ten years. In addition, the long period of political disunity in Japan had shattered its society and economy. Trade with China came to be seen as critical for the survival of many people in Japan. Therefore smuggling and piracy became rampant: all sorts of people – frustrated warriors, discontented soldiers and bankrupt merchants – were pushed by poverty and social instability at home into piracy along the China coast; whenever confronted by Ming coastal defences "they would pillage the coastal areas and abduct men and women for ransom."[68]

The Hongwu Emperor regarded piracy as a sign of disrespect for his authority and blamed it on the Japanese emperor. The Ming court sent a letter of warning to the Japanese emperor, threatening military invasion if the Japanese government did not bring a halt to the piracy.[69] The Japanese response surprised and angered the Hongwu Emperor: "Your great empire may be able to invade Japan, but our small state is not short of a strategy to defend ourselve."[70] The Japanese knew they had nothing to lose as the once-every-ten-year tributary trade (with no more than two ships) did nothing to solve their economic problems. Piracy was the only way to

---

65 Li Longqian 李龍潛, *Ming Qing jingji shi* 明清經濟史 (*An Economic History of the Ming and Qing periods*). (Guangzhou: Guangdong Education Publishing House, 1987), p. 1.

66 *Ming Taizu shilu*, *j.* 5, p. 4b.

67 Gu Yingtai, *Mingshi jishi benmo*, *j.* 55, pp. 1b–2a.

68 *Ming Taizu shilu*, *j.* 36, p. 14a.

69 Ibid., *j.* 138, pp. 2b–3a.

70 *Dongxiyang kao* 東西洋考 (A Study of the Eastern and Western Oceans) by Zhang Xie 張燮 (1574–1640), in *Siku quanshu*, fasc. 594, *j.* 6, p. 3b.

break the maritime interdiction. The threatened military invasion never took place, as the disastrous experience of the Mongol attempt to conquer Japan was still fresh in everyone's memory. All the Ming court could do was to restrict tribute trade further. When the emperor was informed that some Japanese had been discovered hiding in the tribute ships, and that they were allegedly attempting to conspire with his Prime Minister Hu Weiyong 胡惟雍 (?–1380) to overthrow the dynasty, he decided to "to cut off the tribute trade relations and shut the door along the coast, leaving no room for piracy and conspiracy."[71] It was argued that there was no point in maintaining a relationship with a neighbouring state where "the ruler was too young to rule, his officials abused their imperial power, and his subjects bullied their own fellows at home and harassed others abroad."[72] Japan was seen as an enemy, side by side with the Mongols. Maritime prohibition was believed to be a comprehensive defence policy to keep the "eastern barbarians" away.

The resort to this maritime prohibition as a defence policy was also a consequence of the government's strategy to deal with another anti-Ming element: the remaining rebel forces that sought refuge along the coast. The remnants of Fang Guozhen's 方國珍 (1319–1374) and Zhang Shicheng's 張士誠 (1321–1367) forces, who used to be the Hongwu Emperor's political rivals, remained a significant problem for the new regime. The former warlords were said to have some ten thousand warships hiding out at sea waiting to attack.[73] Their military campaigns were not just the 'hit and run' kind of harassment mostly associated with pirates, but rather reflected a much more organised operation. From military bases in Vietnam, Thailand and Sumatra, they joined Japanese pirates, whom they used as their military vanguard, to launch 'international joint force' style operations.[74] The army of Zhang Shicheng, the former King of Wu 吳, had been 180,000 men strong and was credited with five significant victories over the Mongols in 1353. While they had been weakened by the victory of Zhu Yuanzhang 朱元璋 and the formation of the new Ming dynasty, and no longer constituted a direct threat to the young regime, the Hongwu Emperor nevertheless could not ignore the threat of invasion from his former rivals for the throne. They occupied a significant place on the Ming defence agenda. Traditionally, economic gain was always a secondary consideration, subsumed by the need to achieve political stability, and this was even more the case with a newly established administration like that under the Hongwu Emperor. The establishment and enforcement of the prohibition on maritime activity was seen as a price that needed to be paid in order to achieve political stability.

For these reasons, it seems sensible to explain the maritime prohibition solely in terms of defence policy. However, when we explore the issue in more detail we find that there are more questions than answers. For instance, there is a discrepancy

71 Gu Yingtai, *Mingshi jishi benmo, j.* 55, p. 3a.

72 *Ming Taizu shilu, j.* 90, p. 1a–b.

73 Gu Yingtai, *Mingshi jishi benmo, j.* 5, pp. 1a and 9a.

74 *Fengzhou biji houji* 鳳洲筆記後集 (*Random Notes from Fengzhou by Wang Shizhen; Supplement*) by Wang Shizhen 王世貞 (1526–1590), in *Siku cunmu* 集, fasc. 114, *j.* 3, p. 3a.

between the decline in the significance of coastal piracy and the continuation of the policy for 200 years. Harassment by pirates and the irritations caused by rebel activity were a periodical rather than a continuous occurrence. Japanese piracy almost disappeared after 1403 when the Yongle emperor relaxed his father's severe prohibition on tribute trade. In 1392, when Ashikaga Yoshimitsu 足利義満 (1358–1408) had desperately wanted to improve the Japanese economy by encouraging trade with China, he wasted no time in eulogizing the new Ming emperor and vowing to be his loyal subject: "Your majesty is the sun in the sky, there will be no darkness in this world from now on. You are the timely rain, there will be nowhere that will not benefit; you are the greatest ruler of this world who can bring order out of chaos ... Japan is certainly protected by your care."[75] In the second year of his reign, the Yongle emperor took the opportunity to dispatch Admiral Zheng He and his fleet to Japan to help resolve the issue of piracy. A *kanhe* 勘合, a certificate issued as official tributary permission by the Ming government, was issued, which secured Ashikaga Yoshimitsu's promise to crack down on piracy and in return saw the restoration of a full diplomatic and tributary trade relationship.[76] Minamoto Yoshimitsu was rewarded with the title "King of Japan". The results were immediate: "No sooner had the king signed the treaty than he rushed out to suppress piracy. Twenty-two Japanese pirate-merchants were caught and sent to China for execution."[77] This crackdown on piracy was likened to "thunder and lighting".[78] To demonstrate his loyalty and sincerity Minamoto Yoshimitsu continued to pursue and extradite pirates until he died in 1408.[79] His son, Ashikaga Yoshimochi 足利義持 (1386–1408), followed in his father's footsteps, continuing to capture pirates and extradite them to China.[80] A great improvement had taken place along the coast and reports of piracy "greatly decreased."[81] Peace and order were restored, with commentators noting how "the sea has since become calm for a long time."[82] Piracy was no longer a major defence problem. Meanwhile, the rebel forces had also become much weaker by this time. These fugitive forces, hiding out on islands for 30-odd years, could not survive without new recruits: "The old has gone, the strong has

75 "Zheng fa 徵伐" (Military Expedition), in *Riben yijian* 日本一鑒 (*A Mirror of Japan*), *j.* 6, quoted in Pan Qun 潘群 and Shen Haitian 申海田, "Zheng He shi Ri zaitan 鄭和使日再談" (A Further Debate on Zheng He's Mission to Japan), *Haijiaoshi yanjiu* 2 (1985), p. 97.

76 Gu Yingtai, *Mingshi jishi benmo*, *j.* 55, p. 5a.

77 *Ming shi*, *j.* 322, pp. 6a–b.

78 *Ming Taizong shilu*, *j.* 40, p. 6a.

79 *Guoque* 國榷 (*Annalistic Deliberations on State Affairs*) by Tai Qian 談遷 (1595–1658), in *Siku xuxiu*, fasc. 359, pp. 20, 47 and 53.

80 "Wangheng ji 王亨記", in *Mingshan cang* 名山藏 (*Collection Hidden in Jingshan*) by He Qiaoyuan 何喬遠 (1558–1632), in *Siku quanshu jinhui shu congkan* 四庫禁燬書叢刊 (*Banned Books from the Complete Library of the Four Treasuries*) 史, fasc. 46, *j.* p. 21b [hereafter *Siku jinhui*].

81 *Chouhai tubian* 籌海圖編 (*Illustrated Compendium on Maritime Security*) by Hu Zongxian 胡宗憲 (1511–1565), in *Siku quanshu*, fasc. 584, *j.* 12, p. 3b. See also Tan Qian, *Guoque*, in *Siku xuxiu*, fasc. 358–359, pp. 8 and 20.

82 Tan Qian, *Guoque*, in *Siku xuxiu*, fasc. 359, p. 629.

become old, and they have come to rest at last."[83] If the maritime prohibition had been put in place simply for defence purposes, what was the point in continuing to maintain the policy when the threat was no longer present? Why did the Yongle emperor not take the opportunity to abolish the prohibition policy once and for all and encourage international trade to generate state revenue, as had been the case in the preceding Tang, Song and Yuan dynasties?

Maritime prohibition was neither the most effective nor the only option to deal with piracy. Though the policy had been strictly implemented its effects were limited. By 1388, after the policy had been in effect for sixteen years, it was still the case that none of the provinces along the coast escaped pillaging by pirates. Shandong was attacked in 1369, Guangdong in 1371, Zhejiang and Fujian in 1372, and Nan Zhili in 1375.[84] On the other hand, by the time of the Yongle reign the Ming government had gained the military resources and the financial ability to undertake a much more active policy to deal with coastal piracy and did not need to rely on the passive maritime interdiction. It was also the case that by the end of the Hongwu reign the empire was in a much better financial condition: "The government granaries were full, with enough grain to last the whole empire for thirty years."[85] One account claims: "People were content with their lives and there were few criminal cases reported. The society was so abundant that if someone lost his money he would not have to worry as it would stay where it was until he came to pick it up."[86] Zheng He's seven overseas maritime expeditions demonstrated the financial and military strength of the Ming Empire during the Yongle reign. It is hard to imagine that the Japanese pirates would have been able to challenge the Chinese maritime fleet, with its numerous warships, its thousands of marines and its extensive munitions.[87] It is equally difficult to understand why, if piracy was such an issue, the emperor dispatched this fleet to patrol the Indian Ocean rather than confront the problems along the China coast. If Admiral Zheng He's naval power was able to besiege the Ceylonese capital, bombard the palace and defeat a 50,000 strong Singhalese army, as well as capture the Ceylonese King alive, then the Ming navy should have been able to protect merchants from pirate harassment along the China coast, if indeed piracy was a problem and the administration had been concerned to eradicate it.[88] Why, then, did the Ming government keep the maritime prohibition policy in place, despite changed circumstances and the availability of

83 *Zheng Duanjian gong wenji* 鄭端簡公文集 (*The Collected Works of Zheng Xiao, Posthumous Title Duanjian*) by Zheng Xiao 鄭曉 (1499–1566), in Chen Zilong 陳子龍 (1608–1647) (ed.), *Ming jingshi wenbian* 明經世文編 (*A Collection of Ming Writings on State Affairs*). (Beijing: Zhonghua shuju, 1997), *j.* 218, pp. 9b–10a [Hereafter *MJSWB*].

84 Tan Qian, *Guoque*, in *Siku xuxiu*, fasc. 358, pp. 250, 299, 308–309 and 422.

85 *Ming Taizu shilu*, *j.* 83, p. 2b.

86 *Kezuo zhuiyu* 客座贅語 (*Superfluous Words to Entertain my Guests*) by Gu Qiyuan 顧啟元 (1565–1628), in *Siku cunmu* 子, fasc. 243, *j.* 1, p. 35b.

87 *Ming shi*, *j.* 304, p. 3a–b.

88 *Xingcha shenglan* 星槎勝覽 (*The Overall Survey of the Star Raft*) by Fei Xin 費信 (1388–?). (1599–edition), in *Siku xuxiu*, fasc. 742, *j.* 3, p. 5b.

resources? If we concentrate solely on the issue of piracy and coastal defence, we cannot satisfactorily explain the many contradictions surrounding the maritime prohibition policy.

The disjunction between the reality along the China coast and the perceived aim of the prohibition policy adds further confusion. Despite the interdiction there was not a decrease in piracy. Rather, as the dynasty progressed, activity along the China coast grew in intensity. While the original aim might have been to ensure that "not a single piece of wood would float in the sea", in reality "thousands of people were sailing away and hundreds of pirate ships were sailing away fully loaden with people and cargo."[89] While the intention of the law was "to prohibit our people from going overseas to trade with foreigners",[90] the fact was that "all sorts of people were involved with maritime trade, from courtiers in the palace to salt workers on the coast."[91] And "the coastal people regarded pirates not as their enemy, but rather as the suppliers of their 'daily bread'."[92] The stricter the prohibition was maintained, the more violations of it appeared and the more destructive the piracy became. Tang Shu 唐樞 (1497–1574), Grand Coordinator of Fujian, alarmed the court in 1516 when he reported: "Pirates and traders are the same people. When trade flourishes, pirates become traders; and when trade is banned, traders become pirates."[93] This indicated that the 'enemy' was not pirates but merchants. The aim of the policy was to restrict trade not control piracy. More disturbingly, it was obvious that many of the pirates were actually Chinese, not foreigners. Hu Zongxian 胡宗賢 (1511–1565), the Commander-in-Chief of coastal defence in Zhejiang 浙江, made a list of the leaders from more than ten pirate groups. They were not foreign pirates but Chinese merchants.[94] Similarly, it was found that the owners of ocean-going trading ships and the suppliers of cargo were also Chinese.[95] A message from Wang Zhi 王直, the so-called "king of pirates", was more pressing: "Piracy will disappear when the trade prohibition is lifted."[96] This statement was vindicated by what happed after 1568, when the policy was abolished: "The *wo* (Japanese pirates) have disappeared and ceased to cause trouble as people are enjoying doing business."[97]

89 *Qiantai wo zuan* 虔臺倭纂 (*A Record of the Qiantai Piracy*) by Xie Jie 謝傑 (1536–1604), in *Xuanlantang congshu xuji*, *j.* 1, p. 7b.

90 *Ming Taizu shilu*, *j.* 70, p. 40a, *j.* 139, p. 8a, *j.* 231, p. 2b.

91 *Zheng Duanjian gong nianpu*, *j.* 3, p. 29a.

92 Zhu Wan, *Piyu zaji*, in *Siku cunmu* 集, fasc. 278, j. 3, p. 38b.

93 "Fu Hu Hailin lun chu Wang Zhi 複胡海林論處王直" (A Reply to Hu Meilin's Decision on the Punishment of Wang Zhi), in *Yu Wo zazhu* 禦倭雜著 (*Assorted Works on Defence Against Piracy*) by Tang Shu 唐樞 (1497–1574), in *MJSWB*, vol. 270, *j.* 1, p. 4a.

94 "Wozhi 倭志" (*A Record of Piracy*) by Wang Shizhen, in *MJSWB*, *j.* 332, p. 27a.

95 "Yi fang Wo 議防倭" (Debate Over Defence Against Japanese Piracy) by Jiang Bao 姜寶 (1514–1593), in *MJSWB*, fasc. 383, *j.* 1, p. 7a. See also *Wubei zhi* 武備誌 (*Coastal Defence Annals*) by Mao Yuanyi 茅元儀, in *Siku jinhui* 子, fasc. 26, *j.* 214, p. 23b.

96 Hu Zongxian, *Chouhai tubian*, *j.* 9, p. 62a.

97 Tan Qian, *Guoque*, in *Siku xuxiu*, fasc. 361, p. 620.

In other words, the painfully preserved maritime interdiction was not effective either as a defence policy or as a political strategy, and nor was it effective in economic terms, yet the Ming government maintained it for two centuries. What kind of logic would have persuaded Ming policymakers to persevere with such a policy for so long? Were there other reasons that help us understand the commitment to this policy? Research on the European witch-hunts may give us some clues which might help us seek a better explanation and resolve this apparent conundrum. Brian P. Lavack's approach is encouraging in this regard. He suggests that any phenomena that lasted centuries, as did the European witch-hunts, could not be simply the result of the whims of popes or emperors, nor should it be explained away as religious madness or the result of some external impact. He argues that it is now understood that social and economic changes influenced a great deal of activity in the early modern period, and thus the social history of witchcraft "becomes more than a study of deviant behaviour." He goes on to demonstrate how, in seeking to explain many cases of witch-hunting, social and economic considerations have "assumed paramount importance". Instead of focusing solely on politics and/or religion, he emphasizes the impact of a range of socio-economic factors, such as population growth, the rise in commodity prices, urbanisation and the fact that "both mercantile and agricultural capitalism were introduced in many areas."[98] Socio-economic changes rather than political manoeuvring or religious conspiracy thus became the main mechanism employed to try to understand the witch-hunts. Similarly, if we are to understand the consistency and magnitude of the Ming maritime prohibition, a policy that was of great significance and was maintained for such a long time, we need to develop a more coherent, structural and organic explanation than that of the periodic incidence of piracy and banditry.

Government policy is formed within the context of – and reflects – the configuration of political power. The disposition of political power is often made manifest through the power struggles amongst different factions within an administration. As the Chinese civil service system was based on the selection of candidates through an open imperial examination system, one of the factors influencing the formation of political power groups within the government was the conflict amongst various social interest groups. In this way, social and economic circumstances directly determined the political landscape and hence the policy direction of the government.[99] In order to understand Ming maritime policy it is important to explore the social and economic circumstances in which this policy was developed. To explain the policy simply in terms of piracy, what might be termed the 'defence approach', leads to what Lucien Febvre termed *histoire événementielle*, an event-oriented history. "Such a narrative history with its primary political content not only failed to grasp the fullness of human reality but even endangered the status of his-

98 Brian P. Levack, *Witch-hunt in Early Modern Europe*. (London: Longman, 1995), pp. 125–127.

99 For a good case study of this at work see James M. Polachek, *The Inner Opium War*, 1840–42. (Cambridge, Mass.: Harvard University Press, 1992).

tory itself."[100] As Fernand Braudel argued, we should seek an understanding of humanity and human society in terms of all of the social sciences, including economics and sociology. The problem with an event-oriented history is that it can lead to a woefully inadequate and incomplete understanding of the past.[101] Earlier still, James Harvey Robinson, advocate of what was called the "new history", encouraged a comprehensive approach to a historical phenomenon: "Nothing could be more artificial than the scientific separation of man's religious, aesthetic, political, intellectual and bellicose properties. These may be studied, each by itself, with advantage, but specialization would lead to the most absurd results if there were not someone to study the process as a whole; and that someone is the historian."[102] We need to bring these perspectives to bear on a study of the Ming maritime prohibition, as it seems most unlikely that such a policy was introduced and then abandoned simply as a response to fluctuations of a temporary external phenomenon such as Japanese piracy. Braudel reminds us that "we can no longer believe in the explanation of history in the terms of this or that dominant factor. There is no unilateral history. No one thing is exclusively dominant."[103]

A new structural approach is needed to re-interpret Ming maritime policy. It is my intention to undertake such an approach in this book. I will argue that the maritime prohibition policy did not stand alone. The prohibition against trade with foreign countries was a principle that was applied to all states, not just Japan. We need to understand the maritime policy in conjunction with the prohibition on the horse fairs with the Mongols and the prohibition on the tea trade with the "western barbarians". Together, these policies constituted the whole foreign trade prohibition regime. The three policies were instituted and abolished around the same time, and they operated within the same overall environment.

Government policy reflects a particular configuration of political powers of the time, and once that configuration is undermined then the policy is likely to be abandoned. It is only by studying the process of political struggle surrounding a particular policy that we can understand the configuration and reconfiguration of powers within an administration and the consequent shift in policy. And only by analysing the social and economic situation can we understand how new economic circumstances gave rise to new social forces, and hence new power configurations within the administration. Though Japanese piracy was a persistent issue during the Ming period, it was not the fundamental cause for the implementation, continuation and eventual abolition of the maritime prohibition. Studying the policy in isolation can encourage us to place too much emphasis on the effect of piracy. My intention in this book is to study how the inner dynamics of policymaking within the Ming administration can help us reach a broader perspective on the maritime prohibition

100 Ernst Breisach, *Historiography. Ancient, Medieval and Modern.* (Chicago: University of Chicago Press, 1983), p. 370.

101 Arthur Warwick, *The Nature of History.* (London: Macmillan, 1970), p. 121.

102 James Harvey Robinson, *The New History.* (New York: Columbia University Press, 1913), p. 66.

103 Fernand Braudel, *On History.* (London: Weidenfeld and Nicholson, 1980), p. 10.

policy, and how an understanding of the social and economic undercurrents to the landscape of power within the administration can enhance our appreciation of why the policy was implemented, why it was maintained for so long, and why, after two hundred years, it was finally overturned.

CHAPTER II

Socio-Economic Institutions and Foreign Trade Policy during the Early Ming

On the morning of the fourth day of the first lunar month of the year *Wushen* 戊申, in 1368, when Zhu Yuanzhang 朱元璋 (r. 1368–1395) sat for the first time on his throne in Yingtian 應天 to celebrate the founding of the Ming dynasty, he may well have wondered: 'How long can I sit here and how long will it be before I face the next round of peasant rebellions?' Zhu Yuanzhang and his officials had just witnessed the collapse of the Yuan dynasty (1271–1368), once the centre of the great Mongol empire, which encompassed half of Eurasia. This huge empire had not been destroyed by a larger army with better munitions, but rather by an army of disgruntled peasants. Fifteen years after the outbreak of the peasant uprising in southern China in 1351, Toghōn Temür 妥權貼睦爾 (r. 1333–1368), the last Yuan emperor, once master of the magnificent Dadu (the Yuan capital, later to become Beijing) and heir to the throne of both Chinggis Qan and Qubilai Qan, found himself all over again wandering the steppe on horseback. Chinggis Qan would never have forgiven Toghōn Temür for losing the Yuan empire to a bunch of poor peasants led by a former novice from the Buddhist temple of Fengyang 鳳陽 along the barren Huai River 淮河.

Newly enthroned as the first of the Ming emperors, with the title Hongwu, Zhu Yuanzhang may well have reflected on the fact that throughout the last 1,500 years of Chinese history few dynasties, even the most powerful, had survived for long. The Qin dynasty 秦 (BCE 221–206), the very first empire, was the clearest example. Although the Qin had unified China, wiping out six other kingdoms with an astonishing display of force, it vanished within the space of two generations. The first emperor, Qin Shihuang 秦始皇 (259–210 BCE), was confident that his house would "rule China for not one or two but for ten thousand generations."[104] He called himself 'emperor', a title that had been reserved for the deity, indicating that he believed the regime he created would be universal and ever-present. A peasant rebellion ended his grand dream that his dynasty would rule China forever.

The new 'Son of Heaven', Zhu Yuanzhang, found himself in the same position as his predecessors to face the same challenge, to be emperor of China. How could his dynasty stand the test of time, and avoid the curse of peasant rebellion which had sealed the fate of many former dynasties? The new emperor directed his officials: "Political stability is most difficult to maintain … since the ancient times all the great rulers of former dynasties have been confronted by this challenge."[105] Yet the new emperor's desire to hold on to power was as strong as that of Qin Shihuang and Qubilai Qan before him: "My sons and grandsons would like to

104 "Qin Shihuang ben ji 秦始皇本記" (The Biography of Qin Shihuang), in *Shi ji* 史記 (*Records of the Grand Historian*) by Sima Qian 司馬遷 (BCE 145–?). (Beijing: Zhonghua shuju, 1956), p. 236.

105 *Huang Ming baoxun* 皇明寶訓 (*Imperial Instructions of the Hongwu and Yongle Emperors*) by Lu Ben 呂本 (1504–1587) *et. al.* (eds.). (1547 edition), in *Siku cunmu* 史, fasc. 53, *j.* 1, p. 20a.

govern the empire diligently and personally (*gong lan shu zheng* 躬覽庶政)."[106] Political stability therefore became the ultimate goal, determining the shape of early Ming politics and the nature of Ming institutions. The social system, the economic structure and the attitude to foreign trade all reflected the stability-orientated ideology that underlay the formation of the Ming world.

Confucianism and the Prohibition of Foreign Trade

The foreign trade prohibition that was in operation for two centuries could never have survived had it not been guided by a strong stability-orientated ideological conviction. State control of the economy can be traced back to the moral code enshrined in the Confucian canon. Song Ne 宋訥 (1311–1390), the Hongwu Emperor's advisor, pointed out: "The essential political means for us to rule our country is to rule in the Confucian Way … The political system has to be established on the foundation of Confucianism … Confucianism is the source of state politics, social customs and the bedrock of the dynasty."[107] Foreign occupation and the social chaos of the late Yuan period encouraged the early Ming regime to seek order and stability. The Hongwu administration strategically elevated the political function of Confucianism to an unprecedented level. The master himself was deified as a God-like figure and his doctrines regarded in a similar manner to how religious texts were viewed in medieval Europe. The court ordered the construction of Confucian temples all over the country, from the imperial palace to ordinary villages. The *Four Books and Five Classics* (*sishu wujing* 四書五經) became the sole texts used in the imperial examination system, through which people were selected for service in the bureaucracy.[108] Confucius' descendants were even granted immunity from criminal prosecution.[109] A scholar was beheaded for questioning a piece of Confucian doctrine.[110] This promotion of Confucianism was also reflected in what was an unparalleled emphasis on morality in the administration's attitude towards economic policy. The prohibition on foreign trade was one part of the belief.

The prohibition on foreign trade reflected the impact of the notion of "*ren* 仁" (humanity or humaneness), one of the core propositions in Confucian ideology. Commerce was associated with greed and rapacity, the attributes of those of low morality. Thus, commerce was to have no place in foreign relations, which should reflect the moral qualities associated with humaneness. Confucius is said to have

---

106 Chen Wutong 陳梧桐, *Zhu Yuanzhang zhuan* 朱元璋傳 (*A Biography of Zhu Yuanzhang*). (Tianjin: Tianjin renmin chubanshe, 1986), p. 267.

107 *Ming shi*, *j.* 69, p. 21a.

108 *Ming huiyao* 明會要 (*Ming Political and Social Institutions*) edited by Long Wenbin 龍文彬 (1821–1893). (1887-edition), in *Siku xuxiu*, fasc. 793, *j.* 47, p. 3a.

109 *Ming Taizu shilu*, *j.* 232, p. 8b. See also *Ming shi*, *j.* 69, p. 16b, and *Shuidong riji* 水東日記 (*Daily Collection from the East of the Songjiang River*) by Ye Sheng 葉盛 (1420–1474), in *Siku quanshu*, fasc. 1041, *j.* 19, pp. 4a–b.

110 *Guochao dianzhang* 國朝典章 (*Imperial Statutes*), in *Siku cunmu* 史, fasc. 268, p. 25 [no author, no *juan*].

remarked: "If the emperor loves righteousness, his people's customs will be virtuous; if he loves material possessions, his people's customs will be mean and selfish. The Son of Heaven is the model for his people, and his example is to be imitated by the world."[111] According to Confucian ideology, the *tianzi* 天子, or Son of Heaven, had the mandate to rule because he was free from worldly desire, and China was "the greatest civilization under heaven" (*tianchao shangguo* 天朝上國) and should rule "barbarians" (*manyi* 蠻夷) through a display of high ethical values. Similarly, it was believed that political power was a reflection of ethical quality rather than economic strength or military muscle. China was the 'caretaker' for the rest of the world, of those who needed to be 'cared for', therefore international trade was called "*gong* 貢" (tribute) rather than "*shang* 商" (commerce). To base commercial exchange between China and the rest of the world on a position of exchange between equal partners was not only politically improper but also ethically degrading. He Mengchun 何孟春 (1474–1536), a Deputy Minister of Personnel, advised the Wuzong emperor 武宗 (r. 1506–1521) about the consequences of the government involving itself with foreign trade for commercial gain:

> When Han Wudi 漢武帝 (r. BCE 140–87) appointed Qianqiu as Prime Minister [Tian Qianqiu 田千秋 (BCE ?-77), notorious for his policies of trying to enrich the state through trade] our enemy, the Xiongnü, laughed up their sleeves [seeing this as a sign of the weakening of China's moral strength and hence of it becoming conquerable]. When Song Shenzong 宋神宗 (r. 1067–1085) appointed Wang Anshi 王安石 (1021–1086) as Prime Minister [well known for his utilitarian approach to economic matters], the king of Jiaozhi 交趾 [now part of Vietnam] wrote a letter to convey his disrespect for China. The barbarians will look down upon us if we lose our ethical standards.[112]

In a political culture based on such an anti-commercial moral foundation, it was most unlikely that the state would encourage people to pursue business opportunities. In fact, the early Ming rulers tried to distance themselves from all 'corrupt' undertakings. The Hongwu Emperor instructed the Governor of Fujian "not to impose any duties on goods brought in for trade from Champa in order to show the greatness of our conciliation."[113] When the Ming envoy visited Brunei and demanded the local king pay tribute to the Ming court and the king responded with the claim that his country was too poor to have anything valuable enough for a tribute mission, the Ming envoy then proclaimed: "Our emperor is the owner of everything under the heaven and needs nothing from you. What we demand is your obedience, that you become a vassal state and join the 'family'."[114] To conduct for-

111 *Qian Han shu* 前漢書 (*The History of the Western Han Dynasty*) by Ban Gu 班固 (BCE 32–92), in *Siku quanshu*, fasc. 533, *j.* 56, p. 25a.

112 *Yudong xulu zhaichao* 餘冬序錄摘抄 (*Outline of my Works Written during the Winter Days of my Life*) by He Mingchun 何孟春 (1474–1636). (1528–edition), in *Siku cunmu* 子, fasc. 101, *j.* 10, pp. 5b–6a.

113 *Ming huiyao*, *j.* 57, p. 19a.

114 *Huang Ming zhengyao* 皇明政要 (*Personal Statements on Government dministration by Five Ming Emperors – from Hongwu to Yingzong*) by Lou Xing 婁性 (*jinshi* 1481). (1507-edition), in *Siku cunmu* 史, fasc. 46, *j.* 20, pp. 6a–b.

eign trade with the purpose of generating a profit was viewed as both morally wrong and politically incorrect. Such behaviour would lower Chinese civilization to the level of the wicked and greedy. The marked contrast between a thriving international trade environment and the short length of time enjoyed by the Yuan dynasty served to reinforce this belief.

Another central concept in Confucianism, *jun* 均, or the belief that it was necessary to prevent the emergence of an unduly wealthy social grouping, also helped shape the early Ming attitude towards the governing of the realm. *The Analects* records that the Master said: "In running a country what we care about most is not scarcity but inequality, not poverty but instability."[115] For Confucian bureaucrats, wealth was seen in a fixed amount, and accumulation by one group would mean the others would suffer. Confucius had warned rulers about the need to leave more social wealth in the hands of the common people: "If his subjects are enjoying sufficiency and security there is no reason to believe that the ruler still needs anything at all. If his subjects are suffering from insufficiency and insecurity how can we believe that the ruler is able to enjoy sufficiency and security?"[116] Leaving more wealth to the people became one of the driving factors behind the early Ming social reformation. Dong Zhongshu 董仲舒 (BCE 179–104), the great Han dynasty Confucian scholar, observed: "If someone in the society becomes rich it is bound to cause poverty for others. The rich will become too powerful and uncontrollable and the poor will be too precarious and rebellious … the government should adjust the distribution of wealth and make the rich and poor both satisfied in order to maintain a stable situation."[117] Industries that created divisions within society were regarded as politically damaging. Commerce was understood to have this effect. Sima Qian 司馬遷 (145– c. 86 BCE) maintained: "It is not as easy to become rich by working in agriculture as it is through being an artisan, but the quickest way is to engage in trade."[118] Merchants were always considered the lowest of social groups because they would accumulate wealth while not producing anything themselves. The Hongwu emperor declared: "Only when commerce was suppressed could the equal distribution of land be secured. Political stability relies on *zhongnong yishang* 重農抑商 (support for farming and suppression of commerce)."[119] While foreign trade was extremely lucrative and hence politically detrimental, it was right the targeted industry for suppression when political stability rather than economic prosperity was the overriding goal for the Hongwu administration.

---

115 *Lunyu* 論語 (*The Analects*), attributed to Kongzi 孔子 (Confucius, 551–479), in *Sishu zhangju jizhu* 四書章句集注 (*Annotations on the Four Books*) by Zhu Xi 朱熹 (1130–1200), in *Siku quanshu*, fasc. 197, *j.* 8, p. 10a.

116 *Lunyu*, *j.* 6, pp. 14a–b.

117 *Chunqiu fanlu* 春秋繁露 (*Expositions on the Spring and Autumn Annals*) by Dong Zhongshu 董仲舒 (BCE 179–104), in *Siku quanshu*, 181, *j.* 8, pp. 1a–b.

118 *Shi ji*, in *Siku quanshu*, fasc. 244, *j.* 129, p. 18a.

119 *Yudong xulu zhaichao*, *j.* 5, p. 3b.

Confucianism also laid the general principled motif for the early Ming international relations. The concepts of *ren* and *jun* were credited as providing the foundation for China's unchallengeable cultural supremacy. The ideal of the Chinese world order required Chinese administrations to provide a moral example for foreigners to follow. The Hongwu Emperor stated this clearly:

> Since ancient times, China, from the centre of the universe, controlled the 'barbarians' on the periphery. It was ridiculous for the Mongols to rule China. It was against Heaven's will, which decrees that all under Heaven should never bow down to the Mongols. The Mongols were abandoned [by Heaven] because of their political illegitimacy."[120]

As soon as the Ming took power, the Hongwu Emperor sought to arrange the 'world order' through moral force. He sent envoys to all places where "the sun and moon shine" and called upon them to pay tribute to the Ming court and thereby gain access to Chinese products.[121] In order to enact this ideal of cultural supremacy, the Chinese needed a mechanism to demonstrate their ceremonial dominance; therefore the tribute mission became the only legal way to engage in foreign trade. Commercial activity thus became a form of politics. Private trade was condemned, and prohibited, because it was seen to weaken the moral legitimacy of the Ming.

The Redistribution of Social Wealth

The objective of political stability fortified by the principles of "*ren*" and "*jun*" created an environment incompatible with commerce. Under the banner of humanity, the government undertook to transform the social and economic régime it had inherited from the Yuan dynasty. Land nationalisation and decentralisation were the primary means used to achieve the redistribution of social wealth. This great redistribution, similar in both scale and depth to the "*tudi geming* 土地革命" (land revolution) of the early 1950s, transformed early Ming society and produced a community where there was hardly any gap between rich and poor. Land was the most significant form of property in all early modern economies, and in this China was no different. The Hongwu Emperor declared: "Stability comes first of all from people being able to meet their requirement for food and clothing,"[122] and "All that we [the government] need comes from the land."[123] Besides this, the rural peasantry was also the main source for military conscription. The dynasty's political strength, and its stability, was grounded in the contentment of the peasantry and the steady flow of income to the state from the land tax. It was an economy that emphasized self-sufficiency, and de-emphasized commodity exchange and commercial activity. This was a very different world from that of the preceding Song and Yuan dynasties.

History served as a reminder to the Ming decision-makers of the consequences of land centralization. As T. T. Meadows, a British consular official serving in nine-

---

120 *Huang Ming zhaoling* 皇明詔令 (*Imperial Edicts*), in *Siku cunmu* 史, fasc. 58, *j.* 1, pp. 1a–b.

121 *Ming Taizu shilu*, *j.* 71, p. 3b.

122 *Huang Ming baoxun*, *j.* 1, pp. 16b–17a.

123 *Huang Ming zhengyao*, *j.* 17, p. 3a.

teenth century China, observed: in the traditional Chinese political system, "Peasants ... have no right to vote for their leaders but they have the ultimate right of rebellion."[124] Throughout dynastic history, the fortunes of regimes had been directly related to land and land ownership. As Xie Zhaozhe 謝肇淛 (1567–1642) remarked in his famous *Wu zazu* 五雜俎 (*Five Mixed Platters*), "Without land people have no life."[125] The Qin experience seemed to bear this out. The Shang Yang reforms (*Shang Yang bianfa* 商秧變法) instituted under the Qin had denounced the well-field system (*jingtian zhi* 井田制) of antiquity. Thoug more an ideal than an actuality, this system sought to secure 100 *mu* 亩 of land for each peasant, and reflected the ancient political ideal that "If there was no man without land and no woman without a loom then there would be no starvation or suffering."[126] The Hongwu Emperor reminded his administration of this when he argued that the Qin privatisation of farmland had ignited the social disturbances that brought the dynasty to an end: "Social injustice caused peasant rebellion and brought on the final destruction of the Qin dynasty."[127] During the preceding Yuan dynasty, the agglomeration of landholdings had been a significant problem. For instance, it was said that "Fifty landlord families owned as much as five-sixths of the arable land in the whole of Chongan 崇安 county in Fujian."[128] The rich and powerful controlled vast tracts of land; and these were the people most adept at tax evasion. In other words, families with big landholdings intercepted and captured the revenue that should have been directed to the state. The Yuan regime collapsed when the state coffers were hollowed out in this way. By the last years of the dynasty the state received virtually nothing from the land tax.[129] It is in this context that we must understand the purpose of the early Ming land nationalisation. The purpose of this policy was to confiscate land controlled by rich families who controlled large areas of land, and re-allocate this land to the poor and the needy. In this way social wealth was politically distributed and the right to land politically secured.

There were few big landlords in the early Ming years. Existing land titles were nullified under the *Great Ming Code*: "Those who left their homes in wartime have no legal right to re-claim their property. If they need land to work for subsistence the government will allocate a new piece from nearby state holdings (*guantian* 官田). Anyone who dares to reclaim his old land ownership but does not intend to work on it personally will be punished." It also stated: "Anybody who occupied more

124 Cited by Stavrianos, *A Global History* (1991), p. 101.

125 *Wu zazu* 五雜俎 (*Five Assorted Offerings*) by Xie Zhaozhe 謝肇淛 (1567–1642), in *Siku jinhui* 子, fasc. 37, *j.* 4, p. 23b.

126 *Guochao dianhui* 國朝典彙 (*Imperial Decrees and Regulations*) by Xu Xueju 徐學聚 (*jinshi* 1583). (1624-edition), in *Siku cunmu* 史, fasc. 264–266, *j.* 92, pp. 2a–b.

127 *Caiqin lui* 采芹綠 (*Collection of Scholars' Academic Pursue*) by Xu Sanchong 徐三重 (*jinshi* 1577), in *Siku quanshu*, fasc. 867, *j.* 1, p. 19b.

128 See *Daoyuan ji* 道園集 (*Collected Works of Yu Ji, Hao Daoyuan*) by Yu Ji 虞集 (1272–1348), in *Siku cunmu* 集, fasc. 22, p. 27b (no *juan*). See also *Wei xueshi quanji* 危學士全集 (*The Collected Essays of Scholar Wei*) by Wei Su 危素 (1303–1372), in *Siku cunmu* 集, fasc. 24, *j.* 8, p. 5b.

129 Cai Meibia, *Zhongguo tongshi*, *j.* 7, p. 174.

land than he was able to work himself deserves 30 lashes for every three to ten *mu* and up to 80 lashes for every ten *mu* and more. In addition, their surplus land will be confiscated."[130] Land became a national asset under strict political control.

Ming Taizu (Zhu Yuanzhang) was a revolutionary. Whereas Song Taizu 宋太祖 (r. 960–976) had encouraged big landholdings and believed "the rich are the gatekeepers of the country's wealth," whereas the Hongwu Emperor wanted to see the rich disappear.[131] No sooner had he taken the throne than he conducted a ruthless campaign to dispossess large landholders of their land. Some 14,300 landlord families from Zhejiang 浙江 and Yingtian 應天 region were evacuated from their landholdings and resettled in the city of Nanjing 南京. In the 14th year of Hongwu reign (1381), 140,000 wealthy landed families were ordered to leave their hometowns in Jiangnan 江南 and resettle in a backward and remote area in Haozhou 濠州.[132] Following his father's policy, the Yongle emperor later shifted 3,000 landlord families from the same region to the new capital in Beijing and thus removed them from the basis of their social and economic influence.[133] The government did not hesitate to find any excuse to re-gather all the land appropriated by the rich and powerful during the Yuan period. The Hongwu administration executed some 30,000 people from large landholding families in the Jiangnan region by arbitrarily accusing them of colluding with Hu Weiyong 胡惟庸 (Prime Minister, 1377–1380) in order to launch a coup.[134] It was said that "Some people were ill-fated to court disaster just because they were rich, even though they were not at all rebellious."[135]

The Hongwu administration thus undermined the foundations of the social groups that had enjoyed great prerogatives during the Tang, Song and Yuan dynasties. There was no consultation nor was there any effort to generate consensus about this process of land disposition. In the 13th year of the Hongwu reign (1380) the administration reclaimed the land titles had been were granted to officials as part of their annual pay from the third year of the reign (1370).[136] Instead of allowing minsters and officials to become absentee landlords and owners of big estates, the early Ming administration turned them into wage earners. Twelve months later the aristocratic families met with the same fate.[137] The Hongwu Emperor declared:

130 *Da Ming lü* 大明律 (*The Great Ming Code*) compiled by Liu Weiqian 劉惟謙 (Minister of Justice, Hongwu reign, 1368–1398), in *Siku cunmu* 史, fasc. 276, *j.* 5. p. 1b. See also *Huang Ming zhaoling*, *j.* p. 7a.

131 *Huichen yuhua* 揮塵餘話 (*Remaining Words from my Conversations*) by Wang Mingqing 王明清 (1127–?), in *Siku quanshu*, fasc. 1038, *j.* 1, p. 29b.

132 *Ming shi*, *j.* 127, p. 4a.

133 *Ming shi*, *j.* 77, pp. 4b–5a.

134 Ibid., *j.* 308, pp. 5a–b.

135 *Ming Taizu shilu*, *j.* 58, 10b.

136 Cao Renhu, *Qinding xu wenxian tongkao*, *j.* 6, p. 27b.

137 "Tuntian 屯田" (Military Colonies), in *Xiyuan wenjian lu* 西園聞見錄 (*Record of Things Observed by Zhang Xuan, Hao Xiyuan*) by Zhang Xuan 張萱 (1459–1527). (Cambridge, Mass.: Harvard-Yanjing Library-edition, 1940), *j.* 91, p. 13a.

"Arable land is the foundation of our national economy and the asset upon which a benevolent emperor relies. We hereby demand all the land rewarded to you be given back to the government. You will be paid in grain and cloth instead."[138] Princes, princesses, dukes and barons, once proprietors of grand estates, some with as much as 100 *qing* 頃 (10,000 *mu*) or even 1,000 *qing* (100,000 *mu*) of arable land, had their titles to landholdings stripped away and found themselves lining up to receive a monthly allowance of rice and cloth.[139]

Religious groups were not exempt from these confiscations. During the Yuan dynasty Buddhist institutions had large landholdings. It was claimed that some "two thirds of the Yuan state revenue was spent on monks and religious affairs."[140] Buddhist monasteries owned 320,300 *qing* out of the total of 542,920 *qing* of arable land in Shandong 山東 province.[141] This land was targeted by the new Ming administration. Some 3,000 Buddhist and Daoist monasteries were dismantled. In conjunction with this, 214,000 Buddhist and 300,000 Daoist monks and nuns were defrocked and their property confiscated.[142] The law allowed only one temple to remain for every county, and this could be staffed with no more than two monks.[143] Daoists and Buddhists were forced to cram into the same monasteries, irrespective of religious differences.[144] By 1382, those who had previously been privileged politically and held grand estates found themselves virtually landless.[145]

The vast amount of arable land reclaimed from all of these sources was cut into "fish scale" (*yulin* 魚鱗) strips and distributed by the government to peasants on a per capita basis. In the north of the empire, fifteen *mu* was given for growing crops and two *mu* for vegetable gardening, with each allocation being exempt from the land tax for three years.[146] In the south, sixteen *mu* was allocated to each peasant, and, along the border, 50 *mu* was allocated to each soldier.[147] By this enforced nationalisation and redistribution of land, most of the agricultural land within the empire was put under permanent ownership by the peasantry. In Suzhou 蘇州 there were a total 8,986 households during the Hongwu reign, and most of them were petty landholding farmers.[148] There were no real big landlord families left in the

138 Ibid., *j*, 32, p. 13a.

139 Cao Renhu, *Qinding xu wenxian tongkao*, *j*. 6, pp. 26b–27b.

140 *Guitian leigao* 歸田類稿 (*Assorted Writings from Retirement*) by Zhang Yanghao 張養浩 (1270–1329), in *Siku quanshu*, fasc. 1192, *j*. 2, p. 24a.

141 Qian Mu 錢穆, *Guoshi dagang* 國史大綱 (*An Outline of the Nation's History*). (Taibei: Guoli bianyiguan chubanshe, 1977), p. 491. See also *Da Ming huidian*, in *Xuxiu*, fasc. 789, *j*. 17, pp. 4b–5a.

142 Fairbank and Reischauer, *China: Tradition and Transformation* (1989), p. 169.

143 *Ming tongjian* 明通鑒 (*Ming Comprehensive Mirror for Administration*) by Xia Xie 夏燮 (1800–1875), in *Siku xuxiu*, fasc. 364 *j*. 5, p. 10b. See also *Ming Xiaozong shilu*, *j*. 5, p. 1b.

144 *Ming tongjian*, *j*. 5, p. 10b.

145 Cao Renhu, *Qinding xu wenxian tongkao*, *j*. 6, p. 29b.

146 *Ming huiyao*, in *Siku xuxiu*, fasc. 793, *j*. 53, p. 1a.

147 "Yuxing zai hubu zhugongshu 與行在戶部諸公書" (A Letter to all the Officials in the Ministry of Revenue) by Zhou Chen 周忱 (1381–1453), in *MJSWB*, vol. 22, *j*. 1, p. 13a. See also *Ming huiyao*, in *Siku xuxiu*, fasc. 793, *j*. 53, p. 6a.

148 Ibid., pp. 13a–b.

region. He Liangjun 何良浚 (1506–1573) reported that "there is no family that owns more land than the total of ten petty farmers combined."[149] Among 10,600,000 households there were as many as 6,500,000 that were self-sufficient petty landholding peasants, some 64 per cent of the total population.[150] Land nationalization made early Ming society more egalitarian, and the gap between rich and poor was greatly narrowed.

Civil servants were not exempt from this campaign to redistribute the wealth of the empire. Their rate of pay was lowered to around one-fifth of the pay rate during the Han, Tang, Song and Yuan dynasties.[151] However, the bureaucrats had little to complain about as the court had already targeted the royal family. The Treasury cut the princes' pay by 80 per cent, from 50,000 *dan* 石 (1 hectoliter) to 10,000 *dan* per year.[152] A Ming official at rank 5A was paid 180 *dan* of rice a year, which was the pay rate for a position four ranks lower (9A) during the Han dynasty. While a Ming county magistrate was allocated 87 *dan* in cereals as his annual pay, a county magistrate during the Song dynasty could count on at least 900 *hu* 斛 (equal to 450 *dan*) of rice as well as a cash payment.[153] Worse still, with the "*zhezhi* 折支-policy" (payment commuted in paper notes or other items rather than in foodstuffs or cloth) the government sought to cut further the already low-pay rate for officials. This forced officials to accept between 40 and 60 per cent of their pay in the form of paintings, calligraphy or pepper rather than in foodstuffs, cloth, cash or precious metals, which were what they needed most.[154] On top of this the government also blocked all the other possible channels for officials to increase their income: "Officials were banned from engaging in any trade activities involving their families and relatives. They were not even allowed to lend money to others for interest."[155] Military officers serving on the frontier would be banished, along with their families, if it was found that they were engaged in private trade of any kind on the border.[156] Severe punishment for taking bribes deterred most officials from any attempt to supplement their income. The Ming law stated: "Any official who takes a bribe of over 60 *taels* of silver will be skinned and then stuffed and placed as a warning to

149 *Siyouzhai congshuo* 四友齋叢說 (*Miscellaneous Notes from the Four-Friends-Hall*) by He Liangjun 何良浚 (1506–1573), in *Siku cunmu* 子, fasc. 103, *j.* 34, p. 4b.

150 Wang Youye 王有夜, "Lun Mingchu zigengnong daliang cunzai ji dui shehui fazhan de yingxiang 論明初自耕農大量存在及對社會發展的影響" (The Impact of the Scale of Self-cultivated Farming on Early Ming Social Development), in *Liaoning daxue xuebao* 遼寧大學學報 6 (1981), p. 158.

151 *Rizhi lu jishi* 日知綠集釋 (*Record of Knowledge Daily Acquired, with Commentaries*) by Gu Yanwu 顧炎武 (1613–1682), commentaries by Huang Rucheng 黄汝成 (1799–1837), in *Siku xuxiu*, fasc. 1144, *j.* 13, pp. 13a–14a.

152 *Huang Ming diangu jiwen* 皇明典故紀聞 ((*Record of Ming Emperor's Sayings and Deeds as Statutory Precedents*) byYu Jideng 余繼登 (*jinshi* 1577) (compiled in 1601), in *Siku cunmu* 史, fasc. 52, *j.* 5, p. 27b.

153 Gu Yanwu, *Rizhi lu jishi*, in *Siku xuxiu*, fasc. 1143, *j.* 12. p. 14b.

154 Xu Xueju, *Guochao dianhui*, *j.* 35, p. 1b.

155 *Ming Renzong shilu* 明仁宗實綠, *j.* 5, *xia*, p. 2b. See also *Ming Yingzong shilu*, *j.* 66, p. 9b.

156 *Huang Ming baoxun*, *j.* 28, p. 62b.

his successor."[157] The administration believed that corrupt officials were always a key factor in land appropriation, hence the harshness of these measures.

The financial situation for most officials was little short of appalling. Many were so impoverished that their very survival was a problem. Yu Xizhi 魚希直, the magistrate of Kaifeng 開封 prefecture, had saved only eight *taels* of silver by the time of his retirement. He donated this money to the local school and eventually died of hunger.[158] After having served as the Zhenghe 政和 county magistrate for three years, Wu Yi 吳義 found himself without even enough money to bury his deceased mother. He had to accept a donation from his relatives in order to pay for his mother's funeral.[159] Cao Tai 曹泰, an investigating censor in Shandong, reported to the emperor that officials who took office up far away from their hometowns were paid only 2–3 *dan* of rice per month, which was far from enough to feed their families.[160] Li Dongyang 李東陽 (1447–1516), who served as a Grand Secretary during the Hongzhi reign 弘治 (r. 1488–1505), regarded it as shameful to be an official, for he was not able to support himself and his family and had to depend on financial assistance from his relatives and village folks.[161]

It is important to realise, however, that this situation was created for political rather than financial reasons. The early Ming GDP increased by one-third in a mere eight years (from 20,889,617 *dan* in 1386 to 32,789,800 *dan* in 1393).[162] This was two and a half times as much as the output during the best years of the Yuan dynasty (at 12,147,008 *dan*).[163] Officials were not allowed to ride horses for transport, yet the administration's stables were full of horses obtained from the tea and horse trade.[164] Contrary to the discrimination of the rich and powerful, the government upgraded its social welfare system to the highest level ever (taking the sixteenth century as the standard). The law demanded at least one social welfare service centre be instituted in every county to care for the needy. Those who could not support themselves were granted three *dou* 斗 of rice a month, 30 *jin* 斤 (weight unit) of firewood and one bolt of cloth. Those over 80 years old were allocated five *dou* of rice a month, five *jin* of meat, and, in addition, they had to be provided with three *dou* of wine.[165] The wealthy families in the community had to share the cost of meeting these welfare payments. The law reads:

---

157 *Ershi'er zhaji* 二十二札記 (*Reading Notes on the Twenty Two Dynastic Histories*) by Zhao Yi 趙翼 (1729–1814), in *Siku xuxiu*, fasc. 453, *j.* 33, p. 7a.

158 *Liunan suibi* 柳南随笔 (*Random Notes from Liunan*) by Wang Yingkui 王應奎 (1686–1767), in *Congshu jicheng chubian*, p. 55.

159 *Zhenghe xianzhi* 政和縣志 (*Gazetteer of Zhenghe County*) by Li Xi 李熙 (Zhenghe County Magistrate, 1911), in *Zhongguo difangzhi jicheng* 中國地方志集成, vol. 8, *j.* 24, p. 6b.

160 Gu Yanwu, *Rizhi lu jishi*, in *Xuxiu*, fasc. 1143, *j.* 12, p. 16a.

161 Zhang Xuan, *Xiyuan wenjian lu*, *j.* 5, p. 3b.

162 *Ming Taizu shilu*, *j.* 176, pp. 7b–8a.

163 *Yuan shi*, *j.* 93, p. 13a.

164 *Huang Ming diangu jiwen*, *j.* 5, p. 9b.

165 *Ming shu* 明書 (*Biographies, Annals, Records, and Monographs of the Ming Dynasty*) by Fu Weilin 傅維麟 (?–1667), in *Siku cunmu* 史, fasc. 39, *j.* 67, pp. 5a–5b.

> Wealthy families in the community are responsible for the welfare of those who live their lives by begging. No matter if they be merchants, artisans or landlords, if they fail in their responsibility to keep their poor from roaming the streets, the government will confiscate their property to pay the bill.[166]

This was a deliberately engineered policy in order to keep the gap between the various social groups as narrow as possible so as to achieve political stability.

This 'egalitarian' society created during the early Ming years generated little in the way of market forces and thus was not conducive to commercial activity. Peasants managed their family economy in terms of self-sufficiency and the few wealthy people who survived the state's confiscations with some of their capital intact were insufficient to generate much private commercial activity. The economy lacked the basic ingredients for foreign trade. Without financial institutions and a capital market, capital-intensive foreign trade was impractical. For example, the construction of an ocean-going ship would alone cost a thousand *taels* or more, which was more than the total amount of pay a county magistrate received for 12 years service. Without an organized financial sector and specialised production there would have been few commodities available for exchange. Even without the introduction of the prohibition on foreign trade, commercial activity had been constrained by the early Ming social and economic frameworks.

The Suppression of Commerce

Whereas the early Ming was a paradise for petty landholding peasants it was a hell for merchants. Commerce was viewed as a damaging factor, something that threatened the stability-orientated social and economic landscape. It was economic disruption rather than economic stagnation that policymakers feared. They believed that the petty landholding self-sufficiency system was the foundation of socio-economic stability and that it facilitated political control, therefore any industry that posed a challenge to this system was viewed as detrimental. The Hongwu Emperor stated: "We must provide our people with sufficient food. The only way to reach that goal is to restrain commerce and keep people in their paddy fields; we must provide our people with adequate clothes and other necessities but the only way to reach that objective is to promote frugality and constrain luxury."[167] Commerce was incompatible with this principle for its two effects. Firstly, it would breed a wealthy merchant group and turn them into land appropriators and, secondly, it would encourage petty landowners to leave their land.

When communication levels were poor and the market lacked an effective system of checks and balances, commerce was the fastest way to generate wealth. Commodity prices were not determined by a mature market system and could easily be manipulated by merchant speculation. Some commodities were valued far beyond their real worth. Sima Qian had observed that it was possible for grain mer-

166 *Huang Ming zhaoling*, *j.* 2, pp. 5a–b.

167 *Ming Taizu shilu*, *j.* 174, p. 4b.

chants to a make a fortune because "grain prices could differ as much as two thousand times between a year with a bumper harvest and a year with a disastrous one."[168] In the international market Chinese products were always in high demand and the possibility of generating considerable profit was enticing. For example, 500 grams of raw silk worth 5–6 *taels* in silver on the domestic market could fetch as much as 50–60 *taels* in Japan.[169] An A grade Mongol horse was worth about 24 *taels* if paid in silver, but only 8 *taels* if paid for in commodities, meaning it was possible to accrue a profit of 300 per cent.[170] It was also extremely lucrative to sell some foreign goods in China. For instance, *Sumu* (*Caesalpinia Sappan*), a dye material, was worth about one *guan* per *jin* (500 grams) in Japan, but could be sold for about 50 *guan* per *jin* in China, generating a fifty-fold profit.[171]

The quick accumulation of wealth by merchants had unwanted implications. In a society where the government provided no financing facilities, rich merchants naturally became creditors. Land was the only valuable property that most peasants had to use as collateral when they required quick cash, such as following natural calamities and family catastrophes. Merchants were the financiers, ready to provide funds that were mortgaged against a peasant's landholding. For instance, Gu Qingyu 顧青宇, a merchant from Songjiang 松江, made a fortune in five years in his trading business and bought 14,000 *mu* of land (equal to the total land quota for nearly 1,000 peasants).[172] Li Xian 李顯 (1408–1466), a Grand Secretary during the Zhengtong reign, described the phenomenon in his hometown:

> Land in our area is fertile and people are hard working, but very few people have been able to live a self-sufficient life. It is not because we waste a lot by living a luxurious lifestyle or because the government demands too much in taxation. It is a consequence of exploitation by merchants ... when we need money for a funeral or a wedding, merchants provide us with it. Then they come to take our crops away at the harvest and leave little for us to subsist on.[173]

In this way, by the middle of the Jiajing 嘉靖 reign (r. r.1522–1566), merchants had established a reputation as moneylenders, land appropriators and exploiters. By the late Ming years, when commerce was thriving in the Jiangnan region, 90 per cent of petty landowners had been reduced to tenantry.[174]

---

168 *Shi ji*, *j.* 30, p. 11a.

169 *Riben kao* 日本考 (*A study of Japan*) by Li Yangong 李言恭, in *Siku xuxiu*, fasc. 744, *j.* 1, p. 11b.

170 "Tiaofu shou huma shu 條覆收胡馬疏" (Item by Item Memorials on Accepting Mongol Horses) by Wang Chonggu 王崇古 (1515–1588), in *Wang Jiachuan wenji* 王鑑川文集 (*The Collected Works of Wang Chonggu, literary name by Jianchuan*) by Wang Chonggu 王崇古 (1515–1588), in *MJSWB*, vol. 318, *j.* 3, pp. 2a–b.

171 *Ming Xuanzong shilu*, *j.* 114, p. 1b.

172 "Shuo meng yi 說夢一" (Interpreting Dreams) by Cao Jiaju 曹家駒 (Qing), in *Qingren shuohui* 清人說薈 (*Collected Statements of Qing People*) by Fu Jin 富瑾 (ed.). (Shanghai: Saoye shangfang 掃業山房 edition, 1913–1917), p. 20b.

173 "Wuxiang shuo 五鄉說" (Anecdotes of My Hometown), in *Gurang ji* 古穰集 (*Collected Works Named after my Home Town in Gurang County*) by Li Xian 李賢 (1408–1466), in *Siku quanshu*, fasc. 1244, *j.* 9, pp. 4b–5b.

174 *Ming huiyao*, *j.* 54, p. 29a.

Commerce destroyed the *lijia* 里甲-system. *The lijia* system was devised to keep citizens under close surveillance. Merchants were the primary target of the system. Villages were managed in a quasi-military camp style. Peasants were supervised systematically in their daily lives by the *jiashou* 甲首 (head of every ten households) and the *lizhang* 里長 (the head of a 110-household community): "Everyone had to answer the village leader's drum to go to the fields together, work together and go back to their residences together."[175] Commercial activities created a tremendous temptation for peasants to leave their land and engage in non-farming businesses in order to generate a quick cash income. The wealth and lifestyles of merchants made peasants, the so-called 'privileged top social group' look shabby and pitiful. Wang Shuying 王叔英 (Hanlin complier 1387) memorialised the court, stating:

> Merchants make more money and have far more material possessions than they need while peasants working on land are always short of food and clothing. Driven by profit, merchants tend to trade in luxurious commodities that are neither edible nor wearable. A single trip by a merchant generates more income than a peasant can make in a whole year.[176]

Qu Dajun 屈大均 (1630–1696) described the situation in Guangdong thus:

> People here are all following the current fashion to engage in trade. They trade sugar, fruits, chests, ironworks, spices, etc. to Henan and Zhejiang in the north, as well as to Japan, the Ryūkyū Kingdom and Luzon overseas. They make their fortune in this way. Peasants, toiling on land for the whole year, often only meet with a poor harvest. That is why our people have put down their hoes and rakes and gone in for trading.[177]

Though the principle of "*zhongnong yimo* 重農抑末" (emphasising agriculture, the principal, while suppressing commerce, the marginal) was a traditional economic principle, there were few dynasties that carried it out in such a serious manner as the Ming. In the Ming *Huangce* 黃冊 (*Yellow Registers*) the three main occupations were farming, artisanship and soldiering.[178] Merchants were deliberately placed at the bottom of the social echelon, as encapsulated in the "*shi-nong-gong-shang* ideology 士農工商" (scholar, peasant, artisan and merchant).[179] The government intentionally blocked the avenue of social mobility for merchants by disqualifying them from participating in the imperial examinations. Merchants were thus barred from access to political power in a way that was not the case for peasants.[180] Merchants were not permitted to sit the civil examinations during most of the Ming era. For instance, among the 110 new *jinshi* degree holders in the second year of the Jianwen 建文 reign (1400), 83 were from peasant families, 16 from military families, 6 from scholarly families, one from a salt worker family and one from a geomancer's family.

175 *Ming Taizu shilu*, *j.* 177, p. 8b.

176 *Zhaodai jingji yan* 昭代經濟言 (*Economic Issues of a Just Government*) by Wang Shuying 王叔英 (?–1402), in *Congshu jicheng chubian*, *j.* 1, p. 12.

177 *Guangdong xinyu* 廣東新語 (*New Stories from Guangdong*) by Qu Dajun 屈大均 (1630–1696). (Beijing: Zhonghua shuju, 1700–edition, 1983), *j.* 14. pp. 371–372.

178 "Zhuansuan zhi ji 傳算之籍" (Accounting Records), in *Daxue yanyi bu*, *j.* 31, p. 13b.

179 *Zhaodai wangzhang*, p. 54b.

180 *Ming Shizong shilu*, *j.* 545, p. 7a.

There were none with a merchant's background.[181] And in the 23rd year of the Jiajing reign (1544), of the 312 new *jinshi* degree holders there was not a single candidate registered as a merchant or from a mercantile family.[182] The commitment to *zhongnong yishang* also led to the persecution of anyone who was involved in economic matters. Petty officials who were engaged in practical economic administration were also barred from participating in the examination system. The Hongwu Emperor instructed the *zhongshu sheng* 中書省 (the prime minister's office) in the fourth year of his reign (1371): "*lixu* 吏胥" (government petty officials who are engaged in money-making matters) can be corrupted in the process of their occupation hence banned from sitting the civil examination to become an official."[183] Furthermore, merchants were also psychologically humiliated by being forbidden from worshipping their ancestors with rice, due to the fact that they were not engaged in the primary enterprise of farming, even though worshipping ancestors with rice had long been a tradition.[184] Along with servants, they were even forbidden from wearing boots.[185] During the Ming, merchants thus suffered from more discrimination than during any other dynasty.

The government granted full administrative powers to the *lizhang*, in part so that that they could keep a check on unwanted commercial activity. Regulations decreed: "Peasants are not allowed to leave their land and travel beyond their villages. Each family's daily itinerary must be monitored by their neighbours for mutual surveillance." [186] Those involved in activities outside their registered occupations (such as peasants engaging in commercial activity) could be arrested, and their neighbours would face the same penalty for failure to report this to the authorities.[187] "Anyone who travels one hundred *li* (50 km) and beyond must apply for a travel permit, and, if found without this, is to be taken into custody and punished."[188] In addition, "Those who issue a travel permit to an unqualified person will be liable to 80 lashes."[189] For a "*yuanxing dingyin* 遠行丁引" (permit for long

181 *Mingdai dengke lu huibian* 明代登科錄彙編 (*Files on Successful Candidates in the Civil Examinations of the Ming Dynasty*). (Taipei: Taiwan Student Publication 臺灣學生書局, 1969), vol. 1, pp. 11–68.

182 Ibid., vol. 10, pp. 5255–5415.

183 *Guoque* 国榷 (*Annalistic Deliberations on State Affairs*) by Tan Qian 談遷 (1594–1657), in *Siku xuxiu*, fasc. 358. (no *juan*,), p. 298.

184 "Bai gong ji 百工記" (Handicraft Industries), in *Songchuang mengyu* 松窗夢語 (*Dreaming by the Window under the Pines*) by Zhang Han 張瀚 (1511–1593), in *Wulin wangzhe* 武林往哲遺著 (*Posthumous Works of Great Scholars*) edited by Ding Bing 丁丙 (1832–1899). (Hangzhou: Qiantang, 1898), *j.* 4, pp. 12a–12b.

185 *Ming huiyao*, *j.* 23, p. 6b.

186 "Hu zhi dingye, disan 互之丁業, 第三" (Mutual Surveillance of Families Members and their Occupations, Section Three), in *Zhaodai wangzhang*, p. 56a.

187 Ibid., pp. 55a–55b.

188 "Bing lü 兵律" (Law on Armed Forces), in *Da Ming lü* 大明律 (*The Grand Ming Code*) by Liu Weiqian 劉惟謙 (Minister of justice, 1373), in *Siku cunmu*, *j.* 15, p. 2b.

189 *Tangming lu hebian* 唐明律合编 (*The Combined Tang and Ming Law Codes*) by Xue Yunsheng 薛允升 (1820–1891). (Tianjin: Xushi changed jingtan, 1922), *j.* 8, pp. 2a–3b.

distance travel) to be valid it had to provide details about the holder's name, place of residence, the name of the "*baihu* 百戶" (Company Commander) of the county or garrison, the age, height, facial characteristics, complexion and occupation of the holder, as well as the names of all immediate relatives. If, while on a journey, any discrepancy was found between the details recorded in the permit and the appearance of the holder, then the person would be escorted back to his hometown and punished.[190] The grandfather of the scholar Zhu Yunming 祝允明 (1461–1527), faced decapitation for losing his travel document and was only pardoned by the emperor minutes before his execution.[191]

Before embarking on any business trip merchants were required to apply for a licence. For this to be granted, the authorities needed to conduct a thorough examination of the goods to be traded, the destination of the merchant and the pricing structure. Even if an applicant received a licence any of his movements would be tracked: "The military is empowered to check a merchant's permit along the route, at a ferry terminal, in the street or in their shops."[192] Guesthouse owners were required to report detailed information about customers who were merchants, including the specification of their cargo and a detailed business itinerary, to the military officials.[193] Merchants were not allowed to store goods anywhere they liked; the government warehouse was the only legal place where they could keep their cargo.[194] Contrary to the practice during the Yuan and the Song dynasties, the Ming outlawed brokerage. Merchants were not permitted to appoint brokers of any kind.[195] When merchants eventually made their way to a market, they would frequently find that a government-appointed village elder and/or patrolman would question them and check their prices.[196]

During the early Ming years the government limited commerce and controlled prices. Merchants were not allowed to charge the market value for their goods because the government had fixed prices on most commodities.[197] If any discrepancy arose in a transaction, merchants would be accused of swindling.[198] If the items

190 "Minwu juan 民務卷" (People's Livelihoods), in *Lügong Shizheng lu* 呂公實政祿 (*Rules and Regulations for Practical Administration by Lü Kun*) by Lü Kun 呂坤 (1436–1518), in *Siku xuxiu* 子, fasc. 164, *j.* 4, pp. 59b–60a.

191 "Qianwen ji 前聞記" (A Record of Things Heard) by Zhu Yunming 祝允明 (1460–1527), in *Jilu huibian* 紀祿匯編 (*Collections of Essays, Stories,Comments, and Quotations before the Ming Jiajing Reign*) by Shen Jiefu 沈節甫 (Chen Yuting 陳于廷 Publication, 1617), *j.* 202 , pp. 10a–b.

192 Cao Renhu, *Qinding xu wenxian tongkao*, *j.* 10, p. 4b.

193 Zashui bu, section #7" 雜稅部彙考七 (Miscellaneous Levies), in 經濟彙編食貨典, *j.* 223, *Gujin tushu jichen* 古今圖書集成 (*A Collection of Books through the Ages*) by Chen Menglei 陳夢雷 (1651–1723). (Beijing: Zhonghua shuju, 1985), p. 55a.

194 *Ming huiyao*, *j.* 57, p. 7b.

195 "Yahang: dibashi'er 牙行：第八十二" (Brokerage: section 82), in *Yuzhi dagao juanshou* 御制大誥卷首 (*Imperial Admonitions, first section*), in *Siku xuxiu*, p. 125a (no *juan*).

196 *Loushantang ji* 樓山堂集 (*The Loushantang Collection*) by Wu Yingqi 吳應箕 (1594–1645), in *Siku jinhui* 集, fasc. 11, *j.* 12, pp. 6b–7a.

197 *Ming huiyao*, *j.* 57, p. 19a.

198 *Da Ming lü*, *j.* 10, p. 2a.

were found to be in a poor condition or the transaction was conducted in an unfair manner, or if the goods were less durable than claimed, they would be confiscated and the merchant could be liable to no fewer than fifty cane floggings.[199] In such an environment, where the administration feared the disruptive nature of commerce and merchants were regarded as an antagonistic force, foreign trade was unthinkable. The government's commitment in principle to maintaining stability by conserving a self-sufficient land-based economy and an egalitarian peasant-centred society was used to justify its harsh policies on trade.

The Politicised Culture of Consumption

During the early years of the Ming social consumption was under strict control. The government controlled the distribution of social wealth and placed constraints on the rich and the privileged. It feared that unconstrained consumption culture would lead to destructive competition in a society where resources were limited and that this would undermine the social and economic foundations of state and society. This meant that the authorities could not afford to allow free and open consumption. Self-interestedness and self-indulgence were condemned as a prime cause of social antagonism and discontent. All forms of consumption were therefore subject to strict political control. The level and nature of consumption had to be limited to a magnitude compatible with the ideal of a self-sufficient social and economic system. Justification for such policies was drawn from Confucian moral values. For instance, *The Analects* state: "If we allow self-seeking to run rampage there will be conflicts throughout the society."[200] Ming policymakers also justified their policies through reference to the great Song Neo-Confucian authority Zhu Xi 朱熹 (1130–1200), who stated: "Human material desire must be eliminated in order for the Way to prevail,"[201] and that "the first and most important theme for Confucianism is the debate over moral righteousness and selfishness".[202] He warned rulers: "Justice and righteousness are always weakened by egotism and self-interest."[203]

The Hongwu Emperor personally set an example for his subjects to follow, taking guidance from Confucius: "Being an emperor he should suppress his desire for self interest and refrain from indulgence in material enjoyment. His every gesture, every word must be virtuous",[204] and "only when the emperor is virtuous (free from material desire) can he rule the court; only a virtuous court can manage its officials; only the virtuous officials can lead the people; only virtuous people can give rise to

199 Ibid., *j.* 10. p. 4a.

200 *Lunyu*, in *Siku quanshu*, fasc. 197, 'Liren' 4, *j.* 2, p. 12a.

201 *Zhuzi yulei* 朱子語類 (*Conversations of Master Zhu*) by Zhu Xi, in *Siku quanshu*, fasc. 700, *j.* 12, p. 13a.

202 *Er Cheng yishu* 二程遺書 (*Surviving Books by the Cheng Brothers*) by Cheng Hao 程顥 (1032–1085) and Cheng Yi 程頤 (1033–1107), in *Siku quanshu*, fasc. 698, *j.* 11, p. 11a.

203 *Zhuzi yulei* 朱子語類 (*The Sayings of Zhuzi*) by Zhu Xi 朱熹 (1130–1200), *j.* 13, pp. 4a–b.

204 *Qian Hanshu*, in *Siku quanshu*, fasc. 533, *j.* 56, p. 25a.

good social order and political stability."[205] The emperor did his best to adhere to these injunctions. He ordered the gold fittings on his royal coach to be stripped off and replaced with copper in order to save state spending.[206] He refused to eat the top-quality rice, a tribute from Jinhua 金華 county, and refused to consume a top-quality wine and *ginseng*, a tribute from Taiyuan 太原. He insisted that these products cost too much to produce and were too great a burden on his people. He decreed that these goods were an intolerable waste of state revenue and forbade government departments from demanding such luxurious tributes.[207] It was reported that the Empress Ma 馬皇后, who had been a comrade-in-arms of the future emperor during the war against the Mongols, was always seen washing the emperor's clothes at the creek near the palace. Despite her status, the Empress wanted to set an example about frugality and simplicity.[208] Following this example, "the Yongle emperor refused to discard his worn shirt and asked his mother to patch it because he wanted to save money in order that less tax could be levied on his subjects."[209] Self-interest and self-indulgence came to be seen as the trademark of corruption. When an official was caught embezzling public funds and then committed suicide while under investigation, the emperor told the censors: "He deserved to die because a good official should abstain from striving for self interest. What he did shows that he was a selfish person and there is no pity in losing such a corrupted person."[210]

Side by side with this moral and ideological direction, the government launched a comprehensive campaign to restrain material exhaustion. The Hongwu Emperor clarified the imperative: "If the emperor sets a good example, frugality will secure good administration of the empire; if the king does the same, frugality will secure good management of a kingdom; if he refrains from luxury, frugality will secure a scholar's career, and if he adheres to the same principle, frugality will secure a good life for a common person."[211] The emperor was evidently influenced by the great Confucian scholar Dong Zhongshu 董仲舒 (BCE 179–104), who regarded excessive consumption as politically destructive: "We wear clothes to keep us warm, but not for the purpose of beauty. We wear coloured clothes to distinguish our social status, not to satisfy aesthetical desire … human desire will lead to disaster."[212] While Dong Zhongshu was merely a thinker who could only recommend an imagined benchmark level for consumption, the Hongwu Emperor was able to put the ideal into practice. Under his leadership, society during the early Ming was almost akin to an ascetic community. He restricted himself to an unprecedentedly low

205 Ibid., *j.* 56, p. 8a.
206 *Ming huiyao*, *j.* 23, p. 4a.
207 Ibid., *j.* 57, p. 10a.
208 *Huang Ming zhengyao*, *j.* 15, p. 10a.
209 Ibid., *j.* 15, pp. 10b-11a.
210 *Huang Ming diangu jiwen*, *j.* 1, p. 19a.
211 *Wugong ji* 武功集 (*A Collection about Wugong County*) by Xu Youzhen 徐有貞 (*jinshi* 1433), in *Siku quanshu*, fasc. 1245, *j.* 1, p. 9a.
212 Dong Zhongshu, *Chunqiu fanlu*, in *Siku quanshu*, fasc. 181, *j.* 8, p. 2b.

level of material consumption. He made his own menu for breakfast. He would eat neither eggs nor meat, only vegetables: "His bed was no different from that of a well-off peasant except for the two painted dragon symbols on the base".[213] He ordered the crown prince to grow vegetables in the palace in order to save on expenditure. He also banned the construction of any flower gardens, landscaping or dancing platforms in all of his 26 sons' castles.[214] He ordered the closure of the zoo, banned the keeping of animals such as tigers for amusement, and insisted on raising cows for practical use instead.[215]

Moved by the call for political stability and inspired by the emperor's high ethical standards, the government set up a whole set of detailed benchmarks for levels of consumption. The basic categories of life, food, clothing, housing and transport 衣食住行 (*yi shi zhu xing*) were controlled and monitored. Regarding "*yi* 衣" (clothing) the regulations were unmistakable:

> Farmers are allowed to wear silk, but not satin; merchants are allowed to wear cotton but not silk.[216]
> Neither soldiers, peasants nor merchants are allowed to wear boots.[217]
> Anybody found wearing a cloth different from that in general use [among his class] would be fined.[218]

The Hongwu Emperor was irritated on seeing a young man from a noble family wearing a beautiful robe, which was said to cost 500 *guan* 貫 in copper coins. The emperor reprimanded the young man by reminding him that 500 *guan* was more than the total income of a peasant for a whole year and ordered him to refrain from such wasteful spending. [219] On checking the consumption on *shi* 食 (foodstuffs) the law was definite: "Nobody is allowed to eat food above the general accepted standard regardless of his or her financial situation." [220] The local community leader was empowered to fine anybody who consumed luxury foods.[221] Farmers were banned from growing glutinous rice because it was the basis for winemaking. The law only permitted peasants to grow plain rice as a staple food (wine was considered too luxurious a commodity to be tolerated).[222] On limiting the *zhu* 住 (housing) the law

---

213 *Donggu zhuiyan* 東谷贅言 (*Superfluous Words from Donggu*) by Ao Ying 敖英 (*jinshi* 1521), in *Siku cunmu* 子, fasc. 102, p. 18b (no *juan*).

214 Ming zuxun: qin wangfu zhi 明祖訓: 親王府制" (Ancestral Injunctions Regarding Princes' Residences), in *Ming huidian* 明會典 (*Statues of the Ming Dynasty*) compiled by Xu Fu 徐溥 (1428–1499), Li Dongyang 李東陽 (1447–1516) *et. al.*, in *Siku quanshu*, fasc. 617–618, p. 147b, and *Huang Ming zhengyao*, *j.* 15, p. 8b.

215 *Huang Ming diangu jiwen*, *j.* 3, p. 10a.

216 *Ming huiyao*, *j.* 24, p. 5b.

217 Gu Qiyuan, *Kezuo zhuiyu*, *j.* 10, p. 40b.

218 *Chengren sheyue yan* 澄人社約言 (*Moral Standards and Community Regulations to Become an Ideal Community Member*) by Liu Zongzhou 劉宗周 (1578–1645), in *Siku cunmu* 子, fasc. 15, p. 11a (no *juan*).

219 *Huang Ming diangu jiwen*, *j.* 5, p. 90.

220 Liu Zongzhou, *Chengren sheyue*, p. 11a.

221 Gu Qiyuan, *Kezuo zhuiyu*, *j.* 5, pp. 39b–40a.

222 *Huang Ming diangu jiwen*, *j.* 1, p. 14b.

was unfaltering. People were not allowed to build a house in whatever style they preferred.[223] The regulations stated: "Commoners were not authorized to dwell in any kind of buildings but a hut, and the hut was not permitted to have a drawing room."[224] A commoner's house was limited to only three rooms.[225] Anyone who owned a house that was beyond the permitted standard or used unauthorized materials in the building could, together with the builder, face punishment.[226] On the limitation of "*xing* 行" (transport) the law was equally severe. Commoners were banned from riding in coaches or on horses.[227] Nobody was allowed to take a sedan-chair.[228] A donkey was the only permitted form of transportation that a county magistrate could use.[229]

The government also imposed stringent regulations to keep a check on recreational activities: "If a soldier is found playing music his tongue will be cut out, [if he is found] playing sport his foot will be chopped off, [if he is found] playing chess his hand will be broken, [if he is found] engaging in trade he will be banished to a remote area ... even a different hairstyle could incriminate him [and lead to] exile."[230] The regulations also stated that "if somebody is found consuming more than they are entitled to their materials or property will be confiscated and the informer will be rewarded with one-third of the things confiscated. If the confiscation of property is not convenient the culprit will be fined in silver and banished to a remote region."[231] Such control over consumption was unparalleled: never before in China's history had such regulations been imposed.

Consumption in early Ming society was maintained at a mere subsistence level. There was little demand for commodities and services. Even the very rich and powerful consumed little. Gu Qiyuan 顧起元 (1565–1628) said: "Before the Jiajing period, there were few rich families who dared to live in a wrongly-categorized house or have 'excessive' food on their dinner table," and "less than 1–2 per cent of the rich and powerful families in Jiangnan hired entertainers."[232] It was said that Jiang Xingzhong 蔣性中 (*jinshi* 1427), a retired Supervising Secretary (*geishi zhong* 給事中), welcomed his former colleague Zhou Chen 周忱 (1381–1453), Grand Coordinator

223 *Da Ming huidian*, *j.* 62, pp. 1a–3a.

224 *Wujiang xianzhi* 吳江縣志 (*The Gazetteer of Wuxian County*) by Chen Qixiang 陳其纕 (Wujiang county magistrate, 1747), Shen Hong 沈彤 (1688–1752) and Ni Shimeng 倪師孟 (*jinshi* 1723), in *Zhongguo difang zhi jicheng* 中國地方誌集成, vol. 20, *j.* 38, p. 1b.

225 *Huang Ming diangu jiwen*, *j.* 2, p. 27b.

226 *Yuzhi dagao juanshou*, *j.* 11, p. 3b.

227 Zhang Han, *Songchuang mengyu*, *j.* 4, pp. 12a–b.

228 *Huang Ming diangu jiwen*, *j.* 1, p. 14b.

229 "Jinyan 今言" (*Historical Notes Collection on the Reigning Dynasty*) by Zheng Xiao 鄭曉 (1499–1566), in *Congshu jicheng chubian*, pp. 128–129.

230 Gu Qiyuan, *Kezuo zhuiyu*, *j.* 10, pp. 39b–40a.

231 *Baizhai ji* 柏齋集 (*The Baizhai Collection*) by He Tang 何瑭 (1474–1543), in *Siku quanshu*, fasc. 1266, *j.* 1, p. 21a.

232 Gu Qiyuan, *Kezuo zhuiyu*, and *j.* 1, p. 31a and *j.* 5, pp. 39b–40a.

of Jiangnan, not with a banquet but with a plate of boiled weeds.[233] There were too many risks of being charged with 'over consumption'. The well-off families from Wuxian had to hide their wealth from the public. In the *County Gazetteer for Wuxian* it states: "Some middle class families used to build a shabby straw hut in front of their yard in order to cover up their brick house in the back. Wealth had to be hidden from the authorities."[234] The suppression of social consumption consequently suffocated demand and led to low levels of manufacturing and business transactions. For instance, it was recorded that "there were few merchant families in Weishi county 尉氏縣 and only occasionally one or two of them would go to the capital for business,"[235] and "there were few cases of land and house transactions in Nanjing 南京 even though there were many big families and retired officials living there."[236]

The foreign trade prohibition policy directly mirrored the Ming culture of politically constrained consumption. Following the puritan example set by the Hongwu Emperor, the living conditions for the general population were maintained at a subsistence level. The Ming economy was caught in a vicious circle. Reduced demand led to less production, while less production further decreased demand. With little consumption, there was little incentive for manufacturing and very few business transactions. In such an environment, where simplicity and frugality become the mainstream culture, foreign trade was unthinkable. We may think that the maritime prohibition sounds unbelievable, but when we set the policy within the context of the social and economic environment of the early Ming years we will find that the policy was practical in social terms, acceptable in cultural terms and institutionally viable.

Currency Controls

In such a constrained economic environment, money could be a disruptive factor. Thus currency control was a necessary strategy to reign in commerce and help secure a stable and self-sufficient economic system. Because of its strong intrinsic value, silver was feared as a potential destabilisator. Wang Shizhen 王世貞 (1526–1590) said: "Among the four types of money, silver was regarded as the best of all. Paper notes were too prone to inflation, copper was not highly valued and vulnerable to debasement and gold was too rare and expensive."[237] As the most valued form of money, silver constituted a direct threat to the economic system. Commercial forces could undermine political directives and stimulate commodity exchange,

233 *Yunjian zhi luo* 雲間志略 (*A Brief Survey of Songjiang*) by He Sanwei 何三畏 (Prefecture Judge 1583), in *Siku jinhui* 子, fasc. 8, *j.* 7, p. 30a.

234 *Wujiang xianzhi*, *j.* 38, p. 1b.

235 *Weishi xianzhi* 尉士縣志 (*Gazetteer of Weishi County*) by Zeng Jiagao 曾嘉誥 (*juren* 1537) and Wang Xin 汪心 (Ming, Jiajing author, 1523–1573) (*Tianyige* 天一閣, 1548), *j.* 1, p. 36b.

236 Gu Qiyuan, *Kezuo zhuiyu*, *j.* 1, p. 31a.

237 *Fengzhou biji xuji* 鳳州筆記續集 (*A Continuation of Random Notes from Fenzhou*) by Wang Shizhen 王世貞 (1526–1590), in *Siku cunmu*, 114, *j.* 3, p. 4b.

and if money was allowed to rule it would produce a strong counterforce to the politically controlled social and economic system of the early Ming period. In such circumstances, the much-feared widening of the social gap and escalating social conflict would be unavoidable.

Huang Zongxi 黄宗羲 (1610–1695) depicted an ideal picture of the kind of barter economy anticipated by the early Ming regime: "Trade should be based on the model by which men barter for their requirements with grain and women with cloth … the former great rulers have all prohibited the circulation of gold and silver in their society to achieve political stability."[238] This was what the early Ming administration carried out. Money in any form except the government-issued paper notes was strictly banned from circulation from the 8th year of the Hongwu reign (1375). The law was severe: "Offenders against the prohibition on the use of silver and gold will be punished and their goods confiscated, while informers will be rewarded."[239] The emperor ordered the arrest of Ding Yan 丁炎, a Supervising Secretary who was accused of sending his men to Sichuan 四川 to trade with silver.[240] A peasant from Jiangxia 江夏 who buried his father with some silverware was prosecuted for violating the silver prohibition law. He was only saved from banishment by the emperor's timely pardon after considering his piety towards his father.[241] Copper-cash was also banned. In the 27th year of the Hongwu reign (1394), a directive was issued on copper: "Copper coins must be handed back to the authorities within fifteen days in exchange for paper notes. Anyone found hiding or burying copper coins will be punished by law."[242] Precious metal that could be used for money became so politically sensitive that most silver mining was banned. When the local officials from Shandong 山東 reported to the emperor in the fifteenth year of the reign (1382) that silver had been discovered in the province, the emperor declined the opportunity to mine the metal. He also declined another proposal for the mining of silver in Jiezhou 階洲. And five years later, in 1388, when a silver mine was discovered in Shanxi 山西, he again rejected the proposition to mine.[243]

The only legal money was the government-issued *Da Ming tongbao* 大明通寶 (*Great Ming Circulating Currency*). It was a paper note issued against neither gold nor silver deposits, hence it was not convertible to any form of precious metal.[244] It carried no intrinsic value: "The paper notes' circulation was made compulsory by law."[245] Though the *Da Ming tongbao* gave the authorities an opportunity to control economic activity, its credibility was very low. The original exchange rate between silver, rice and paper notes was fixed at the rate of 1:1:1 (one tael of silver: one *dan*

238 Huang Zongxi, *Mingyi daifang lu*, p. 34a (no *juan*).

239 Cao Renhu, *Qinding xuwenxian tongkao*, *j.* 10, p. 2a.

240 *Chunming mengyu lu* 春明夢余祿 (*Writings After a Bright Spring Dream*) by Sun Chengze 孫承澤 (1592–1676), in *Siku quanshu*, fasc. 868, *j.* 47, p. 3.

241 *Qinding xu wenxian tongkao*, *j.* 10, p. 8b.

242 *Ming Taizu shilu*, *j.* 234, p. 2b.

243 *Mingshu*, *j.* 82, pp. 8b–9a.

244 *Da Ming huidian*, *j.* 31, pp. 3a–b.

245 Cao Renhu, *Qinding xu wenxian tongkao*, *j.* 10, pp. 1a–b.

of cereal: one *guan* of paper notes). But this was an ideal that was never matched in practice. In the 2nd year of the Chenghua 成化 reign (1466), the exchange rate was lowered to one *guan* of paper notes for 0.003 *taels* of silver. The inflation rate was 330 times. [246] Merchants hesitated to accept the notes and refused to retain them, as they were devalued almost on a daily basis.[247] The frustrated traders were not alone; the government itself did not trust the money either. For example, in order to stop counterfeiting of the paper notes, the authorities would reward informers with silver rather than the handy paper notes.[248] Similarly, those who provided information leading to the arrest of merchants for violating the silver prohibition were rewarded with the confiscated goods rather than paper notes.[249]

As the politically backed paper currency lost ground, the socially valued silver bullion gained in value. The monetary value of the *Da Ming tongbao* decreased dramatically, while silver's worth increased significantly. During the Song and Yuan dynasties, from 1075 until 1346, one *dan* of rice was worth 1.84 *taels* of silver, but under the Ming, between 1436 and 1589, it was worth only 0.94 *taels* of silver.[250] Similarly, between 1068 and 1156, silk was worth 1.83 *taels* per bolt of cloth, but during the Ming, between 1395 and 1644, it was worth only 0.60 *taels* per bolt.[251] The exchange rate between gold and silver was around 1:10 between 979 and 1346, then increased to as much as 1:4 in the period between 1375 and 1644. This increase in the value of silver in Ming China was also evident in the international exchange rate. For instance, the gold-silver exchange rate was 1:10.34 in Japan in 1575, but it was 1:4 in China.[252] This meant there was much profit to be made in bringing silver to China, and the attraction of such profits meant the trade in silver was difficult to control.

For the Ming administration, silver reflected the difficulty in trying to constrain the economy and this made it politically irritating. This monetary metal could power the commercialisation of the economy and, in the process, by drawing peasants away from their paddy field into commercial activity as an unwanted consequences, it could lead to disrupting the self-sufficient society based around the *lijia* community. Although the self-sufficient system was painstakingly upheld the power of silver was still annoyingly commanding. Silver was so expensive and so sought after in China that Chinese merchants wanted nothing but silver in return

---

246 Ibid., *j.* 10, p. 26a.

247 *Ming huiyao*, *j.* 55 p. 3b.

248 Cao Renhu, *Qinding xu wenxian tongkao*, *j.* 10, pp. 1a–2a

249 Gu Yanwu, *Rizhi lu*, in *Siku quanshu*, fasc. 858, *j.* 11, p. 21a.

250 Quan Hansheng 全漢升, *Zhongguo jingji shi yanjiu* 中國經濟史研究 (*Studies in Chinese Economic History*). (Taibei: Xinyan yanjiusuo, 1987), pp. 578–579.

251 Ibid.

252 Tetsuo Kamiki and Kozo Yamamura, "Silver Mines and Sung Coins: A Monetary History of Medieval and Modern Japan in International Perspective", in John F. Richards, ed., *Precious Metals in the Later Medieval and Early Modern Worlds*. (Durham: Carolina Academic Press, 1983), p. 346.

for the Chinese products they had to sell.[253] And Japanese and Spanish American silver could readily be supplied to meet the Chinese demand for the metal driven by the great demand for Chinese products in the international markets. Silver's damaging impact was so grave that a political interference was desperately needed to curb the disturbing situation. A prohibition on foreign trade became an indispensable political tool to block the circulation of the metal by invalidating its financial function. And maritime prohibition was believed to be a handy and efficient policy to weaken its supply by plugging up the overseas inflow of the metal. Silver, the currency of the previous economies was thereafter calculatingly made redundant, and the trade of it illegal. Maritime prohibition was intentionally structured as an inextricable part of the Ming government strategy to maintain its stability-orientated social and economic ideals.

Self-Sufficiency

The early Ming years saw the principle of self-sufficiency in full operation. In the 18th year of the Hongwu reign (1385), the emperor instructed the Minister of Revenue:

> We should maintain a system by which men can work in the fields and women weave at home. It is the fundamental guarantee for a better society. Recalling history, the life quality of our ancestors was always good because during their time there was no man without farming and no woman without weaving. The situation has changed only since the introduction of a commerce-driven, money seeking phenomenon, which has led to the abandonment of the self-sufficiency system.[254]

The Hongwu administration regulated the peasant landholding and self-sufficient pattern of production:

> Those who own land of 5–10 *mu* must plant half in staple crops and half in mulberry trees, or in cotton or hemp for making handcrafts for self-consumption; if they own more than 10 *mu* they are required to plant more than half in mulberry, cotton or hemp. If a peasant fails to plant the required trees, cotton or hemp, they will be fined two bolts of cotton cloth or linen for their failure to plant the required cotton and hemp, and one bolt of silk for their failure to plant mulberry trees.[255]

The objective was more than clear: peasants would need no commodities from outside and their own landholding should provide the source for everything they needed. A society without commercial activities would be a society free from exploitation and contradictions.

The self-sufficient principle was all-inclusive. The military was no exception. To weaken the power of commerce, the military, which consumed nearly half of the total revenue, was the biggest consumer of commodities (apart from the state it-

253 Zhang Xie, *Dongxiyang kao*, *j.* 7, p. 3a.

254 Xu Xueju, *Guochao dianhui*, *j.* 92, pp. 2a–b.

255 Ibid., p. 2b.

self).[256] The government required that it be self-sufficient, independent of the market. In the 6th year of the Hongwu reign (1373), every soldier was granted 50 *mu* of land, one cow and seeds for his farming needs. It was required that 70 per cent of soldiers work in agricultural activity along the border regions while the remaining 30 per cent served on guard duty. In the hinterland, 80 per cent were required to engage in farming with the remaining 20 per cent to serve on guard duty.[257] The aim of this policy was to "feed a million troops without costing the government a single grain of rice."[258] To undermine further any chance of commercial activity, every soldier was required to plant mulberry trees, persimmons, chestnuts, peaches and dates.[259] In the 24th year of the Hongwu reign (1391), instead of purchasing lacquer in order to make towlines for the warships, the emperor ordered the military to plant 500,000 lacquer trees near Beijing to produce lacquer itself.[260] In the 25th year of the Hongwu reign (1392) the central administration ordered that every garrison plant 200 mulberry, date and persimmon trees for their own consumption.[261]

Just as each peasant family and each soldier was required to rely on their own production to provide what they needed, so the state, the biggest consumer in the society, also sought to meet it own needs. The monopoly imposed on state-run industry was devised to keep commercial forces at bay. It was a sophisticated state-run manufacturing system instituted to provide what the state required in every possible category. Manufacturing ranged from office stationery to military equipment. Six government departments were in charge of the different industries, from mining and warehousing to manufacturing, with 62 different trades all told.[262] For instance, for the provision of textiles, twenty-eight textile bureaus were established, equipped with 3,500 weaving machines, manned by 10,000 employees and with an annual output reaching as much as 35,000 bolts of cloth in various styles.[263] With such extensive state-run manufacturing, there was no need to purchase anything on the open market.

The state-run manufacturing industry was exceptionally competitive. Private manufacturers were never able to compete with the state-run firms. Whereas raw materials were a main factor for pricing products in the private sector, these materials were provided free to the state industries. The tribute and taxation

---

256 Tang Shunzhi, *ChongkanJjingchuan xiansheng wenji*, *j.* 8, p. 57b.

257 *Ming huiyao*, *j.* 53, p. 7a.

258 Zhang Xuan, *Xiyuan wenjian lu*, *j.* 91, p. 18a.

259 Xu Xueju, *Guochao dianhui*, *j.* 92, p. 2b.

260 Ibid.

261 Ibid., p. 2b.

262 *Zhuozhong zhi* 酌中志 (*A Eunuch's Unbiased Description and Observation of the Court Institutions, Events, and Policy Processes*) by Liu Ruoyu 劉若愚 (Eunuch, 1622), in *Qingchao Mingji yeshi huibianben* 清朝明季野史匯編本 (*The Qing edition of the Collected Unofficial Histories of the Ming*), in *Siku xuxiu*, fasc. 437, *j.* 16, pp. 142–173.

263 Fan Jinmin 范金民, "Ming-Qing liangdai guanying zhizaoye shengchan guimo de bijiao yanjiu 明清兩代官營織造業生產規模的比較研究" (A Comparative Study of the Magnitude of the Ming and Qing State-Run Silk Manufacturing Industries), *Shilin* 史林 4 (1990), p. 62.

systems provided everything needed. Materials were collected from all parts of the country by three kinds of tribute system. The "*tugong* 土貢"-system provided local products from each county to the court on an annual basis.[264] The "*eban* 額辦"-system required a fixed amount of tax be paid in local products. Finally, the "*zaban* 雜辦"-system was an unfixed amount of tax in local produce demanded randomly according to circumstances.[265] If the *tugong*, *eban*, and *zaban* were still not enough the state industry would be supplemented with the "*choufen* 抽分"-policy, which required that a fee for transportation licences be collected, in kind as a percentage of the total goods, at road and river checkpoints.[266] High-ranking government officials supervised the *Choufen jiu* 抽分局 (Collection Bureau) in order to secure the supply of raw materials for the state-run industries.[267]

The state-run industries also enjoyed a free supply of labour. Workers and artisans were unpaid corvée labourers.[268] The state imposed two kinds of corvée obligations that together guaranteed a supply of artisans. One obligation related to the rotating artisans, who were obliged to serve a three month term once every two to five years, depending on their profession. The other obligation related to the permanently registered paid artisans, who were available for all the sixty-two trades, and resulted in a labour pool involving as many as 232,089 men across the different trades.[269] To give an example of the scale of this activity, in the 26th year of the Hongwu reign (1393), 4,541 blacksmiths, 33,962 carpenters and 465 tailors were discharging their corvée liability in the capital. This source of labour was relatively stable, as anyone who fled the worksite would face punishment.[270]

The free supply of raw materials and labour were not, however, the most important factors that ensured the competitiveness of the state-run industries. It was the monopoly system of production licences that secured the dominant position for these industries. The state-enforced monopoly over production gave the state industries their crucial advantage. For example, the production of salt and tea, the two most lucrative commodities in the empire, were strict monopolies, and the regulations stipulated that "anyone who boils salt privately deserves the death penalty."[271] The salt fields themselves, as well as the supply of fuel for the boiling

264 *Renhe xianzhi* 仁和縣志 (*Gazetteer of Renhe County*) by Shen Chaoxuan 沈朝宣 (Magistrate of Jiangling county, Jiajing reign 1521–1567; Jiajing edition 丁氏嘉惠堂，武林掌故叢書, 1875–1907), *j.* 3, p. 38a.

265 *Quanzhou fuzhi* 泉州府志 (*Gazetteer of Quanzhou Prefecture*) by Huang Ren 黄任 (*juren* 1702) and Huai Yinbu 懷蔭布 (*jinshi* 1736), in *Zhongguo difangzhi jicheng*, vol. 22, *j.* 21, pp. 87a–88a. See also Cao Renhu, *Qinding xu wenxian tongkao*, in *Siku quanshu*, fasc. 626, *j.* 29, pp. 1a–b.

266 Cao Renhu, *Qinding xu wenxian tongkao*, *j.* 24, p. 21b, and *Gujin tushu jicheng*, *j.* 223, p. 55b.

267 Cao Renhu, *Qinding xu wenxian tongkao*, *j.* 24, p. 28b.

268 *Ming Yingzong shilu*, *j.* 39, p. 9b; see also *Han* [xx] *zoushu* 韓 xx 奏疏 (*The Memorials of Han* [xx]), by Han Dazhang 韓大章 (*jinshi* 1493), in *MJSWB*, vol. 1 (Supplementary Volume), *j.* 2, p. 4b.

269 *Da Ming huidian*, *j.* 189, pp. 1a–5a.

270 "Kaogong dian 考工典", disan juan 第三卷" (Artisan Regulations, volume 3), in *Jingji huibian kaogongdian* 經濟彙編考工典, in *Gujin tushu jicheng*, *j.* 3, p. 10b.

271 *Da Ming huidian*, *j.* 34, p. 14b.

process were both under strict government supervision.[272] The government organized the salt workers in military fashion: "Once registered, salt workers are not permitted to alter their occupations. Anyone who is deceitful about his identity (in order to work for others) will receive 80 strokes of the cane."[273] And with regard to tea production, the government controlled the industry by prohibiting private tea farming: "Tea farmers are required to sell only to government-appointed merchants and at a fixed price. Otherwise, their tea gardens will be confiscated."[274] The government imposed a tax of two *liang* of dried tea for each tea-tree.[275] "Tea farmers worked day and night in their gardens but still have no way to pay the high tea tax."[276] The heavy tax on private tea production was intended to discourage individual tea farming. Many private tea farmers were forced into bankruptcy.

With such an emphasis on self-sufficiency, there was little need for commerce in the early Ming economy. And under such circumstances, where there was little market-driven demand and supply, foreign trade was unlikely to thrive. Like other commercial activities, maritime trade was stifled by the self-sufficiency system well before the harassment along the coast by Japanese pirates.

The Wider World

The early Ming pursued an introverted foreign policy. Foreign contact and foreign trade were viewed in a unilateral way. The Hongwu Emperor told his court:

> The foreign countries surrounding us are separated from us by mountains and seas. Foreigners stay in remote locations of their own. Their land is too barren to be taxed and their people are not good enough to be employed. If they do not come to harrass us, we will never have war with them. We should defeat invaders and never pursue them.... We have no need to conduct war with Japan, Korea, Vietnam and the other fifteen countries."[277]

The empire needed no foreign products and the administration showed no desire for territorial expansion and colonisation, therefore international affairs were not at the top of the government agenda.

However, the so-called "barbarians" were extremely interested in China and put trade with China at the very top of their own agendas. For this reason, the Ming policy of disengagement gave rise to continual grievance and conflict. The trade prohibition fuelled confrontations. The Ming government could not afford to wage war with its neighbors on all its borders over trade, as its military was not as strong as supposed, therefore national security relied on a more effective politicized tribute trade, which seemed to have more deterrent power than the threat of war. The Ming admini-

---

272 Gu Yanwu, *Tianxia junguo libing shu*, *j.* 26, p. 38a.
273 *Da Ming huidian*, *j.* 19, pp. 19a and 23b.
274 *Da Ming huidian*, *j.* 37, p. 4a.
275 *Ming Taizu shilu*, *j.* 70, p. 4b; *j.* 72, p. 5a.
276 Gu Yanwu, *Tianxia junguo libing shu*, *j.* 18, p. 70a.
277 *Huang Ming zuxun*, pp. 5b–6a.

stration was concerned about its ability to engage in sustained military campaigns. As Morris Rossabi points out:

> From the North Mongols' history of tribute trade we can see... the Chinese soldiers could not pursue the fleeing Mongol troops because they were unaccustomed to the desert and steppe lands of Mongolia and did not have the supply lines necessary to conduct a lengthy pursuit of the elusive nomadic cavalry. The overwhelming victories described in the Ming sources must therefore be discounted. [278]

This was also the case in the war with the Japanese pirates. Tang Shunzhi 唐順之 (*jinshi* 1529), Right Assistant Censor-in-Chief and the Grand Coordinator of Fengyang, admitted that "our naval force did not want to engage in sea battles because few of our generals and soldiers have experience of fighting at sea."[279] Such weak military faculties heightened Ming sensitivity about foreign contact. It was partly due to this sensitivity that the trade prohibition was enhanced and value was placed on tribute trade as a political instrument to gain sway vis-a-vis foreign powers.

The high demand from abroad for Chinese commodities also generated greater potential for leverage. Holding out the possible opportunity for trade was a much more persuasive means of winning over foreigners than any emphasis on philosophical or ethical values. However, the Ming authorities were faced with a dilemma. Satisfying foreigners' aspirations for trade required a greater degree of commercial engagement, yet conducting business with "barbarians" on an equal footing for the sake of profit violated the principles on which the early Ming administration was founded. The government was convinced that only by prohibiting private trade and increasing the difficulties foreigners faced in gaining access to Chinese goods could they achieve a more powerful position. As Rossabi has observed, court officials acquiesced over the trade fair in the belief that they could more readily control the Mongols.[280] Trade prohibition and tribute trade were the two pillars of international relations under the early Ming, and they were maintained for nearly two centuries.

The three tribute trade institutions were established: the "*mashi* 馬市" (horse trade fairs) in the north, the "*chamashi* 茶馬市" (tea-horse trade) in the west, and the "*shibo* 市舶" (maritime tribute trade) along the coast. Tribute became a compulsory pre-condition to gain permission to trade.[281] In order to facilitate the prohibition on trade and the operation of a tribute system, a full interdiction was imposed on all the borders. The law was severe: "Those who transport horses, cattle, iron-

---

278 Morris Rossabi, "Ming China and Inner Asia," in Frederick W. Mote and Denis Twitchett (eds.), *The Cambridge History of China, Volume 8: The Ming Dynasty*, 1368–1644, Part 2 (Cambridge: Cambridge University Press, 1998), p. 226

279 See "Tiaochen hai fang jinglüe 條陳海防經略" (An Itemized Statement of Strategies about Coastal Defence) by Tang Shunzhi 唐順之 (1507–1560), .in *Tang jingchuan jia cang ji* 唐荊川家藏集 (*The family Collection of Tang Jingchuan*) by Tang Shunzhi, in *MJSWB*, 260, *j.* 2, pp. 2a–b.

280 Morris Rossabi, "Ming China and Inner Asia" (1998), p. 226.

281 "Huiyi Riben chaogongshi yi liu 會議日本朝貢市宜疏" (Memorial on a Court Debate about Japanese Tribute), in *Nangong zouyi* 南宮奏議 (*Memorials from the Secretariat*) by Yan Song 嚴嵩 (1480–1565), in *MJSWB*, vol. 219, *j.* 1, pp. 30b–31b.

works, copper coins, silk, satin and cotton beyond the border and trade with foreigners warrant 100 lashes."[282] The law also stated: "Those who sail out on the sea, contact foreigners or trade with them will face capital punishment and their families will be banished to the frontier for penal servitude."[283] Along the border with the Mongols the prohibition on trade was accordingly strengthened: "Officers and soldiers on the border are prohibited from contacting foreigners or undertaking private trade in the name of official errands, and so on. Otherwise, they will be punished, along with their families, for a violation of the law."[284] On the western border the prohibition against private trade was put into effect through harsh regulations: "The law requires not only the execution of the smuggler but also dismemberment of the commander of the garrison through which the smuggling took place."[285] Tea consumption on the border was also restricted so as to prevent the locals from smuggling: "The law allows each household to keep no more tea leaves than what they normally consume in a month."[286] To further enhance the prohibition, people from Shanxi were not even allowed to consume tea at all.[287] "If tea cultivators are found selling their products to private merchants without permission, their products will be confiscated."[288] The notion that "everybody is equal before the law" was not just a cliché as far as the prohibition on trade was concerned. The husband of the princess Anqing 安慶公主, son-in-law of the Hongwu Emperor, was among those whom smugglers captured. All the emperor could do to comfort his grieving daughter was giving permission to allow her husband to commit suicide within 24 hours so as to preserve his dignity.[289] The court authorized the regional inspecting censor to report to the emperor directly if he found anyone going across border to trade with foreigners.[290] Many officers and soldiers were executed for violating the prohibition policy. [291]

The tribute trade was not a normal trade by any category. The *Ming shi* records: "There was no trade between China and other countries in a true commercial sense."[292] The horse trade with the Mongols was no exception. Traders from both sides had to go through complicated formalities to apply for a permit. The specification of all the goods to be traded had to be declared to the Ming military officials prior to the fair. The types and volumes of the commodities were meticulously

282 *Huang Ming shifa lu* 皇明世法祿 (*Rituals, Laws and Regulations of State Administration in the Ming Dynasty*) by Chen Renxi 陳仁熙 (1581–1676), in *Siku jinhui* 史, fasc. 15, *j.* 47, p. 26a.

283 Ibid., *j.* 8, p. 10b.

284 *Da Ming huidian*, *j.* 132, p. 12b.

285 "Chama shiyi 茶馬事宜" (Issues of the Tea and Horse Trade) by Liang Cai 梁材 (*juren* 1505), in *MJSWB*, vol. 106, *j.* 5, p. 1b.

286 Ibid., *j.* 5, p. 2a.

287 Ibid., *j.* 5, p. 3a.

288 *Ming shu*, in *Siku cunmu* 史, fasc. 39, *j.* 82, p. 2a.

289 *Guochao huidian*, *j.* 11, p. 1b.

290 *Da Ming huidian*, *j.* 130, p. 5b.

291 *Ming Xiaozong shilu*, *j.* 150, p. 8a. See also *Huang Ming baoxun*, *j.* 28, p. 62b.

292 *Ming shi*, *j.* 81, p. 22a

regulated. For example, Mongol traders were limited to 150 members with no more than 500 horses for trade. The trade venue was appointed by the government and was heavily guarded.[293] Once permission had been granted the items for trade were not to be changed. If traders wanted to alter items they had to lodge an application to the Ming emperor himself. The only exception was the grain petition of Mongol chieftains to the Yongle emperor in the winter of the fourth year of the Yongle reign (1407). When the Mongol regions were short of grain, the Mongols' leaders lodged an application to change the commodities for trade from silk to grain. The Yongle emperor granted their petition.[294] Secondly, the Ming government unilaterally controlled the trade timetable. The Chenghua (1465–1488) administration demanded that the Mongols pay tribute and trade once in every nine years, irrespective of changing circumstances.[295] Commodity prices were also pre-determined and no bargaining was allowed. For instance, in 1406 the government stipulated that an A^+ grade Mongol horse was valued at eight bolts of silk or twelve bolts of cloth, while an A grade horse was worth four bolts of silk or six bolts of cloth, and a B grade horse was worth three bolts of silk or five bolts of cloth.[296]

The tea and horse trade was managed in exactly the same way. Trade was used as a political tool. The Xifan 西番 (western non-Han nomad people) occupied a strategic position in the war with the Mongols. They were assessed as the 'right arm' of the Mongols and their territories were seen as a second frontier.[297] The government wanted to cut off the Mongols' right arm by winning Xifan support. The tea trade was devised to bring the Xifan under Chinese control, and the Ming administrators believed they could not survive without access to Chinese tea: "Tea is the imperial sword which provides the power to control the barbarians."[298] "Tea is what the barbarians need to digest their meat, dairy products and barley."[299] "If they disobey China they will have nowhere to get tea and will get sick and die."[300] A Ming official stated: "We should never underestimate the power of tea. Although other materials were also important to them, they were replaceable. If we do not provide them with grain they still have meat and cheese; and although fabric is much needed their blankets and felts can do the job. Tea is the only thing they must get from us to digest their daily food intake."[301] But the tea and horse trade was not a trade at all.

293 *Da Ming huidian*, *j.* 130, p. 5b.

294 Zhang Xuan, *Xiyuan wenjian lu*, *j.* 71, p. 27b.

295 *Da Ming huidian*, *j.* 107, pp. 3a–b.

296 Zhang Xuan, *Xiyuan wenjian lu*, *j.* 71, pp. 26a–27b.

297 *Guangzhi yi* 廣志繹 (*Extensive Interpretation of my Travel Diaries*) by Wang Shixing 王士性 (1546–1598), in *Siku cunmu* 史, fasc. 251, *j.* 1, p. 15a.

298 *Ming shu*, *j.* 82, p. 4b.

299 Zhang Xuan, *Xiyuan wenjian lu*, *j.* 66, p. 15a.

300 *Xuanghuai suichao* 雙槐歲抄 (*Colletion of Annually Studying Notes from the Two Pagoda Trees Pavillion*) by Huang Yu 黄瑜, in *Siku cunmu* 子, fasc. 239, *j.* 5, p. 16a.

301 "Yan cha 嚴茶" (Stricter Control of the Tea Trade), in *Wangshi jiacang ji* 王氏家藏集 (*The Treasured Collection of the Wang Family*) by Wang Tingxiang 王廷相 (1474–1544), in *MJSWB*, vol. 149, *j.* 2, p. 22a.

The Ming called the selling of horses by the Xifan "*make* 馬課" (horse tax) and the tea used to pay for the horses was called "*shang* 賞" (a reward).[302] The two sides involved in the exchange were not on an equal footing. The Ming court granted "*jinpai xinfu* 金牌信符" (a golden trade permit plate) to those dependent states that were judged obedient and worthy of reward through such exchange.[303] The price for the Xifan horses was fixed. Every 5,000 *jin* of tea was to be paid for with 13,500 horses.[304] The exchange of tea and horses was allowed to occur only at three places, Taozhou 洮州, Xining 西寧 and Hezhou 河州, and was limited to three-yearly intervals.[305]

The tribute trade with the maritime countries was also not a free and open trade. The *kanhe*-system allowed the Ming government to unilaterally control it. Japan was allowed to pay tribute and trade once every 10 years and with no more than two ships and 200 people.[306] Vietnam and Korea were permitted to visit once every three years and the Ryūkyū Islands once every two years.[307] Tribute missions would not be allowed into port if they arrived earlier than scheduled.[308] All missions were directed to enter the Chinese empire through a specified location. The Japanese had to enter via Ningbo 寧波, while missions from Thailand, Champa and other western states had to enter via Guangzhou. Quanzhou 泉州 was reserved for missions from the Ryūkyū Islands.[309] Goods brought in with the tribute mission were free from all duties, and 60 per cent of their cargo was reserved for "*guanmai* 官買" (government procurement), with the rest available for unofficial trade through designated public fairs.[310] Some goods, such as ironwork and weaponry, were not to be brought into China through such missions.[311] No brokerage of any kind was permitted in the transactions.[312]

The institutions of the *mashi*, *chamashi* and *shibo* and the full-scale prohibition on all private trade constrained and deformed foreign trade. They became an indispensable part of the government's political strategy in international politics and were championed by the landed conservatives, the then prevailing political faction in the early Ming government. They believed that China's ability to control foreign

302 Zhang Xuan, *Xiyuan wenjian lu*, *j.* 70, p. 13b.

303 Ibid.

304 "Xifan kao 西番考" (A Study of the Western Barbarians), in *Cangxia zheng xuji* 蒼霞正續集 (*Continuation of Collected Works of Ye Xianggao, Named After the Village Pavillion of my Hometown, Cangxia*) by Ye Xianggao 葉向高 (1559–1627), in *MJSWB*, vol. 461, *j.* 1, p. 16a.

305 Zhang Xuan, *Xiyuan wenjian lu*, *j.* 66, pp. 15a–b and *j.* 70, p. 13b.

306 Ibid.

307 *Ming huidian*, *j.* 105. p. 1b and p. 6b.

308 "Fangxing huibian, bianyi dian: Riben bu 方形匯編, 邊裔典, 日本部" (A collection Detailing Regulations Regarding Neighbouring states: Japanese Section), in *Gujin tushu jicheng*, *j.* 47, p. 17b.

309 Cao Renhu, *Qinding xu wenxian tongkao*, *j.* 26, p. 25b.

310 Ibid., *j.* 26, p. 26a.

311 *Huang Ming shifa lu*, *j.* 47, p. 26a.

312 Cao Renhu, *Qinding xu wnxian tongkao*, *j.* 26, p. 26a.

powers was a reflection of its moral superiority rather than of its military strength or economic prosperity, yet trading with foreigners on a basis of equality simply for the sake of business would undermine the moral standing of the 'middle kingdom' and violate the China-centred 'world order'. The twin policies of the tribute missions and the prohibition on private trade were painstakingly guarded for more than a century against a politically cultivated and orchestrated context of the social culture and the economic system. It was a compatible background meticulously protected where commercial activity of any kind was condemned for creating economic dissonance and social polarization, hence being responsible for politcal instability. The desired political stability was firmly believed to hinge on the preservation of a self-sufficient economic system and a closely controlled society. The situation of the maritime prohibition policy would fluctuate with the circumstances of the general foreign policy agenda, which was determined by the operating conditions of the established social and economic institutions.

CHAPTER III

The Collapse of the Early Ming Institutions and Foreign Trade Policy

The strictly controlled nature of foreign trade of the early Ming, constrained into the *shibo*, *mashi* and *chamashi* arrangements, was not the manifestation of an isolated defence policy nor was it the product of a deliberate trade policy. Foreign trade was an integral part of the overall superstructure that was established on a much deeper social foundation. This embodied a set of consistent and interrelated institutions pertaining to every aspect of the administration: the institutions relating to the enforcement of the state ideology, the decentralization of land ownership and the petty landholding system, the institutions designed to enforce an economy based around self-sufficiency, the state control of industry and the campaign to supress commerce. These interrelated institutions were politically engineered and maintained; however, after about a century of enforcement, the structure supporting them began to decay. Confucian values began to be questioned, peasant landholdings were beginning to be centralized, state-industries could no longer operate effectively, the self-sufficiency system became more and more awkward and less and less sufficient, and the prohibitions on trade were challenged by wars. Against this background of the decay of the early Ming structures, it was inevitable that foreign policy would also begin to change.

Land Centralization

The politically enforced landholding system was bound to collapse when the conditions on which the system depended changed. By the Jiajing 嘉靖 period (1522–1567) land title changes had gone full circle, from a high level of land centralization during the late Yuan through to the extensive decentralisation under the early Ming administration and then back to the amalgamation of landholdings by the late Ming years. Farmland was the primary form of property and the main source of state revenue in an early modern economy, and land policy was the foundation for all aspects of administration. The re-configuration of land ownership thus shook the very base of government institutions. The collapse of early Ming land policies initiated a transformation of all aspects of the administration, and foreign policy was not different.

The gradual centralisation of landholdings during the Ming was predestined. It resulted from factors inherent in the nature of the early Ming institutions. Ironically, it was the political ideals underlying the early Ming institutions that encouraged literati officials to become the main culprits in the appropriation of land. The court faced a dilemma over how to maintain the petty landholding system. The government had intentionally impoverished the educated social élite in order to prevent them from appropriating land. Nevertheless, it badly needed the support of the educated élite in order for the machine of bureaucratic administration to function effectively, especially when these positions had been vacated by the Mongols and Central and Western Asians (*semu ren* 色目人) following the overthrow of the Yuan dynasty. To compensate for the élite's loss of wealth during the early Ming years, the court had to work out a means to maintain their support. This was the reason why the educated élite were given exemption from the "*yaoyi* 徭役" liability (corvée, service levy), an exemption designed to make up for their economic losses by enhancing their privileged status.

This was a meticulously engineered system. The Hongwu Emperor instructed the Prime Minister's office in 1382: "The scholars and officials and their families are different from the common people. The *corvée* are the liability of commoners. Officials are '*junzi* 君子' (gentlemen) and should not be liable, though they should pay land tax."[313] Freedom from the *yaoyi* obligation became a symbol of political superiority, which helped satisfy the bureaucrats and restore their psychological sense of social elevation. This was further enhanced by many other regulations: "Commoners were not allowed to sit side by side with the educated elite at the community meetings. In the community's ritual ceremony (*xiangyin* 鄉飲) a special table had to be prepared for the educated elite to differentiate their superior status. Any slight disrespect towards literati and officials would result in severe prosecutions no matter whether they are in office or in retirement."[314] Marriage between the educated élite and commoners was considered unacceptable. Li Yi 李宜, Grand Coordinator of Jiangxi 江西, was demoted for marrying his daughter to a non-official clerk.[315] The *yaoyi* exemption for the ruling group was undoubtedly good politics at the time. As a result of this exemption, the financially crippled political élite enjoyed their supremacy in social status and their prerogatives but at the same time they constituted no threat to the decentralised landholding system. However, contrary to the government's wish, the *yaoyi* exemption laid the seeds of future land centralisation.

The more privileged élite group worked out how to use their prerogatives in order to generate personal material gain. Their abuse of their privileged status constituted the biggest threat to the early Ming system. The *Yaoyi* obligation was one of the pillars of state income and, along with the "*fu* 賦" (land tax) was critical for the welfare of the state. Under the early Ming system, the financing of local administration and of most of the empire's public works was achieved through these service levies rather than from the state treasury. These levies were one of the biggest financial burdens imposed on landowners and were allocated on a per capita basis and according to the area of land owned.[316] The "*lijia zhengyi* 里甲正役" (the *corvée* and service levy imposed on *lijia* members) and the "*zafan* 雜泛" (miscellaneous service levies) covered much of the general cost of the operation of the state, including "cash levies for the operation of local administration, labour services for the construction and repair of roads and city walls, the construction and maintenance of water facilites, the construction and repair of granaries, the labour required for postal work, guarding shops, archers and whatever else the government

313 *Ming Taizu shilu*, *j.* 111, p. 7a.
314 Ibid., *j.* 126, p. 2b.
315 Ibid., *j.* 159, p. 7b.
316 *Da Ming huidian*, *j.* 20, pp. 10a–11a.

needed."[317] In Putian county 莆田, the discharging *jia* 甲 (11 households) shared more than a thousand *taels* for the *lijia zhengyi*.[318] It was a devastating strain. Wen Baozhong 溫寶忠 (Ming) warned: "Without a family member who is a scholar or in an official robe [thus qualifying for exemption], a peasant household with 20 *mu* of farmland will be crushed immediately they are required to discharge their *lijia zhengyi* liability."[319]

Nevertheless, there were many privileged people that were exempt from these dues, and the numbers snowballed as the government became bigger and bigger. For instance, the number of "*shengyuan* 生員" (government students) had grown from 35, 820 during the Zhengde reign 正德 (1507–1520) to 500,000 by the late Ming years.[320] According to the regulations, "the lowest degree-holder was qualified for 200 *mu* of *corvée*-exempted land as soon as he left school."[321] Besides, the number of "retired officials who continued to enjoy the same privileges had increased ten-fold by the later Ming years."[322] The multiplication of degree-holders and officials retirees was accompanied by an inflation of their exemption quota.[323] In this way, large areas of arable land officially became *corvée*-free, and the consequences of this were crtitical for the state. In effect, the registered taxable land decreased by 50 per cent, dropping from 8,846,023 *qing* and 6,000 *mu* in the early Hongwu period to 4,292,318 *qing* and 75 *mu* in 1502.[324] In order to maintain the fixed state annual income there was an equivalent and dramatic increase in land tax. The "*jinhuayin* 金花銀" (grain and cloth tax collected in silver) increased four-fold, rising from 0.25 *tael* per *dan* of rice in 1436 to one *tael* of silver per *dan* in 1487.[325] Similarly, the "*jiahao* 加耗" levy was introduced, which involved an extra amount of tax allocated on top

---

317 Li Longqian 李龍潛 *Mingqing jingji shi* 明清經濟史 (*An Economic History of Ming and Qing*). (Guangzhou: Guangdong Tertiary Eduction Publication, 1988), p. 64.

318 "Luogang xiebian szhi 落綱協辦志" (The Records of Coordinated Levy Implementation), in *Tianma shanfang yigao* 天馬山房遺稿 (*Surviving Works of Zhi Zhe, Named After the Tianmashan Mountain of his Home Town*) by Zhu Zhe 朱浙 (1486–1552), in *Siku quanshu*, fasc. 1273, *j.* 4, pp. 25a–b.

319 *Wen Baozhong yigao* 溫寶忠遺稿 (*The Posthumous Works of Wen Baozhong*) by Wen Baozhong 溫寶忠 (Ming), in *Qiankun zhengqi ji* 乾坤正氣集 (*Collected Works to Demonstrate the Spirit of Universal Integration*) by Pan Xien 潘錫恩 (?–1867) (ed.). (Jingxian County: Pan family printer 潘氏刻本, 1849), *j.* 5, p. 10a.

320 Martin Heijdra, "The Socio-Economic Development of Rural China during the Ming," in Frederick W. Mote and Denis Twitchett (eds.), *The Cambridge History of China,* Volume 8 (1998), p. 561. See also, "Jicun 積存" (Storage and Savings), in Zhang Xuan, *Xiyuan wenjian lu*, *j.* 34, p. 2b.

321 *Yujian jumu chao* 雲間據目抄 (*Happenings on Songjiang Observed through my Eyes*) by Fan Lian 范濂 (born 1540), in *Biji xiaoshuo daguan sanji* 筆記小說大觀 (*A Grand Collection of Notes and Stories*), volume 3 (Shanghai: Progress Publishers, 1912–1949), *j.* 4, p. 5a.

322 *Siyou zhai congshuo*, *j.* 13, p. 12a.

323 *Xiaoxia xianji zhaichao* 消夏闲記摘抄 (*Extracts from a Summer Resort Diary*) by Gu Gongxie 顧公燮 (*juren* 1703) (Shanghai: Shanghai Commerical Press, 1924), *shang*, pp. 6a–b.

324 *Huang Ming jiluo* 皇明紀略 (*A Brief Account of the Imperial Ming Dynasty*) by Huang Pulu 皇甫錄 (1470–1540), in *Siku cunmu* 子, fasc. 240, *j.* 85, p. 1a.

325 "Fu yi 賦役" (Taxes and Corvée), in *Qianlong xu wenxian tongkao*, *j.* 2, p. 7b, p. 28a and pp. 28b–30b.

of the fixed amount in order to make up for any loss during transportation and storage. These changes almost doubled the tax rate. He Liangjun 何良俊 (1506–1573, *jinshi* 1542, and Director of the Ministry of Rites in Nanjing), who was once a *liangzhang* 糧長 (tax captain) himself, complained: "After the 10th year of Zhengde Reign (1507), the land tax rate was 0.5 *dou* per *mu* but the *jiahao* surcharge was three times more at 1.5 *dou* per *mu*."[326]

The tax increase became unbearable for many peasants and the centralisation of land holdings thus became inevitable. To avoid the land tax liability petty landowners had no option but to give their land to the privileged in order to gain exemption from the associated levies. Similarly, the practice of "*guiji* 詭寄" (false registration commendation) became widespread. Thousands of families voluntarily left their land under the ownership of the privileged families so as to gain relief from the levies.[327] In order to cope with this increase in their landholdings, the privileged worked out a set of strategies to enlarge their exemptions from the levies. The phenomenon of "*lanmian* 濫免" (abuse of the exemption quotas) gained considerable momentum. For instance, "If an élite family was eligible for 1000 *mu* of levy-free land, they would claim the same exemption in a number of different *lijia* communities, and eventually claim ten times more than they were due."[328] The phenomena of *guiji* and *lanmian* transformed many degree-holders into absentee landlords with large landholdings in many different places. For instance, it was reported that Xu Jie 徐階 (1503–1583, a Senior Grand Secretary) employed 1,000 tenants and enjoyed a yearly income of 9,800 *taels* in silver from land rent. Similarly, Dong Fen 董份 (*jinshi* 1541, a Minister of Rites) was said to possess a million *mu* of farmland in Suzhou 蘇州 and Huzhou 湖州 and employed 1,000 tenants. And Wang Yuanmei 王元美 (who served as an Assistant Minister of War during the Jiajing reign and whose father was a Chief Censor of the Surveillance Office), earned an annual income from rent of at least 300,000 *taels* of silver.[329] Some landowners in Jiangnan 江南 came to own as much as 36,000 *mu* of arable land."[330] Reflecting on this phenomenon, Gu Yuanwu 顧炎武 (1613–1682) noted that "as soon as a scholar became an official there would be thousands of peasant families that wanted to leave their lands in his care to avoid the levy liability."[331]

As more and more small landowners lost their landholdings and disappeared from the *lijia* registration, the *lijia* system gradually collapsed. The numbers of taxpayers dropped from 60,545,812 in 1393 to 50,207,934 in 1488.[332] And this occurred

326 *Siyou zai congshuo*, *j.* 13, 10a.

327 *Ming shi*, *j.* 77, p. 8b.

328 Tang Shunzhi, *Tang jingchuan wenji*, in *Siku quanshu*, fasc. 1276, *j.* 5, p. 26b.

329 Quwei xinwen 曲洧新聞" (News from Quwei), in *Yu Zilong ji* 禦子龍集 (*The Collected Works of Yu Zilong*) by Fan Shouji 范守己 (*jinshi* 1574), in *Siku cunmu* 集, fasc. 162, *j.* 2, pp. 13b–15a.

330 "Nan sixian fengjian lun 難四賢封建論" (Questioning the Four Masters on Feudalism), in *Wuyue Shanren ji* 五岳山人集 (*Collection of the Huang Shengzeng, Hao Wuyue, the Hermit*) by Huang Shengzeng 黄省曾 (1490–1540), in *Siku cunmu* 集, fasc. 94, *j.* 28, p. 12a.

331 Gu Yanwu, *Tianxia junguo libing shu*, *j.* 13, p. 29a.

332 *Ming Xiaozong shilu*, *j.* 21, p. 13a.

during a period of continued population growth, even in the poorest region. For instance, the population of Gongxian county 鞏縣 in Henan had doubled, from 20,000 in 1391 to 40,000 in 1547.[333] Land appropriation created more big landlords and more landless people. Gu Yanwu reported that in Fujian between 70 and 80 per cent of the petty landowners of the early Ming had lost their allocated land to absentee landlords by the late Ming period.[334] Unfortunately for the petty landowners seeking service levy relief, giving away their land did not improve their situation. Though the new landlords shouldered their levy liability, they demanded high rents from their tenants. For instance, during the Jiajing reign "absentee landlords in Nanjing demanded rent as high as 50 per cent of the total harvest."[335] And when tax breaks came during years of natural disasters, the tenants rarely benefited. As Gu Yanwu again notes, this time for the Jiangnan region, the absentee landlords were the recipients of the tax deduction, but under no circumstances did they decrease the rent for their tenants.[336] It was reported that 190,170 refugee families swarmed into Jingxiang 荊襄 during the Xuanzong 宣宗 period (r. 1426–1434).[337] By 1438, more than half of the population of Fanshi county 繁峙 in Shanxi had fled the county.[338] Similarly, there were as many as 126,000 people who left the four counties in Taizhou prefecture 台州 in Zhejiang Province in 1441, which meant the population of the region was reduced by two-thirds.[339] It seemed that "the court could do nothing but allow the rich to have more and more farmland and the poor to have no land at all."[340]

The bankruptcy of the *lijia* system and land centralisation destroyed the 'egalitarian' society of the early Ming. The rich became richer and the poor poorer. This had an impact on all aspects of life in Ming China, including foreign trade policy. The breakdown of the self-sufficient economic system meant that commercial activity became much more central in people's lives. Many landless people went into craft making and peddling to generate income for their families, and the richer landlords tended to shift their investments into manufacturing and trade so as to garner greater profits. The official history for the Shizong reign (1506–1521), the *Ming shizong shilu*, records that "some landlords tended to invest their capital in commerce rather than farming while the poor sell their property and become labourers for others."[341] With the fracturing of the structures of the self-sufficient economic

333 "Jiajing gongxian zhi 嘉靖鞏縣志" (Gongxian Annals, the Jiajing reign), *j.* 3, quoted in Qin Peiyan 秦佩珩, *Mingdai jingji shi shulun cong chugao* 明代經濟史述論從初稿 (*The First Draft of Collected Essays in Ming Economic History*). (Zhengzhou: Henan People's Publishing House, 1959), p. 38.

334 "Nanqing zhi 南靖志" (Gazetteer of Nanqing), in Gu Yanwu, *Tianxia junguo libing shu*, p. 122a.

335 Gu Qiyuan, *Kezuo zhuiyu*, *j.* 5, pp. 30a–b.

336 Gu Yanwu, *Rizhi lu*, *j.*10, pp. 22a–b.

337 *Ming Xianzong shilu*, *j.* 167, p. 1b.

338 *Ming Yingzong shilu*, *j.* 45, p. 2a.

339 *MingYingzong shilu*, *j.* 85, p. 8a.

340 Zhang Xuan, *Xiyuan wenjian lu*, *j.* 25, p. 2a.

341 *Ming Shizong shilu*, *j.* 545, p. 6a.

system, commercial activity sprouted into life once more. As the society and the economy became less government-controlled and more market-oriented, the prohibition on trade became more and more impractical.

Commercialisation of the Economy

The collapse of the petty landholding and *lijia* community system gave rise to a reconfiguration of the economy and society. The disappearance of the self-sufficient petty landowners with their "fish scale" landholdings ushered in the growth of big landlordism. Increasing social polarisation produced two main social groups: the big estate owners and the landless peasantry. The economy increasingly came to reflect these new social circumstances, and with commerce no longer politically constrained the concentration of social wealth saw more investment in commercial activity. The momentum behind this was such that it proved to be too powerful to be stopped. After a century-long period where the emphasis had been on creating a self-sufficient economy and supressing commerce, there was something of a commercial vacuum, which provided a great opportunity for investment in trade and the generation of considerable profit. In such an environment, farming was no longer so attractive because of its low returns and heavy tax liabilities. Two phenomena soon surfaced: "The rich are pressured to sell farmland to engage in commerce and the landless participate more in a market-orientated farming on their rented land."[342] The price of land in Huizhou 徽州 dropped 50 per cent between the period from 1501–1525 and 1551–1576, from 12.39 *tael* of silver per *mu* to 7.51 *tael* per *mu*. The price was later to drop even lower, to 5–6 *liang* per *mu*, but it was still difficult to find buyers. [343] There were fewer and fewer people who could afford to own land and who wanted to invest in it. A landlord from Huizhou 徽州, Zhang Xikong 張習孔, left the following instructions in his "*Family Precepts*" (*jiaxun* 家訓): "Land is too burdensome in Huizhou, we should never buy too much of it but only own enough to produce food for our own consumption."[344] This decrease in the demand for land reflected the changed direction of capital flows. When a rich man bought a new piece of land in Changshu 常熟, Jiangnan, people sneered at him and sent him a poem by way of congratulation, which reads: "How lovely seeing you obtaining new land, being a tax captain may be on your mind, but in three, four or five years time, you will beg others to buy it but nobody will be so kind."[345] Farming had clearly lost its attraction as investments in commercial enterprises became more and more attractive.

342 *Ming Shizong shilu*, *j.* 545, p. 5a.

343 Wu Chengming 吳承明, *Shichang, jindaihua, jingji shilun* 市場, 近代化, 經濟史論 (*Markets & Modernisation: Essays on Economic History*). (Kunming: Yunnan University Press, 1996), p. 253.

344 "Jiaxun 家訓" (Family Regulations) by Zhang Xikong 張習孔, in *Tanji congshu* 檀幾叢書 (*Collection of Important Books Worth to be Offered on a Sandlewood Table*) by Wang Zhuo 王晫 (born 1636), Zhang Chao 張潮 (Qing). (Shexian 歙縣: A Zhang Family publication 張氏霞舉堂, 1695), *j.* 18, p. 8b.

345 *Shanqiao xiayu* 山樵暇語 (*Leasure Talk by a Firewood-Gatherer-Style Scholar*) by Yu Bian 俞弁 (a Ming Budhist scholar), in *Siku cunmu* 子, fasc. 152, *j.* 8, pp. 2a–b.

Big landlords, with the capital they accumulated from their land tenancy, either went into the banking industry or invested in trade in order to make more profit. Loans for trade became an attractive investment. And despite high interest rates being around 20–30 per cent there was no shortage of borrowers.[346] Fan Lian 范濂 (b. 1540) described the situation: "Landlords tend to invest in more profitable commercial activities. Xu Jie 徐階 (1503–1583, a Senior Grand Secretary) and his family participated in commerce by financing merchants with bank loans. His family issued a bank draft in Jiangnan and his client would get the finance in Beijing."[347] Dong Fen 董份 (*jinshi* 1541, Minister of Rites) operated as many as 100 banking services.[348] The manufacturing industry was also favored by the rich and powerful. Yu Shenxing 于慎行 (1545–1607) observed: "Many official families are involved in market-orientated manufacturing and have become very rich. Silk manufacturing is very popular," and he noted that "Xu Jie employed many women in his silk factory."[349] Zhang Han 張瀚 (1511–1593, a Minister of Personnel) and his family managed twenty textile machines which generated around 20 per cent profit, and his family remained involved in the business for three generations.[350] The politically powerful spearheaded the transition from a landed economy to a commercial one. And local people followed the example of these 'big families', also engaging in trade and commodity production if they could afford to.[351] The privileged social group deserves the credit for leading the late Ming economic transformation.

The élite group was also very active in the highly lucrative overseas trade. The prohibition policy did little to deter them. An Guo 安國 (1481–1534), the father and grandfather of two famous government officials, owned a big printing business in Wuxi 無錫, and was engaged in the export of classical texts and other printed material to Japan.[352] Zhang Siwei 張四維, a coastguard commander, voluntarily provided goods for Wang Wufeng 王五峰 (also known as Wang Zhi 王直), a pirate merchant, for his smuggling trade with Japan.[353] Yang Ji 楊稽, a Deputy Grand Coordinator in Guangdong, organized his family to engage in the illegal maritime trade

346 *Jin Zhongjie gongwen ji* 金忠節公文集 (*Collection of Jin Sheng, Shihao Zhongjie*) by Jin Sheng 金聲 (1598–1645). (明末邵鵬程刻本, End of Ming Edition, Printed by Shao Pengcheng, 1889), *j.* 4, pp. 34a–b.

347 Fan Lian, *Yunjian jumu chao*, *j*, 3, p. 12b.

348 Fan Shouji, *Yu Zilong ji*, *j.* 2, p. 14a.

349 *Gushan bichen* 穀山筆塵 (*My Undertanding of Ming History from a Mountain Valley at Gucheng*) by Yu Shenxing 于慎行 (1545–1607), in *Siku xuxiu*, fasc. 1128, *j.* 4, p. 10a.

350 "Yi wen ji 異聞記" (Fantastic Stories), in *Songchuang mengyu* 松窗夢語 (*Collected Works Recalling the Dream-like Old Days at my Window under a Pinetree*) by Zhang Han 張瀚 (1511–1593), in *Siku xuxiu*, fasc. 1171, *j.* 6, p. 15a.

351 *Wujiang xianzhi*, *j.* 38, p. 7b.

352 Wu Ren'an 吳仁安, *Mingqing jiangnan wangzu yu shehui jingji wenhua* 明清江南望族與社會經濟文化 (*The Relationship between Jiangnan Prominent Families and the Society, Economy and Culture During the Ming and Qing Periods*). (Shanghai: Shanghai renmin chubanshe, 2001), pp. 222–223.

353 *Haikou yi* 海寇議 (*Discussion on Piracy*) by Wan Biao 萬表 (1498–1556), in *Siku cunmu* 子 31, p. 3a (not in *juan*).

and then persecuted some officials who exposed him.[354] Zhang Dexi 張得熹, a judge in Ningbo 寧波 prefecture, was a business partner of his uncle who was a big maritime smuggler. In order to assist his uncle's business with the Japanese he tried to frame and even instigate Japanese to murder Zhu Wan 朱紈 (1494–1549), Supreme Commander of the coastguard in Zhejiang and Fujian, and Grand Coordinator of Zhejiang.[355] On the Mongol border official involvement in the smuggling trade was no different in its intensity. In 1499, Liu Huan 劉瓛, a Chief Censor and Sun Zhen 孫振, the Grand Eunuch, were caught trading iron goods with the Mongols. Officials actually became leaders of smuggling rings, each with a large group of local followers.[356] Some military officials even confronted the invading Mongols with trade rather than battle. Zhao Chang 趙昶, a Deputy Regional Guard Commander at Datong, and Shen Ying 神英 (1435–1512), a regional commander at Datong, organized a commercial contest with the Mongols, in iron goods and silks.[357] The two commanders made a huge profit out of the 'battle'. In 1513, the Duke of Ningyang 寧陽候 dispatched 20 soldiers and equipped each with two horses to travel to Hangzhou 杭州 to procure commodities for foreign trade.[358] It was said: "There is not much difference between officials and merchants … Official family members travelled far and wide to engage in trade, in goods ranging from salt to pearls, timber, textiles and foodstuffs."[359] Zhu Wan reported to the court: "The owners of the illegal maritime traders were *guiguan daxing* 貴官大姓, powerful families with a strong social background."[360] In the north, Luo Jinshi 羅禁時, an Investigating Censor, examined the illegal horse trade in Guangning 光寧, Kaiyuan 開原 and Fushun 撫順 and discovered that the primary participants were the local influential and literati families.[361]

While the privileged landed proprietors thronged to market-oriented production and trade, landless peasants also actively participated in commerce by shifting to growing cash crops on their rented land. Their status as tenants placed pressure on them to engage in more profitable commercial farming in order to cope with the high rents.[362] Production for the market became the main driver in farming. People from Yanzhou 兗州 in the north gave up weaving and turned to specialised cotton farming, as they were less skillful in the former but more in the later. They tended

354 *Ming Yingzong shilu*, *j.* 244, p. 8b.
355 Zhu Wan, *Piyu zaji*, *j.* 5, pp. 6a–7b.
356 *Ming Xiaozong shilu*, *j.* 150, p. 8a.
357 *Ming Xiaozong shilu*, *j.* 150, p. 8b.
358 *Ming Xuanzong shilu*, *j.* 76, p. 11b.
359 *Gui xiansheng ji* 歸先生文集 (*Collected Works of Mr. Gui*) by Gui Youguang 歸有光 (1506–1571), in *Siku cunmu* 集 138. *j.* 31, p. 13b.
360 *Ming shi*, *j.* 81, p. 28b.
361 *Ming Xiaozong shilu*, *j.* 154, p. 9b.
362 "Lun wenyi jin dicang liang shu 論文邑禁糴倉糧書" (A Comment on Banning the Purchase of Grain for the Granary) by Ye Xianggao 葉向高 (1559–1627), in *Huangzheng bu yiwen* 荒政部藝文, 8, in *Jingji huibian shihuo* 經濟彙編食貨, in *Gujin tushu jicheng*, *j.* 101, p. 463b.

to sell their cotton to the southerners and buy their textiles instead.[363] On the opposite side, southerners were more competent in making textiles but less skillful in growing cotton. They therefore concentrated on textile manufacturing but purchased cotton from the north. To make the best use of their rented land people of Jinxing 嘉興 (Zhejiang) turned from their principle industry of crop farming to tending mulberry trees. In Zhenze town 震澤 (near Suzhou) raising silkworms became a profession: "People never visit each other in March or April because every family is busy raising silkworms."[364] By the Jiajing period the division of labor and the specialisation of production had reached a very high level. It was said that "people from Jiading county 嘉定縣 in Suzhou prefecture relied solely on the farming of cotton,"[365] and "millions of *taels* of land tax comes from nowhere but the girls' looms".[366] Cash crops generated a great deal more income for the people in Jiading, and the shift from rice farming to silk production and the cultivation of mulberry trees produced a three-fold increase in income.[367] In Dongwan 東莞 county, in Guangdong, the rise of the more profitable candy-making industry turned a thousand *qing* 頃 of paddyfields into sugarcane plantations.[368] The silk industry gradually divided up into four independent sectors: the growing of mulberry leaves, silkworms farming, the making of raw silk, and silk weaving. Silkworm farmers needed only to go to the market to buy mulberry leaves provided by the specialist growers, while silk weavers also bought the raw yarn they needed at the market.

The market became the pivot place to coordinate each specialized sector of the commercialised economy. Wu township 烏鎮 in Zhejiang was such a commercial center, where everything was available for trade.[369] The deepening of the division of labour brought a greater flow of regional and international commodities. Petty farmers in Linqing 臨清, Shandong province, specialized in brewing spirits but relied on cereals imported from other regions.[370] Commercial development was a nationwide phenomenon. The Zhu 朱 brothers, a Huizhou merchant family, went to Fujian and became involved in iron mining and smelting in the mountains. They soon became millionaires as metal goods were always in hot demand, both at home

363 "Yanzhou fubu fengsu kao 弇州府部風俗考" (Local Customs of Yanzhou Prefecture), in *Gujin tushu jicheng*, *j.* 230, pp. 12a and 16a.

364 "Feng su 風俗" (Local Customs), in *Zhenze bian* 震澤編 (*A Collection on Zhenzhe*) by Cai Sheng 蔡昇 (Ming), re-edited by Wang Ao 王鏊 (1450–1524), in *Siku cunmu* 史, fasc. 228. *j.* 3, p. 1b.

365 Gu Yanwu, *Tianxia junguo libing shu*, p. 25a.

366 *Nongzhen quanshu* 農政全書 (*A Complete Handbook on Agricultural Administration*) by Xu Guangqi 徐光啟 (1562–1633), in *Siku quanshu, fasc.* 731, *j.* 35, pp. 13a–b.

367 *Jiading fuzhi* 嘉興府誌 (*Gazetteer of the Jiading Profecture*) by Wu Yangxian 吳仰賢 (1812–1887), in *Zhongguo difangzhi jicheng*, *j.* 32, pp. 23b–24a.

368 Qu Dajun, *Guangdong xinyu*, *j.* 2, p. 32a.

369 *Nanxun zhenzhi* 南潯鎮誌 (*The Annals of Nanxun Township*) by Wang Zizhen 汪自楨 (1812–1881), (1858–edition), in *Siku xuxiu*, fasc. 717, *j.* 22, pp. 5a–b.

370 *Ming Yingzong shilu*, *j.* 256, p. 3a.

and abroad.[371] Many regions concentrated on specialised production but depended on importing the products they needed. Whereas people from Quanzhou 泉州 in Fujian province specialized in sugarcane farming and sugarmaking, people from Huizhou 徽州 in Anhui province specialised in tea farming and papermaking. They relied on imported grain from Nanzhili 南直隸, Huguang 湖廣 and Jiangxi 江西 where people specialised in commercial grain production.[372] Ming China's division of labour also directly affected the international market. Guangzhou 廣州 was the commercial center for exports to Japan, Thailand and the Ryūkyū archipelago, but was also the destination for rice imported from Vietnam.[373]

The late Ming economic transformation, from a self-sufficient to a commercialised economy, made the institution of the prohibition on foreign trade incompatible with the requirements of the domestic economy. The economic structure in which the prohibition was an integral part was no longer there. The mature division of labour and the commercialised economy destroyed the old social relations as *lijia* community members of the early years and transformed the late Ming interactions between employers and workers, landlords and tenants from a personally bonded relationship to an indispensable partnership in a market-oriented commercial economy. Workers could easily walk away if the conditions did not suit them,[374] and they were paid in cash (in silver) rather than in goods and accommodation. For instance, an average weaver's daily wage was one *fen* 分 (a hundreth of a *tael*) in silver, and nothing else.[375] Trade was no longer primarily a form of barter. The thriving commercial activities revolutionised the old methods of transaction, and the introduction of a credit system greatly facilitated trade. A silkworm farmer could use credit to purchase mulberry leaves and pay nothing until selling the raw silk yarn he produced.[376] Merchants increasingly began to use the "*huipiao* 匯票", a quasi-bank draft, to pay their accounts in different places without knowing their clients and business partners personally.[377] The enthusiastic participation in commerce by both the rich and poor propelled the commercialisation of the economy. A maturing financing system and the enlarged scale of domestic trade provided the important foundation for a flourishing foreign trade.

371 "Haiyang xinxi Zhu chushi muzhiming 海陽新溪朱處士墓誌銘" (The Tomb Inscription of Mr. Zhu from Xinxi, Haiyang), in *Taihan ji* 太函集 (*A Collection of Maximised Containment*) by Wang Daokun 汪道昆 (1525–1593), in *Siku cunmu*, 集, fasc. 117, *j.* 47, p. 14a.

372 *Quannan zazhi* 泉南雜志 (*Random Notes about Quannan*) by Chen Maoren 陳懋仁 (1573–1619), in *Siku cunmu* 史, fasc. 47, *shang*, p. 11b (no *juan*). See also "Jiangnan ping wujia yi 江南平物價議" (A Comment on the Levelling of Commodity Prices in Jiangnan) in Wu Yingqi, *Loushan tang*, *j.* 12, pp. 7a–b.

373 Qu Dajun, *Guangdong xinyu*, *j.* 14, pp. 1a–2a.

374 *Xitai manji* 西臺漫記 (*Sketches by a Retired Censor*) by Jiang Yihua 蔣以化 (*juren* between 1567 and 1573), in *Siku cunmu* 子, fasc. 242, *j.* 4, p. 5a.

375 Ibid., *j.* 4, p. 5a.

376 Wang Rizhen, *Nanxun zhen zhi*, *j.* 22, pp. 5a–b.

377 Fan Lian, *Yunjian jumu chao*, *j.* 3, pp. 8b–9a.

The Silver-Based Tax Reform

The late Ming years saw great changes to the early Ming taxation system which had been based on payments in kind. The barter economy that had been maintained for a century after the establishment of the dynasty eventually went into decline. A taxation system based on payments in kind rather than money and the ban on silver were devised to secure the ideal of a land-based self-sufficient economy. Whereas individual families were required to support themselves by family farming and handcraft making, the state relied on the land tax, paid in kind, and the labor service obligations. An economy without reliable money was awkward and expensive. The maintenance of such an economy drained the state coffers and consumed much of people's income. As the dynasty progressed, this politically enforced economic mode became more and more unworkable and unbearable. For example, the shipping of millions of *taels* worth of tax revenue in kind from the south to the north of the empire was extremely burdensome. The requirement that peasants transported their tax to an appointed state granary was also a great burden to many peasant families. The state income in 1385 amounted to 20,889,617 *dan* of grain, almost half of which was left in local granaries, but the rest had to be taken great distances. Four million *dan* were earmarked and transported to the capital, while a further eight million was assigned to the military and had to be transported to the northern border regions."[378] With oceanic, or maritime, transportation prohibited, all of this grain had to be carried via the *caoyun* system 漕運 (transportation of land tax grain collected from the south)). Li Chunfang 李春芳 (1510–1584, who served as a Grand Secretary) criticized the system: "Since the sea route is blocked by maritime prohibition, the *JingHang* canal 京杭運河 is the only means of transportation, but it is too shallow and narrow for big ships, and the operation is extremely strenuous."[379] The canal transportation was highly costly. "Every *dan* of rice received in the capital would cost three times more [to transport] than the tax itself."[380]

To reduce the spending on transportation the government entrusted the supply for the military to the "*tuntain* 屯田"-system (military colonies). The government had granted 29 *mu* of arable land for each of its 3,100,000 troops, which amounted to 899, 000 *qing* of land in total and comprised around 10 per cent of all of the empire's arable land. There was also the "*mintun* 民屯" (organized peasant farming) system managed by the central administration, which involved immigrants recruited from the hinterland and relocated to border regions. "The state treasury provided them with tools and seeds. The *tuntian* was valued as a ready granary on the borders

378 *Ming Taizu shilu*, *j.* 176, p. 6a, and *Ming Muzong silu*, *j.* 15, pp. 7b–8a.

379 "Haiyun 海運" (Maritime Transportation), in *Yi'antang ji* 貽安堂集 (*Collection from the Yi'antang Ancestry Hall*) by Li Chunfang 李春芳 (1510–1584), in *Siku cunmu* 集, fasc. 113, *j.* 4, pp. 24b–25a.

380 "Yu Li Longgang yiling shu 與李龍崗邑令書" (A Letter to County Magistrate Li Longgang), *Tang Jinchuan wenji* 唐荊川集 (*The Collected Works of Tang Shunzhi, Hao Jingchuan*) by Tang Shunzhi 唐順之 (1507–1560), in *Siku quanshu*, fasc. 1276, *j.* 5, p. 23b.

for the military."[381] However, the deteriorating situation along the borders disrupted the *tuntian* system. In 1568, Pang Shangpeng 龐尚鵬 made a case study of this process. He noted that the collapse of the *tuntian* system in Yansui 延綏 resulted from frequent Mongol harassment, which led to desertion by the *tuntian* farmers. With 50 per cent of the *tuntian* in shutdown mode, financial difficulties in feeding the military pressurized the government either to increase the tax rate on the *tuntian*, or put the land up for sale.[382] The collapse of the system saw the gradual shift from the military being self-sufficient to it being dependent on the state coffers. Financial pressure forced the government 'to kill the hen to get the eggs' by selling the *tuntian* land to officials for their pay. More and more state land was thus officially transformed into private property.[383] In other cases the *tuntian* land was illegally appropriated: "Thousands of *mu* of *tuntian* land were infringed by officials in Zhejiang 浙江, Jiangxi 江西, Shandong 山東, Shanxi 山西 and Henan 河南. They utilized the land either for cash crop farming or the cultivation of fruit for cash."[384] Wei Qing 魏清, the Regional Military Commissioner of Tiancheng garrison 天城衛, occupied two *qing* of *tuntian* land and employed 50 soldiers.[385] Cao Jian 曹儉, an Assistant Regional Commander at Datong 大同 appropriated 150 *qing* of *tuntian* and illegally employed 100 men to farm for him.[386]

With the bankruptcy of the *tuntian* system the government, out of helplessness, enhanced the "*minyun* 民運"-system. It demanded taxpayers themselves to organise the transportation of their land tax to the appointed destination.[387] The *minyun* system was not only logistically a far more inefficient way of supplying the military, but it was also a crushing encumbrance for taxpayers. Wang Ao 王鏊 (1450–1524: a Grand Secretary), worked out the cost by the *minyun* system: "If soldiers can harvest one *dan* of rice on the border by themselves, the taxpayer will save 30 *dan* from transporting one *dan* to the border."[388] In some mountainous areas the transportation situation was even worse. Every *dan* of grain from Shanxi 山西 cost as much as 60 *dan* to transport to the garrisons in Datong 大同 and Xuanfu 宣府. The *minyun*

381 *Shi dong ji wenxuan* 石洞集文選 (*Extracts from the Rock Cave Collection*) by Ye Chuanji 葉春及 (1532–1595), in *Siku quanshu*, fasc. 1286. *j.* 2, p. 35b. See also *Ming huiyao*, *j.*53, p. 7a.

382 "Qing li Yansui tuntian shu 清理延綏屯田疏" (A Memorial Requesting the Military Colonies in the Yansui Region be Put in Order), in *Pang zhongcheng zhaigao* 龐中丞摘稿 (*Excerpts from the Writings of Pang Shangpeng, the Grand Coordinator*) by Pang Shangpeng 龐尚鵬 (*jinshi* 1553), in *MJSWB*, 359, *j.* 3, pp. 11a–b.

383 *Ming Xiaozong shilu*, *j.* 75, p. 5b. See also "Tuntian 屯田" (Military Colonies), in *Huang Ming shifa lu*, *j.* 30, p. 31b.

384 *Ming Xuanzong shilu*, *j.* 57, p. 11a.

385 Ibid., *j.* 10, p. 15a.

386 *Ming Xuanzong shilu*, *j.* 108, p. 15b.

387 "Wei huiji yanchen jiyi yulu fanglüe yi jue dazhong shu 為匯集廷臣計議禦虜方略以絕大患疏" (A Memorial to Gather Courtiers' Proposals for a Strategy to Terminate the Calamity caused by the Mongols) by Ma Wensheng 馬文昇 (1426–1510), in *MJSWB*, vol. 64, *j.* 3, pp. 7a–b.

388 Zhang Xuan, *Xiyuan wenjian lu*, *j.* 91, p. 1b.

carriers had to spend as long as a year on their arduous thousand *li*- long trip.[389] Despite these costs, the *minyun* system began to play the main role in military supply. Taking Xuanfu garrison as an example: in 1529 the *minyun* provided 745,273 *dan* of grain while local farming by the military could only contribute 62,320 *dan*.[390] But the *minyun* system was not only burdensome to the carriers, it was also costly to the military. Lin Shi 林時 (an Assistant Surveillance Commissioner in Shanxi) observed in 1432 that even if the supply arrived at the granary in time, soldiers had to travel a long way from their posts to receive their provisions: "Soldiers at Ganzhou garrison 甘州衛 have to collect their provisions from the fortress at Lanxian Pass 藍縣關 a thousand *li* [about 500 km] away. Sometimes they have to borrow from wealthy locals and pay high interest (in order to finance the trip). Sometimes 70–80 per cent of their pay was spent paying the interest."[391] Besides this, the *minyun* system depreciated an officer's pay, since they had to sell their silver rations in order to purchase other things they needed. They would lose some of the value in selling the grain and cloth as part of their salaries.[392]

The kind-based taxation system became more and more burdensome; therefore conversion to a monetary taxation system became more and more imminent. The problem was that there was no reliable money available. The only form of money permitted, the *Da Ming tongbao*, was incapable of supporting a monetisation of the taxation system. A currency without intrinsic value which, by the Hongzhi reign (1488–1505), had been devalued some 750 times, and was only used in those transactions where it was made compulsory, in particular in official salaries and the pay for *corvée* labourers.[393] In such circumstances, silver ingots had emerged to play a powerful role in the economy. Silver was the precious metal that was most valued within the society and was the most preferred medium for exchange. Consequently, some officials campaigned to convert the taxation system into a silver-based regime. Tang Shunzhi 唐順之 (1507–1560) advocated the conversion of the four million *dan* of grain sent annually from the south to the capital into a payment in silver: "The taxpayers in the south can save their transportation costs while the state revenue is guaranteed by receiving income in valuable silver."[394] It was also argued that "the system will save the huge costs expended on grain storage".[395] If the state received its income in silver, that would enable the Treasury to convert payments in

389 *Ming Renzong shilu*, *j.* 7, p. 7b. *Ming Yingzong shilu*, *j.* 55, p. 3b.

390 "Huiyi wang lu jun liang ji neifu shouna shu 會議王祿軍糧及內府收納疏" (A Memorial About the Income of the Emperor's Warehouses, the Military Food Supply and the Princes' Remuneration), in *Liang Duansu gong zongji* 梁端肅公奏議 (*The Collected Memorials of Liang Cai, Shihao Duansu*) by Liang Cai 梁材 (*jinshi* 1505), in *MJSWB*, vol. 103, *j.* 2, pp. 7a–b.

391 *Ming Xuande shilu*, *j.* 87, pp. 5b–6a.

392 *Ming yingzong shilu*, *j.* 21, pp. 7b–8a.

393 Wang Shizhen, *Fengzhou biji xuji*, *j.*3, pp. 4b–5a. Note: 3,000 *guan* of paper notes were worth only 4 *taels* of silver instead of the 3,000 *taels* stipulated by the official exchange rate. See *Qinding xuwenxian tongkao*, *j.* 10, p. 4b.

394 Tang Shunzhi, *Tang Jingchuan wenji*, in *Siku quanshu*, fasc. 1276, *j.* 5, p. 23b.

395 Zhang Xuan, *Xiyuan wenjian lu*, *j.*32, p. 2b.

kind made to officials into payments in silver and thus would help officials avoid losing income through the process of exchange. Gu Yanwu records that "officials always sell their salary paid in rice to exchange it for silver for other purposes", and "the officials' pay is inevitably reduced from the commutation into silver, as ten *dan* of rice is only worth one or two *taels* of silver while they are paid at the official ratio of one *tael* per one *dan*."[396] Tang Jingchuan wrote to the court: "The military supply should be operated by the market mechanism of demand and supply while the Treasury should pay the military in money, therefore the spending on transportation can be saved."[397]

The difficulties of tax collection and transportation were an ongoing problem. Many approaches were experimented with. In 1440, Nian Fu 年富, a Provincial Administrative Commissioner in charge of food supply, memorialized that the court had suggested that soldiers be paid in silver at the rate of 2.5 *dan* of grain for 1.2 *tael* of silver.[398] Li Min 李敏 (*jinshi* 1454, Minister of Revenue) started a pilot policy of collecting tax in silver in the north and transporting 90 per cent of it to the frontier.[399] In the first year of the Zhengde reign (1506), the "*jinhuayin* 金花銀" (land tax converted to silver) policy was introduced. Every *dan* of rice was converted to a payment, at a rate of 0.25 *tael* of silver.[400] The century-old *kaizhong* system 開中鹽 (transporting grain to the border in return for a permit to trade salt) was scrutinized in line with the increasingly silver-based system. Yeqi 葉淇 (1426–1501, Minister of Revenue) memorialized the court suggesting it sell salt permits for silver and that the government buy grain locally to supply the military.[401] By 1503, tax and *corvée* liabilities were publicly sold.[402] Three months *corvée* liability was sold for 1.8–2.4 *taels* of silver.[403] Finally, the Single Whip Reform, implemented gradually during the late Ming years, converted all taxes and levies into a single silver payment, which relieved taxpayers and also the government itself from the frustrations of an increasingly redundant fiscal system.[404]

Silver became the center of the economy. The shift to a silver-based economy destroyed the early Ming social landscape and liberated people from their land-

396 Gu Yanwu, *Tianxia junguo libing shu*, *j.* 8, p. 12a.

397 Tang Shunzhi, *Tang Jingchuan wenji*, in *Siku quanshu*, fasc. 1276, *j.* 5, p. 20b.

398 *Ming Yingzong shilu*, *j.* 74, pp. 1b–2a

399 "Li Min zhuan 李敏傳" (The Biography of Li Min), in *Ming shi*, *j.* 185, pp. 2a–b.

400 Can Renhu, *Qinding xuwenxian tongkao*, *j.* 2, p. 29a.

401 *Ming huiyao*, *j.* 55, pp. 14a–16a. See also, "Hami shu 哈密疏" (A Memorial about Hami) by Huo Tao 霍韜 (1487–1540), in *MJSWB*, vol. 186. *j.* 2, p. 28a, and "Jiu wang wu ke ji shi jiang qiu yi yan min ling shu 救荒無奇及時講求以延民命疏" (There Is No Magic Wand, Only a Practical Way to Save People's Lives) by Wang Dewan 王德完 (1554–1621), in *MJSWB*, vol. 444, *j.* 1, pp. 4a–b.

402 Gu Yanwu, *Tianxia junguo libing shu*, *j.* 22, p. 10a, and Cao Renhu, *Qinding xuwenxian tongkao*, *j.* 2, p. 29a.

403 *Da Ming huidian*, *j.* 189, pp. 5b–6a.

404 Ray Huang discusses the implementation of the Single Whip Reform in *Taxation and Governmental Finance in Sixteenth-Century Ming China.* (London & New York: Cambridge University Press, 1974), pp. 111–122.

bound occupations: "People rushed to engage in commerce to obtain silver to pay tax and the state relied on money to provide military supplies."[405] Silver revolutionized the taxation and military supply systems. The weakening of the *minyun* supply system turned the frontier into a huge commercial zone. Millions of soldiers were shifted to the government pay role, receiving payments in silver, and "most of the Ming land tax collected in silver was spent there."[406] Merchants from all corners of the country, such as Shanxi 山西, Henan 河南, Zhengding 正定, Baoding 保定 and Linqing 臨清, swarmed to the border regions to trade in grain, silk, cotton, handcrafts, tea, horses, cattle and so on.[407] The border trade was not only extremely large in volume but also exceptionally profitable. For instance, along the far northern border one *dan* of rice was worth 0.8–0.9 *taels* of silver, but its price were nearly four times cheaper in Liaodong 遼東.[408] "The nine defence regions boasted as flourishing an economy as the commercial heartland of Jiangnan."[409] Tang Shunzhi described the border circumstances: "Merchants provide the basic conditions for military supply. If merchants have problems, there will be no provisions available and the situation on the frontier will become problematic."[410] The Shanxi merchants, drawing on the geographical advantage and the opportunity of commercialisation in the Ming military logistics, grabbed a big piece of pie in the trade and soon gathered tremendous wealth. They were immediately followed by Huzhou merchants, merchants from Jiangxi, Fujian, Guangdong and others.

However, the tax reforms encountered a substantial problem: a shortage of money. Neither the geological nor the historical conditions favoured the Ming in this aspect. Centuries-long mining in the previous dynasties had depleted the silver mines so that the Ming miners were forced to work with ore that was only 1/100,000th in terms of silver content of the ore of the Spanish American mines.[411] Moreover, during the Song and Yuan dynasties, silver and copper were exported in large quantities and over a time span of a few centuries. During the Song paper notes became an efficient currency and the copper currency was in high demand in neighbouring countries. The great outflow of copper coins dried up the state's cop-

---

405 *Shanxi Shangren yanjiu* 山西商人研究 (*A Study of Shanxi Merchants*) by Terada Takanobu 寺田隆信 translated by Zhang Zhengming 張正明, Dao Feng 道丰, Sun Yao 孫燿 and Yan Shoucheng 閻守誠. (Xi'an: Shanxi People's publishing House, 1986), p. 122.

406 Ibid., p.120. During the Xiaozong period the total number of soldiers on the border was 2,700,000 (cf. *Ming shi*, *j.* 91, p. 22a); during the Muzong reign, the total number of soldiers on the border was 3,138,300 (*Muzong shilu*, *j.* 35, p. 8b); at the end of the Wanli reign the total number of soldiers on the border was 1,160,000 (*Shenzong shilu*, *j.* 577, p. 2b).

407 *Ming Yingzong shilu*, *j.* 236, pp. 9b–10a.

408 *Ming Xianzong shilu*, *j.* 208, p. 7a.

409 Xie Zhaozhi, *Wu zazu*, *j.*4, p. 38a.

410 Tang Shunzhi, *Tang Jingchuan shansheng wenji*, in *Congshu jicheng xubian* 叢書集成續編 (*The Continuation of the Grand Collection of Books*). (Shanghai, Shanghai Bookstore Publication, 1994), fasc. 116, *j.* 10, p. 8a.

411 *Ming Xuanzong shilu*, *j.* 83, p. 7a. See also Earl J. Hamilton *American Treasure and the Price Revolution in Spain*, 1501–1650. (Cambridge: Cambridge University Press, 1934), p. 36.

per resources.[412] With the Yuan dynasty, this outflow of copper was immediately followed by the export of silver. It was a time when the Yuan paper money became a compulsory medium in transactions while the silver-gold exchange rate in the world market made the export of silver very profitable.[413] During the Ming, the value of silver reached the highest level in Chinese history. Whereas the Japanese gold/silver exchange rate was 1:10.34, it was 1:4 in the Ming and even reached 1:1.67 during Yingzong years (r. 1435–1449 and 1457–1464).[414] Hao Jing 郝敬 (1558–1639), complained of the situation: "Where silver was most needed, it was in shortest supply."[415] Smilarly, Gu Yanwu later noted:

> There is not enough silver to pay the land tax ... In Dengzhou 登州 and Laizhou 萊州 people sold their children to get silver ... there is no silver in the mountain areas or on the coast in Shandong. Even in a bumper harvest year peasants still have no way to clear their tax obligations ... whenever the due day approaches people would sell their sons to the army in order to get the metal ... what the peasants harvest from their landholdings is useless for paying tax. Silver does not come from the sky and the existing silver resources have already been exhausted, especially when maritime shipping is prohibited and merchants have long vanished.[416]

However, silver was abundant beyond the border. It was the maritime prohibition policy that deliberately blocked the inflowing of the metal: "Ever since the advent of Toyotomo Hideyoshi 豊臣秀吉 (1536–1598) gold and silver have gushed forth from the mountains and from the plains in the land of Japan."[417] Whereas the Chinese silver ore content was 0.003–12.5 per cent, the ore content from the newly discovered silver mine in Potosí in Peru was more than 50 per cent.[418] The Spanish court received the equivalent of one million *taels* a year from the Royal Fifth from Peru alone, which was ten times more than the total output of the Ming silver production.[419] The trade prohibition had a destructive impact on all societies. Without sufficient monetary metal, the Ming economy was becoming paralyzed. At the same

---

412 *Qunshu kaosuo houji* 群書考索後記 (*Postscript to the Investigation and Scrutiny of Assorted Documents*), by Zhang Ruyu 章如愚 (*jinshi* 1196), in *Siku quanshu*, fasc.937, *j.* 61, p. 2a. See also Peng Xinwei 彭信威, *Zhongguo huobishi* 中國貨幣史 (*A Monetary History of China*). (Shanghai: Shanghai renmin chubanshe, 1988), p. 650.

413 Huang Zongxi, *Mingyi daifang lu,* pp. 42b–43a (no *juan*). See also Gernet, *A History of Chinese Civilization* (1982), pp. 371–372, and Peng Xinwei, *Zhongguo huobishi* (1988), p. 570.

414 Tetsuo Kamiki and Kozo Yamamura, "Silver Mines and Sung coins" (1983), p. 346.

415 Sun Chengze, *Chunming mengyu lu*, *j.* 47, p. 9b.

416 *Tinglin wenji* 亭林文集 (*Writings from Tinglin*) by Gu Yanwu 顧炎武 (1613–1682), in *Siku xuxiu*, fasc. 1402, *j.* 1, pp. 13a–13b.

417 Quoted from George Elison, "The Cross and the Sword: Patterns of Monoyama History", in George Elison and Bardwell L. Smith (eds.), *Warlords, Artists and Commoners: Japan in the Sixteenth Century*. (Honolulu: University of Hawai'i Press, 1981), p. 55.

418 *Ming Xuanzong shilu*, *j.* 83, p. 7. See also Hamilton, *American Treasure and the Price Revolution in Spain*, 1501–1650 (1934), p. 36.

419 Quan Hansheng 全漢昇, "Ming Qing meizhou baiyin de shuru zhongguo 明清美洲白銀的輸入中國" (*Imports of American Silver to China during the Ming and Qing Eras*), in *Zhongguo Jingjishi luncong* 中國經濟史論叢 (*Collected Essays on Chinese Economic History*). (Hong Kong: Xinya chubanshe, 1972), pp. 613–616.

time, it was suggested that "Japan would stop functioning properly without Chinese products."[420] Similarly, "the Spanish Governor-General of the Philippines told the local chiefs that the Spanish could not run the country without Chinese products and blamed them for failing to attract Chinese merchants."[421] When the state and the economy depended on silver, it seemed ridiculous to intentionally obstruct the import of the metal. It was politically senseless to fight off foreign traders who brought silver bullion to China, and who could wage war if trade was obstructed.

Paralysis of the State-run Manufacturing Industries

The state-run manufacturing industry was an important part of the early Ming institutions that was used to buoy up the self-sufficient system. It was a monopolized industry used to sustain the independence of the state from commerce, a political actuality rather than an economic entity. However, the state-run industries could not help but be influenced as the forces of commercialisation became too strong to resist. The basis on which the state industries depended was rapidly crumbling away and it was becoming impracticable to run any industry according to a state-enforced demand and supply system, using forced labour and tax revenue to sustain competitiveness when land was increasingly centralised, taxation increasingly monetised and political surveillance increasingly enfeebled. With such a radically different social and economic context from that instituted during the early Ming years, the state-run industries could not survive.

Labour shortages became a serious problem from the Hongzhi reign (1488–1505) onwards. The *yaoyi*-system of forced labour was generally hated. Those obliged to serve were not only unpaid but also had to pay for their own travel to the work site and their own accommodation during the period of their labour service. To make matters worse, the discharge of this service would also ruin their yearly income by taking them away from their landholdings during the sowing and harvest seasons.[422] These industries were also operated in an extremely hostile environment. On one side, there was the government department which was anxious to accomplish the project, while on the other side there were the unpaid *corvée* workers who lacked motivation and were anxious to get out of doing the work. For instance, "a foreman was accused of beating as many as 13 artisans with a hammer at different occasions in only two days."[423] Such confrontational labour relations and the associated financial burden drove more and more people to avoid the *yaoyi*. As this evasion of service escalated, the labour source for the state industries disappeared. This was recognised by the government: "Although there is a great number of *corvée* labourers on the roll, those who actually arrive at the worksite are less than 2–3 per

420 *Haifang zuanyao* 海防纂要 (*Essentials of Writings on Coastal Defence*) by Wang Zaijin 王在晉 (*jinshi* 1592), in *Siku jinhui* 史, fasc. 17, *j.* 7, pp. 32b–33a

421 *Min shu* 閩書 (*Documents on Fujian*) by He Qiaoyuan 何喬遠 (*jinshi* 1586), *in Siku cunmu* 史, fasc. 204, *j.* 39, p. 34b.

422 *Ming Yingzong shilu*, *j.* 153, pp. 7a–b.

423 *Ming Shizong shilu*, *j.* 173, pp. 8a–b.

cent."[424] Of those artisans with permanent jobs in the capital half fled between 1466 and 1488. The ammunition department had a fixed number of artisans, 5,787 between 1437 and 1449, but there were only 2,000 left by 1485.[425]

The poor quality of the goods manufactured in these state industries also meant that demand was dramatically curtailed. The *Ming shilu* 明實錄 records many cases where military equipment from the state-run factories was returned because of its unacceptable quality. In the third year of the Wanli reign 萬歷 (1575), five thousands shields were handed back to the state factories for re-making as they were too poor to be used in battle.[426] Zhao Shixun 趙世勛 (*jinshi* 1571, Supervising Secretary in the Ministry of War), memorialised the emperor, stating that soldiers discarded arrows made by the state-run factory and asked that the court give money directly to soldiers so that they could make their own equipment.[427] The impracticability and difficulties of the state industries encouraged private business, and more and more government orders were shifted to the private sector. The policy of "*zhaoshang maiban* 召商買辦" (government purchase from private merchants) recognised the degree to which the state had come to rely on the market. The textile industry was a good example. By the Jiajing years the monetisation of the tax system enabled the government to purchase whatever cloth it needed with silver. The bankruptcy of the *Su-Hang guanju* (the state manufacturing departments in Suzhou and Hangzhou) led to the mushrooming of private silk mills. The burgeoning "*lingzhi jihu* 領織機戶" (government commissioned silk manufacturers) took over the state-run business and organised silk weaving in accordance with government orders.[428] The *zhaoshang maiban* policy allowed government departments to grant money directly to merchants for supply.[429] State purchases during the late Jiajing years boosted the local silk price as the government spent a great amount of money in this market. In some cases, a single deal was worth as much as 10,000 *taels* of silver.[430] Increasingly, the government relied on a regular supply of silver in order to maintain the supply of commodities that could no longer be supplied by the state-run manufacturing industries. This pressure gave rise to the conversion to paying in silver for the labour service, and also local tribute, which was no longer needed.[431] A market-orientated and silver-based commercial mechanism was slowly coming about. Merchants were now under no other pressure to accept or decline deals with business partners, including the government departments, it became a true business no more than a

424 *Ming Yingzong shilu*, *j.* 239, p. 9b.
425 *Ming Xianzong shilu*, *j.* 261, p. 3b.
426 *Ming Shenzong shilu*, *j.* 110, p. 2b.
427 Ibid., *j.* 45, p. 8a.
428 *Ming Shizong shilu*, *j.* 172, pp. 4a–b.
429 "Ti wei tiao chen bian wu yi xia an rang shi 題為條陳邊務以狎安攘事" (Policy Suggestions for Frontier Security), in *Zhao Gongxiang wenji* 趙恭襄文集 (*Collected Works of Zhao Bingran, Shihao Gongxiang*) by Zhao Bingran 趙炳然, (?–1569), in *MJSWB*, vol. 252, *j.* 1, p. 9b.
430 *Ming Xianzong shilu*, *j.* 155, pp. 4a-b.
431 *Da Ming huidian*, *j.* 189, p. 10a.

concern with profitability. Sometimes they simply walked away from a deal.[432] With manufacturing industries now competiting for government orders, prices were lowered and the quality of commodities improved.

Trade boomed as the disintegration of the government monopoly paved the way for commodity manufacturing and export. During the Wanli 萬歷 period (r. 1573–1620) private manufacturing grew to be of gigantic magnitude. It was reported by Lü Kun 呂坤 (1536–1618), the Grand Coordinator of Shanxi, that "thousands upon thousands of people in the Zhaolan 洮藍 region participated day and night in jacquard weaving and cloth dyeing."[433] Qu Dajun 屈大均 observed a similar situation in the ironwork industry in Guangdong: "Some ironworks were established on a grand scale for massive production, one of which was financed with 10,000 *taels* of silver, manned with as many as 1,000 blacksmiths and supported by three hundred families."[434] This enhancement of the manufacturing sector stimulated the export business. The border region stretching for thousands of miles was like a huge magnet for both Chinese and foreign merchants. Silks, porcelains and spices changed hands in great quantites. "Silk from Huzhou, in Zhejiang, was loaded on board the 'silk galleons', each with more than a thousand cases, sailing for Manila [where it was sold for further shipment] on to Mexico and Peru."[435] From 1560–1640, it is estimated that 10,000 tons of silver went across the Pacific, 9,000 tons of which ended up in China. But the annual silver flow from Japan to China during these years was 6–7 times more than that from America.[436] Japanese merchants earned profits as high as six times their initial investment from their China trade.[437] With private manufacturing propelling commodity exports, the prohibition on foreign trade was increasingly little more than an anachronism. André Gunder Frank estimates that 60,000 tons of the 137,000 tons of silver produced in the world from 1550–1800 arrived in China to pay for the equally valued exports.[438]

The Weakening of Conventional Values

The dissemination and imposition of its ideology was a crucial constituent of the administration's strategy to maintain political stability. But as the dynasty progressed, social and economic changes posed a serious challenge to the official Confucian values that had been established with such vigour during the Hongwu ad-

432 *Ming Xizong shilu*, *j.* 25, p. 7a.

433 *Ming Shenzong shilu*, *j.* 309, pp. 1b–2a.

434 Qu Dajun, *Guangdong xinyu*, *j.* 15, pp. 7b–10a.

435 Quan Hansheng, 全漢昇 *Mingqing jingji shi jianju* 明清經濟史研究 (*Studies in Ming and Qing Economic History*). (Taibei: Lianjing Publishers, 1987), p. 23.

436 André Gunder Frank, *ReOrient: Global Economy in the Asian Age*. (Berkeley: California University Press, 1998), p. 205.

437 George Samson, *A History of Japan, 1334–1615* (Stanford: Stanford University Press, 1961), p. 271; for later periods, see also George Samson, *A History of Japan*, 1615–1867. (Stanford: Stanford University Press, 1963), pp. 142–146.

438 André Gunder Frank, *ReOrient* (1987), p. 208.

ministration. Increasingly, political thinkers came to question these values and suggest miodifications to them. Wang Yangming 王陽明 (1472–1529) was one of the most prominent Ming philosophers to question the functionality and practicability of some long-held principles. He denounced the deification of Confucianism and its institution as an unchangeable and universal belief system. For instance, he argued that "the Way cannot be the private property of Confucius"[439] ..."what Confucius instructs is not necessarily correct, let alone the words from those who claim to speak in his name"[440]. He emphasized the power of self-consciousness over the doctrinarism of the sages: "There is nothing beyond our heart and nothing beyond our senses (*xinwai wuwu, xinwai wushi* 心外無物, 心外無事)."[441] Such a shift in values, as exemplified in the arguments of Wang Yangming, helped liberate people from the confinement of conventional values and encouraged them to follow their own inclinations rather than the sage's doctrines. Wang suggested that "if we learn Confucianism only by the book ... we will get further and further away from the truth (*tianli* 天理)."[442] He saw current problems as a consequence of people blindly following old principles: "Our country is not ideally managed and our officials have become corrupted because the interpretation of Confucianism is incorrect."[443] Such challenges led people to explore other values. For instance, Li Zhi 李贄 (1527–1602) went even further in denouncing the rigidity of keeping Confucianism as an immutable creed. He stated: "Each dynasty has a different emperor; every administration has its own guidelines for administration. They do not have to follow others but should adopt changes when needed."[444] Li Zhi considered Qin Shihuang 秦始皇 the best emperor in a thousand years in Chinese history because of his practical and sensible approach to the economy and to administration, regardless of his notoriety for executing Confucian scholars and burning Confucian books.[445] Li Zhi also exposed the hypocrisy of the doctrine on self-interest:

> Selfishness is natural and there is nothing wrong with it ... There would be no motivation for peasants to toil hard developing their lands if they were not selfish, wanting to harvest more. It is the same for a homemaker, who would not try to accumulate more without the motivation to become richer, and for a scholar studying for a degree ... the so-called selfless mentality is only a mirage and pretence.[446]

---

439 *Wang Yangming xiansheng quanji* 王陽明先生全集 (*The Complete works of Wang Shouren, Hao Yangming*) by Wang Shouren 王守仁 (1472–1529), in *Siku cunmu* 集, fasc. 50. *j.* 1, p. 52a.

440 Ibid., *j.* 1, p. 47b.

441 Ibid., *j.* 1, p. 17b.

442 Ibid., *j.* 21, p. 46b.

443 Ibid., *j.* 5, p. 57b.

444 *Cang shu* 藏書 (*A Book to Conceal*) by Li Zhi 李贄 (1527–1602), in *Siku cunmu* 史, fasc. 23, *j.* 2, p. 4a.

445 Ibid., p. 1b.

446 Ibid., *j.* 32, pp. 42a–b.

> The desire to have good materials and beautiful women, to buy more farmland and houses, and to save more money and pursue degrees by studying hard ... is human nature and is shared by everybody.[447]
> The value of a person is decided by himself, not Confucius.[448]

Many high-ranking officials followed this new way of thinking, at least to some degree. Xu Jie 徐階 (1503–1583), for instance, who served as a Senior Grand Secretary from 1562, argued: "We should be guided by our own desires and restrained by our own feelings."[449]

This challenge to inherited values had a significant impact on the economy, especially the idea that it was part of human nature to pursue self-interest. A prosperity-motivated economy and a self-seeking social culture replaced the mentality of controlled stability. This gave rise to the prevalence of materialism, pragmatism and utilitarianism: "Everybody respects rich merchants while nobody cares about the poor and lonely scholars, and since there has never been such a phenomenon in history [of scholars being poor and socially downgraded], it may be the true world outlook anyway."[450] In late Ming society people were inclined to judge social status not in terms of scholarship but rather by wealth. Money worship was no longer shameful; it had become a social trend. Those who made little money were looked down upon. Peasants who were at the top of the social echelon during the early years of the dynasty were downgraded to the very bottom: "The social trend is for luxurious spending hence those who are still toiling on their landholdings are laughed and sneered at,"[451] and "farmers are despised as foolish and numb."[452] With commerce becoming the driving force that propelled social mobility and economic development, this new value system transformed people's understanding of the world.

The decay of the inherited and conventional value system indicated the changing nature of social ethics. People became more and more self-obsessed and money-orientated. Economic commercialisation generated tremendous wealth and helped breed a new culture of consumption. The moral barrier of frugality crumbled in this environment. A retired high-ranking official named Shi 石 is a good example. He often patronised a deluxe restaurant with his acquaintances and never hesitated to give tips to the chef, sometimes as much as 200 *taels* (a county magistrate's annual

---

447 *Li Wenling ji* 李溫陵集 (*Collected Works of Li Zhi, Literary and Buddhist Name by Wenling, the Monk at Residence*) by Li Zhi 李贄 (1527–1602), in *Siku xuxiu*, fasc. 1352, *j*. 3, p. 19a.

448 Ibid., *j*. 2, pp. 1a–b.

449 *Shijingtang ji* 世經堂集 (*The Shijingtang Collection*) by Xu Jie 徐階 (1503–1583), in *Siku cunmu* 集, fasc. 79, *j*. 18, p. 32b.

450 *Gaitang qian,hou,xu ji* 溉堂前後續集 (*Collected Writings Consisting of the Former, the Later and its Continuation Parts, Named After my Dwelling House, the Gaitang*) by Sun Zhiwei 孫枝蔚 (1620–1687), in *Siku cunmu* 集, fasc. 206, *j*. 4, p. 23b.

451 *Wu xing zhanggu ji* 吳興掌故集 (*The Collected Anecdotes of Wuxing*) by Xu Xianzhong 徐獻忠 (1483–1559), in *Siku cunmu* 史, fasc. 188, *j*. 12, p. 1a.

452 *Ming shan cang*, p. 9a (no *juan*).

salary was 87 *taels* of silver).[453] The polarisation of society in terms of wealth was obvious. A rich merchant could afford to spend on one private party as much as a peasant family's income for a whole year.[454] The betrothal gift and dowry for a rich family could reach as high as 500–700 *taels* of silver, an unthinkable amount during the early years of the dynasty.[455] But this culture of consumption did gradually infiltrate all levels of society: "Students used to wear cotton robes but now they look too shabby. They have to wear silk even if they cannot afford it. Social fashion has changed people's aesthetic tastes."[456] In the first month of the 24th year of the Jiajing reign (1545) the emperor endorsed a memorial by Cha Bingyi 查秉彝 (1504–1561, Supervising Secretary at the Ministry of Revenue) suggesting banning luxurious spending: "Luxurious spending led by the gentry and officials has corrupted our people and lured them away from their registered occupations … political stability comes from people abiding by the ethics and prosperity in which frugality was the prerequisite."[457] However, such good intentions could do little to stop the overwhelming current of commercialisation.

Late Ming officials took a new approach to the social and economic issues. For example, the long-held virtue of frugality was questioned. Lu Ji 陸楫 (1515–1552) noticed the contradiction between frugality and prosperity:

> Since ancient times, the rulers have always advocated frugality while prohibiting luxurious spending. They always claim that wealth is a fixed quantity. One person's luxurious consumption is bound to lead to the scarcity of another person. Frugality was the only trait that could bring out overall prosperity. However, I can never figure out how luxurious consumption will cause poverty … It may be the case for an individual or an individual family … but it would be a much different story if it is for the country as a whole … Now look at the situation in WuYue 吳越. It is where great wealth comes from. People there enjoy a luxurious lifestyle, which provides the chance for others to make a living. Frugality will cause exactly the opposite."[458]

Wei Shaoshi 魏昭士 (1628–1693) argued the same point:

> Consumption will benefit society more than maintaining subsistence because it increases social spending ... While frugality helps an individual accumulate more wealth, it is not good for society as a whole. If an individual is frugal in his life, it may make little difference to society, but society will become poor if everybody is frugal. If an individual pursues a luxurious lifestyle in his home, his clothing and in a love of good food and wine, many people will benefit

453 *Hai Shi xiansheng wenji* 海石先生文集 (*Collected Literary Works of Qian Wei, Hao Haishi*) by Qian Wei 錢薇 (1502–1554), in *Siku cunmu* 集, fasc. 97, *j.* 26, p. 1a.

454 Xie Zhaozhe, *Wu zazu*, *j.* 11, p. 11a.

455 *Xu Wenchang wenji* 徐長文集 (*Collected Literary Works of Xu Wei, Hao Changwen*) by Xu Wei 徐渭 (1521–1593), Wanli 42 edition, in *Siku cunmu* 集, fasc. 145, *j.* 20, p. 30b.

456 Fan Lian, *Yunjian jumu chao*, p. 2a.

457 *Xinke Ming zhengtongzong* 新刻明政統宗 (*Newly Printed Unoffical Veritable Records of the Ming Dynasty*) by Tu Shan 塗山, in *Siku jinhui* 史, fasc. 2, *j.* 25, p. 31a.

458 *Jianxiatang gao* 蒹葭堂稿 (*Writings from my 'Reeds House'*) by Lu Ji 陸楫 (1515–1552), in *Siku xuxiu*, fasc. 1354, *j.* 6, pp. 2b–3a.

> from producing and selling these goods to satisfy these demands. As a consequence, wealth will be generated in society at large.[459]

These commentators argued that commerce helps drive an economy through the beneficial circle created by the mechanism of demand and supply. Huang Zongxi 黄宗羲 (1610–1695) strongly condemned prejudice against commerce: "Those bookish scholars always follow tradition and advocate the suppression of commerce. They subjectively reached such an irresponsible conclusion before investigating the role of commerce. Commerce is also fundamental to industry."[460] Zhang Juzheng 張居正 (1525–1582, Senior Grand Secretary) observed the dialectical relationship between farming and commerce: "Farming will suffer without a good commercial exchange and commerce is undermined without a healthy farming industry."[461] Wang Shixing 王士性 (1546–1598, Supervising Secretary in the Ministry of Rites) made the observation that "although the land tax is much heavier for the Wu 吳 region, people there are not poor because it is a commercial center where 30 per cent of the population are artisans and merchants who benefit from trade."[462] Yang Wei 楊巍 (1514–1605, Minster of Revenue) stressed the importance of supporting merchants and protecting private property: "The rich provide the vitality in the capital; these merchants today are the rich of the past. They are the ones we need to take care of. We should never exhaust their energy. Only by enhancing their wealth can we have resources to draw upon."[463] Economic benefit replaced virtue, becoming the standard for judging a social institution. For instance, some officials publicly praised the much disliked absentee landlords and usurious loans. Gu Qiyuan 顧起元 (1565–1628, Vice Minister of Personnel) argued:

> Absentee landlords are indispensable to tenants. They were accused of evading the labour service levy but, if they hadn't, they would not have wanted to buy more land. [Without absentee landlords] Our landless people would have no land to rent therefore no chance to make a living. They would not have support to buy seed, feed their cows or maintain their residences ... money lenders should not be abolished as they provide the shoulder on which the poor are able to lean in emergency ... the rich are not bad if they abide by the law, and there is no reason to drive them away and take over their property, as this will impoversish hundreds or thousands of needy peasants.[464]

By the late Ming there was a new social culture and a very different economic climate. Commerce became the focus of the economy and money played a crucial role.

---

459 *Wei Shaoshi wenji* 魏昭士文集 (*Collected Literary Works of Wei Shaoshi*) by Wei Li 魏禮 (1628–1693), in Lin Shiyi 林時益 (d. 1691) (ed.), *Ningdu san-Wei ji* 寧都三魏全集 (*Complete Collection of the Three Wei Brothers from Ningdu*), *in Siku jinhui* 集, fasc. 6, *j.* 7, p. 1a.

460 Huang Zongxi, *Ming yi daifang lu*, p. 47a–b (no *juan*).

461 *Xinke Zhang Taiyue wenji* 新刻張太岳文集 (*Newly Printed Collected Literary Works of Zhang Juzheng, Hao Taiyue*) by Zhang Juzheng 張居正 (1525–1582), 1612 edition, in *Siku xuxiu*, fasc. 1345, *j.* 8, p. 1a.

462 *Guang zhi yi* 廣志繹 (*Extensive Local Chronicles Unravelled*) by Wang Shixing 王士性 (1546–1598), in *Siku cunmu* 史, fasc. 251, *j.* 2, pp. 27b–28a.

463 Zhang Xuan, *Xiyuan wenjian lu*, *j.* 34, p. 11b.

464 Gu Qiyuan, *Kezuo zhuiyu*, *j.* 5, pp. 31a–31b.

The new values that went with this destroyed the ideological foundation for the trade prohibition policy. Without ideological constraints from the government people would pursue activities that enhanced their material lives; it was impossible to prevent people from engaging in market activity. Similarly, without politically enforced constraints, people would engage in business to generate more income for themselves, and it was impracticable to prevent people, especially those in border regions, from contacting foreigners for more profitable exchange. When foreign vessels fully loaded with silver were approaching Ming waters and merchants were eager to pay any price to engage in trade, the authorities would have a great deal of difficulty in restraining Chinese people from violating the maritime interdiction.

The Pursuit of Politics and Social Influence by Merchants

A government's trade policy directly reflects the political status of merchants. The early Ming prohibition on trade reflected the administration's adherence to the principles of self-sufficiency and the suppression of commerce. Commercialisation of the economy and society during the mid and late Ming periods elevated the social and political standing of merchants. Merchants became the biggest political beneficiary from the economic transformation and the associated changes in social values. And merchants were well aware of the value and consequences of political engagement. The Ming political system determined money to be secondary to the significance of political participation: "Officials are the eyes, the ears and backbone of the dynasty."[465] It was also argued that it was "the Confucian literati who executed the real power in the administration", even though the court provided the focus for authority.[466] The experience that merchants underwent during the early Ming years made them well aware of the imperativeness of keeping politically active. Only by becoming officials themselves could they participate in policy-making; only by becoming the ruling social élite could they protect themselves, their families and their properties. The late Ming merchants were successful in using their wealth to gain office, either through the examination system or through the "*juanguan* 捐官"-system, the system that allowed the purchase of office. The rise of merchants to political importance became a late Ming phenomenon.

Scholars and officials were the social élite who enjoyed constitutional privileges that were not available to any other social group, even the wealthy. Merchants especially envied the political prerogatives of literati-officials, particularly their immunity from prosecution by the local judiciary. The law on this was clear: "Officials at rank 5 and above cannot be subject to persecution without the emperor's personal endorsement. Officials at rank 6 or below cannot be subject to questioning except by investigation by the "*xun'an yushi* 巡按禦史" (Touring Censor) and the "*ancha si* 按察司" (Provincial Surveillance Commission). Penalties were solely for de the em-

465 *Ming Shizong shilu*, *j.* 30, p. 3b.

466 *Qianfu lun* 潛夫論 (*Discussion [on Political Matters] by Wang Fu, the Hermit, Hao Qianfu*) by Wang Fu 王符 (85–162), in *Siku quanshu*, fasc. 696, *j.* 2, p. 6a.

peror to decide."[467] For example, Fu Sheng 福生, a convicted criminal, was pardoned only because he was a university student, a would-be official whom the régime needed most.[468] Privilege could even be delegated to the relatives of officials. A case in point was demonstrative. The persecution of a suspect was dropped because the accused happened to be the uncle of a government official named Liu Zhong 劉仲 (Bureau Director of the Ministry of Revenue).[469] As soon as a man was awarded the *juren* or *jinshi* degree he would become a member of the privileged club of the "*jinshen* 縉紳" (the landed gentry with an official title), overshadowing the rest of his fellows, even local minor officials. Because of this immunity, everyone had to show respect to such people.[470] In some cases official titles were also inheritable, thus a man's sons or even his parents could assume his privileges or be rewarded with a position in the government.[471] Exempted from the heavy labor service levy, officials and degree-holders also enjoyed security of their property. Wang Shixing 王士性 (1546–1598) observed: "Without producing a current degree holder, a family of the gentry or an official can never secure their wealth. Their hold on their property is only temporary."[472] Li Mengyang 李夢陽 (1473–1529) pointed out the significance of this for merchants: "Lacking a connection with the politically powerful, merchants may encounter difficulties that they themselves are not able to overcome. For example, merchants have to sell goods on credit, but there is no guarantee that their loans will be repaid without the powerful and influential working on their behalf."[473] It was reported that in Songjiang 松江 "drapers could not prosper without running their business in the name of the local *jinshen*."[474] A scholar's degree or an official's title became the political shield for both his social status and the security of his property.

Many merchants were only too well aware of their insecurity and vulnerability without either a proper political position or political influence. They had a burning desire to get into the political circle of the government. However, merchants were not in the category for officialdom. The Hongwu administration set up the standardized qualification to recruit its officials. "Officials have to be selected from those who make a living by farming and have upright and integral characters."[475] Those who were profit-orientated were obviously not in the category. The legal

467 *Tang Ming lu hebian*, *j.* 2, p. 4a.

468 *Ming Taizu shilu*, *j.* 181, p. 1a.

469 *Ming Taizu shilu*, *j.* 131, p. 7b.

470 *Yueshi bian* 閱世編 (*Collected Writings Examining the World*) by Ye Mengzhu 葉夢珠 (Qing), in *Shanghai zhanggu congshu* 上海掌故叢書 (*Collected Anecdotes of Shanghai*) edited by Chen Tao 陳陶 (1881–1946). (Shanghai: Zhonghua shuju, 1935), *j.* 4, p. 1b.

471 *Tang Ming lu hebian*, *j.* 9, p. 7b.

472 Wang Shixing, *Guang zhi yi*, *j.* 4, p. 6a.

473 "Qianqiu shanren ji 潛虬山人記" (The Diary of an Unemployed Great Man of Letters), in *Kong tong ji* 空同集 (*Collected Works with Nothing in Common with the Fashionable Style*) by Li Mengyang 李夢陽 (1473–1529), in *Siku quanshu*, fasc. 1262, *j.* 48, pp. 48a–b.

474 "Shihuo wu," 食貨五 (Economic Issues, section 5), in *Yueshi bian*, p. 5b.

475 *Ming shi*, *j.*71, 3a.

occupations eligible for the Ming civil examination was limited to the family of *jun* 軍 (military) *min* 民 (farmer) and *jiang* 匠 (artisan).[476] Qian Maowei 錢茂偉 observed: "During most of the Ming era there were no merchant candidates in the civil examination; most of them listed themselves as farmers."[477] Merchants had not made their debut as a registrated occupation in the civil examination until the 35th year of the Wanli reign (1607) when Zheng Maohua 鄭茂華, a candidate from Yangzhou 揚州 earned a *jinshi* degree in the registration as a merchant after the government's introduction of the *shangji* 商籍 (merchant registration).[478] He was the *only* registered merchant among the 22,404 Ming *jinshi* degree holders, of whom 14,765 registered as farmers, 5,372 from the military, 808 from official families and 801 from artisanal backgrounds.[479] The early Ming discriminating political culture forced the merchants to take many different detours to reach their goal. Tang Lixing 唐力行 points out: "Merchants, the group at the bottom of the social echelon, look mean and low even if they have a great amount of wealth. Hence merchants have a strong desire to assimilate themselve into the *shi* 士 (scholars) or *nong* 農 (farmers) groups to upgrade their social status. What they could do was to purchase land to become landowners, participate in the civil examination system to become scholars or buy office with cash...."[480]

Once merchants became affluent they invested in education for themselves and for their sons, or even their relatives, so that they could pursue office through the imperial examination system. They might also provide financial support for any 'talented potentials' as an indirect way of gaining political influence. As a consequence, merchants came to dominate the examination process in the late Ming period. The merchant group was accused of 'stealing' the examination system in the late year when the civil examination court was full of unabashed 'unqualified' merchants. Huo Tao 霍韜 (1487–1540, Minister of Rites), who himself was from a merchant family, complained of the situation: "The recruitment of officials relies on the civil examination system but so many positions have been stolen by merchants through the system."[481] The 'theft' was made possible via the practice of "*maoji* 冒籍" (assuming another person's registration in the civil examination). It became a

---

476 *Ming shi, j.* 77, 3a. *Daming huidian, j.* 77, pp. 24b–25a.

477 Qian Maowei 錢茂偉, *Guojia, keju yu shehui: yi mingdai wei zhongxin de kaocha* 國家，科舉與社會：以明代為中心的考察 (State, Society and the Civil Examination System: a study foused on the Ming dynasty). (Beijing, Beijing Library Publication 北京圖書館出版社, 2004), p. 167.

478 *Wanli sanshiwu nian dingwei ke jinshi luli bianlan* 萬曆三十五年丁未科進士履歷便覽 (A brief guide on the *jinshi* degree holders of the 35th year of the Wangli reign). (Shanghai, Shanghai Library digital consultation on ancient books), p. 9. Also Qian Maowei, *Guojia, keju yu shehui: yi mingdai wei zhongxin de kaocha* (2004), p. 167.

479 Qian Maowei, *Guojia, keju yu shehui: yi mingdai wei zhongxin de kaocha* (2004), pp. 167 and 310.

480 Tang Lixing 唐力行, *Shangren yu zhongguo jinshi shehui* 商人與中國近世社會(Merchants and China's Modern Society). (Beijing: Commercial Publication, 商務印書館，2003), pp. 25–26.

481 *Xu wenxian tongkao* 續文獻統考 (*Compilation of Dynastic Government Administration Documents, Continued*) by Wang Qi 王圻 (*jinshi* 1566), Xi Huang 嵇璜 (1711–1794) *et al*, in *Siku xuxiu*, fasc. 762, *j.* 48, p. 17a.

handy and efficient way for merchants to sit the civil examination registered in other people's occupation category and compete in a less competent community. Most of the merchants registered as farmers to meet the civil examination category. The well-known Pan Huang 潘潢 (*jinshi* 1521) was the son of a millionaire timber merchant. But he sat the civil examination in his hometown in *minji* 民籍 (farmer registration).[482] Wang Daokun 汪道昆 (*jinshi* 1547), the son of a great salt merchant, instead of registering himself as a merchant in his hometown of Shexian 歙縣, listed himself in Lianghuai 兩淮 as a farmer. Jiang Zhen 江珍 (*jinshi* 1544), the son of a rich businessman even registered himself in *junji* 軍籍 (military occupation) and sat the civil examination far away from his hometown where he was supposed to be. [483]

Although "the law prohibited examinees from sitting exams in locations other than their registered birthplace"[484] more and more merchants and their sons, taking advantage of their jobs, travelled to other places for the examination. The father and brother of Xu Wei 徐渭 (1521–1593), a well-known scholar of the late Ming period, left their hometown in Shaoxing 紹興 of Zhejiang 浙江 and went to Guizhou 貴州 and registered there for the civil examination. Xu Wei's father earned a *juren* degree there and was appointed to a post of prefect while his brother followed in his father's footsteps... [485] It was a phenomenon that lasted for a century. We can only see the tip of the iceberg from the information on a few who were caught and punished. As early as 1465, Fengshi 馮詩 and his seven compatriots from Zhejiang who were accused of gaining their degrees by impersonating others' registration categories, were demoted to the status of commoners.[486] Tao Dashun 陶大順 (*jinshi* 1566) was dismissed from his post after being exposed for impersonating another person's registration in the "*xiangshi* 鄉試" (provincial civil examination) in Shuntian 順天 prefecture. He returned to his hometown in Huiji 會稽, Zhejiang, where he sat the examination with his son Tao Yunchun 陶允淳 (*jinshi* 1566), both of whom got the *jinshi* degree in the same year, in 1566.[487] The late Ming period saw a snowballing of the *maoji* phenomenon and a great upsurge of merchants taking up government posts through this illegal practice. Even the Jiajing Emperor could do little about it, so he changed his attitude, stating: "There are no

482 *Mingdai denke lu huibian*, p. 3073.

483 Ji Shan, *Lianghuai yanfa zhi*, *j.* 47, pp. 21b–22b.

484 "Xiang shi 鄉試" (Provincial civil examination), in *Da Ming huidian*, *j.* 77, p. 25a.

485 "Tan mingdai de weiji 談明代的衛籍" (A discussion on the garrison registration of the Ming dynasty) by Gu Cheng, in *Beijing Normal University Journal* 5 (1989), p. 63.

486 "Siyou jingshi maoji 已酉京試冒籍" (The impersonation of other people's registration category in the metropolitan civil examination in 1585), in *Yehuo bian* 野獲編 (*Collected Harvest from the Wildness*) by Shen Defu 沈德符 (1578–1642), *j.* 16, p. 16b, in *Siku jinhui* 史, fasc. 4, pp. 1–702.

487 "Yuzhong xiangshi 雨中鄉試" (The provincial civil examination in the rain), in *Yehuo bian*, *j.* 16, p. 7b. Wu Renan, *Mingqing jiangnan wangzu yu shehui jingji wenhua* (2001), p. 205.

such things as *maoji* in the domain of our empire because every talent from all corners of the country belongs to the court."[488]

Merchants did not only 'steal' degrees but did it overwhelmingly. The consequence was disastrous for the farmers' group. As quotas for degrees (for both *juren* and *jinshi*) were mainly fixed by region, merchants taking a greater share meant correspondingly less for other social groups. The *jinshi* quota was fixed at 100 degrees for the whole nation in the 3rd year of the Hongwu (1370), 60% of them was allocated to the South and 40% for the North.[489] The quota was increased to 300 degrees for each civil examination (with the exeption of a few years) after the Chenghua reign 成化 (14665–1488).[490] It was changed to 150 each for the South and North since the 3rd year of the Zhengde (1508).[491] The quota of *juren* degrees was also permanently fixed on each degree for every 20 to 30 candidates.[492] The Lianghuai 兩淮 area was a good example. The region yielded 286 *juren* 舉人 in the Ming era, 213 of whom were from merchant families who were not natives, taking 74% of the total quota (162 holders were from Anhui merchants, 42 from Shaanxi 陝西 merchants and 9 from Shanxi 山西 merchants while 73 were from local residents). Furthermore, among the total 137 *jinshi* holders from the region, 106 were from migrant merchant families, taking 77% of the total quota (70 degrees were taken by the merchants from Anhui 安徽; 30 by the merchants from Shaanxi 陝西 and 6 by the Shanxi 山西 merchants while only 31 were from the local population).[493]

Armed with a legalized 'status impersonation', merchants cleared themselves from the discriminated restriction in civil examinations. Wang Daokun demonstrated the late Ming merchants' determination and confidence in gaining higher economic status and more political power. He claimed: "Our people (merchants) aim at the highest degree in education through the civil examination system or be-

488 "Jiyuan qu xiangren 畿元取鄉人" (The first prize in the provincial civil examination should be given to a Northerner from the capital), in *Yehuo bian*, *j.* 16, p. 27a.

489 "Fan hui shi eshu 凡會試額數" (The quota for the metropolitian civil examination), in *Libu zhigao* 禮部志稿 (*Draft Monograph of the Ministry of Rites Containing Administrative and Ceremonial Regulations, Imperial Edicts, Memorials, etc*), *j.* 23, p. 31b, in *Siku quanshu*, fasc. 597, pp. 433–444.

490 Ibid., *j.* 23, p. 32a–b.

491 "Xuanju er 選舉二" (Recommendation and Examination, section 2), *Ming shi*, *j.* 70, p. 8a.

492 "Jiangxi xiangshi xiaolu ji 江西鄉試小錄序" (A brief description of the provincial civil examination in Jiangxi), in *Xiangyi wenji* 襄毅文集 (*Collected Works of Han Yong*) by Han Yong 韓雍 (1422–1478), *j.* 10, p. 2a, in *Siku quanshu*, fasc. 1245, pp. 730–731; "Jingsheng shi gebi shiyi 京省試革弊事宜" (The issue of the elimitation of malpractice in the metropolitian and provincial civil examinations), in *Libu zhigao*, *j.* 71, p. 42b. The rate was 1/20 in the 7th year of Jingtai 景泰 (1456) and 1/25 for the 43rd year of the Jiajing year (1564).

493 '科第表上，人物六' (The list of the successful civil examination candidates, 1st section; in the People, section six) *Lianhui yanfa zhi* (1870) *j.* 47, pp. 1a–48b. Also Wang Rigen 王日根, "*Mingqing keju zhidu dui minying jiaoyu de cujin* 明清科舉制度對民營教育的促進" (The promotion to private education by the civil examination system during the Ming and Qing eras), *Xiamendaxue xuebao* 廈門大學學報 4 (2001), p. 102.

coming as rich as a "*sufeng* 素封" (princely status in wealth) by doing business." [494] In Shaxian 沙縣 merchants concentrated on two enterprises: "While merchants were proud of leaving for overseas for trade, those who stayed home were also proud, preparing themselves for the civil examinations."[495] Their financial capacity gave merchants an unequal advantage. As Shen Yao 沈垚 (1790–1840) observed: "Unless his ancestors engaged in business, a man could never afford to study to become a scholar or an official. There used to be discriminations between the four social groups [scholar-officials, peasants, artisans and merchants]. The differences have by now vanished. Merchants are no longer at the bottom of the social strata. In the old days the sons of officials were always scholars but now the situation has changed. The sons of merchants are always officials."[496]

The local gazetteers from Zhejiang and Fujian describe the same process, whereby the rise in influence of merchants enabled them to compete in increasing numbers in the imperial examination. If we take Fujian, for example, we find that spending on education became one of the primary investments for merchant families. Xiao Lougong 小楼公 (The Revered Mr Lou), a maritime merchant from Anping 安平, would not allow his children to follow in his footsteps and become merchants but rather wanted them to become officials. And when he was away from home for business, his wife spent a substantial amount of money on their sons' education. The sons finally made it into the *Guozijian* 國子監, the Imperial Academy.[497] Qian Qiu 潜虬, a rich merchant from Fujian, gave up his business and rented a ten-room house in the mountains to teach his children poems and Confucian doctrine in order to prepare them for the official examinations.[498] By the mid- to late Ming years, the efforts of merchants were paying off. For example, the Pans 潘, a rich merchant family of Wuyuan county 婺源, produced eleven *jinshi* and four government ministers. Pan Yu 潘鈺 (*jinshi* 1483, Assistant Surveillance Commissioner of Fujian) had two sons, Pan Dan 潘旦 (*jinshi* 1505) was a Deputy Minister of War and Supreme Commander in Guangdong and Guangxi, while another son, Pan Jian 潘鑒 (*jinshi* 1508) was a Minister of Works. His grandson, Pan Huang 潘潢 (*jinshi* 1521), served as Minister of Works, Minister of War, Minister of Personal and

494 *Taihan ji*, *j.* 34, p. 10b.

495 *Chongzhuan Fujian tongzhi* 重纂福建通志 (*The Recompiled Fujian Gazetteer*) by Sun Erzhen 孫爾准 (1772–1832)and Chen Shouqi 陳壽淇 (1771–1834), (Zhengyi 正誼 Academy, 1868), *j.* 57, p. 3b.

496 "Fei-Xi xiansheng qishi shuangshou xu 費席先生七十雙壽序" (A Preface for the Double Seventieth Birthday Celebration of Mr. Fei and Mr. Xi), in *Luofan lou wenji* 落帆樓文集 (*Collected Literary Works from the Luofan Mansion*) by Shen Yao 沈垚 (1790–1840), in *Siku xuxiu*, fasc. 1525, *j.* 24, pp. 11b–12a.

497 "Shimu Shen ru ren shou xu 史母沈孺人壽序" (A Preface to the Birthday Celebration of Madame Shen), in *Jingbi ji* 景壁集 (*Scenic Wall Collection*) by Li Guangjin 李廣晉 (Ming), (1637–edition), *j.* 4, pp. 9a–b.

498 *Kongtong ji*, *j.* 48, pp. 48a–b.

Minister of Finance.[499] The Xu family produced six officials in five generations in a row. Xu Jie 徐階 (*jinshi* 1523, Senior Grand Secretary), was a big landlord, a merchant, a factory owner and a banker. His brother Xu Zhi 徐陟 (*jinshi* 1547) was a Minister of Justice.[500] His son Xu Yangzhai 徐仰齋 took a hereditary post as Minister of the Court of Imperial Sacrifices, while his grandson Xu Anyang 徐晏陽 (*jinshi* 1574) took the same office. Xu Jie's great-grandson, Xu Langao 徐蘭皋, was given a position as Commander of the Imperial Guards, and his great-great-grandson, Xu Tanning 徐澹寧, became a Grand Mentor to the heir apparent and Left Military Commissioner.[501]

Similar inter-generational success occurred in the family of the business tycoon An Guo 安國 (1481–534). He made a fortune by smuggling Chinese products to Japan and produced two *jinshi* in his next two generations. His son An Rushan 安如山 (*jinshi* 1529) served as magistrate of Zhizhou 裕州 and his grandson An Xifan 安希范 (*jinshi* 1586), served as Director of the Ministry of Rites and was of the leading members of the Donglin 東林 party.

Desire for profit and enthusiasm for office became a prominent characteristic of merchants during the middle and late Ming years. In regions known for commercial activity, it was said that "everyone is engaged in trade and every family is striving for a degree."[502] Consequently merchant families became numerous degree-holders and officials. Fujian produced 2,436 *jinshi* degree-holders, nearly one tenth of the whole quota of the empire during its 276 years of history.[503] Rather than Beijing or Nanjing, it was Fujian that claimed the two most prolific counties in terms of producing degree holders. Putian county 莆田 contributed 493 *jinshi*, while Jinjiang 晉江 368.[504] Putian county alone produced more *jinshi* than the combined numbers for Guangxi (201) and Yunnan (240) provinces.[505]

Some inland regions experienced a similar phenomenon. Huizhou 徽州 is a good example. According to Ye Xian'en 葉顯恩, Huizhou, the home of the well-known *Huishang* 徽商 (Huizhou merchants), produced 392 *jinshi* degree-holders during the Ming years from a small population of 65,861 (statistics, 1491), comprising 1.55 per cent of all *jinshi* degree holders (yet the prefecture had only 0.00107 per

499 *Guochao xianzheng lu* 國朝獻徵錄 (*Ming Biographies up to the Wanli Reign Compiled by Jiao Hong, The Hanlin Academician*) by Jiao Hong 焦竑 (1541–1620), in *Siku cunmu* 史, fasc. 102, *j.* 43, pp. 49a–b.

500 *Yueshi bian*, *j.* 5, p. 2a.

501 *Benchao fensheng renwu zhikao*, *j.* 26, pp. 18a–b.

502 *Chongzhuan Fujian tongzhi*, *j.* 57, p. 3b.

503 Ibid.

504 Qian Maowei 錢茂偉, *Guojia, keju yu shehui: yi Mingdai wei zhongxin de kaocha* 國家，科舉與社會：以明代為中心的考察 (*State, Society and the Civil Examination System: a study focused on the Ming dynasty*). (Beijing: Beijing Library Publication, 2004), p. 167.

505 Duo Luoken 多洛肯, *Mingdai Fujian jinshi yanju* (*A Study on the Ming jinshi degree holders from Fujian*). (Shanghai: Shanghai cishu chubanshe, 2004), p. 73.

cent of the total population of the empire – 61,416,735 [statistics, 1502]).[506] The Pan 潘 village, a merchant village, alone produced 40 *jinshi*, more than a hundred officials at ranks 9 or above from Chenghua (1465–1488) to the Chongzhen (1628–1644) eras. *She* county 歙縣, known as 'the county of merchants' with a population of just 2,365 households, since the Jiajing years produced one grand secretary, one government minister, nine deputy government ministers and ministers of the court of review, four supervising secretaries and compliers, five grand coordinators, six circuit inspectors, four surveillance commissioners and three prefects.[507]

Merchants took up more and more important positions in the administration. As their number and influence rose, they formed a close and powerful network in the Ming decision-making process. Wang Chonggu 王崇古 (1515–1588), a merchant official from Shanxi, took the position of Vice Minister of War and Supreme Commander of Shaanxi 陝西 in 1567. His nephew Zhang Siwei 張四維 (*jinshi* 1553), the son of a big merchant, was a Senior Grand Secretary at court. Zhang's daughter married the son of Ma Ziqiang 馬自強 (*jinshi* 1553) who was the Longqing emperor's advisor and a Senior Grand Secretary at the Wanli court.[508] Even in the military, officials with merchant backgrounds were as powerful as they were at court. While this was undoubtedly a boast, Wang Daokun 汪道昆 (*jinshi* 1547) and Wang Shizhen 王世貞 (*jinshi* 1547) were considered the two best ministers of war 'under the heavens' (*tianxia liang sima* 天下兩司馬). They shared the same merchant family background.[509] Another legend that circulated wide and far claimed that "among all the officials from the twelve departments of the government in Nanjing there is only one, Wang Shu, who can say 'no' to the emperor." Wang Shu (*jinshi* 1448) was a government minister under four emperors and was closely related to a prominent salt merchant's family.[510] The highest-ranking official serving the Jiajing Emperor, Yan Song 嚴嵩 (*jinshi* 1505, a Senior Grand Secretary for 20 years) was from a merchant family. He was the grand secretary to whom the Jiajing emperor delegated most of his power. Both he and his son, Yan Shifan 嚴世播 (a Deputy Minister of Works), engaged in large-scale trade and owned many shops and trading sites in Yangzhou 揚州, the most thriving commercial center in the South.[511] Li Mengyang 李梦陽 (*jinshi* 1493) and Kang Hai 康海 (*jinshi* 1502), who were respected and admired as being among the seven most talented scholars within the empire, were

506 Ye Xian'en 葉顯恩, *Mingqing huizhou nongcun shehui yu dianpu zhi* 明清徽州農村社會與佃仆制 (*The Tenant and Servant Systems of Huizhou during the Ming and Qing dynasties*). (Hefei: Anhui renmin chubanshe, 1983), p. 192.

507 Ye Xian'en, *Mingqing huizhou nongcun shehui yu dianpu zhi* (1983), p. 192.

508 For the alleged cooperation between Wang Chonggu and his merchant brother-in-law see *Guochao dianhui*, *j.* 42, p. 48b. For Zhang Siwei's merchant background see *Guochao xian zheng lu*, *j.* 17, p. 72b.

509 Wang Daokun, *Taihan ji*, *j.* 17, p. 18b, and *j.* 43, pp. 9a–10b. See also *Yanzhou sibu gao* 弇州四部稿 (*Notes in Four Sections by Wang Shizhen, Hao Yanzhou*) by Wang Shizhen, in *Siku quanshu*, fasc. 1280, *j.* 85, pp. 8b–9a.

510 *Ningdu san Wei quanji*, *j.* 18, p. 1a. See also *Guochao xianzheng lu*, *j.* 24, pp. 61a–63b.

511 *Ming shi*, *j.* 210, pp. 27a–b; *Ming Shizong shilu*, *j.* 4, p. 7b.

from the same type of background, Shanxi merchant families.[512] In the ideological arena there was nobody that was more controversial and influential than Li Zhi, who, as we noted before, was well known for his open challenge to Confucianism. Li was a son of a maritime merchant.[513] As these examples show, the late Ming era witnessed merchants' active engagement in the examination system and the snowballing of their influence in every corner of the administrative system.

While merchants were increasing their influence through the examination system, many were still not satisfied with their political influence and wanted more control over the administrative processes. Education was not necessarily the most efficient way to obtain office, because it required years of work to prepare for the examinations, and even then success was not guaranteed. For this reason, the purchase of office became an increasingly common practice, especially when wars with the Mongols and the Japanese exhausted the state coffers and the government began to sell administrative positions in order to generate a quick income. It was said that "anyone can get an office as high as a county magistrate if he can afford the cost."[514] The door thus opened wide and merchants had a short cut to gain more prestige and influence. Wang Qi 王琦 (1432–1499) provides a description of this process: "Though we deem the office of a county magistrate at rank 7 as a high position, merchants are still not satisfied. Without much effort, they can obtain an office of general commander at rank 3 by paying cash in silver. People call them 'silver commanders', indicating the way they got the office."[515] The desperation to generate income in the quickest way possible to meet the costs of the war forced the government to sell high offices and to sell them cheaply. A position of rank 3 was priced as worth only 20,000 *dan* of rice around 1559. It was an unbelievably low price when compared to just 30 year earlier when an office at rank 7 was worth as much as 100,000 *hu* 斛 (50,000 *dan*).[516] Moreover, the privilege of tertiary education was also under the hammer and merchants were the biggest clients. In 1495, there were 2,068 students registered in the National University in Nanjing (Nanjing *Guozijian* 南京國子監), but only 496 of them were studying at the campus. Some 75 per cent of the students had paid for their enrolment but seldom studied.[517] The unconditional sale of student qualifications caused a lot of complaints: "We feel shamed seeing these people who have neither academic nor personal qualities crowded into the government school … University used to be the place for the best

512 *Kongtong ji*, *j.* 37, pp. 3a–5b.

513 *Lishi zupu* 李氏族譜 (*The Li Clan Genealogy*) by Li Zhi 李贄 (1527–1602). (Handwritten copy from the Library of the Fujian Normal University 福建師大圖書館), p. 4a.

514 *Shi Wei* 世緯 (*World Orderliness*), by Yuan Shi 袁袠 (1502–1547), in *Siku quanshu*, fasc. 717, *xia*, p. 9b (no *juan*).

515 *Yupu zaji* 寓圃雜記 (*Miscellaneous Writings from my Garden*) by Wang Qi 王琦 (*juren* Yongle reign), in *Siku cunmu* 子, fasc. 239, *j.* 10, p. 3a.

516 *Jingzhai zhizheng zhiji* 靜齋至正直記 (*An Unbiased Observation of the Zhizheng Reign* (1341–1368) *by Kong Qi, Hao Jingzhai*) by Kong Qi 孔齊 (Yuan), in *Siku xuxiu*, 239, *j.* 4, p. 34b.

517 *Nanyong zhi* 南雍志 (*Annals of the Imperial Academy in Nanjing*) by Huang Zuo 黃佐 (1490–1566), in *Siku cunmu* 史, fasc. 257, *j.* 4, p. 42b.

candidates but now it is only for merchants' sons, who swarm in with nothing but money."[518]

Merchants also increased their share of political influence by investing in official candidate. Education was too expensive an undertaking for a peasant family with no capital except for a small landholding. Apparently, Wang Shizhen spent 300 *taels* per annum on his years of schooling. Even the poorest candidates had to spend at least 100 *taels* or so; most of peasant families could hardly afford the expenses and had no choice but to borrow.[519] It was reported that "an official candidate is a mere commoner before he gets his degree. He has to borrow for his education-related spending ... [then] as soon as he steps into their office, he would be followed immediately by creditors."[520] The creditors were merchants. The creditors were serious in using their financial leverage to get what they invested for: "When a new magistrate in Yuzhou 余州 took office he was followed by his seven creditors ... in a few months he was accused [of corruption] and out of office, even though he was an honest and competent official."[521] This episode demonstrates the power of merchants. They were able to help finance a candidate to get into office; no doubt, they were equally capable of driving him out of office if the creditors did not feel they were getting a suitable reward for their investment. In some cases, the financial strength of merchants even empowered them to attempt to sway appointments to office.

> Pan Hongye 潘鴻業, a rich merchant with a *juren* degree, wanted the office of the magistrate of a sub-prefecture (zhi zhou 知州). He 'lent' 8,000 *taels* of silver to the officials in the court, with 1500 *taels* for each official and 2,200 to the son of the Senior Grand Secretary to ask them for assistance in his appointment to the office. [522]

The dependence of official candidates on the financial help of merchants was wide-ranging. Even if a candidate gained the *jinshi* degree he would still probably need a loan to negotiate the first year in office. Wang Shizhen observed: "The low pay for new officials is far from enough to meet the costs of entertaining their teachers and

---

518 "Yongzheng 雍政" (Harmony-orientated Government), in *Yongzhuang xiaopin* 涌幢小品 (*Minor Essays from the Portable Kiosk*) by Zhu Guozhen 朱國禎 (?–1632), in *Siku cunmu* 子, fasc. 106, *j.* 11, pp. 2b–3a.

519 *Gubugu lu* 觚不觚錄 (*Nostalgia, Recalled from the Grand and Trivial Matters of Past Days*) by Wang Shizhen 王世貞 (1526–1590), in *Siku quanshu*, fasc. 1041, *j.* 24, pp. 24b–25a.

520 *Loushan tang ji* 樓山堂集 (*Collection from the Loushantang Hall*) by Wu Yingqi 吳應箕 (1594–1645), in *Siku xuxiu*, fasc. 1388. *j.* 9, pp. 21b–22a. See also "Yu Wu gong ru shu er 与吳公如書二" (A Second Letter to the Respected Mr. Wu), in *Zhou zhong jie gong jin yu ji* 周中介公燼余集 (*The Written Remains of Zhou Zhongjie*) by Zhou Shunchang 周順昌 (1584–1626), in *Siku quanshu*, fasc. 1295, *j.* 2, p. 8a.

521 *Yutang huiji* 玉堂薈記 (*Assorted Unoffical Materials and Casual Commentaries to Supplement the Official History by a Hanlin Scholar*) by Yang Shicong 楊士聰 (1597–1648), in *Siku xuxiu* 1175, *j.* 3, p. 12b.

522 "Tan heng yang chen qi jun nang guo shu 貪横瘾臣欺君囊國疏" (A Memorial to Expose these Sinister and Crafty Officials who Mislead the Emperor and Destroy the Dynasty), in *Zou zhongcheng zoushu* 鄒中承奏疏 (*Memorials of the Grand Coordinator Zou*) by Zou Yinglong 鄒應龍 (*jinshi* 1556), in *Ming jingshi wenbian*, vol. 329, *j.* 1, p. 2b.

friends and flooding them with gifts."[523] Money cemented the cooperation between merchants and officials, from the time of the future official's schooling through to further on down the road in their career as an administrator. It was a good match, as merchants needed political assistance from officials and the officials needed merchants to arrange business on their behalf. By the later years of the dynasty, official involvement in money making was no longer seen as a form of corruption and something shameful.

> As soon as the *jinshi* candidates get their degree they tend to say good-bye to those friends with whom they used to talk about poetry and philosophy. Instead, they would rush to receive new friends interested in how to make money. The new visitors were interested in nothing but how to generate more income by providing loans and arranging official cooperation. The new administrator loves merchants because they will do business as the official's representative or have a business partnership with the official's family and relatives, without the official's personal involvement.[524]

Such joint ventures drew officials and merchants into the same interest group. Officials would lobby the government to make conditions favourable for merchants: "It has become a trend that officials are not only interested in their ranking and promotion but more so in fattening their purses. There is not a single one who would do otherwise. The tendency is irresistible."[525] The partnership formed between the political élite and merchants helped lift merechants to unparalleled high social status. Zhu Yuanming 祝允明 (1460–1527, Vice Prefect of Yingtian 應天 Prefecture), one of the four famous scholars in the South, witnessed his aunt's marriage to Tang Juan 湯琯, a descendent of the biggest merchant family in the central Zhejiang region.[526] This marriage would hardly have been possible during the early Ming years. Wang Daokun described the situation in his hometown: "We always regard a scholar higher in social status than a merchant, but the fact is now we respect merchants more in our place. Those who are not physically able to engage in trade study for a degree[527] [...] There is no reason at all to regard a rich merchant as less respectful than a well-known scholar."[528] Through dominance in the examination system, the financial capacity to buy government positions and to invest in powerful networking merchants was able to secure for them unmatchable political influence.

Along with their rising political power merchants also saw their social influence grow. Wealth enabled them to accomplish tasks of great social value, especially as

523 *Gubugu lu*, *j*. 24, pp. 24b–25a.

524 "Zhengsu yi 正俗一" (Rectification of Customs), in *Siyouzai congshuo*, *j*. 34, pp. 5a–5b.

525 *Linju manlu* 林居漫錄 (*Random Notes from my Retirement Days in the Countryside*) by Wu Yuancui 伍袁萃 (*jinshi* 1580), in *Siku cunmu* 子, fasc. 242, *j*. 1, p. 5b.

526 "Shou zhai chu shi tang jun wen shou sheng guang zhi 守齊處士湯君文守生壙志" (The Inscription on the Memorial Tablet for Mr Tang Wenshou, the Great Scholar in Seclusion), in *Huaixingtang quanji* 怀星堂全集 (*Complete Collection of Zhu Yunming, Named After the HuaixingAncestral Hall*) by Zhu Yunming 祝允明 (1460–1527), in *Siku quanshu*, fasc. 1260, *j*. 17, p. 22b.

527 Wang Daokun, *Taihan ji*, *j*. 54, p. 18a.

528 Wang Daokun, *Taihan ji*, *j*. 55, p. 1a.

they could render timely financial assistance to a local community when most needed. This practice grew more common during the late years when natural disasters, such as drought and flood, struck frequently and the government was unable to provide sufficient relief. Merchants gained more and more sway at the expense of the local administration. For instance, Cao Fu 曹傅, a powerful merchant, spent a large amount of his family fortune providing financial support for the needy in his local community. No matter who died, he would pay the bills if the deceased's family was unable to afford the funeral; whenever locals suffered from famine he would arrange for relief and paid for it out of his own pocket. He loaned 1,000 *taels* of silver to the poor and cancelled their debts when he was informed about his debtors' destitute situation. His financial support for the poor earned him great power and influence in local affairs. And when there was a local dispute, no matter who was involved, his personal presence meant a quick settlement.[529] Similarly, the grand uncle of Han Wenluo 韓文洛 (1479–1555), a Ming official, was another powerful merchant who involved himself in various aspects of local administration. Whereas the local government found it difficult to pressurize the influential and powerful to return land they had appropriated from petty landowners, Han Wenluo's uncle could be counted on for this. His power stemmed from his extensive sponsoring of local famine relief for many years and maintaining a very high ethical standard with his own employees.[530] Merchants could often provide more extensive financial assistance to local society more swiftly and hence more effectively than the local administration could. During a year of severe drought, a certain Mr. Wang 王, a powerful merchant and banker, ordered each of his debtors to pay 100 *taels* of silver for the local famine relief. His generosity saved many people. In addition, his funding of many public facilities, such as bridges and temples, gained him much popularity and increased social status.[531] What is more, the involvement of merchants in cultural activities helped transform their image as simply money-obssessed indivuals and enabled them to take a leading part in the community's cultural affairs. Wu Mianxue 吳勉學, a Huizhou merchant, invested 100,000 *taels* of silver to set up a publication house, the *Shigu zhai* 師古齋, to print medical and classical books.[532] Mao Jin 毛晉 (1599–1659), a merchant from Suzhou, also established a publishing house, the *Jigu ge* 汲古閣 and employed hundreds of specialists to make printing blocks to print classics for export to countries overseas.[533] In a related way, the

529 Wang Daokun, *Taihan ji*, *j*. 32, pp. 12b–13b.

530 *Han Yuanluo quanji* 韓苑洛全集 (*The complete works of Han Bangqi, literary name by Yuanluo*) by Han Bangqi 翰邦奇 (1479–1555). (Xihe Academy, Chaoyi county, 1828), in *Siku quanshu*, fasc. 1269, *j*. 6, p. 2a.

531 Wang Daokun, *Taihan ji*, *j*. 8, pp. 1a–2a.

532 *Jiyuan ji suo ji* 寄園寄所寄 (*Collection of Accumulated Materials from the Jiyuan Garden by Zhao Jishi, Hao Jiyuan*) by Zhao Jishi 趙吉士 (1628–1706), in *Siku cunmu* 子, fasc. 155, *j*. 11, p. 38b.

533 *Luyuan conghua* 履園叢話 (*Collection of Stories Named After my Residence, the Luyuan House*) by Qian Yong 錢泳 (1759–1844), in *Siku xuxiu*, fasc. 1139, *j*. 22, p. 1a.

merchant Wu Ji 吳季 became a clan leader by spending 10,000 *taels* of silver on the construction of the clan temple.[534]

The social power of merchants increased dramatically when local administrations granted political prerogatives, such as education or even judicial immunity, to those who could provide financial help.

> During famine years anyone who can contribute 1–2 *dan* of grain to the community will be immune from criticism; and a certificate will be awarded to anyone who can make a donation of 1–10 *dan* that will give exemption from punishment for violating the village laws. A donation of 10 *dan* will save him from flogging; and 1,000 *dan* will secure for him or his children a place in the government school.[535]

Wealth raised merchants up to the same status as the educated élite and local administrators. It was widely accepted that "successful businessmen, such as the lacquer craftsman Wang 王 or the porcelain potter Wu 吳, would be rated as influential as a *jinshen*."[536] The reality was that merchants always got the upper hand in competition for power. An incident occurred in Zhejiang during the late Ming that provides a significant footnote to this claim. Zou Donghu 鄒東湖, a wealthy merchant, and a Mr. Rong 榮, a retired government minister, were members of the same community, but competing for influence within that community. Mr. Rong, the high-ranking retiree, tried to exercise his political sway through his networks so as to exclude Zou Donghu, the merchant. In response to Mr. Rong's hostility, Zou used his financial power to buy up everything in the local food market one day. As a consequence, Mr Rong could get neither fresh fish nor fresh vegetables for several days. The antagonism ended with the retired official admitting defeat.[537] There was little doubt that the merchants held much power in community affairs. And their power was still increasing as commercialisation was gathering more momentum.

This increase in power by merchants, with regard both to the administration and the wider society, meant that the prohibition of foreign trade came to seem more and more incongruous. With more and more officials taking office from merchant families, or with merchant backgrounds, the numbers of officials who were zealous advocates of trade and effective promoters of the interests of merchants in the government increased. Eventually, once the political landscape changed remarkably in merchants' favor, the trade prohibition became redundant: "Merchants from Zhangzhou 漳州 and Quanzhou 泉州 conducted their trade in the name of

534 "Wu Ji gong Cheng ruren zhuan 吳季公程孺人傳" (The Biography of Madam Cheng, Wife of the Honourable Wu Ji), in *Taimi shanfang ji* 太泌山房集 (*Collection of Works from Taimishan*) by Li Weizhen 李維禎 (1547–1626), in *Siku xuxiu* 集, fasc. 152, *j.* 74, p. 20b.

535 *Taiquan xiangli* 泰泉鄉禮 (*Regulations and Rituals of Taiquan*) by Huang Zuo 黃佐 (1490–1566), in *Siku quanshu*, fasc. 142, *j.* 4, pp. 2b–4a.

536 *Tao'an mengyi* 陶庵夢憶 (*Dream Recollections from Tao's Hermitage*) by Zhang Dai 張岱 (1597–1667), in *Siku xuxiu*, fasc. 1260, *j.* 5, p. 3b.

537 *Huacun tanwang* 花村談往 (*Recalling the Past from Huacun, the Blossom Village*) by Zhang Junheng 張均衡 (1872–1927), in *Congshu jicheng xuxian* 史, fasc. 26, *j.* 2, pp. 12a–12b.

local officials or their families. Their ships were marked with an official's name; cargoes were sealed up on an official's behalf and the official's private staff escorted the voyagers. Nobody dared to question them."[538] The undermining of the prohibition law reflected the political influence of merchants and those cooperating with them. Wang Zaijin 王在晉 (*jinshi* 1592) admitted: "The authorities cannot compete with the influence of the powerful locals … The power of the local political forces was more influential than the law."[539] It is not difficult to comprehend the mechanism of the thriving smuggling trade. Wang Zaijin made the observation: "It is impossible for ships to sail out of the harbour without the coastguard noticing it; it is impossible for ships to be built locally and crews recruited locally without assistance from powerful local families; it is impossible for merchants to be allowed to sail to the seas without support … it is impossible for the building of ships, which takes months to complete, not to be discovered by the authorities, and it is impossible for the military to leave smugglers untouched without their superiors knowing they were violating the law."[540] The long maintained maritime prohibition policy was constantly violated by all and sundry as they sought to benefit from the extremely profitable foreign trade. Thus the question of whether or not to continue the maritime prohibition became a central issue in late Ming politics. It sparked a wide-ranging policy debate involving all sectors of the élite, the landed conservatives, the pro-trade merchant group and the various imperial factions. The nature of this policy debate will be the subject of the next chapter.

538 "Hai fang 海防" (Coastal Defense), in *Wubei zhi* 武備志 (*Notes and Data on Military Defence*) by Mao Yuanyi 茅元儀 (*Chongzhen* period Hanlin official), in *Siku jinhui* 子, fasc. 26, *j.* 6, p. 23b.

539 Wang Zaijin, *Haifang cuanyao*, in *Siku jinhui* 史, fasc. 17, *j.* 8, p. 28b.

540 Ibid., *j.* 8, pp. 28a–b.

CHAPTER IV

The Grand Policy Debate

Part One: The Problem

The late Ming era witnessed sweeping policy changes, from socio-economic affairs to international relations. These constituted an unprecedented policy overhaul. By the sixteenth century the early Ming institutions were under intense pressure, both from within the empire and from beyond it. Many argued that it was time that these institutions were reformed so that they might better respond to the changed socio-economic and political contexts. Externally, destructive foreign wars with the "*beilu nanwo* 北虜南倭" (Mongols in the north and Japanese in the south) generated an unparalleled political and financial plight, as "there has not been a single day without war with the Mongols in the north and west since the year of *gengshu* 庚戍 (1550) and there has not been a single day without war with the Japanese pirates on the southeast coast since the year of *renzi* 壬子 (1552)."[541] These enemies "besieged our capital, captured our emperor and massacred our people. Our dignity has not been insulted to this extent by the barbarians for the last 250 years."[542] These combined threats meant that most of the revenue of the empire flowed to the frontier. The state coffers were drained and the government could only resort to tax surcharges in the case of extra need.[543] Internally, the conflict between the long-maintained institutions and much changed social economic circumstances dragged the empire into a difficult economy and a discordant society. The difficulties caused by the wars inflamed the situation, generating not only political and financial pressures from outside but also setting off political challenge within the government. The dynasty came to a stage when it was obvious that the continuation of existing policy was bound to lead to crisis while change became the only hope of alleviation. Moreover, the difficulties caused by the wars inflamed the situation, not so much in terms of providing external pressure but rather by generating an earthquake within the internal political landscape. It was a time when wars were going on along the borders and also inside the walls of the imperial palace. A new political force emerged, composed of men with merchant family backgrounds, and they became more and more dominant in the policymaking process. These men challenged the old institutional forms on all fronts. The Jiajing era (1521–1567) witnessed for the first time during the Ming era the appearance of a dual situation in government. Whereas members of the old guard regarded themselves as the defenders of established principles, the new guard justified their defiance in terms of the urgent need to find relief from the current crises. The political struggle between these two factions became a dominant feature of late Ming politics.

541 "Ce – yulu 策禦虜" (Defence Strategy against the Mongols) by Wang Shizhen 王世貞 (1526–1590), in *MJSWB*, vol. 332, *j.* 4, p. 1a.

542 *Chou Liao shuohua* 籌遼碩畫 (*Memorials about the Liaodong Defence*) by Cheng Kaigu 程開祜 (Ming). (Beijing: Commercial Press, reprinted from Wanli edition, 1936), *j.* 8, p. 50a.

543 Sun Chengze, *Chunming mengyu lu*, *j.* 42, p. 39b.

External Pressure, the Trade Prohibition and the Wars

The external pressure was crushing. The prohibition on foreign trade had long been the main cause of grievance and war. Enmity between the Ming and the *beilu nanwo* fluctuated in accordance with the relaxation and intensification of the trade prohibition. The abolition of the Mongol and Japanese tribute missions dragged the Ming into protracted wars. The unsuccessful outcome of Esen Tügel's tribute mission in 1449 led to the *Tumu zhibian* 土木之變 (Tumu debacle), and the refusal of a Japanese tribute mission caused the *Ningbo zhi luan* 寧波之亂 (Ningbo Incident) in 1522. Driven by their desperate demand for Chinese products, the Mongols and Japanese both sought to test the Ming trade prohibition by waging numerous military campaigns. The Jiajing administration found itself under extraordinary pressure as it sought to cope with these challenges. As Wang Shizhen remarked, "The Mongols in the north and the Japanese in the south posed the biggest threat to our national security. There is no way we can win the war with the Mongols, while we can win the war against Japanese pirates but we do not know how."[544]

The Mongol's looting became a yearly occurrence. During the three months from June to August in 1542, Altan Qan broke the Ming defences and took 10 Ming garrisons (*wei* 衛) and 38 counties. In the process it was estimated that his forces killed 200,000 people, looted 2 million animals, burnt 80,000 houses and ravaged 10,000 *qing* 頃 of crops.[545] The government organised a few offensive operations, but most ended in defeat. The *Tumu* debacle saw 500,000 foot soldiers slaughtered by Esen's cavalry before the Yingzong emperor 英宗 (r. 1436–1449) was captured. The chief advocate of the war, the grand eunuch who refused to trade with Esen, was killed in the battle.[546] Morris Rossabi points out that the Mongols "continued to pose a challenge, if not a threat, throughout much of the history of the dynasty. Complete suppression of the various nomadic Mongol groups was exceptionally difficult, if not impossible."[547] The Ming generals themselves were even less confident of their chances. When Anta's cavalry was conducting a massacre on the outskirts of Beijing, the supreme commander Chou Luan 仇鑾 (?-1552) and his 50,000 soldiers were too intimidated to challenge the enemy. They locked themselves within the city walls and did not shoot a single arrow. The senior grand secretary suggested to the emperor that the best strategy was to wait until the Mongols got what they wanted and then left of their own accord.[548]

The situation along the coast had also deteriorated. When their desire to trade with the Ming was dashed, the frustrated Japanese plunged themselves into smuggling and armed confrontations. They were far from an ordinary bunch of bandits, looting whatever they came across, but rather were a powerful international joint force that put considerable strain on the Ming coastal defences and upset the politi-

544 *Yanzhou shiliao qianji*, in *Siku cunmu*, *j.* 18, p. 37b.

545 Gu Yingtai, *Mingshi jishi benmo*, *j.* 60, p. 5a.

546 Ibid., *j.* 32, pp. 3–6a.

547 Morris Rossabi, "The Ming and Inner Asia" (1998), p. 225.

548 Gu Yingtai, *Mingshi jishi benmo*, *j.* 59, pp. 4a and 9a–b.

cal order in the coastal regions. In February 1556, after their appeal to trade was again declined, a force of some 50,000–60,000 pirates on board more than 1,000 ships moved into Zapu 乍浦 in Zhejiang 浙江 and completely overpowered the government troops.[549] Immediately following this, there was an attack by 3,000 pirates on the cities of Zhenjiang 鎮江, Zuazhou 瓜州 and Yizhen 儀真. They burnt 34,000 *dan* of rice in government granaries, and went on to sack the city of Yangzhou 楊州 before executing the magistrate of the prefecture.[550] They controlled 200 *li* (about 100 km) of the busy sea route from Taicang 太倉 to Kunshan 昆山.[551] The following year, in 1567, Zeng Yiben 曾一本, a merchant-pirate commanding an army of around 10,000 pirates, openly defied the maritime interdiction. Confronted by a government force, he captured Haicheng county 海澄 and took the magistrate hostage. The local government had no option but ask the emperor to offer to pardon them in order to avoid bloodshed. The emperor granted the petition right away so as to disarm the pirates, but within three months they had broken their promise and resumed their attack.[552]

The political pressure to maintain the trade prohibition was deeply felt. But political pressure was not the only factor. Closely intertwined was the mounting financial predicament. By the late Jaijing years the Ming finances were on the verge of collapsing, as military spending had surpassed the state's annual income. With a revenue system that was still based on payments in kind, the state could not prosecute these wars for long. In the 30th year of Jiajing reign (1551) the war bill reached as high as 5,950,000 *taels*, at a time when the Neifu ke 內府庫 (Palace Storehouse) was maintained at around 2,000,000 *taels*.[553] By 1567 spending to support these conflicts was reliant on borrowing from the Taicang treasury 太倉 (Imperial Grnaeries, National Silver Vault, for administration of the capital). In 1567 Ma Sen 馬森, (1506–1580), the Minister of Revenue, reported to the emperor:

> There are 1,346,520 *taels* of silver in the National Silver Vault. An official's pay amounts to 1,350,000 *taels*; the military along the frontier needs 2,360,000, and 1,820,000 more is required to pay for the default from last year. The total annual budget is 5,530,000 taels. What is left will be barely enough to run the country for another three months.[554]

The situation was drastic. When the Mongol cavalry was marching to Beijing the emperor ordered a reward be paid to the soldiers to encourage them to fight. But he was shocked to learn that the government coffers had little that could be used to fund such a reward. Not only that, most of the soldiers had not been fed properly.

549 *Xu Hai benmo* 徐海本末 (*Topically Arranged Histories on Xu Hai, the Pirate Chief*) by Mao Kun 茅坤 (1512–1610), in *Siku cunmu* 史, fasc. 128, pp. 1a–2b (no *juan*).

550 Tan Qian, *Guoque*, p. 562.

551 Ibid., p. 535.

552 *Chaozhou zhi* 潮州志 (*The Annals of Chaozhou Prefecture*) by Rao Zongyi 饒宗頤 (1917–). (1522 edition, reprint, Guangdong: 1949), p. 34b.

553 *Ming Shizong shilu*, *j.* 456, pp. 4a–b.

554 *Ming Muzong shilu*, *j.* 15, pp. 5b–6a.

The emperor fired the Minister of Revenue and ordered all responsible officials to atone for their faults.[555]

The financial situation along the coast was no better. In 1559, when the time for tribute trade with Japan came around again, Tang Shunzhi 唐顺之 (*jinshi* 1529, Right Assistant Censor-in-Chief), reported to the court:

> We have prepared for war against the Japanese without a single year of relief. Even if we always won the battles we could no longer afford this. The government has to budget for 2,000,000 *taels* in Jaingnan 江南, Jiangbei 江北, Zhejiang 浙江 and Sanzhen 三鎮 to pay the government troops (*guanjun* 官軍) and the mercenary forces (*kebing* 客兵 and *mubing* 募兵).[556]

This was at a time when the total cash income of the state coffers stood at only 2.5 million *taels*, which included the *zhese* 折色 (tax in kind converted to silver) from the land tax and salt levies.[557]

Internal Pressure, the Two Camps and the Memorial System

Pressure from within the empire to lift the prohibition on foreign trade gathered increasing momentum. Political and financial difficulties prompted the escalation of the 'war' between the two factions in the government. Members of the government were increasingly divided over whether to continue the wars in the hope that success would eventually relieve the country from the crisis, or take a completely new approach and try to eliminate the causes of the conflicts. On one side was the new pro-trade group, whose members warned the court that without strong military backing and abundant material resources the maintenance of the trade prohibition was unfeasible. On the other side were the landed conservatives, who stood firmly behind maintenance of the trade prohibition, convinced that, in safeguarding the dynasty's political stability and national security, war with the 'barbarians' was inevitable. The debate between the two forces gradually intensified and it seemed that the Ming court had never been so eager to engage in policy consultation with its officials. The Jiajing emperor encouraged officials to use the *zoushu* 奏疏 (personal memorial) system in order to involve more and more voices in the policymaking process. He strengthened the memorial system by demanding every official of rank 4 and above, those in the supervising departments of the six ministries and the governors of all the thirteen administrative regions to send in memorials expressing their opinions about how to deal with the crises.[558] It was stipulated that these offi-

555 Gu Yingtai, *Mingshi jishi benmo*, *j.* 59, p. 5a.

556 *Chongkan Jingchuan xiansheng wenji* 重刊荊川先生文集 (*The Reprint of Mr Jingchuan's Collected Works*) by Tang Shunzhi 唐顺之 (1507–1560). (Shanghai: Hanfen loucang, Wanli edition), in *Sibu congkan* 四部叢刊. (Beijing: Commercial Press, 1919), *j.* 8, p. 57b.

557 "Qing tingqu yin liangshu 請停取銀兩疏" (Memorial Requesting an End to the Withdrawal of Silver [from the Treasury]), in *Zhang Wenzhong gongji* 張文忠公集 (*Collected Works of Zhang Juzheng, Shihao Wenzhong*) by Zhang Juzheng 張居正 (1525–1582), in *MJSWB*, vol. 324, *j.* 1, p. 14a.

558 Xu Xueju, *Guochao dianhui*, *j.* 29, p. 19a.

cials had "to lodge their memorials within five days of receiving the emperor's instruction, otherwise they would be subject to impeachment."[559]

The memorial system had long been an important part in the policymaking process. The Hongwu Emperor had said: "The memorials from officials assist the emperor in making important decisions for the sake of the country and hence are critical for the destiny of the dynasty."[560] He also stated that "the prosperity of the empire depends on whether it opens or blocks the channels for officials to advise the court in time,"[561] and "those who do not memorialize the emperor directly on the point of the issue cannot be regarded as loyal to the emperor."[562] When a proposal was introduced by an official in a memorial it would be discussed in the *baiguan tingyi* 百官廷議 (court policy discussions), in which the *jiuqing* 九卿 (the nine government ministers) participated along with other high-ranking officials from the ministries and military officers from the *zhongjun dudu fu* 中軍都督府 (Chief Military Commission), as well as some concerned officials in the capital. The result of the debate was submitted to the emperor for final endorsement, which would make it policy.[563] Memorials from all ministers were registed in the Grand Sectretariat (*Neige* 内閣), and then submitted by the Grand Secretariat to the Emperor. However, the Grand Secretarait had no power over the Six Ministries, which were directly accountable to the Emperor and the Emperor alone.[564] The Jiajing Emperor was reminded of this: "Important decisions should be handed down to an assembly of Court Ministers for decision."[565] Discussion in this assembly marked the final stage in the decision-making process. However, the memorial system was never used to its full extent during the early Ming years, when the landed conservatives dominated the bureaucracy, and thus there was no real opposition that might generate proper debate about issues. This was especially so after the abolition of the prime minister's office in 1380, when decision-making was centralized in the hands of the 'imperial faction'. The decision-making process allowed little room for discussion or debate over different policy directions. The memorial system became more of an institution for eulogizing the emperor and

559 Ibid., *j.* 110, pp. 5b–6a.

560 Ibid., *j.* 29, p. 2a.

561 "Kai yan lu du jian meng yi quan sheng de shu 開言路杜姦萌以全聖德疏" (A Memorial on how to Provide Better Means for Officials how to Stop Evil Practices in order to Safeguard the Virtue of the Emperor) by Wang Jiabin 王嘉賓 (*jinshi* 1562), in *Huangming liutai zouyi* 皇明留台奏議 (*Memorials from Ming Censors*) edited by Zhu Wubi 朱吾弼 (*jinshi* 1589), in *Siku xuxiu*, fasc. 467, *j.* 11, p. 6a.

562 Ibid., *j*, 29, p. 2b.

563 "Hui yi bei lu qiu gong 會議北虜求貢" (A Debate about the Mongols's Requests to Pay Tribute), in *Xu Wenzhen gong ji* 徐文貞公集 (*Collected Works of Xu Jie, Shihao Wenzhen*) by Xu Jie 徐階 (1503–1583), in *MJSWB*, vol. 245, *j.* 2, p. 7a. See also Charles O. Hucker, "Government Organization of the Ming Dynasty", *Harvard Journal of Asiatic Studies* XXI (1958), pp. 1–66.

564 Li Konghuai 李孔懷, *Zhongguo gudai zhengzhi yu xingzheng zhidu* 中國古代政治與行政制度 (*Politics and Administrative Systems in Traditional China*). (Shanghai: Fudan University Press, 1993), p. 102.

565 *Ming shi*, *j.* 196, p. 21a.

echoing established beliefs, rather than an institution for challenging, debating and improving on exisiting policy. But the war crises of the mid-to-late Ming years no longer allowed the government to rely on timeless politically correct clichés. The government badly needed a more competent policymaking system to help develop strategies that might alleviate the crises. The emergence of a group of officials with merchant-family backgrounds saw the rise of a new faction in the government and witnessed the development of a new policymaking culture. The upgraded memorial system provided a platform for the different political factions to influence policymaking in the court through intensive debate.

Officials from the two camps sought to influence the policymaking process by utilising the memorial system for networking, political lobbying and to try to gain a monopoly over decision-making. As Jung-pang Lo points out, "Power – actual power – was not the monopoly of one political group. It seesawed between the imperial faction and the bureaucratic faction, fluctuating with the personalities of the political leaders."[566] The memorial system allowed the rival factions to organise and exchange attacks so as to generate more weight in their own favour in the decision-making process. The process of using memorials to attack one's opponents and advocate one's own beliefs became a dominant feature of political culture in the Jiajing era.

Zhu Wan 朱紈 (*jinshi* 1521) complained to the court of the resistance in implementing a government decision: "Obstruction to a government decision always precedes its execution."[567] He also condemned 'piracy' within the administration: "It is more difficult to fight the 'pirates' in official robes than foreign pirates out at sea."[568] The late Ming political factions were drawn into a conflict or 'war' situation via the memorial system. Their writing to the court was sharp and acute. Wang Shizhen, on behalf of the pro-trade faction, condemned the conservatives for their impractical and unrealistic mentality: "Our officials boast of winning the war by drilling soldiers, enhancing fortifications and inspiring troops by rewarding the brave and punishing the undisciplined. Such a suggestion produces nothing useful but some bookish empty talk."[569] Wang indicated that trade rather than military confrontation was a more effective means to relieve the crisis. Yang Jisheng 楊繼勝 (1516–1555), a spokesman for the conservatives, retaliated by denouncing the pro-trade camp for "tarnishing the dignity of a heavenly ordained empire and disturbing the holy world order by trading with the animal 'barbarians' … It is ridiculous and foolish."[570] The formation of the two camps in the government was striking.

566 Jung-pang Lo "Policy Formulation and Decision-Making on Issues Respecting Peace and War,' in Charles O. Hucker (ed.), *Chinese Government in Ming times: Seven Studies* (New York: Columbia University Press, 1969), p. 45.

567 Zhu Wan, *Piyu zaji*, *j.* 2, p. 15a.

568 Shen Yue, *Huang Ming Jia-Long liangzhao wenjian ji*, *j.* 7, p. 45b.

569 Wang Shizhen, *Yanzhou shiliao quanji*, in *Siku cunmu* 史, fasc. 112, *j.* 18, p. 37b.

570 "Qing ba mashi shu 請罷馬市疏" (A Memorial Calling for the Abolition of the Horse Fair), in *Yang Jiaoshan ji* 楊椒山集 (*Collected Works of Yang Jisheng, Hao Jiaoshan*) by Yang Jisheng 楊繼勝 (1516–1555), in *MJSWB*, vol. 293, *j.* 1, p. 2b.

Feng Qi 馮琦 (1558–1603; Minister of Rites) remarked on the clear demarcation with regard to relations with the Mongols: "Half of the officials want to trade with the Mongols while the other half insists on war."[571] There was an obvious divide in the official debate over whether or not to begin trading with the Mongols. When the trade proposal was introduced in March of the 5th year of the Longqing reign (1571), the emperor presided over the grand debate. Twenty-three officials supported the trade proposal, led by Xu Wenbi 徐文壁, Duke of Dingguo 定國公, who was supported by Zhang Luo 張羅 (Deputy Minister of Personnel), Li Chongji 李崇極 (Censor-in-Chief), Gao Gong 高拱 (Grand Secretary) and Zhang Siwei 張四維 (Minister of Rites and Grand Secretary). But the pro-trade faction met with powerful opposition from twenty-two high-ranking officials, seventeen of whom opposed the trade proposal. They were led by Zhang Rong 張溶, Duke of Yingguo 英國公, who was supported by Zhang Shouzhi 張守直 (Minister of Revenue). Another group of five, led by Zhu Heng 朱衡 (Minister of Works) backed a proposal to grant the Mongols tribute status but to refuse to trade with them.[572] The two sides were fighting on equal terms and no one was able to gain the upper hand. The final decision was left to the emperor.[573]

The debate on the maritime prohibition policy was also evenly matched in intensity. Liu Tao 劉燾 (*jinshi* 1538, Supreme Commander in Huguang and Grand Coordinator of Fujian), observed the forming of the two rival sides:

> On one side are officials who support the lifting of the trade prohibition and advocate engaging in trade with the pirates, while on the other are those who insist on a military campaign to strengthen the maritime interdiction. Neither side is restrained from attacking its rival camp."[574]

Xu Guangqi 徐光啟 (*jinshi* 1604, Minister of Rites) named the leading participants from both camps:

> There has been a distinction among officials on the trade policy with the Japanese since the 1553 incident. The camp of the conservatives was headed by Zhang Jing 張經 (*jinshi* 1517, Minister of War and Censor-in-Chief), Ruan Er 阮鶚 (1509–1567: Right Assistant Censor-in-Chief and Grand Coordinator in Fujian and Zhejiang), and Yu Dayou 俞大猷 (1504–1580: Regional Commander in Zhejiang, Fujian and Guangdong). They asserted their stance to main-

---

571 "Zeng yushi dafu shaoquan Hao gong ru li rong zheng xu 贈禦史大夫少泉郝公入理戎政序" (A Preface Dedicated to the Honourable Censor Hao Shaoquan Who Is to Engage in Military Administration) by Feng Qi 馮琦 (1558–1603), in *MJSWB*, vol. 442, *j.* 3, p. 22b.

572 *Shanxi tongzhi* 山西通志 (*A Comprehensive Record of Shanxi*) edited by Chu Dawen 儲大文 (1665–1743), in *Siku quanshu*, fasc. 549, *j.* 181, pp. 62b–63a. See also *Mingshi juan erbai ershi'er kaozheng* 明史卷二百二十二考證 (*Textual Research on Volume 222 of Mingshi*) by Yan Fu 嚴福 and Fang Wei 方煒, in *Siku quanshu*, fasc. 300, *j.* 222, p. 39a.

573 "Yu Wang Jianchuan ji sishi siyao 與王鑑川計四事四要" (Four Points and Four Issues in My Discussion with Wang Jianchuan) by Zhang Juzheng 張居正 (1525–1582), Zhang Juzheng, *Zhang Wenzhong gongji*, in *MJSWB*, vol. 326, *j.* 3, p. 24a.

574 "Da Hu Meilin fu chao woyi shu 答胡梅林撫剿倭夷書" (A Reply to Hu Meilin about How to Appease and Pursue Japanese Pirates), in *Liu Daichuan shugao* 劉帶川書稿 (*Policy Statements of Liu Tao, Hao Daichuan*) by Liu Tao 劉燾 (*jinshi* 1538), in *MJSWB*, vol. 308, *j.* 5, p. 12b.

> tain the maritime prohibition by military force. On the rival side there was also a politically powerful group, led by Hu Zongxian 胡宗憲 (*jinshi* 1538, Right Assistant Censor-in-Chief and Supreme Commander in Zhejiang), Zhao Wenhua 趙文華 (*jinshi* 1529, Minister of Works), Tang Shunzhi 唐順之 (*jinshi* 1529, Right Assistant Censor-in-Chief and Grand Coordinator of Fengyang) and Lu Tang 盧鏜 (Regional Commander of Zhejiang). They campaigned for the lifting of the trade prohibition and for engaging in trade with the enemy.[575]

The memorials from these political and military 'heavyweights' constituted the basis for the formation of government policies. The court had no alternative but to rely on their judgement. However, there was a price to pay for being granted such a high political honour. Far from being merely a game of words or an academic pursuit, the memorial system was a life-or-death engagement. It was a political gamble in which participants risked their positions, their property, and even their lives and the lives of their family members. They were responsible for formulating policy that could involve a considerable amount of resources and affect the lives of millions of people. It is no exaggeration to say that the destiny of the dynasty was in their hands. Many officials paid the ultimate price for expressing their views through the memorial system. Zeng Xian 曾銑 (*jinshi* 1529, Supreme Commander of the three defence regions in Shanxi), and Xia Yan 夏言 (*jinshi* 1517, Senior Grand Secretary) were two of the many. They opposed the proposal to trade with the Mongols in order to alleviate the cross-border conflict and expressed their belief that the best policy was to to defeat the enemy on the battlefield. Both of them submitted memorials to the court and eventually they won the court's approval. A massive military operation was immediately instigated. A 60,000 strong force costing around 300,000 *taels* of silver was sent deep into Hetiao 河套, but the Ming army still failed to check the Mongol incursions. Even worse, these actions provoked the Mongols to seek revenge by taking the Xuanfu 宣府 garrison. Pro-trade officials, led by Senior Grand Secretary Yan Song, memorialised the court demanding Zeng Xian and Xia Yan be punished for their ill-calculated advice which had led to such a devastating outcome. In September of the 27th year of the Jiajing reign (1548) the two were beheaded in the capital.[576]

The debates about maritime policy could also have deadly consequences for individual officials. Zhu Wan (*jinshi* 1521, Supreme Commander on the coast and Grand Coordinator of Fujian and Zhejiang) was hated by the pro-trade officials for his upgrading of the maritime interdiction through the infamous *baojia* 保甲 system, so that the neighbours of anyone who violated the interdiction were to be equally guilty and subjected to the same punishments. Zhou Liang 周亮 (a Censor) and Ye Tang 葉鏜 (*jinshi* 1541, Supervising Secretary at the Ministry of War) headed the operation to oust him from office. They petitioned the court to strip him of his position as Grand Coordinator of Fujain and Zhejiang, leaving him only with his

575 "Hai fang yu shuo 海防迂說" (An Expanded Discussion on Coastal Defense), in *Xu Wendinggong ji* 徐文定公集 (*Collected Works of Xu Guangqi, Shihao Wending*) by Xu Guangqi 徐光啟 (1562–1633), in *MJSWB*, vol. 491, *j.* 4, pp. 31a–b.

576 Gu Yingtai, *Mingshi jishi benmo*, *j.* 58, pp. 10b–14a.

military post. Zhu Wan was immediately demoted.[577] In 1549, when Zhu ordered the execution of 96 merchants who were engaged in illegal activity, the rival faction finally found a pretext to get rid of him. The Censor Chen Jiude 陳九德 accused him of killing innocent people and carrying out the executions without informing the court beforehand. The emperor ordered the Ministry of War and the Three Judicial Offices (*san fasi* 三法司: the Ministry of Justice, the Censorate and the Court of Judicial Review) to conduct an investigation. Pro-trade officials, led by Du Luzhen 杜汝禎 (*jinshi* 1538, Supervising Secretary at the Ministry of War) and Xu Zongkui 徐宗夔 (a Regional Inspector), supported the accusation made by Chen Jude. Zhu Wan was arrested and committed suicide in custody pending trial.[578] Just before his death he remarked mournfully: "Even if the emperor doesn't want my life the officials from Fujian are bound to have me executed."[579] He was right. His misfortune was partly a consequence of his inattention to the changing distribution of power in the government and he paid for going against the new trend.

In the 33rd year of the Jiajing reign (1554) two of the most powerful officials assigned to the coast, Zhang Jing 張經 (*jinshi* 1517, Minister of War in Nanjing and Censor-in-Chief) and Li Tianchong 李天寵 (*jinshi* 1538, Grand Coordinator of Zhejiang), were executed for showing sympathy to the pirates and avoiding confrontation.[580] Nevertheless, the death penalty had never deterred some officials from expressing their views. The late Jiajing years saw more and more memorials flowing to court, and more officials were escorted to the execution ground. The memorialists were always proud of being loyal to their beliefs and taking a stand for the sake of the country while caring little about the cost, whatever it might lead to. In order to comprehend the nature of late Ming politics and to understand the mentality of those pushing for policy changes it is necessary to consider the memorials they wrote to advance their positions.

Trade Prohibition and Prejudice about 'Barbarians'

How to stop the war with the Mongols and the Japanese was at the top of the Ming administration's agenda. Pro-trade officials reminded the court that the solution to these wars depended on how policymakers understood the causes of the war. They blamed the breakdown in international relations that resulted in these wars on the conventional cognition of foreigners as 'barbarians' and the self-imposed cultural superiority associated with this. They argued that the hostilities stemmed from this biased attitude towards foreigners. Pro-trade officials found themselves engaged in

577 Shen Yue, *Huang MingJia-Long liangchao wenjian ji*, *j.* 8, p. 5b.

578 *Ershi'er shi zhaji* 二十二史札記 (*Commentaries on the Twenty-two Dynastic Histories*) by Zhao Yi 趙翼 (1729–1814), in *Siku xuxiu*, fasc. 453, *j.* 34, pp. 18a–b. See also Shen Yue, *Huang Ming Jia-Long liangchao wenjian ji*, *j.* 81, pp. 5a–b and 12b.

579 *Ming tongjian* 明通鑒 (*The Ming Comprehensive Mirror*) by Xia Xie 夏燮 (1800–1875), in *Siku xuxiu*, fasc. 365. *j.* 59, p. 29a.

580 Gu Yingtai, *Mingshi jishi benmo*, *j.* 55, p. 21a.

a bitter conflict over foreign relations. For the conservatives, the 'middle kingdom' was the centre of civilization, and those inhabiting the peripheries, the 'barbarians', were dependent on China's civilization for survival. As previously noted, they believed that China's morality and propriety-based political system was superior to that of the barbarians. The end of the Yuan occupation after a short period of only 125 years further reinforced such convictions. The foreign trade prohibition and the control of tribute missions were therefore regarded as legitimate ways to arrange the relationship between the *tianchao shangguo.* 天朝上國 (the heavenly endorsed empire) and the barbarians. As Shen Jia 沈佳 pointed out: "The Son of the Heaven should stick to the 'Way', with China at the center and the barbarians on the periphery, and China should rule by both ethical and physical power."[581] The Hongwu Emperor initiated Ming relations with Japan by ordering the Japanese to pay tribute to the 'Son of the Heaven,' otherwise he would "dispatch a heavenly-assigned army to wipe out the undisciplined and ill-natured barbarians."[582] In the fifth year of his reign (1373) he sent monks on a mission to Japan to 'educate' the Japanese."[583] Zeng Xian 曾烍 (*jinshi* 1529, Supreme Commander of the three defence regions in Shanxi) asserted in his memorial:

> China was the 'head' while the foreigners were the 'feet' in the body of the world, and this order cannot be turned upside down. Our Emperor himself is the symbol of heaven, the sun and moon; our officials who are assigned with a holy duty should exterminate the barbarians and safeguard the separation between China and the uncivilised to demonstrate our empire's significance … [Therefore] the Emperor should not waver in his determination in the military campaign, even though it may cost a great amount of resources.[584]

The conservatives viewed foreigners as a destabilising factor and legitimised their position on the grounds of maintaining stability. For instance, in a memorial Feng Zhang 馮璋 (*jinshi* 1538) reinforced the disservice to the empire that came from foreign contact: "Contact with the barbarians will confuse the division between Chinese and aliens, and the damage could become uncontrollable if we allow such a trend to grow."[585] The prohibition on private trade, which reversed the historical trend of international exchange between Chinese and others, was instituted on such a strong prejudice. In another memorial, Zhu Wan tried to convince the emperor of the necessity of blocking all contact with foreigners, no matter what the cost:

> The Chinese political system can never be applicable in foreign lands, while China will never apply an alien system. Our social system is based on orders and a code of ethics. Our foreign policy should therefore be instituted according to guidelines that prevent our people from

581 *Mingru yanxing lu* 明儒言行錄 (*Statements and Implementations of the Confucian Principle by the Ming Literati*) by Shen Jia 沈佳 (*jinshi* 1690), in *Siku quanshu*, fasc. 458, *j.* 1, p. 20a.

582 Hu Zongxian, *Chouhai tubian*,, *j.* 2, p. 6b.

583 Ibid., *j.* 2, p. 7a.

584 "Yi shoufu hetao shu 議收復河套疏" (A Memorial on Recapturing the Ordos) by Zeng Xian 曾烍 (?–1548), in *MJSWB*, vol. 237, *j.* 1, pp. 4a–5a.

585 "Tongfan boyi 通番舶議" (My Comment on the Proposal for Allowing Foreign Shipping Trade) by Feng Zhang 馮璋 (*jinshi* 1538), in *MJSWB*, vol. 280, *j.* 1, pp. 18b–19a.

engaging with the 'barbarians'. If they are here to pay tribute and show their obedience we will reward them with kindness but we will strike them if they invade our territory. Our coastal people should always abide by the principle of the maritime interdiction. Not a single piece of wood is allowed to float in the sea.[586]

Yang Jisheng 杨繼盛 (*jinshi* 1547, Vice Director in the Ministry of War) opposed establishing the horse trade with the Mongols on similar grounds.

Our country is the centre of the universe and the master of the world. It is so great that foreign countries are willing to be subjugated. Our heavenly dynasty (*tianchao*) should never conduct equal trade with the barbarians, who are akin to animals. It will disturb the holy cosmic order if we do so. The whole world will laugh at China.[587]

This biased preconception about foreigners was applied to anyone foreign, irrespective of who they were and what they did. When in the sixteenth century Portuguese merchants, newcomers in China's waters, sought permission to trade they were immediately branded as a danger. Pang Shangpeng 龐尚鵬 (*jinshi* 1553, who served variously as a Regional Inspector, A Right Assistant Censor-in-Chief, and AS Grand Coordinator of Fujian) alarmed the court when he informed it that:

They [the Portuguese] look dishonest in their weird clothes … their swords are sharp and shining, their cannon powerful. When displeased they behave like a wild animal, while they tend to be human only when they are satisfied. This reflects their inner quality. Collaborating with Chinese traitors they bully our locals and disrespect our officials. They seem uncontrollable. If one day they are no longer interested in making money but organize an invasion of Xiangshan 香山 and control our strategic fortresses, and then march to Guangzhou, catastrophe cannot be far away."[588]

Suspicion and xenophobia made conservative officials fear the 'barbarians' and determine to do whatever was required to hold them at bay. Yang Jisheng wrote in this vein to the emperor: "What we know about the Mongols is their horrible holocaust of our people, their rape and torture of our women. Our attitude towards them should be nothing but hatred. No matter where we are, even aboriginals in the remote mountains, we are inspired to fight the Mongols."[589] Zhang Chong 張翀 (*jinshi* 1553, a Bureau Secretary in the Ministry of Justice during the Jiajing reign, and Deputy Minister in the Ministry of Justice during the Longqing reign) did not even support the demonstration of tolerance towards foreigners through the tribute system:

---

586 "Yi chu yizei yi Ming dian xing yi xiao huo shi 議處夷賊以明典刑以消禍事" (a Debate on How to Punish Foreign Pirates to Respect the Law to Avoid More Disaster), in *Zhu Zhongcheng piyu ji* 朱中丞甓餘集 (*Collected Works of Zhu Wan, the Chief Censor*) by Zhu Wan (1494–1549), in *MJSWB*, vol. 205, *j.* 1, p. 10b.

587 Yang Jishan, *Yang Jiaoshan ji*, *j.* 1, pp. 2a-b.

588 "Tiwei chenmo yi yi bao hai yu wanshi zhian shu 題為陳末議以保海隅萬世治安疏" (My Humble Opinion on How to Conserve National Security and Stability for a Thousand Generations), in *Pang zhongcheng zhaigao* 龐中丞摘稿 (*Excerpts from the Writings of Pang Shangpeng, the Grand Coordinator*) by Pang Shangpeng 龐尚鵬 (*jinshi* 1553), in *MJSWB*, vol. 357, *j.* 1, pp. 8b–9a.

589 *MJSWB*, vol. 293, *j.* 1, p. 2b.

> Japanese are greedy, ruthless ... and they are cunning and brutal .... They hide themselves in caves on remote islands waiting to attack China. They will rob and kill our people wherever they have the chance, but then pretend to pay tribute when they are overpowered. They satisfy their desire for booty by looting and pay tribute so as to be rewarded with goods. They get what they need from both activities.[590]

Some officials wanted to "block the narrowest section of the port at Macao with rocks in order to prevent Portuguese ships from sailing into and out of the harbour", while others proposed burning down the Portuguese houses and driving them away. Others wanted to set up road blocks to supervise Chinese and foreigners from coming and going from foreigners' residential areas.[591] Preserving political stability by avoiding foreign contact became a political priority. The horse trade with the Mongols was denounced as a "betrayal",[592] while violation of the maritime prohibition was categorised as one of the two biggest crimes of the time, on a par with inciting rebellion. Supreme Commander on the coast, Zhu Wan, warned the locals: "Violating the trade prohibition by making ships with two masts or more and smuggling goods across the border deserves capital punishment."[593]

By the Jiajing period, however, numerous crises had unsettled this orthodox belief. The inability of the military to maintain the disengagement policy discredited the self-imposed notions of Chinese 'superiority'. When open violation of the trade prohibition became uncontrollable the pro-trade officials were encouraged to challenge the policy. They questioned the leverage of cultural factors in international relations and noted the difficulty of implementing the trade prohibition. Liu Tao 劉燾 (*jinshi* 1538, Supreme Commander of Huguang) reminded the emperor that 'cultural superiority' carried little weight with the Mongols: "The Mongols have been begging for tribute trade for many years but is not a consequence of their respect for China's morality nor through fear of China's military might. It is only because of their need for Chinese goods."[594] Gao Gong 高拱 (*jinshi* 1541, a Grand Secretary) said, "Though the Mongols are 'animals', the power to control them lies in meeting their desires. In doing so they will behave like a poodle, begging for pity, otherwise they will bite us like a wolf. For the sake of our national security we have no option but to meet their needs in order to control them. They are not the type that we can control by ethics and principles."[595] Yang Shouchen 楊守陳, a conservative official,

---

590 "Duxia yiyi an zhong tu shu 杜狡夷以安中土疏" (My Memorial on Blocking the Cunning Foreigners to Enhance our National Security), in *Zhang dujian zoushu* 張都諫奏疏 (*Personal Memorials of Zhang Chong, the Supervising Secretary*) by Zhang Chong 張翀 (*jinshi* 1553), in *MJSWB*, vol. 292, *j.* 1, pp. 1b–2a.

591 *MJSWB*, vol. 357, *j.* 1, p. 9a.

592 *MJSWB*, vol. 293, *j.* 1, pp. 2b–3a.

593 Zhu Wan, *Zhu zhongcheng ji*, in *MJSWB*, vol. 205, *j.* 1, p. 11a.

594 "Da zhu lao beilu qi gong shi shu 答諸老北虜乞貢市書" (A Reply to Your Opinion about the Northern Barbarians' Plea for Tribute Trade) by Liu Tao 劉燾 (*jinshi* 1538), in *MJSWB*, vol. 305, *j.* 2, p. 3b.

595 Gao Gong, "Lu zhong nei fu bian huan shao ning qi ji shi daxiu bian zheng yi yong tu zhi an shu 虜眾内附邊患稍寧乞及時大修邊政以永圖治安疏" (A Memorial on the Timely

also admitted that "The Japanese are not motivated to pay tribute out of respect. They have never been willing to do so. What they want is to use tribute as a precondition for trade."[596] Hu Zongxian 胡宗憲 (*jinshi* 1538, Right Assistant Censor-in-Chief and Supreme Commander of Zhejiang), remarked thus on what he felt was the true intention of the Mongols: "The submissive relationship between a master and his subordinates depends on either the latter's respect or fear of the master ..., however, this is not the nature of the relationship between the Ming and the Mongols. They neither respect our culture nor fear our military power, because we have never defeated them in a decisive way ... what leads to the situation [of being submissive] is their desire for our commodities."[597]

Pro-trade officials stressed that it was the foreigners' desire for commodities rather than their appreciation of Chinese cultural values and philosophies that would enable the Ming administration to gain control of the situation. Gao Gong warned the court of the outcome if the government failed to realise this critical point:

> Their [the Mongol's] different culture and their value-regime deprived our government of the power to control them through rites, philosophy and law, which they would never believe and respect. In the 19th year of the Jiajing reign (1540), the Mongols came to ask to pay tribute; it was nothing but an honest intention to get what they needed from trade. Unfortunately, our officials on the border did not see this and refused their request, executing their emissaries. This resulted in the Mongols' prompt invasion of Datong 大同, Shanxi 山西, Jichang 薊昌 and Beijing. We had to pay for our misjudgement by going through the suffering of war and conflict for the next thirty years.[598]

Zhang Wei 張位 (*jinshi* 1568, Minister of Personnel and a Grand Secretary) emphasized the 'containing' power of trade. He advised the court: "The best way to control foreigners is to know what is in their minds. Though the Japanese beg for the status of a tribute state, do they simply want an empty title? Do they really intend to invade China? Their ultimate goal is to gain permission to pay tribute in order to obtain Chinese goods, and that is all."[599]

Rectification of Frontier Administration when Tension along the Border is somewhat Relaxed as the Mongol's Frustration has been Subdued) by Gao Gong 高拱 (*jinshi* 1542), in *MJSWB*, vol. 301, *j.* 1, p. 1b.

596 Qian Wei quotes Yang Wenyi 楊文懿, in "Yu dang dao chu wo yi 與當道處倭議" (A Discussion with the Official in Charge about how to Deal with Japanese Piracy), in *Chengqitang ji* 承啓堂集 (*Collected Works from the Chengqi Hall*) by Qian Wei 錢薇 (1502–1554), in *MJSWB*, vol. 214, *j.* 1, p. 15b.

597 "Tiwei xia lu jin bian gan yan qiu gong shi 題為黠虜近邊甘言求貢事" (My Opinion on the Deceitful Mongol's Plea with Honeyed Words for Tribute Trade), in *Hu Shaobao zoushu* 胡少保奏疏 (*The Memorials of Hu Zongxian, the Tutor of the Heir Apparent*) by Hu Zongxian 胡宗憲 (1511–1565), in *MJSWB*, vol. 266, *j.* 2, p. 2a.

598 *MJSWB*, vol. 301, *j.* 1, pp. 1b--2b.

599 "Lun dong wo shi qing jie tie 論東倭事情揭帖" (A file Directed to the Emperor from the Sectretariat about the situation of Japanese Piracy), in *Zhang Hongyang wenji* 張洪陽文集 (*Collected Works of Zhang Wei, Hao Hongyang*) by Zhang Wei 張位 (*jinshi* 1568), in *MJSWB*, vol. 408, *j.* 1, pp. 20a–b.

Pro-trade officials broke the enchanting bubble of China's sense of cultural superiority. They challenged the once conventional political mindset and attacked the very ideological foundation of the trade prohibition policy. They tried to convince the court that cultural superiority and military pressure held little sway and that it was the policy of forceful disengagement and trade prohibition that created hostilities. The feared expansion by foreigners and their supposed desire for political domination were mere products of the imagination. What was on their minds was simply trade. Unless the court sanctioned productive commercial relations war would continue and the costs to the empire would be even greater.

The Foreign Tribute Missions

The distress of war forced policymakers to review Ming foreign policy. Why was it that foreigners did not respect China's world order? Why did they not become submissive in the way they were supposed to be? By the sixteenth century, the grand design of the international political order established at the beginning of the dynasty, with its principle of "no trade without tribute", had been called into question. Tribute trade and the trade prohibition were the twin pillars of early Ming foreign affairs. And the system had indeed had its good days. Ma Wensheng 馬文升 (*jinshi* 1451, Vice Censor-in-Chief and Grand Coordinator of Shanxi) recalled that "The Hongwu Emperor had the foreign powers under control by asserting Ming authority through both *wei* 威 (force) and *de* 德 (morality/virtue/ethics). Foreigners became obedient because of the tribute trade system, by which they would show political subordination in order to get the goods they wanted most: tea, silk, utensils and other ironworks."[600] However, the tribute trade failed to remain effective simply through the Ming administration's attempt to engineer control over foreigners in such a way. The policy was a political institution not a reflection of commercial imperatives, and because of this it was subject to political requirements rather than market demands. In 1592 Feng Qi 馮琦 (*jinsh,* 1577, Minister of Personnel) noted:

> The tribute system will either produce great benefits or cause dreadful consequences. The wise use tribute trade to control an enemy while the stupid use it to please an enemy; the intelligent use it to win time to strengthen the defences while the brainless use it as an excuse for ignoring the defences. The competent will benefit from tribute trade for decades, but the foolish will damage the country for more than a century. The wise use the system while the foolish are used by the system.[601]

Pro-trade officials condemned the system for worsening Ming foreign relations by completely ignoring foreigners' commercial needs. They criticized its tailored politi-

600 "Jin tong fan yi mian bian huan shu 禁通番以絕邊患疏" (Prohibiting Foreigners from Trading to Avoid Frontier Encroachments), in *Ma Duansu gong zoushu* 馬端肅公奏疏 (*Collected Memorials of Ma Wensheng, Shihao Duansu*) by Ma Wensheng 馬文升 (1426–1510), in *MJSWB*, vol. 62, *j.* 1, pp. 18a–b.

601 "Zeng yu shi da fu shao quan Hao gong ru li rong zheng zu 贈禦史大夫少泉郝公入理戎政序" (A Preface Dedicated to the Grand Master Hao, the Censor-in-Chief, on Engaging in Military Administration), by Feng Qi 馮琦 (1559–1603), in *MJSWB*, vol. 442, *j.* 3, p. 25a.

cal function, such as the arbitrary limitation on trade missions, the restriction on the kinds of goods that could be traded and the compulsory price controls.

Hu Zongxian attacked the unreasonable limitation on tribute missions. He criticized the 'once-every-ten-years-with-no-more-than-three-ships' restriction on the Japanese for being indifferent to their legitimate grievances, arguing in 1562, when his *Chouhai tubian* 籌海圖編 (*Illustrated Compendium on Maritime Security*), went to print:

> There is not a single day in which the Japanese don't need commodities from China, ranging from utensils for daily use to the indispensable textiles. How can they survive with only one trade mission every ten years? How can a mission of just three ships meet the demands of a whole country for ten years? Prohibiting trade is bound to cause piracy and smuggling. Even if Japan is a small country it still has a complete bureaucracy to maintain and state rituals to perform: how can we imagine a country without silk and other fabrics? How can we still call such a place a country when it lacks such commodities? How can we possibly stop smuggling when the trade prohibition has increased the profit from trade so dramatically?[602]

Contrary to the wishes of the early Ming policymakers, foreigners did not become more controllable under the tribute trade system, owing to the rigid nature of the trade missions. An undersupply of goods and an increasing demand for Chinese products in foreign countries fuelled smuggling and looting along the borders of the empire. Qian Wei 錢薇 (*jinshi* 1532, Supervising Secretary in the Ministry of Rites) pointed out the inevitability of illicit trade:

> Since the whole country [i.e. Japan] relies on Chinese products, we can well imagine the enormous profit such trade generates. Traders cannot wait for ten years to come with a tributary mission. Of course they will come so long as the wind is favourable … Chinese merchants too will make a good income in trade, so they certainly will not just wait for the foreigners to come. Their collaboration with the Japanese smugglers is unstoppable. They will try all possible ways to get business done regardless of the enhanced interdiction.[603]

Tang Shu 唐樞 (*jinshi* 1526, Bureau Director at the Ministry of Justice) observed the failure of the restricted tribute trade system:

> Whether it was in the Hongwu years when the tribute trade was abolished or in the Taizong years when the institution was restored, smuggling was always in operation. The illicit private trade was so intensive and extensive that the coastguards have been unable to stop it and the garrison patrols did not dare to check it. The maritime prohibition has been openly violated for 110 years. It resulted from the attraction for foreign silver, with which the illicit trade was conveniently conducted, and trade became a good way to make a living. This was common sense.[604]

The compulsory restriction of trade missions was hardly attainable on the frontier. Both the Japanese and the Mongols refused to abide by the fixed timetable. The precarious trade arrangement on the northern border engendered frustrations and clashes as the high demand for Ming goods encouraged the Mongols to break any

602 Hu Zongxian, *Chouhai tubian*, *j.* 12, p. 113b.

603 "Hai shang shiyi yi 海上事宜議" (A Debate on Maritime Issues) by Qian Wei 錢薇 (1502–1554), in *MJSWB*, vol. 214. *j.* 1, pp. 23b–24a.

604 *MJSWB*, vol. 270, *j.* 1, pp. 3b–4a.

prohibition. The Chenghua 成化 administration (1465–1488) demanded the Mongols pay tribute and trade only once every nine years, but Batu Möngke 巴圖蒙克 (d. 1520) came in 1465, 1467, 1468 and 1473, ignoring the prescribed timetable.[605] In its 30th year (1551), the Jiajing administration allowed the Mongols to have a horse fair twice a year, but Anta 俺答 (1507–1582) wanted it to occur four times a year.[606] The following year, Anta came in January, ahead of the scheduled time, and asked for trade. Li Fengshi 李逢时 (Regional Inspecting Censor, Datong) told Anta that according to imperial decree no trade was allowed except during the officially regulated period. As a result, Anta looted Datong.[607] The restriction on trade missions, which was devised to reduce contact and avoid trouble, ended up generating even more hostility and conflict.

The failure of the tribute trade system was also engendered from the strict regulation on trade items. The Ming government never granted the tribute countries the right to choose what commodities they would need in the trade that accompanied the tribute missions. The commodities for trade were unilaterally decided on by the Ming administration and were under political direction rather than market demand. The pro-trade officials condemned this policy for its unresponsiveness to foreigner's grievances. In July of the 30th year of the Jiajing reign (1551), Anta submitted two requests to the Xuanda 宣大 garrison, one to allow the Mongols to trade horses for cereals instead of fabrics, and the other to trade sheep and cattle rather than horses. Shi Dao 史道 (*jinshi* 1517, Left Assistant Censor-in-Chief and Grand Coordinator of Datong) asked the court to grant permission for this, and explained the reasons for this request. He noted that only 20 per cent of the Mongols who came with the tribute mission could trade horses while the other 80 per cent were poor people who could only trade the sheep and cattle that their families raised. And they were also those who most needed grain and cereals. This was not just a commercial issue; it was also an urgent security issue. Shi Dao warned the court that if the request from the poor Mongols was not satisfied they maight be inclined to disobey their chieftains and resume looting (regardless of what their leaders told them). But the Ministry of War did not see the point and refused the request. The emperor sacked Shi Dao for lacking judgment. Looting and attacks by the Mongols immediately ensued.[608]

Similar restrictions were inflicted on those countries which approached the Ming Empire from the coast. Even though tribute trade existed with Japan, smuggling remained phenomenal because the Japanese were unable to get what they wanted through the tribute trade system. The Japanese did not mint money and badly needed Chinese copper coins, which they used as currency. In the 5th year of the Chenghua reign (1469), the Japanese envoy came to ask for 5,000 *guan* of copper coins in their tribute mission, which was a very modest amount by the standards

605 *Da Ming huidian*, *j.* 107, pp. 3a-b.

606 Shen Yue, *Huang Ming Jia-Long jianwen ji*, *j.* 8, p. 40b.

607 Ibid., *j.* 9, p. 1a.

608 Ibid., *j.* 8, pp. 46b–47a.

of the time. The Ministry of Rites declined this request straight away. When the case was reported to the Xianzong 憲宗 Emperor (r. 1466–1486), the emperor cut their request by 90 per cent and granted them only 500 *guan*.[609] The Japanese had no choice but to rely on smuggling as the only way to obtain monetary metal. The restrictions on trade drove up the value of Chinese copper coins in Japan fourfold and caused a serious economic deflation.[610] In the 3rd year of the Tianshun 天順 reign (1458–1464), the King of Ryūkyū sent a long list of tribute goods to please the emperor and asked the court to allow them to trade for 100,000 *guan* of copper coins. The Chinese court flatly refused his request.[611] Trade in which only one party dictated the Chinese commodity to be exchanged was not really considered trade.

The notorious price control system was another excessive condition imposed on all tribute trade, which pro-trade officials argued was another cause of the ill feeling foreigners felt towards the Ming administration. During the Hongwu reign, the administration established a "*chama si* 茶馬司" (Horse and Tea Trading Office) in Taozhou 洮州 and Hezhou. 河州 to regulate the trade price. Every 5,000 *jin* of tea were fixed as equivalent to 13,500 horses, or 185 grams of tea per horse.[612] This was an arbitrarily imposed exchange rate, and far below the market value. Smuggling was soon thriving and the tribute trade went into disarray. This resulted in difficulties for the Horse Trading Office, which could not get enough horses, as the 'western barbarians' showed little interest in the tribute missions.

Liang Cai 梁材 (*jinshi* 1505, Minister of Revenue) sent his men to investigate this case and was told that smugglers were everywhere. A single day saw the interception of sixty smuggled horses in Taozhou and forty in Xining. Liang attributed the collapse of the official tea-horse trade to a lack of commercial incentives. He reported to the emperor: "Tea piled up in the stores and trade was slow ... it went rotten and had to be incinerated. 20,002,000 *jin* were burnt to ashes, worth tens of thousands of *taels* of silver ... what a terrible waste."[613] Wang Tingxiang 王廷相 (*jinshi* 1502, a Minister of War) tried to convince the court of the failure of the system: "Smugglers are travelling through the fortresses, in and out of the border; tea boats are sailing on all the waters ... A single custom's raid can confiscate as much as 100,000 *jin* of smuggled tea ... The leverage to control the barbarians through trade has now shifted into the hands of illicit merchants."[614] In the 3rd year of the Hongzhi reign (1490) the government, out of desperation, attempted to increase the price of horses 270 fold, from 185 gram per horse to 50 kilograms per horse.[615] But

609 Cao Renhu, *Qinding xu wenxian tongkao*, *j.* 11, pp. 9a–b.

610 *Riben kao*, *j.* 1, p. 12b.

611 Ibid., *j.* 11, p. 8a.

612 "Xifan kao 西番考" (A Study of the Western Barbarians), in *Cangxia zheng xuji* 蒼霞正續集 (*Continuation of Collected Works of Ye Xianggao, Named After the Village Pavillion of my Hometown, Cangxia*) by Ye Xianggao 葉向高 (1559–1627), in *MJSWB*, vol. 461, *j.* 1, p. 16a.

613 "Yi chama shiyi shu 議茶馬事宜疏" (A Memorial on the Tea and Horse Trade) by Liang Cai 梁材 (1470–1540), in *MJSWB*, vol. 106, *j.* 5, pp. 4b–5a.

614 Zhang Xuan, *Xi yuan wenjian lu*, *j.* 66, p. 15a.

615 *Ming shi*, *j.* 80, p. 26b.

this did not improve the situation, as it was too little too late. The *Ming shi* records: "The situation had worsened to such an extent that by the 13th year of the Wanli 萬歷 reign (1586) the tribute trade had lost its attraction and foreigners no longer wanted to pay tribute in horses."[616]

The geographic nature of the boundaries between the Ming Empire and both the Mongols and the Japanese also facilitated smuggling and thus helped undermine the success of the tribute trade system. Mao Kun 茅坤 (*jinshi* 1538, Assistant Surveillance Commissioner of Guangxi) pointed out: "There are no mountains and rivers between the Mongol steppe and China's border. Whenever their horses are strong and our harvest is ready during August and September they are bound to come to loot."[617] Tang Shu also observed that "Dinghai 定海 is a place where there are ten thousand peasants living on the sea … The north-easterly will take a ship from Japan to Dinghai only in 5–6 days."[618] Enforcing the maritime prohibitions in such circumstances was exceptionally difficult. Hu Zongxian noted that "Tuolin 拓林 in Zhejiang 浙江 was a center for merchants. Whenever the westerly wind comes, there will be 200–300 smuggling ships in the port, busy preparing their overseas trips … there were about ten thousand smugglers there."[619] Since the ten-yearly official tribute trade was far from enough to satisfy its needs, the Japanese government became ever more zealous in encouraging its people in their trips to China. The authorities simplified their procedures for foreign trade by allowing any merchant with 10,000 *taels* or more in capital to engage in overseas trade, after payment of 1,000 *taels* tariff in advance. Imported or exported goods were free from custom duties and other taxes.[620] Qian Wei noticed that "the Liangzhe 兩浙 region is closely connected with Japan by sea. As they [the Japanese] depend on our products, trade is always in high demand. The 'once-every-ten-years' tribute trade is rather impractical. During every intercalary month ships will arrive on China's coast … It is hard to prevent our own people from collaborating and cooperating with them."[621]

The pro-trade officials declared their position clearly. They argued that the politically controlled tribute system and trade prohibition dragged the country into war with its neighbours and the situation would become even worse if the policies remained in place. Hu Zongxian warned the court: "So long as the Japanese rely on

616 Ibid., p. 31a.

617 "Tiaoshang Li Jiquan zhoncheng haikou shiyi 條上李汲泉中丞海寇事宜" (A Submission to Li Jiqian, Vice Censor in Chief, on the Issue of Pirates), in *Mao Lumen wenji* 茅鹿門文集 (*Collected Works of Mao Kun, Hao Lumen*) by Mao Kun 茅坤 (1512–1601), in *MJSWB*, vol. 256, *j.* 1, p. 2a.

618 *MJSWB*, vol. 270, *j.* 1, pp. 18b–19a.

619 "Tiwei dufu dachen kou yang min kenqi jiu zhi shishu 題為督撫大臣寇殃民懇乞究治事疏" (A Memorial Requesting that the Court Investigate and Impeach Governors who bring Calamity to the People), in *Hu Shaobao zoushu* by Hu Zongxian (*jinshi* 1538), in *MJSWB*, vol. 266, *j.* 2, pp. 23b–24a.

620 Li Yangong & Hao Jie, *Riben kao*, *j.* 2, p. 29b.

621 *MJSWB*, vol. 214, *j.* 1, pp. 23b–24a.

us for consumable goods, the lucrative business [of providing these goods] will motivate people to do anything to take a part in it. The longer the prohibition is implemented, the more rampant the illicit trade will become. People will risk their lives to participate in it. How can we stop them?"[622] Jiang Bao 姜寶 (*jinshi* 1553, a Minister of Rites) reminded the emperor: "The barbarians can hardly be deterred from harassing us if they no longer rely on the tribute missions to get what they need."[623] He implied that it was an urgent necessity to replace the faulty tribute trade system with a more efficient and more reasonable relationship.

Motivation for War

The exact motivation behind the conflicts along the borders of the empire was a subject of considerable debate amongst officials and the issue divided the government. Pro-trade officials challenged the mainstream view of foreigners as 'barbarians'. Li Chengxun 李承勳 (*jinshi* 1493, Deputy Censor-in-Chief and Grand Co-ordinator of Liaodong) noted: "They come in dozens of big ships, fully armed and loaded with expensive commodities, looking for trade and resorting to killing only when their trade has declined."[624] Regarding the Portuguese, Pang Shangpeng 龐尚鵬 (*jinshi* 1553, Grand Co-ordinator of Fujan) observed:

> They have been trading in the south of Guangdong for a long time and have never caused any trouble. They are here for trade without any intention to do us any harm. The best way for us to deal with them is through 'no interruption' [...] If the foreigners are allowed to trade, why would they risk their licences to do us harm? We should not discourage the barbarians from admiring China and we should use trade to pacify them. We should resume trade with them and levy tariffs on the trade to generate revenue ... the barbarians will then be controlled and their evil intentions will disappear, as will the conflict. [625]

The debate focused on whether the foreigners came for trade or to invade the empire; whether it was the innate nature of the 'barbarians' or Ming policies that generated the hostilities; whether their aggression was a product of their desire for trade or an indication of the intent to conquer the empire. Even after the lifting of the maritime prohibitions, this was an issue that could still generate strong opinions. The editors of the *Ming jingshi wenbian* only rarely inserted editorial commentaries about the documents included in the collection, but Chen Zilong 陳子龍 (*jinshi* 1638) was moved to do so following a memorial by the Censor Song Yiwang 宋儀望 (*jinshi* 1547) in which Song had emphasized the malign intentions of foreigners. Chen felt he had to correct what he saw as Song's misguided understanding of the issue:

622 Hu Zongxian, *Chouhai tubian*, *j.* 12, p. 113b.

623 "Chafa yi 茶法議" (A Discussion about the Law on Tea Trade), in *Jiang Feng'a ji* 姜鳳阿集 (*The Collected Works of Jiang Feng'a*) by Jiang Bao 姜寶 (1514–1593), in *MJSWB*, vol. 383, *j.* 1, p. 3b.

624 Zhang Xuan, *Xiyuan wenjian lu*, *j.* 56, p. 13b.

625 *MJSWB*, vol. 357, *j.* 1, pp. 10a-b.

> The Japanese come to China for trade rather than for piracy. Our people violate the trade interdiction in order to trade with the Japanese rather than to collaborate with them in illegal activities. It is our trade prohibition policy that drives them to do such things. It is the maritime prohibition that caused the problem. We have to work out a policy to get benefit from trade while avoiding its detrimental effects.[626]

Pro-trade officials argued that the foreigners could be managed through trade, no matter how different they were. For instance, Wang Chonggu 王崇古 (*jinshi* 1541, Supreme Commander of the three defence regions of Shaanxi, Yanning and Gansu) made his voice heard on relations with the Mongols:

> Although the Mongols have weird clothing and unusual customs, their basic materials, such as cloth and utensils, come only from China ... that is why they resort to looting. Thousands of ordinary Mongols will have nowhere to get what they need if we only allow tribute trade, from which the reward goods only go to the chiefs. It is inevitable that these people will harass our borders. Only by trading with them all can peace be guaranteed.[627]

Similarly, in 1558, Zheng Xiao 鄭曉 (*jinshi* 1523, a Minister of Justice and Acting Minister of War) wanted to release captured Japanese pirates, arguing: "As far as I know, the Japanese came here only for trade. Their parents, brothers, wives and children sent letters to them, not knowing they were in jail. We should keep a few and send most of them back to Japan."[628] Wang Shizhen also identified the so-called 'pirates' as merchants: "The Japanese who came to China did not board warships. Some of them came as a business partners who rented a place on board the "*gongbo* 貢舶" (tribute ships) for private trade, while others managed to board a private commercial vessel."[629] Zheng Ruozeng 鄭若曾 (an assistant of Hu Zongxian) objected to the long held images of 'pirates': "They are a rather special type. They travelled 3,000 *li* throughout eight prefectures and were well informed on the situation of our human and material resources (helped by our people), they did not kill people, did not rape women and did not loot property."[630] Lin Xiyuan 林希元 (*jinshi* 1517, a Director of the Grand Court of Review) joined in with an even more forceful declaration, this time with regard to the Portuguese: "Our people love the Portuguese. They come with spices to trade with our people at a good price. Our peo-

626 "Hai fang shan hou shiyi shu 海防善後事宜疏" (My Memorial on the Aftermath of the Coastal Defense Issue), in *Song dufu zoushu* 宋督撫奏疏 (*Memorials of Song Yiwang, Governor and Inspector General*) by Song Yiwang 宋儀望 (*jinshi* 1547), in *MJSWB*, vol. 362, *j.* 1, p. 2a.

627 "Wei beilu na kuan zhi pan qiu jiang shu 為北虜纳款執叛求降疏" (A Memorial Regarding the Mongols Paying Tribute, Sending over Defectors and Asking for Surrender), in *Wang Jiachuan wenji* by Wang Chonggu 王崇古 (1515–1588), in *MJSWB*, vol. 316, *j.* 1, pp. 23a–b.

628 "Da Jingchuan Tang yintai 答荊川唐銀臺" (Reply to Tang Jingchuan, the Transmission Commissioner), in *Zheng Duanjian gong wenji* by Zheng Xiao 鄭曉 (1499–1566), in *MJSWB*, vol. 218, *j.* 2, pp. 1b–2a.

629 *MJSWB*, vol. 332, *j.* 1, pp. 30a–-b.

630 "*Jiangnan jingluo* 江南經略" (*Strategies for Jiangnan*), by Zheng Ruozeng 鄭若曾 (1503–1570), in *Siku quanshu*, fasc. 728, *j.* 8, *xia*, p. 24b.

ple sell daily commodities to them … the local people made much more money than usual. Our people love to trade with them."[631]

Wang Shizhen was one among many of the pro-trade officials who argued that the 'barbarians', both Mongols and Japanese, were motivated neither by conquest nor territorial expansion.[632] He noted that although their cavalry was extremely powerful, they had no desire to control China politically; their interests were purely commercial.[633] Reinforcing the point, he suggested that what the Mongols wanted was China's products, not its land or its people.[634] Nevertheless, some conservative courtiers approached the issue differently. Unlike Wang Shizhen, they believed that the Mongols wanted only one thing: to take control of China and rule over Chinese people. Morris Rossabi notes that the Ming court was sensitive to any sign that the Mongols might attempt this. In 1550, the court declined a Mongol request for grain in trade, and Rossabi suggests that the court's response

> was conditioned on the fear that Mongol grain purchases were designed for Chinese defectors – that is, prisoners, law-breakers, or ordinary citizens who served the Mongols. The skills in administration, craftsmanship and financial affairs offered by Chinese defectors could prove to be a challenge to China because they offered the Mongols the means not only to conquer but also to govern the Middle Kingdom.[635]

Defectors were a serious concern for the Ming administration because of the possibility that they might help the Mongols to run a sedentary empire. Defectors such as Xiao Qin 蕭芹, Wang Dedao 王得道, Qiu Fu 丘富 and Qiao Yuan 喬遠 were put on the most wanted list.[636] However, events were to prove the conservatives' worries groundless. The Mongols did not value the defectors as much as was suspected. When the defector issue became a pre-condition for trade, Anta immediately sent them straight back over the border. From the 30th year of the Jiajing reign (1551, when Xiao Qin, Zhao Quan 趙全 and thirty others were returned) one group of defectors after another was deported back across the border.[637] This again confirmed that the Mongols were interested in trade rather than domination.

Regarding the question of what it was that motivated the coastal pirates, Xu Guangqi asked the emperor to get a fairer picture by listening to those in uniform serving along the border rather than officials in robes stationed at the court:

> We have never understood the key reason for piracy … we should listen to Lu Tang, the general who has fought the pirates his whole life and is well informed about the situation along the coast. Lu says that Wang Zhi, the king of pirates, has never personally led an invasion. We

631 "Yu weng jian yu bie jia shu 與翁見愚別駕書" (My Humble Farewell Letter), in *Lin Ciya xiansheng wenji* 林次崖先生文集 (*Collected Works of Lin Xiyuan, Hao Ciya*) by Lin Xiyuan 林希元 (*jinshi* 1517), in *MJSWB*, vol. 165, *j.* 4, pp. 5a–b.

632 *Wang Yanzhou wenji*, *j.* 1, p. 30b.

633 Ibid., *j.* 4, p. 4a.

634 Ibid., *j.*4, p. 11a.

635 Morris Rossabi, "The Ming and Inner Asia" (1998); p. 237.

636 Shen Yue, *Huang Ming Jia-Long liangchao jianwen ji*, *j.* 8, p. 45a.

637 Gu Yingtai, *Mingshi jishi benmo*, *j.* 60, pp. 11a–b, 21b and 26a.

> should appoint him to a minor office to wipe out the illicit traders and then openly trade with the Japanese.[638]

Tang Shunzhi argued that "if the Japanese knew there was a legitimate channel to get what they needed, then their evil intentions would automatically disappear and the illegal local collaboration with the pirates would cease."[639] Debating the objectives of the Japanese pirates, Hu Zongxian reported to the emperor that the Japanese harassment was not a state-organized campaign for political purposes but rather a product of economic difficulties: "A captured Japanese, named Tasuku Shiryō 助四郎, claimed that Japan was suffering from drought, and they came to China for trade to make a living. Their King knew nothing about it."[640] Similarly, Lin Xiyuan protested about the military offensive against the Portuguese ships and petitioned the court to treat them as traders rather than intruders: "The Portuguese did not come to attack us. They have never done anything illegal … It was our coastguard who wanted to attack them … a sudden attack on them by our military was no more than a low trick, it is deplorable. The Portuguese have never taken our territories, killed our people or looted our property."[641]

The prohibition on trade underlay illegal activities, as looting and smuggling became the only way to break the interdiction. Pro-trade officials criticized the politically destructive trade prohibition for fuelling these confrontations. Tan Lun 譚倫 (*jinshi* 1544, Vice Commissioner in charge of Coastal Military Defence, Supreme Commander of Jiliao and Minister of War) pointed out:

> There are no silk or cotton textiles produced in the foreign countries; how can they be called a state without these necessities? Whenever we police our prohibition policy with greater vigilance, the profit from smuggling increases, and more and more people become involved in the illicit trade. If smuggling is blocked there will more piracy and looting. The old saying is right: if you want to block up a rat hole you have to leave the rats a way to escape, otherwise they will destroy everything on their way out. The prohibition policy follows the principle.[642]

In the 18th year of the Jiajing reign (1539), after sixteen years without any trade, once again a mission was sent to China to beg for tribute trade. The mission was sent on the order of the Japanese ruler Ashikaga Yoshiharu 足利義晴 (1511–1550).[643] The court allowed the Japanese to pay tribute once every ten years and with no more than 100 people and three ships. (There was no restriction on the

---

638 *MJSWB*, vol. 491, *j.* 4, pp. 31a–b.

639 "Tiaochen haifang jing shi shu 條陳海防經事疏" (An Ordered Memorial on the Issue of Coastal Defence) by Tang Shunzhi, *MJSWB*, vol. 260, *j.* 2, p. 6a.

640 "Tiwei xian yu zhong yi tu rang shi shu 題為獻愚忠以圖攘事疏" (A Humble Memorial on Resisting Foreign Aggression to Show My Blind Loyalty), in *MJSWB*, vol. 266, *j.* 2, p. 20b.

641 *MJSWB*, vol. 165, *j.* 4, p. 5b.

642 *Tan xiangmin zouyi* 潭襄敏奏議 (*The Memorials of Tan Xiangmin*) by Tan Lun 譚倫 (1520–1577), in *Siku quanshu*, fasc. 429. *j.* 2, p. 46b.

643 For details see Oláh Csaba, *Räuberische Chinesen und tückische Japaner. Die diplomatischen Beziehungen zwischen China und Japan im 15. und 16. Jahrhundert.* (Wiesbaden: Otto Harrassowitz, 2009), chapter II, esp. pp. 109–116. *East Asian Maritime History* 7.

number of people on board the tribute ships before). Of course the Japanese could not wait for ten years. They came after six years, in the 23rd year of the Jiajing reign (1544), but were refused straight away. They returned in 1546 and again were sent back.[644] When the legal tribute year finally came in the 27th year of the Jiajing reign (1548), the Japanese could not wait any longer, they turned up in four ships with 600 people on board and a few months earlier than scheduled. They were told to go back for violating the rules. It was only then that they went in for looting around Ningbo 寧波 and Taizhou 臺州 out of desperation and frustration.[645] This was a typical example of the 'rat-hole-plugging' theory. The trade prohibition went hand in hand with piracy and smuggling, and it was not an isolated phenomenon. In 1559 Tang Shunzhi noted that "for the last ten years there has been not a single year without piracy."[646]

The situation with the Mongols was no different. In the 20th year of Jiajing reign (1541), after decades of not being allowed access, the Mongols came to beg for trade. But their request was declined. When they sent their diplomat back to negotiate in 1547 he was executed.[647] In 1550, the Mongols marched their cavalry to Beijing, besieged the capital and conducted a massacre on the outskirts of the city. They captured eight officials and released them so that they would tell the emperor that the only condition for their retreat was a trade agreement.[648] Pro-trade officials persistently blamed the trade prohibition policy for inducing such grievance-orientated wars. Weng Wanda 翁萬達 (*jinshi* 1526, Right Assistant Censor-in-Chief and Supreme Commander of Xuanfu, Datong, Shanxi and Baoding) complained: "The devastation from their failure to get a trade agreement gave the Mongol chiefs power to inspire their men to seek revenge by attacking us hard."[649] Pro-trade officials wanted to clarify their stand that the barbarians came neither for conquest, nor simply for profit from trade. They came to satisfy their basic needs. Trade was the only antidote for the calamity of war. "If they can get what they want by peaceful means, who will then want to try to get it in a violent way?"[650]

Legitimate Grievances?

Pro-trade officials challenged the officially maintained prejudice against foreigners as 'bellicose barbarians'. They campaigned for their colleagues to recognize the need that foreign people felt to rectify the underlying justification for Ming foreign

644 Gu Yingtai, *Mingshi jishi benmo*, *j.* 55, p. 9a. See also Zhu Wan, *Piyu zaji*, *j.* 2, pp. 37a-38b.

645 Zhu Wan, *Piyu zaji*, *j.*2, pp. 38a–b and *Ming shi*, *j.* 322, pp. 13b–14b.

646 Hu Zongxian, *Chouhai tubian*, *j.* 11, p. 11a.

647 Shen Yue, *Huang Ming Jia-Long liangchao jianwen ji*, *j.* 6, p. 32a, *j.* 7, p. 44a. See also "Da lu qiu gong shu 大虜求貢疏" (A Memorial about the Mongols' Request for Tribute), in *Weng Dongya wenji* 翁東涯文集 (*Collected Literary Works of Weng Wanda, Hao Dongya*) by Weng Wanda 翁萬達 (1498–1552), in *MJSWB*, vol. 224, *j.* 2, pp. 7b–8a.

648 Gu Yingtai, *Mingshi jishi benmo*, *j.* 59, pp. 5a–b.

649 *MJSWB*, vol. 224, *j.* 2, p. 11b.

650 "Lun tongshi 論通市" (On Allowing Trade with Japan), in *Gujin tushu jicheng*, *j.* 40, p. 17b.

policy, a policy which placed considerable constraints upon them. While they offended the conservatives, they also increased awareness of the legitimate grievances of the foreigners. They stressed the 'enemy's' unique geographical, social and economic circumstances and associated these factors with their 'barbarism' and their desire for trade with China. According to Wang Shizhen, the natural geographic situation and economic situation made these foreigners 'looters' rather than 'occupiers of territory'.[651] In his memorial, Wang Chonggu argued that the different social system and different level of economic development determined the Mongols' feverish desire for trade:

> The Mongols are located in the open lands of the far north. Their people do not know how to plant crops and know nothing about raising silkworms and making cloth … They make no products themselves. Cooking pots and other commodities in daily use were all traded from China. When normal trade is blocked, looting is the only way for them to obtain the cotton textiles and ironware they need.[652]

Qian Wei argued in a similar way with regard to the Japanese. "Japan is located in the sea in seclusion … Only the eastern side of the mountains is cultivatable and the rest of the country is barren. Though the southerners make their living by fishing, most people rely on trade."[653]

This shortage of basic commodities that the Mongols and the Japanese suffered from aroused great sympathy among officials. Pro-trade officials softened the image of them as enemies by portraying them as victims of the prohibition on trade. This new approach weakened the justification for the trade prohibition policy. Whereas the prohibition on trade was a means by which the Ming administration was able to manipulate its relations with foreigners, for the Mongols and the Japanese it was much more serious, as they relied on China for so many of their basic commodiites. Pro-trade officials wanted the government to become aware of their vulnerability. Wang Tingxiang explained the pathetic situation in the north. "The Mongols and the Xifan indulge in looting because they cannot survive a single day without tea and tea only grows in China. Their geographic location has made them reliant on meat and dairy products. Without tea, they cannot digest their food properly."[654] Similarly, Gui E 桂萼 (*jinshi* 1511, a Minister of Rites and a Grand Secretary) observed: "Tea, rhubarb and musk were the three principle commodities that the people of Turfan relied on. Without musk there is no cure for snake bites, without rhubarb both humans and animals will suffer from constipation, and without tea peo-

651 *MJSWB*, vol. 332, *j*.4, p. 11a.

652 Wang Chonggu, "Que yi feng gong shi yishu 確議封貢事宜疏" (Memorial on Confirming the Granting of a Title Conferring Tribute Status to the Mongols) in *MJSWB*, 316, *j*. 1, p. 29b and *j*. 2, p. 10a.

653 *MJSWB*, vol. 214, *j*. 1, .pp. 15a–b and 20b.

654 "Yan cha 嚴茶" (Strict Enforcement of the Prohibition on the Tea Trade), in *Wang shi jiacang ji* 王氏家藏集 (*Family Collection of Wang Tingxian*) by Wang Tingxiang 王廷相 (1474–1544), in *MJSWB*, vol. 149, *j*. 2, p. 22b. See also Gu Yingtai, *Mingshi jishi benmo*, *j*. 60, p. 22b.

ple cannot digest their food."[655] Pro-trade officials repeatedly emphasized the fact that foreigners were sensible human beings rather than cold-blooded monsters, who were made to suffer by the prohibition on trade. Looting and smuggling were taken up only as matters of last resort.

Pro-trade officials argued that a lack of understanding of these legitimate grievances led to poor political decisions. For instance, disengagement would not produce security but rather the opposite. The prohibition on trade was despised and generated conflict. And there was plenty of evidence to show that an active engagement with foreigners could turn trade into a source of power for the Ming. When smallpox devastated Mongol society and undermined its economy in the sixteenth century, Anta tried every possible way to save his people by arranging trade with China. In 1541, he sent his envoy Shi Tianjue 石天爵 to visit the Supreme Commander Shi Dao 史道 to beg for permission to trade. Out of desperation the messenger claimed that the shaman had prophecied that tribute trade with the Ming would please the gods and save the Mongols from the epidemic.[656] He vowed not to wreak war on China if trade was permitted. Otherwise, they would shift their base further to the north and repeat military attacks and lootings. Shi Dao sent an urgent memorial to the court: "The 40 years from the Hongzhi reign since we cut off tribute trade relations with the Mongols has been a period during which we have suffered from Mongol attacks. If the Mongols are genuine in asking for tribute, there can be no better fortune for us than this."[657] Wang Chonggu emphasized the urgency with which it was necessary to rectify the injustice of the prohibition on trade with the Mongols: "Cooking pots are the first thing Mongols loot when they invade a city. How can they survive when they cannot cook food and when they do not have enough clothes to wear?"[658] But the conservatives refused to change the official position. Tan Xuefu 譚學復 (a Regional Inspector) argued: "To decline the Mongols' trade request would prevent disaster in the long run, though it may cause some temporary trouble at present. Getting ready for war is the most urgent imperative."[659] His memorial was approved at the court meeting and endorsed by the emperor. The conservatives led the court to believe in an illusion: that the trade prohibition would keep the Mongols away. In reality, the opposite occurred. Forced to confront the hard-line policy of the Ming administration, the Mongol cavalry marched towards the Ming border instead of retreating from it, and turned commerce into war.[660] The resultant bloodshed reinforced the pro-trade adherents about the reality of the situation along the land border. The experience reinforced their

655 "Jin Hami shiyi shu 進哈密事宜疏" (A Memorial on the Issue of Hami) by Gui E 桂萼 (*jinshi* 1511), in *MJSWB*, vol. 181, *j.* 3, p. 3b.

656 "Ti bei lu qiu gong shu 題北虜求貢疏" (A Memorial on the Mongols' Request for Tribute Status), in *Shi dufu zouyi* 史督撫奏議 (*Memorials of Shi Dao, the Supreme Commander and Grand Coordinator*) by Shi Dao 史道 (1485–1554), in *MJSWB*, vol. 166, *j.* 1, p. 8b.

657 Shen Yue, *Huang Ming Jia-Long liangchao jianwen ji*, *j.* 6, p. 32a.

658 *MJSWB*, vol. 316, *j.* 2, p. 23b.

659 Shen Yue, *Huang Ming Jia-Long liangchao jianwen ji*, *j.* 6, p. 32a.

660 *Ming shi*, *j.* 204, p. 7a; *j.* 238, p. 2b; *j.* 198, p. 2b; and *j.* 173, p. 19b.

belief that only by redressing the legitimate grievances of the Mongols through the opening of trade relations would it be possible to extinguish their war drive.

Trade was also the most important pre-condition for good security along the coast. Trade granted China a tremendous leverage in its relations with Japan. Qian Wei noted that the Japanese "relied on China for supply. They need Chinese products as much as the Xifan barbarians need Chinese tea. Just as the Xifan barbarians will loot whenever they are short of tea, so the Japanese will loot for what they need. From the Tang and Song dynasties onwards we have seldom encountered problems with piracy when the tribute trade was in good operation."[661] The Japanese were forced to engage in illicit trade in order to get what they failed to obtain through normal transactions. And these politically destructive undertakings would always constitute a security problem as long as their legitimate grievances were not realized. Li Yangong depicted the organization of pirates thus: "The pirates organise themselves into many groups, with around thirty members each, to loot everything they find. The pirates are required to hand in what they obtain through looting to the leader without daring to hide anything."[662] What the pro-trade officials wanted to emphasize was that the 'barbarians' had no option but to engage in piracy and it became routine and institutionalized. Such disasters could have been avoided had the authorities become a little more caring and tolerant.

The pro-trade officials tried to persuade the court to have more empathy toward the foreigners' requests for trade. Qian Wei petitioned the emperor, requesting: "Even if they come again in less than ten years, there is no reason to send them back, as they undergo so much hardship at sea and have travelled from so far away. In addition, we also need their goods."[663] When Zhu Wan was impeached for killing ninety-six illegal merchants, he became the target of criticism for his lack of sympathy for the legitimate grievances of these 'enemies'. Following Zhu Wan's suicide, Xu Guangqi noted: "He [Zhu Wan] may have been an upright official ... but he did not understand the true situation [of trade] and hence was unable to make the right decision."[664] Wu Guifang 吳桂芳 (*jinshi* 1544, a Magistrate of Yangzhou 揚州 and a Deputy Minister of War) petioned the court, stating: "If the foreigners are truly obedient and they present no great threat to us, why can we not accept their tribute?"[665]

The Portuguese did not often go in for piracy, even though they were an increasingly powerful force in the region by the mid- to late sixteenth century. Their cannons were ten times more powerful than those of the Ming navy.[666] But Pang

661 *MJSWB*, vol. 214, *j.* 1, p. 20b.

662 Li Yangong and Hao Jie, *Riben kao*, *j.* 1, p. 14a.

663 *MJSWB*, vol. 214, *j.* 1, pp. 24a-b.

664 *MJSWB*, vol. 491, *j.* 4, p. 31a.

665 "Yi zu Aoyi jin gong shu 議阻澳夷進貢疏" (A Memorial Commenting on Refusing to Allow the Barbarians at Macau to Pay Tribute), in *Wu sima zouyi* 吳司馬奏議 (*Memorials for Court Debate by Wu Guifang, Minister of War*) by Wu Guifang 吳桂芳 (1521–1578), in *MJSWB*, vol. 342, *j.* 1, p. 14b.

666 *MJSWB*, vol. 280, *j.* 1, p. 8b.

Shangpeng reported to the emperor: "The Portuguese will become obedient, their war drive will vanish, and the war tension will go away once we restore the old trade system."[667] Instead of piracy, the Portuguese resorted to deception in order to get into the China trade. They impersonated the envoy of Malacca, a tribute state which, since its annexation by another kingdom, had long since failed to turn up to pay tribute. The Portuguese pretended to be envoys from Malacca, but were kicked out as soon as their true identity was discovered.[668] This setback did not discourage the Portuguese. In order to please the Ming officials, and gain favour at court, they lined up their war-ships with the Ming navy to help eradicate the priates. Lin Xi-yuan commented: "For the last twenty years there have been so many pirates, and the government had no way to clear them up. The Portuguese fought the pirates on our side rather than going in for piracy themselves. They brought us benefit, not damage."[669] The pro-trade officials denounced the long-held biases about foreigners as unjustifiable. They continually argued that if the foreigners' legitimate grievances were not properly remedied, war would never end.

Social Injustice and Insurgency

The prohibition on trade not only inflicted suffering on the 'barbarians'. It also adversely affected people within the empire. In other words, the policy not only created international conflict, it also produced social discord within the empire. The court had long been alerted to the fact that the so-called foreign war was all too often fought between government forces and its own people. When Tan Lun once called on the court to demand that the Japanese ruler prevent pirates from coming to China's shore, some officials regarded such a demand as ridiculous: "It is hilarious to ask others to prevent their people from engaging in piracy when you yourself fail to stop your own people from sailing out for the same illicit activity."[670] The reason was simple. "When the prohibition has blocked the flow of commodities in and out [of the empire], our local people tend to collaborate with the pirates in smuggling goods."[671] However, these Japanese pirates "are not here to invade but for trade; and our people who cooperate with them are not on any purpose but business."[672] The maritime prohibition policy brought about the open violation of the maritime interdiction by Chinese people living along the coast. For instance, in the 25th year of the Jiajing reign (1546), a merchant ship was wrecked along the coast of Korea. On board were 613 merchants from Zhangzhou 漳州 and Quanzhou 泉州. A similiar incident happened again the following year, when 341 smugglers from Fujian were saved from storms. The ship was loaded with all sorts of

667 *MJSWB*, vol. 357, *j.* 1, p. 10b.
668 *MJSWB*, vol. 342, *j.* 1, .pp. 13b–15a.
669 *MJSWB*, vol. 165, *j.* 4, p. 5b.
670 "Wo zhi 倭志" (Notes about Japanese) by Tan Lun 譚倫 (1520–1577), in *Xuanlantang congshu xuji* 玄覽堂叢書續集, pp. 15b–16a.
671 Hu Zongxian, *Chouhai tubian*, *j.* 11, pp. 4b–5a.
672 *MJSWB*, vol. 362, *j.* 1, p. 2a

Chinese commodities the Japanese wanted.[673] The Jiajing emperor, astonished by the situation, dispatched Chen Zhang 陳璋 (Vice Prefect of Tongzhi prefecture) and Ren Huantong 任寰统 (Vice Prefect of Suzhou prefecture) to conduct an investigation in 1553. They reported to the emperor that most of the pirates were Chinese.[674] Tang Shu pointed out how the smuggling was snowballing. "The pirates in the *renzi* 壬子 year (1552) were frustrated maritime merchants, those in the *guichou* 癸丑 year (1553) were people from other businesses trying to increase their income, those in the *jiashen* 甲申 year (1554) were just common people and those in the *yimao* 乙卯 year (1555) were people from everywhere."[675]

Economic difficulties engendered by the prohibition policy undermined its justification. The policy hurt the most vulnerable section of society hardest, the landless coastal people. Tang Shu pointed out: "We have a great number of people making their living from the sea, sailing wherever they can fish and collect things. The prohibition policy has unsettled them."[676] Dai Chongxiao 戴冲霄, a Fujian official, petitioned the emperor on behalf of the poor:

> The poor people of Fujian rely on the sea for subsistence, either by salt works or by fishing … these are low-profit activities only undertaken by the poor and the weak. The powerful and rich will engage in foreign trade to make ten times more income. However, the maritime interdiction has outlawed people's way of making a living. And these frustrated people become the very source of piracy. They are not going to wait for death. The stricter the prohibition is maintained, the more intensified piracy will become.[677]

Lin Xiyuan denounced the policy for overriding the common people's basic welfare. "Our authority is unable to prevent foreigners from coming in for trade hence [the imposition of the] interdiction along the whole coast. The policy restricts all coastal people from contacting outsiders for trade, leading to their misery. It seems as if one gives up eating to avoid the accident of suffocation."[678] Tan Lun pointed out the impracticality of enforcing the prohibition policy, owing to the fact that it pushed ordinary Chinese people on to the side of the 'pirates':

> There are numerous people from Fujian who live by the sea and have no way to make a living without being involved in maritime trade … foreigners are not the only people who need maritime trade; our own people do too. The local people need to trade their fish products, Guangdong merchants need to trade their rice and spices, Zhangzhou merchants need to trade their sugar. All these activities are now prohibited, so how can we avoid people from collaborating with foreign illicit traders? How can we stop people from engaging in smuggling and piracy?[679]

---

673 *Jiajing woluan beichao* 嘉靖倭亂備抄 (A Back-up Copy of Records of the Unrest Caused by Japanese Piracy), in *Siku cunmu* 史, fasc. 49, p. 552 (no author, no *juan*).

674 Shen Yue, *Huang Ming Jia-Long liangchao jianwen ji*, *j.* 9, p. 18a.

675 *MJSWB*, vol. 270, *j.* 3, p. 5a.

676 Ibid., *j.* 3, p. 5a.

677 Mao Yuanyi, *Wubei zhi*, in *Siku jinhui* 子, fasc. 26, *j.* 214, pp. 21b–22a.

678 *MJSWB*, vol. 165, *j.* 8, p. 6b.

679 *Tan xiangmin zouyi*, in *Siku quanshu*, fasc. 429, *j.* 2, pp. 46b–47a.

Looking back on this situation, Gu Yanwu 顧炎武 (1613–1682) accused the government of turning a blind eye to people's distressing circumstances. "Those poor peasants were smuggling for subsistence. The prohibition on trade prevented them from making a living."[680] Xu Fuyuan 許孚遠, the Grand Coordinator of Fujian, requested the court to consider the trauma that the policy could lead to:

> I received a report from Yu Fan 余樊 (the Assistant Surveillance Commissioner of Fujian coastal defense), which petitioned on behalf of merchants from Haicheng 海澄 county. It claims that his county is a place where most of the farmland is salty and barren. With little yield from their poor crops, people rely on fishing and trade in order to pay the land tax and maintain themselves. When the prohibition was strictly enforced it led to much antagonism. Thanks to the relaxation of the trade provision, revenue has increased and people are wealthier. If the maritime prohibition is again enhanced it will bankrupt our merchants and people will lose their income … they will become rebellious.[681]

The merchant group persecuted by the policy naturally provided the main opposition to it. Organizing smuggling and collaborating with foreigners, they had a head-on collision with the government forces. Wan Biao 萬表 (*jinshi* 1520, Assistant Commander of Ningbo garrison and Vice Secretary in the Central Military Commission in Nanjing) reported that the pirates were led by Chinese merchants, such as Xu Er 许二 and Wang Wufeng 王五峰 (Wang Zhi 王直).[682] Tu Zhonglü 屠仲律 reported to the court: "I have been told that the powerful and the wealthy along the coast have begun harbouring pirate merchants. They provide them with cargos and warehousing facilities. They are the source of smuggling."[683] Many of these smugglers enjoyed a high social and political status and tended to organise their overseas business on a grand scale. An Guo 安国, the seventeenth richest man in the country, with five million *taels* of silver in assets, was found openly violating the prohibition policy by managing the book trade with Japan. This was a protected trade. Though the sea port was a thousand *li* away from his home in the inland city of Wuxi 無錫, the magistrate of Taizhou prefecture 台州 became his personal friend and the backstage supporter for his trade.[684]

Mao Kun reported to the court that most of the so-called 'Japanese' pirates were in fact Ming merchants:

> A coastal peasant, who was abducted by the Japanese pirates and stayed on board the pirate ship for fifty days, reported to the authorities that on board his ship there were about 200 people including both the chiefs and crew, who were Chinese rather than Japanese pirates from Fujian, Wenzhou, Taizhou, Ningbo and Huizhou, among which sixty to seventy per cent

680 Gu Yanwu, *Tanxia junguo libing shu*, in *Siku xuxiu*, fasc. 597. p. 103b.

681 "Shu tong haijin shu 疏通海禁疏" (A Memorial on Lifting the Maritime Prohibition), in *Jinghetang ji* 敬和堂集 (*Collected Works by Xu Fuyuan, from the Jinghe Ancestral Hall*) by Xu Fuyuan 許孚遠 (1535–1604), in *MJSWB*, vol. 400, *j.* 1, pp. 1b–2a.

682 *Haikou yi*, in *Siku cunmu* 子, fasc. 31, pp. 1b–2a (no *juan*).

683 "Yu Wo wushi shu 御倭五事疏" (A Memorial to Interpret the Five Main Points in Resisting the Japanese), in *Wen Tu ergong zoushu* 聞屠二公奏疏 (*The Memorials of Wen and Tu*) by Tu Zhonglü 屠仲律 (*jinshi* 1550), in *MJSWB*, vol. 282, *j.* 1, p. 4a.

684 Wu Renan, *Ming-Qing Jiangnan wangzu yu shehui jingji wenhua*, pp. 218–223.

> were from Fujian. They employed only a dozen or so native Japanese who were dressed with their cone hair style for their ferocious image [to intimidate the coastguards].They were our own merchants with a fat purse for trade capital yearning for a fat dividend…It was the prohibition policy that deterred these Ming merchants from returning home, as they feared that they had committed great crimes [by collaborating with the foreigner] … but their families are all on the mainland.[685]

The movement of Fujian merchants thus became a weathercock, a means of determining the operation of the Japanese pirates. Tu Zhonglü said in his memorial: "Whenever Fujian people are busy building big ships, the Japanese pirates will come soon to invade. I did not believe this at first but what happened soon proved this prediction."[686] Similarly, Mao Yuanyi remarked: "If you want to know when the Japanese will come, just dress yourself up like a merchant and go to Nan Au 南澳 and convince the locals that you want to do business [with the Japanese]; you will be told when the Japanese will come and how many. What will happen within a year can easily be forecasted."[687] The war with the 'barbarians' was indeed a war between the government and its own frustrated merchants.

Pro-trade officials argued that the maritime prohibition policy was not sustainable when so many people co-operated in the campaigns and when there were sound warehousing and wholesale systems. Merchants from throughout the empire were involved. Wang Zaijin 王在晋 (*jinshi* 1592, Right Censor-in-Chief and Grand Co-ordinator of Shandong) reported: "Merchants from all over the country came to Zhangzhou 漳州 and Chaozhou 潮州. Here they stored their goods in the local residents' homes and then traded them with Japanese merchants for silver as soon as they came. Silver made the trade more efficient, and much easier to conduct than that with the western merchants, where goods had to be exchanged by barter."[688] Merchants from all over the country also swarmed into Guangzhou, which was the only port left to receive the tribute mission. "As soon as any foreign ships arrived in port, merchants from other provinces would rush to load silk, porcelain, gunpowder and other prohibited goods on board the foreign ships. It always took place during the night … when the customs officers got to the site the transaction was nearly over … It became common practice and nobody dared question it."[689] Pro-trade officials pursued the government to face this reality. Hu Zongxian stated: "It is impossible for a thousand foreign pirates to get here themselves. There must be our people who support and guide them, providing them with provisions so they will be able to stay longer, supplying them with goods so that they can trade, and working as their guides so that they will be able to go to the hinterland."[690] And

685 *MJSWB*, vol. 256, *j.* 1, pp. 2a–b.

686 *MJSWB*, vol. 282, *j.* 1, p. 4a.

687 Mao Yuanyi, *Wubei zhi*, in *Siku jinhui* 子, fasc. 26, *j.* 214, pp. 19a–b.

688 Ibid.

689 "Shang fan da xun Guangzhou shiyi 上潘大巡廣州事宜" (Problems Regarding the Guangzhou Inspection) by Huo Yuxia 霍與瑕 (*jinshi* 1559), in *MJSWB*, vol. 368, *j.* 1, pp. 5b–6a.

690 Hu Zongxian, *Chouhai tubian*,, *j.* 4, p. 26b.

Wan Biao tellingly observed: "The pirates carefully selected the places for looting. They looted Guanhai 觀海, but left Yuyao 餘姚 alone; they looted Ruian 瑞安, but skipped Leqing 樂清. Pirates never attacked merchant families."[691] In other words, the illict trade along the coast was far from simply a case of Japanese piracy. It was a complex and well-engineered smuggling network, with good coordination between people within and those from abroad. The failure of the government campaign was predicable.

The Military's Involvement in the Illicit Trade

The poverty-stricken coastal peasants and frustrated merchants, however, were not the most essential factor in counteracting the trade prohibition. It was the protests from the military that struck at the heart of the institution. Tang Shu noticed that the military showed great sympathy for both the devastated poor peasants and also for the merchants. Witnessing peoples' suffering weakened the military's sense of duty. Tang noted that "They were always in favour of abolishing the prohibition policy and they cared about the poor."[692] The military criticized the trade prohibition policy for causing great distress. Gao Gong observed, "They [the military] showed great commiseration for the coastal people and complained of the injustice of the policy for causing poverty. Meanwhile they denounced the rich and powerful for engaging in the protected illicit trade, taking advantage of the trade prohibition to monopolise trade and pocket great wealth. If the situation remains unchanged it will be impossible to stop people from becoming pirates and smugglers."[693] The military was under great stress, having to fight its own people. Zhu Wan noted that "The coastal people regard smugglers as their *yishi fumu* 衣食父母 (parents who provide food and clothes) but the coastguards as their enemy."[694] Therefore, the military tended to take every opportunity to protect and assist the local people.

Wang Zaijin asked the question: "An ocean-going ship is not something that can be finished in the dockyard in half a month, so how can the military not notice such a big ship in port? Why does the military not pursue them?"[695] The military always tried to avoid engagement with its own people. Tang Shunzhi reminded the court: "We always talk about defeating the enemy at sea but why have we never been able to do so? Our generals always try to avoid conflict at sea, and order the petty officers to engage the 'enemy', who in turn tend to take the opportunity to hide themselves in nearby ports instead of going out to the deep sea."[696] Similarly, Zhu Wan notes that "Even a little boy understands the state of affairs, in which the local people rely on smugglers for a living by providing them with cargo or guiding

691 Ibid., *j.* 11, p. 8a
692 *MJSWB*, vol. 270, *j.* 1, pp. 3b–4a.
693 "Yu Yin Shiting lun wo zei 與殷石汀論倭賊" (My Discussion with Yin Shiting over Japanese Pirates), in *MJSWB*, vol. 301, *j.* 2, p. 9a.
694 Zhu Wan, *Piyu zaji*, *j.* 8, p. 64a.
695 *Haifang cuanyao*, in *Siku jinhui* 史, fasc. 17, *j.* 8, p. 28b.
696 *MJSWB*, vol. 260, *j.* 2, pp. 2a–b.

them for trade. If smugglers are arrested they will be released immediately by the coastguarded on the excuse of their having been abducted and forced to engage in smuggling by the Japanese. The military provides the internal contacts for the smugglers."[697]

The military's compassion for the poor was also a result of its composition. The coastguards stationed in the fifty-nine garrisons from Denglai 登萊 in Shangdong to Zhejiang were all recruited from the local communities by a 'one-out-of-every-four' draft, while those who guarded the sixteen garrisons from Fujian to Guangdong were enlisted from the local regions by a 'one-out-of-every-three' rule.[698] The coastguard's families and relatives were the direct victims of the trade prohibition policy; hence their sympathy with the situation of their families and relatives drove them to render assistance to the so-called 'enemy'. Zhang Huan 章煥 (a Censor-in-Chief) remarked: "The foreign merchants come and leave without trace. Not a single soldier from the fortress wants to question them so that their little boat sails without obstruction. Our coastguards are supporting them."[699] Sun Chengze made a similar observation. "Our border is under close scrutiny. Nobody would be able to come and go without first informing the coastguards. Yet the military always avoid their opponents, only following them after their departure and pretending to shoot an arrow or two. The military are actually protecting them and helping them to escape. Is there any hope of getting rid of the smuggling and piracy?"[700]

The military itself suffered from the trade prohibition too. When the state's income fell below its expenditure level there were fewer resources to maintain the troops. The financial crisis forced the government to reduce its support for the military, and this had become a serious problem by the Jiajing years. In 1531, Li Chengxuan 李承勳 (*jinshi* 1493, Minister of War) reported to the emperor:

> Since the conversion of the army's income from kind to silver, our soldiers' pay has decreased by 40 per cent. Every *dan* of rice was paid for at a rate of 0.6 *tael* of silver, while the market price for a *dan* of rice fetched one *tael*. This indicates that our pay has decreased from one *dan* to 0.6 *dan*. And in a disastrous year when a *dan* of rice will cost as much as 3 *taels*, soldiers actually starve."[701]

Tang Shunzhi complained that because of this the military were not able to feed the troops properly: "The soldiers enlist in the military and risk their lives in battle for nothing but a small amount of rice. Yet we simply cannot honour such low payments. A month's delay in paying our troops on the southeast coast has been a problem."[702] Many soldiers did indeed die of starvation.[703] Tang Shunzhi also re-

697 Zhu Wan, *Piyu zaji*, *j.* 8, p. 64a.
698 *MJSWB*, vol. 218, *j.* 2, p. 7a. See also *Ming shi*, *j.* 322, p. 4b.
699 Hu Zongxian, *Couhai tubian*, in *Siku quanshu*, fasc. 584, *j.* 11, p. 5b.
700 *Chunming mengyu lu*, *j.* 42, p. 39a.
701 *Ming Shizong shilu*, *j.* 122, pp. 7b–8a.
702 *MJSWB*, vol. 260, *j.* 2, p. 7b.
703 *Ming Shizong shilu*, *j.* 122, p. 8a.

marked on the difficulty of solving this problem because of the overburdened taxpayers, noting that as there were no reserves, even a shortfall of ten *taels* would mean that one soldier would be without food and clothing for a year.[704] Tang also complained about the inability to collect the assigned taxes: "The military budgets for 160,000 *taels* of silver … but only 10,000–20,000 could actually be collected."[705] Li Lian 林燫 (*jinshi* 1547, Examining Editor) protested the unjustness of the military pay situation: "We often delay the pay for soldier's rewards for 5–6 years, or even ten years. Even after a soldier's death his wife and children are still not paid."[706]

Involvement in the lucrative smuggling trade became a handy way for the military to supplement its limited income. Luo Jinshi 羅禁時 (Investigating Censor and Grand Coordinator of Liaodong) told the court:

> Government officials and military officers are deeply involved in private trade with the Mongols in the garrison area of Guangning 廣寧, Kaiyuan 開元, and Fushun 撫順, as are officers in Datong 大同. They even smuggled prohibited goods to the Mongols … the situation prompted the government to punish those who traded illicit goods worth more than 200 *guan* in value.[707]

Zhu Wan said in his memorial: "Now the commanders of our garrison on the coast respect merchants who smuggle and treat them as their dear guests. Pirates publicly marry the local girls and openly invite an opera troupe to perform at the celebration. The Portuguese sold their cargoes and repaired their ships in the dock in broad daylight in Duanyuzhou 斷嶼州."[708] In order to improve the welfare of their soldiers many high-ranking officials allowed their men to engage in illicit trading. At the Datong garrison in May 1499, Zhao Xu 趙用昶 (Assistant Commissioner of the Regional Military Commission), Shen Ying 神英 (Regional Commander), Song Cheng 宋澄 (Commissioner-in-Chief), Li Jing 李敬 (Regional Military Commissioner), Sun Zhen 孫振 (a eunuch) and Liu Xian 先劉獻 (a Censor-in-Chief) were all accused of being involved in the illegal trade of iron-works and silk for horses, and for allowing the Mongols to come and go without question.[709] Hou Xianchun 侯先春 (*jinshi* 1580, Supervising Secretary of the Ministry of Personnel and Ministry of War) observed some of their operations: "Our officials assigned their men to purchase silk and silk cloth inland in Suzhou and Hangzhou to exchange for horses

704 *MJSWB*, vol. 260, *j.* 2, p. 8a.

705 *Chongkan jingchuan xiansheng wenji*, in *Sibu congkan*, *j.* 8, p. 54b.

706 "Chen yan bian tao shu," 陳言邊計疏 (A Memorial on Frontier Policy), in *Lin xueshi wenji* 林學士文集 (*Collected Works of Scholar Lin Lian, the Chancellor of the Hanlin Academy*) by Lin Lian 林燫 (*jinshi* 1547), in *MJSWB*, vol. 313, *j.* 1, p. 8a.

707 *Ming Xiaozong shilu*, *j.* 154, pp. 8a–b.

708 Zhu Wan, *Piyu zaji*, *j*, 2, p. 19a.

709 *Ming Shizong shilu*, *j.* 150, pp. 7a–8a.

with the 'barbarians'. The 'mismanaged' funds amount to as much as 4,000–5,000 *taels*. The actual magnitude of the trade can only be imagined."[710]

Whereas the troop's enthusiasm for smuggling was great, their fighting spirit was poor. Their sympathy toward the 'enemies' and their personal involvement in the operations that they were supposed to suppress meant that they were confused about their role and their identity. Wu Shilai 吳使來 (*jinshi* 1553, a Supervising Secretary of the Ministry of Justice) described the situation: "Our officials and the Mongols at Duoyansan 朵顏三 garrison are closely connected. Some of them are even related by marriage. There are thousands of Chinese who fled to the Mongols. The Datong garrison allowed the Mongols to come and go. They are in collaboration with them."[711] Wang Chonggu made this observation: "Our soldiers and officers are convinced that the best way to avoid conflict with the Mongols is to trade with them. This has been the case for a long time. Some officials have even assigned quotas to their subordinates to do business with Mongols … Those who insist on fighting the enemy are often regarded as outsiders and persecuted."[712] The relationship between the military and the smugglers on the border was far from that anticipated by the policymakers at court. Wu Shilai reported to the court that the soldiers on duty were not doing what they were supposed to do.[713] Similarly, Wan Biao did not see any enmity between the Ming military and the smugglers or pirates:

> Smugglers are left to do their business without any worry, as there is seldom any questioning at the check-points. Zhang Siwei 張四維 (Garrison Commander) kowtowed to Wang Zhi, the Huizhou merchant-turned- pirate king and demonstrated his admiration by presenting him with a red robe and a waist-belt dotted with jade. The commander became his subordinate. Upon getting his instructions he would rush to arrange the cargo for him … even law-abiding citizens sought a career in the illicit trade.[714]

This was a clear evidence of why it was not possible to maintain and enforce the trade prohibition. Lin Xiyuan sent a memorial to the court expressing his concern at the lack of a military ethos amongst troops stationed along the coast, noting that the main reason for this was their involvement in smuggling.[715] Similarly, Tu Zhonglü told the court that fishermen and salt workers along the coast would rather fight for the pirate faimilies than for the government.[716] The Grand Secretary Xu Jie 徐階

710 "An bian ershisi yishu 安邊二十四議疏" (A Memorial to Illustrate the Twenty-four Points on How to Achieve Frontier Security), in *Hou geijian zoushu* 侯给谏奏疏 (*The Memorials of Hou Xianchun, the Supervising Secretary*) by Hou Xianchun 侯先春 (1545–1611), in *MJSWB*, vol. 428, *j.* 1, pp. 12a–b.

711 "Ying zhao chen yan bian wu shu 應詔陳言邊務疏" (My Submission on Frontier Policy by the Order of the Emperor), in *Wuzhai wenji* 悟齋文集 (*Collected Literary Works of Wu Shilai, Hao Wuzhai*) by Wu Shilai 吳時來 (*jinshi* 1553), in *MJSWB*, vol. 385, *j.* 2, pp. 3a–b.

712 *MJSWB*, vol. 316, *j.* 1, pp. 11a-b. For similar comments from Gao Gong see *MJSWB*, vol. 301, *j.* 2, p. 9a.

713 *MJSWB*, vol. 385, *j.* 2, pp. 3a–b.

714 *Haikou yi*, in *Siku cunmu* 子, fasc. 31, pp. 2b–3a (no *juan*).

715 *MJSWB*, vol. 165, *j.* 4, p. 27b.

716 *MJSWB*, vol. 282, *j.* 1, p. 8a.

(*jinshi* 1523) was disappointed at the poor morale and lack of fighting spirit of the troops: "Soldiers are neither able to kill enemies at sea nor to guard their fortresses ashore … We have only 40–50 per cent of the required forces available but they are not only unable to combat the enemy but also unable to protect their own ships. Our war-ships are only there to facilitate the pirates."[717]

Worse still, whereas the soldiers showed little inclination to confront the enemies they were much more enthusiastic in finding ways to defy the authorities. Tang Shunzhi warned the government that the unjust trade prohibition policy and people's destitution would prompt its own people to turn against it:

> Nowadays the coastguards in Wusong 吴淞 and Dinghai 定海 behave like mutineers. They capture officials and blackmail administrators. People's characters seem to have changed. The Suzhou people are typically mild in disposition and gentle because of their local culture, but now they are actually fighting alongside the pirates, taking part in robbing the state granaries and breaking into jail to rescue prisoners. It looks like a rebellion[718]

The unpopularity of the trade prohibition and the low pay in the military made the coastguards a very unappealing occupation. The late Jiajing years witnessed a surge in desertion from the military. Wu Shilai reported that nearly half of the garrison soldiers had deserted and that this persisted despite increased penalties.[719] Ma Wensheng 馬文升 (*jinshi* 1451, Vice Censor-in-Chief and Grand Coordinator of Shaanxi) told the court:

> The defence situation went downhill when our officers and soldiers became engaged in private trade with the enemies, who obtained silk, ironworks, weapons and shields from our military personnel or their family members. Duty officials and soldiers were sometime paid to cooperate. That is why foreign powers do not obey our government's orders and launch attacks … if this is not stopped, people will follow suit one after another, and we will meet with a catastrophy.[720]

Inability to Maintain the Policy

Offending the conventional mainstream mentality, the pro-trade officials openly acknowledged the incapacity of the government and its inability to implement the trade prohibition by force. They broke the taboo by conceding the incompatibility between ambition and actuality, between the political agenda and the inability of the military to implement that agenda. They criticized the China-centered focus of the conservatives' arguments and their ignorant confidence in China's ability to hold sway over others – a view which was still quite influential. For instance, the conservative official Xu Zongjun 涂宗濬 (*jinshi* 1583, Minister of War) believed that the "barbarians fear our emperor as much as they fear Heaven, and they fear China as

717 "Fu wen guan suo 復問觀所" (Revisiting the issue of Observation Posts), in *Xu Wenzhen gong ji* by Xu Jie 徐階 (1503–1583), in *MJSWB*, vol. 245, *j.* 2, p. 24b.
718 Hu Zongxian, *Chouhai tubian*, *j.* 11, pp. 10b–11a.
719 *MJSWB*, vol. 385, *j.* 2, pp. 6b–7b.
720 *MJSWB*, vol. 62, *j.* 1, pp. 18b–19b.

much as they fear a tiger."[721] Similarly, Shen Yiguan 沈一贯 (*jinshi* 1568, Minister of Revenue and Grand Secretary) argued that the "Japanese pirates are just like mosquitos; what we need to do is just brush them away."[722] Hu Zongxian showed a similar confidence about the government's Mongol policy: "The Mongol's [territory] is so small, no bigger than one of our counties. Our empire contains everything in the world and is thousands of times bigger. Our emperor has the mandate from heaven. Such a humble one as Anta would be scared to death once our emperor makes a policy to deal with him; why are we worrying about this?"[723] The illusionary self-confidence behind such statements served to sanction the political ideal, and the prohibition on foreign trade and the institution of tribute missions were employed to maintain it. There was little ground for equal trade or diplomacy. Any proposals other than demanding tribute or war were regarded as "weakening the military, damaging the empire and encouraging the enemy.[724]

However, the deteriorating situation along the borders, with frequent crises and much conflict, encouraged some officials to question whether the exisiting policy should be maintained any longer. Wang Chonggu explained it to the emperor:

> Though we are the masters positioned at the center of the world and the barbarians are our subordinates on the peripheries, the Mongols are, however, special. They are too tough and powerful so we can never subjugate them … Although the Yongle emperor campaigned three times into the steppe and laid the foundation of security … they have remained a worry to our empire. It is their military operations that determinate our security situation.[725]

Pro-trade officials wished the court to become aware of the country's actual military potential and admit the strain on the empire in trying to conserve the current foreign policy. Qi Jiguang 戚繼光 (1528–1587, Commander-in-Chief of Fujian) was more frank about the circumstances: "For the last 200 years we have never even dared to have a field battle with the Mongols."[726] Zhang Ding 張鼎 (Director of the Ministry of Justice and Assistant Censor-in-Chief) conceded the struggle in continuing the war on the coast: "Zhejiang and Nan Zhili were assaulted by Japanese pirates in November. For the past six or seven years, many supreme commanders were replaced and our government has spent thousands of *taels* of silver on war preparations, but we have not seen one victory so far."[727] Tang Shu also got on the

721 "Yi gui qiu gong shu 夷酋求貢疏" (A Memorial about the Mongol Chieftain's Request to Pay Tribute), in *Tu sima beilu fenggong shimo shu* 涂司馬北虜封貢始末疏 (*Itemised Memorials about Title Conferring and Tribute Status Grants to the Mongols by Tu Zongjun, the Minister of War*) by Tu Zongjun 涂宗濬 (*jinshi* 1583), in *MJSWB*, vol. 450, *j.* 4, p. 12b.

722 "Lun wo gong shi bu ke xu shu 論倭貢市不可許疏" (A Memorial to Insist on Refusing Tribute-Trade with Japan), in *Shen jiaomen wenji* 沈蛟門文集 (*Collected Works of Shen Yiguan, Hao Jiaomen*) by Shen Yiguan (1531–1615), in *MJSWB*, vol. 435, *j.* 1, p. 1b.

723 *MJSWB*, vol. 266, *j.* 2, p. 2b.

724 *MJSWB*, vol. 293, *j.* 1, pp. 6a–b.

725 *MJSWB*, vol. 316, *j.* 1, pp. 21a–b.

726 *Guoque* 國榷 (*Annalistic Deliberations on State Affairs*) by Tai Qian 談遷 (1595–1658) annotated by Zhang Zongyang 張宗祥. (Beijing: Zhonghua shuju, 1958), vol. 4, p. 4143.

727 Ibid., p. 3984

conservatives' nerves: "We deployed 200,000 soldiers on the 2,000 *li* of coastline, and spent 500,000 *taels* annually but we could hardly defend the country, and we have to employ salt workers, monks and miners to carry out the fighting."[728] The pro-trade officials objectively analysed the weakness of the Ming military in order to convince the court to face up to reality.

Tan Lun highlighted the costs involved in stopping the Mongols' invasion. "We have less than 100,000 soldiers, half of whom are old and weak. They are stationed along a two thousand *li* border, while the Mongols can concentrate 100,000 cavalry to attack us at one point. We have no way of coping."[729] Wang Gong 萬恭 *(jinshi* 1544, Deputy Minister of War) made the same point: "We deploy 30,000 soldiers to defend a border of 800 *li* in length, while the enemy attacked our defences with 100,000 soldiers on horseback and targeted a very tiny section of no more than 10 *li* along the border to make a breakthrough. Once they gor through the defence line, their troops could no longer be stopped. They had five times more soldiers and twenty times more cavalry."[730] Zhang Siwei questioned the feasibility of both defensive and offensive strategies along the coast:

> The strategy to deal with the 'barbarians' is either defensive or offensive. However, we are unable to execute either of them … Our army is incapable of waging an offensive by fighting them at sea because the cunning enemy is able to hide out in remote islands, coming and going without trace … Defense is also extremely difficult … they come and attack us without any pattern along the thousands of miles of border, therefore defense cannot be effective either.[731]

In highlighting this, Zhang Siwei unveiled a controversial but long-denied fact, that China had never established a decent permanent naval force for maritime defence. Qian Wei reflected on the historical circumstances for this: "Piracy had never been a problem in the past, as Japanese tribute missions had been in operation from the Tang to the Song. China had met no enemies from the sea therefore there had never been a sophisticated defence system on the coast … We provided what they needed, so why would they go in for piracy?"[732]

Whereas the Mongols were too powerful to defeat, the pirates posed too new a threat for the Ming army to confront. In addition, as has been argued, the conflict was with opponents who were driven by legitimate grievances. Pro-trade officials

728 *MJSWB*, vol. 270, *j.* 1, p. 4b. See also Hu Zongxian, *Chouhai tubian*, *j.* 11, pp. 103b–105a.

729 "Shi shu 事疏" (A Memorial on Current Issues), in *Wan sima zouyi* 萬司馬奏議 (*Memorials for Court Debate by Wan Gong, the Minister of War*) by Tan Lun 譚綸 (1520–1577), in *MJSWB*, vol. 322, *j.* 1, p. 2b.

730 "Tiaochen sanguan tong bian deng shu 條陳三關通變等疏" (Memorials on Lifting of the Interdiction on Trade at the Three Strategic Passes) by Wan Gong 萬恭 (1515–1591), in MJSWB, vol. 352, *j.* 2, p. 7b.

731 "Fang yu wokou yi 防禦倭寇議" (A View on Guarding against Japanese Pirates), in *Tiaolutang ji* 條麓堂集 (*The Tiaolutang Collection*), in *Tiaolutang ji* 條麓堂集 (*Collected Works from my Study at the Foot of Tiaoshan Mountain*) by Zhang Siwei 張四維 (1526–1585), in *Siku xuxiu*, fasc. 1351, *j.* 9, pp. 19a–b.

732 *MJSWB*, vol. 214, *j.* 1, pp. 20b–21a.

argued that Ming foreign policy was established on a shaky footing and continued conflict was the result, yet legitimizing trade was ignored as a way of resolving this situation and bringing new power to the Chinese state. Though the Japanese were not militarily superior they proved themselves a formidable adversary. Mao Kun memorialized the court:

> We are facing two enemies: one of them is powerful [the Mongols], but the more difficult one is the Japanese pirates. Though the defence against the Mongols takes more than half of our military budget, fortunately the worst period for war with the Mongols is only from August to September, about 100 days, when their horses are strong and our harvest is ready. We can see the enemy's movements beforehand because there are no mountains and hills in between, [and thus] we can station troops for patrol. The defence against Japanese piracy is a different story. They come anytime, riding the tide along the three thousand *li* coastal border from Yangzhou to Wenzhou. When we deploy troops in the west, they will attack from the east; when we patrol the north, they harass the south. It is simply beyond our defence capability.[733]

The army's inability to cope with the challenge led the government to resort to some extreme tactics. Officials viewed these as shameful and incompatible with the dynasty's 'superior' status. For instance, Tu Zemin 涂澤民 (Censor-in-Chief in charge of military affairs), posted a reward of 1,000 *taels* of silver for anyone who could poison the food of those on board a pirate ship.[734] And instead of organising the troops to confront the pirates, the Imperial Commisioner Zhao Wenhua went to sacrifice at the altar of the Sea God.[735] These things indicate the extent of the helplessness of the government.

Moreover, Ming military competence was also badly offset by its engagement with its own people. Victimised by the trade prohibition policy, the local people created a united front with foreign smugglers, breaking the trade prohibition in order to make a living. The Censor-in-Chief Zhang Huan 章瑍 noted: "It is easier to discover the enemy if they are in the open but much more difficult to find them if our people hide them. They [the Japanese pirate-merchants] seemed to be well advised of government decisions, military deployment and travel information. When thousands of pirates suddenly appeared before us, we knew they were hiding amongst our people. It is a sign of rebellion."[736] Hu Zongxian described the detrimental situation: "It has become a common phenomenon that all local people are good citizens before the arrival of the Japanese pirate-merchants and then suddenly they turn themselves into collaborators, only to become normal citizens as soon as the Japanese depart."[737] Zhang Huan seemed to despair at this situation: "When the

---

733 *MJSWB*, vol. 256, *j.* 1, p.2a. See also *Tiaolu tangji*, *j.* 9, pp. 19a–b.

734 "Xing xun hai dao 行巡海道" (From the Inspection by the Coastal Patrol Circuit), in *Tu zhongcheng junwu jilu* 涂中丞軍務集錄 (*Collected Works on Military Affairs by Tu Zemin, the Grand Coordinator*) by Tu Zemin 涂澤民 (?–1569), in *MJSWB*, vol. 355, *j.* 3, pp. 21b–22a.

735 *Haifang cuanyao*, *j.* 3, p. 19b.

736 Hu Zongxian, *Chouhai tubian*, *j.* 11, pp. 5a–b.

737 Ibid., *j.*11, p. 5b.

military came to investigate the smugglers and pirates they were not welcomed by the locals. They tended to be misled and were provided with false information."[738] It was becoming impossible to maintain such a hated policy, especially with the collusion of the army and the local people. As Yuan Zhi 袁袠 (1502–1547) noted: "The pirates always attack in a small band of less than a thousand members, their boats are small, their weapons are inferior, their tactics awkward, and their logistics inefficient, yet they always defeat us."[739] The reality of this had long been denied. Hu Zongxian reminded the emperor that it was the time to review the situation: "We can defeat the Japanese with all our troops but we cannot defeat our own discontented people."[740] The pro-trade officials' argument was explicit: there was no way out of the many crises unless a revolutionary change in policy was undertaken.

---

738 Ibid., *j.* 11, pp. 5b–6a.

739 "Jiedao yi 詰盜議" (Remarks on the Interrogation of Pirates and Outlaws), in *Yuan Yongzhi ji* 袁永之集 (*Collected Works of Yuan Zhi, Zi Yongzhi*) by Yuan Zhi 袁袠 (1502–1547), in *MJSWB*, vol. 271, *j.* 1, pp. 7b–8a.

740 Hu Zongxian, *Chouhai tubian*, *j.* 11, p. 6b.

CHAPTER V

The Grand Policy Debate

Part Two: The Solution

The maintenance of the prohibition on trade had undoubtedly engendered the late Ming crises. By the late Jiajing years an unprecedented demand in the government for change was accelerating. The arguments from both camps had become louder and more strident. The Minister of War, Wan Gong (1515–1591), appealed to the emperor: "Your humble subject understands such a truth: the strings on a *se* 瑟 (harp) have to be adjusted from time to time in order to make good music, and by the same law a flawed policy should be adjusted in order to avoid its worsening impact."[741] Fu Yuanchu 傅元初, a Supervising Secretary, made a similar comment: "As for the maritime policy, we have to review it to see whether it is beneficial or detrimental. It is obvious that the on-going prohibition is giving rise to disaster whereas opening up trade will stop the turmoil."[742] Having failed to safeguard the country by military operations, more and more officials, including hard-line military officers, had become convinced by the power of the argument in favour of freeing up trade. Wang Shizhen noticed the transformation: "The old days have gone when the literati insisted on making peace with the barbarians by *heqin* 和親 (marrying a princess to the nomad chieftains) while the military officials stood firm on fighting … the military nowadays want to make peace with the enemy by allowing them to trade but lack the courage to speak out about it frankly."[743]

Mao Kun was one of many who questioned the rationality of following the old practice: "There have to be different reasons for each case of social turmoil and insurgency in history. Our authorities have to figure out the origin of the problem. Only by doing so can the government have the justification to implement a policy."[744] He implied that the government had been blindly following obsolete rules, ignoring the present situation. The late Jiajing years saw a transformation in official opinion about this changed situation. For instance, Hu Zongxian attached great importance to the need for flexibility rather than loyalty in appointing an official. Commenting on the appointment of the new Minister of War, he advised the emperor to pay particular attention to the candidate's adaptability.

> The post of Minister of War is vital during the wars with the Mongols in the north and the Japanese in the south. [The holder of] this office must be able to act according to circumstances; [he must possess] the ability to judge the circumstances as well as the trait of integration … as far as I know, we have had ministers who were obviously short of the ability to adopt timely changes even though they were indeed upright. This led to grave consequences … when the Mongols become as aggressive as they are today, we can no longer afford to appoint a dogmatic and pedantic literati official [who can only] cause more disasters.[745]

---

741 *MJSWB*, vol. 352, *j.* 2, pp. 7a–b.

742 Sun Chengze, *Chunming meng yu lu*, *j.* 42, p. 39b.

743 Wang Shizhen, *Wang Yanzhou wenji*, *j.* 4, p. 3a.

744 *MJSWB*, vol. 256, *j.* 1, p. 1b.

745 *MJSWB*, vol. 266, *j.* 2, pp. 3a–b.

Tang Shunzhi praised Weng Wanda as an extraordinary official who accomplished much for the dynasty in trying circumstances: "He is the kind of official who has the courage to memorialise the court with a timely suggestion to trade rather than fight the enemy."[746] This proposal, to consider the need to lift the prohibition on trade, which was proposed by all the pro-trade officials of the time, came to be seen as a cure-all that would alleviate the difficult situation for the country.

The Power of Trade

The pro-trade officials, equipped with a whole range of specific historical examples, railed against the trade prohibition policy. One of the examples they drew on was the superpower status of the empire during the Yongle 永樂 reign (r. 1403–1424) and its dramatic trade policy changes. It was a golden era of peace and prosperity, when there was a thriving international trade and when China was powerful in international affairs. When the Yongle emperor altered his father's injunction on prohibiting trade, he created a situation in which foreign powers submitted to Chinese authority rather than one in which they sought to intrude into the Chinese realm. The Yongle administration not only allowed the Japanese to break the once-every-ten-years rule for tribute trade but also permitted them to trade any commodity they liked. "The Japanese actually undertook tribute trade in every single year during the first three years of the Yongle reign."[747] They were even allowed to trade weapons on China's soil, which was strictly prohibited in the *Da Ming lü* (the Great Ming Code).[748] The pro-trade officials looked back nostalgically on the peaceful days of the Yongle era. One official noted that "there was seldom Japanese piracy during the years of the Yongle reign when trade was taking place,"[749] while another remarked that "foreigners could not wait to go ashore to do business as soon as they arrived; why would they intend to do illicit things?"[750] Tang Shu attributed the hundred years of peace following the Yongle reign to the open and enthusiastic breaching of the prohibition policy: "The century-long peace since the Tianshun reign [1457–1464] has resulted from the open violation of the maritime trade pro-

746 "Da Weng Dongya zongzhi 答翁東崖總制" (A Reply to Supreme Commander Weng Dongya), by Tang Shunzhi, *MJSWB*, vol. 260, *j.* 2, p. 16b.

747 Tan Qian, *Guoque*, in *Siku xuxiu*, fasc. 358–359: 1st year (1403), in *Siku xuxiu*, fasc. 358, p. 629; 2nd year of the reign (1404), in *Siku xuxiu*, fasc. 359, p. 8; 3rd year of the reign (1405), in *Siku xuxiu*, fasc. 359, p. 20.

748 Cao Renhu, *Qinding xu wenxian tongkao*, *j.* 26, p. 29b.

749 "Woyi rong liu panni jiujie ru kou shu 倭夷容留叛逆糾結入寇疏" (A Memorial about how the Japanese Barbarians Detain our Defectors and Gather them for Invasion), in *Wang sima zoushu* 王司馬奏疏 (*Personal Memorials by Wang Yu, Minister of War*) by Wang Yu 王忬 (1507–1560), *MJSWB*, vol. 283, *j.* 1, p. 31b.

750 "Zhe xunfu yi 浙巡撫議" (A View from the Grand Coordinator of Zhejiang), in *Hai Shi xiansheng wenji* 海石先生文集 (*The Collected Works of Mr Hai Shi*), in *Haishi xiansheng wenji* 海石先生文集 (*Collected Works of Qian Wei, Hao Haishi*) by Qian Wei 錢薇 (1502–1554), in *Siku cunmu* 集, fasc. 97, *j.* 10, pp. 20a–b.

hibition, when eunuchs were more influential in the Maritime Trade Supervisorate and private trade flourished."[751]

Along the northern frontier, people on both sides of the border benefited from the improved trade relations. Though the Yongle emperor himself led a few successful military campaigns into the steppe, he dispensed with his father's hostile attitude and used trade as a key policy to deal with the Mongols. From the first year of his administration he instructed that sentry posts be set up side by side with trade fairs. The emperor showed great concern that trade be open and above board in order to ensure its long-term maintenance. "The emperor ordered the commanders of the Fuyu garrison 福餘衛 to open trade fairs where there was grass and water to enable the Mongols to come for trade. The Mongols were excused from going to the capital to pay tribute because the weather was too hot for them. The Ming authorities also restrained their officials from interrupting the trade fairs."[752] Generating profit from this trade was never the government's top priority. The emperor forbade government departments from making extra profit by trading low quality tea for high quality Mongol horses.[753] What occupied the minds of the policymakers during the Yongle reign was the political function of trade, the way it helped in the maintenance of security along the borders of the empire. In the 4th year of the Yongle reign (1407) the Mongols were suffering from starvation and asked to trade horses for grain at the three garrisons [the Sanwei 三衛: i.e. Duoyan 朶顏, Fuyu 福餘 and Taining 泰宁]. Though trading cereals with the Mongols was a politically sensitive issue, the Yongle emperor not only immediately sanctioned the trade but he also ordered that the Mongols be paid twice as much as they asked for their horses.[754] Contrary to the predictions of conservative officials, such trade did not weaken the security of the empire. What did result, however, was conflict between the eastern and western Mongols, as they fought each other to gain favour with the Yongle court. The Ming government was the biggest beneficiary of this conflict.[755]

Trade Diminishes Conflict

The policy debate between the two factions in the administration focused on whether trade diminished conflict or made a state vulnerable to incursions from outside. The conservatives were distrustful of any non-military approach to dealing with those accustomed to looting. They believed that the only secure approach was to undermine the enemy's capacity for engaging in conflict and warfare. Trade was obviously not the right strategy to achieve this objective. Moreover, it was feared that trade would generate a negative impact, undermining the psychological attitude necessary to fortify the empire. Yang Jisheng advised the emperor of this:

751 *MJSWB*, vol. 270, *j.* 1, pp. 9a–b.
752 Cao Renhu, *Qinding xu wenxian tongkao*, *j.* 26, p. 30b.
753 Ibid., p. 31a.
754 Ibid., p. 31b.
755 Tan Qian, *Guoque*, in *Siku xuxiu*, fasc. 359, p. 188.

> Trade will lead to a belief that the hostilities have ended and military preparation is no longer necessary; it will mislead us into relying on trade as a way to bring about peace, which is bound to slacken our vigilance and undermine our military defences by compromising our military's fighting spirit and determination. And it may encourage our armed forces to depend on expedient factors for temporary security. But how will we then restore their fighting spirit in case of war? [756]

Zhang Shiche 張時徹 (*jinshi* 1523, Minister of War in Nanjing) criticized the proposal to free up trade for what he saw as a flawed understanding of what was necessary in order to reduce war tension.

> It is wrong to believe that our trade policy can stop pirates from attacking ... pirates do not fear death and want nothing but trade and money. It may be possible to stop them before they come to trade but we will be unable to curb them once trade has commenced. Thousands upon thousands of them would come; can we really trade with each and every one of them? ... If we allow a hundred of them to come we have to prepare a thousand troops to ensure security; if we allow a thousand to come we have to prepare ten thousand troops in case of emergency. Do we have the financial capacity to organise such a deployment? And trade is not an event which lasts only a few days or months. If trade persists will we be able to maintain the army in such a state forever?[757]

The conservatives opposed the proposals to free up trade on the grounds that this would water down the preparedness for war, both psychologically and institutionally.

The pro-trade camp, on the other hand, sought to disprove this allegation. They were convinced that trade would help pacify the enemies. The Mongols from the north, the Japanese from the east and the Portuguese from the south were propelled to China's borders for one purpose only: trade. Without understanding this fact there could be no basis for a better security policy. Wang Minghe 王鳴鶴 considered that trade would help curb the 'barbarians': "If we want to have good defences we have to stop the illegal collaboration between our people and foreigners, but if we want to stop this we have to establish official trade. The foreigners come with their ships loaded with cargo in order to make a profit. They would never dare to break our laws [if we granted them permission to trade]."[758] Similarly, Su You 蘇祐 (1492–1571, Surveillance Commissioner for Xuanfu and Datong, and Minister of War) was convinced that resolution of the conflict with the Mongols lay through the opening up of trade. He urged the government to consider the value of commercial relations:

> The Mongols have made great efforts to persuade us to set up trade fairs in the Xuanfu, Datong and Shanxi region so that they can trade their lamb, mules, cows and horses. I hereby ask our emperor to order the Ministry of War to investigate whether there are still invasions and lootings during the trading period ... If there are no invasions please meet and consider es-

756 *MJSWB*, vol. 293, *j.* 1, p. 3a.

757 Hu Zongxian, *Chouhai tubian*, *j.* 12, pp. 108b–109a.

758 "Fang wo 防倭" (Guarding Against Piracy), in *Xiyuan wenjian lu* by Zhang Xuan, *j.* 56, p. 5b.

> tablishing trade fairs there … Trade fairs will enable our government to establish good relations with each of the tribes and consolidate our commanding influence.[759]

The pro-trade officials discredited the old principles about defence and emphasized the role of a non-military means. For instance, Liu Tao argued that "appeasement through trade is still the best policy … [as] it can pacify the enemy, prevent our people from enduring the suffering that comes with war and spare us the casualties of war."[760] Pang Shangpeng believed trade would be a useful way of preventing the Portuguese from harassing the Chinese coastal regions: "How can the Portuguese dare to create unrest if they want trade? Our military should not obstruct them from admiring China; instead we should make them change their hostile attitude by treating them with even more favourable trade conditions ... business should be allowed to go on as before."[761] This claim was further substantiated by the special phenomenon in Guangdong: "When tribute trade was banned in Fujain and Zhejiang, Guangdong was the only region left open for tribute trade, which consequently became the only place immune from piracy. It is a strong proof."[762] Wang Chonggu declared: "They [Ming soldiers] have sought to engage in trade with the Mongols and sometimes cared little about their patrol duty … I intend to abolish all the sentry posts to save tens of thousands of *dan* in provisioning. Instead, I want to pay three *taels* of silver for each soldier and allow them to go deep into the steppe in order to trade, while still requiring them to provide us with information about the enemy."[763]

However, the conservatives' opposition to the opening of trade was based on seemly credible grounds: that trade might facilitate the military needs of the enemy. It was feared that trade was a process that would enhance the enemy at the expense of the Ming. Feng Zhang expressed such concerns in his memorial:

> There had never been gunpowder as such in the foreign lands until they got it from our merchants, who breached the trade prohibition and smuggled it across the borders. It was our merchants who taught them how to use the explosives. Now we meet the Portuguese who come with cannons, muskets and handguns ten times more powerful than ours. What we get from the trade is nothing but some cheap and useless things. Fortunately, thanks to the maritime prohibition, they have not yet got too much gunpowder. If we allow merchants to trade with them, it means that we are handing over our weapons to our opponents.[764]

759 "Jie bao yi qing shu 楼報夷情書" (A Statement upon Receiving a Report on the Situation with the Barbarians), in *Su sima zouyi* 蘇司馬奏議 (*Memorials of Su You, Minister of War*) by Su You 蘇祐 (1492–1571), in *MJSWB*, vol. 216, *j.* 1, pp. 9a–b.

760 *MJSWB*, vol. 308, *j.* 5, pp. 12b–13a.

761 *MJSWB*, vol. 357, *j.* 1, p. 10a (see editors' comments).

762 "Lun tongshi, riben bu, bianyi dian 论通市, 日本部, 边裔典", in *Gujin tushu jicheng* 古今图書集成 (Beijing: Zhonghua shuju, 1934, reprint of the Kangxi 康熙 edition), *j.* 40, p. 18a.

763 Wang Chonggu, "Jin tong lu zhuo bian shao yi cheng su wan shu 禁通虜酌邊哨以懲夙玩疏" (My Memorial on Forbidding Contact with the Mongols, Selecting Responsible Border Patrols and Punishing those who are Negligent), in *MJSWB*, vol. 316, *j.* 1, pp. 11b–14b.

764 *MJSWB*, vol. 280, *j.* 1, p. 18b (see editor's comments).

Conservative officials were thus fearful that trade would help oil the enemy's war machine. The export of saltpetre and lead always had them on high alert. Many memorials streamed into the court warning the emperor of the potentially catastrophic aftermath of such trade.[765] In a similar manner, the conservatives one after another sent memorials to the court to express their concern over the selling of iron cauldrons to the Mongols, as these could possibly be used to make weapons.[766] He Dongxu 何東序 (*jinshi* 1553, Prefect of Huizhou and Grand Coordinator of Yulin) credited the growing Mongol military power to the illicit trade with China: "Our people are greedy and care little about selling ironworks to the Mongols. For the last 20 years the Mongols have grown increasingly stronger and now they can march anywhere without meeting challengers."[767] Yang Jisheng could not hide his agitation: "Since the olden days the people from the Xuanda region have attempted to breach the trade prohibition but they were prevented by our policy. Now the abolition of the trade prohibition will legalise their trade and collaboration. The repercussions could be disastrous."[768]

The conservative's anxieties were unfounded. Wang Chonggu called such attitudes bigotry and a misreading of the true situation. He refuted the claims that the Mongols wanted to smelt the iron pots they purchased to make weapons: "Iron cooking pots are a necessity for daily life. Whenever they loot a city they rush to get them as the most treasured booty … our officials now feel concerned about them possibly recasting these ironworks into weapons; how ridiculous this is! Everybody understands that the Mongols know nothing about metallurgy. They hold cooking pots so dear that they will rush to mend them once broken."[769] Wang Chonggu also consolidated his argument in a technological way.

> The Mongols have no metallurgical industries, thus they cannot manufacture cooking utensils themselves … besides, the very commodities we trade with the Mongols in Jilaio 薊遼 are cauldrons from Guangdong, which are very light and not good for recasting. An experiment reveals that only five *jin* of iron can be obtained from a 10 *jin* smelted piece of cooking pot. Moreover, the cauldrons from Shaanxi, which are the main commodity we trade in Datong and Xuanfu, are even poorer. Only three *jin* can be acquired from a 10 *jin* cauldron … It is impossible for the Mongols who cherish the cauldrons so much to melt them down ... The shortage of enough cooking utensils forces them to share one cooking pot amongst many families.[770]

Regarding the maritime prohibition policy, Xu Fuyuan found fault with the concern that trading with the Japanese would help them enhance their arsenal. "We are not

765 *MJSWB*, vol. 400, *j.* 1, p. 6a.

766 *MJSWB*, vol. 316, *j.* 2, p. 23b.

767 "Tao lu shu kuan qiu gong shu 套虜輸款求貢疏" (A Memorial about the Request by the Ordos Mongols to Pay Tribute and Trade), in *He zhongcheng jiuyu shanfang ji* 何中丞九愚山房集 (*The Collected Works of He Dongxu, the Censor*) by He Dongxu 何東序 (*jinshi* 1553), in *MJSWB*, vol. 382, *j.* 1, p. 10a.

768 Yang Jisheng, *Yang Jiaoshan ji*, in *MJSWB*, vol. 293, *j.* 1, p. 13a.

769 *MJSWB*, vol. 316, *j.* 2, p. 23b.

770 Ibid., *j.* 3, pp. 7a–b.

the only source of lead and saltpetre for the Japanese. The Portuguese are the biggest middleman in Guangdong dealing with smuggled goods ... the smugglers travel widely overseas. Cambodia is abundant with the products and so is Thailand. The Japanese also dispatch ships to get the goods to Vietnam and Luzon where we have no control whatsoever."[771]

The strained social relations and political unrest on the coast became a serious challenge to the government. The pro-trade officials blamed the trade prohibition policy for making two social groups suffer, prompting them to become destabilising factors. They were the landless coastal people, whose lifeline was cut off, and the frustrated merchants whose business was blocked. Whereas the conservatives regarded them as enemy, the pro-trade group held that their grievances had to be redressed. Among all the possible options, allowing them to trade was the most efficient solution. Many pro-trade officials submitted memorials about this. For instance, Xu Fuyuan told the court:

> People searching for a means to make their living are pressing on with a forceful momentum, like water flowing to the valley. It is impossible to stop them ... we should strictly prohibit them from trading forbidden goods while we have to encourage a lawful trade ... the trade prohibition is rather unfeasible when the common people want to make a living, which we should never obstruct. It is better to open up trade and have it controlled by the authorities. If it is done in the right way these smugglers and pirates will disappear. I am told by the older generations that trade will turn pirates into merchants while the prohibition will turn merchants into pirates. It is manageable when dealing with merchants, but much harder in dealing with pirates.[772]

Zhang Lian 张濂, a retired official in Hangzhou, sent a memorial to stress the importance of lifting the maritime prohibition.

> I am a native of Hangzhou and have spent five years here in retirement. I have witnessed the deteriorating process of piracy and become clear about its cause ... the government should restore maritime trade to demobilise the followers of the pirates ... and trade will provide a way for the poor to make a living, which will restrain them from becoming desperados.[773]

Similarly, Tang Shu argued that trade was the pivotal institution to get the dissenting people back on the right track: "We have great numbers of people making their living on the sea, drifting wherever they can go fishing and collecting. The prohibition policy has unsettled them. So long as they have a chance to work for the merchants they will be engaged in trade and settle down."[774]

There was no shortage of memorials that spoke for the distressed merchants. Those who submitted these memorials argued that lifting the maritime prohibition would turn these people from outlaws into legal merchants. When the Ming products became more profitable through ever-increasing overseas demand, the maritime interdiction was condemned for contributing to more and more antagonism

771 *MJSWB*, vol. 400, *j.* 1, pp. 6a–b.
772 Ibid., *j.* 1, pp. 4b–5b.
773 Gu Yingtai, *Mingshi jishi benmo, j.* 55, pp. 18a–19b.
774 *MJSWB*, vol. 270, *j.* 1, p. 5a.

amongst China's own merchants. Song Yiwang pointed out the destructive consequences when the government attempted to control the uncontrollable: "The desire for wealth is uncontrollable, even in an intimate relationship between father and son … The rewards from doing business with Japan are too tempting for both the Japanese and our own people. Collaboration with foreigners for illicit trade cannot be prevented."[775] Wan Biao unveiled the partnership between the local people and the foreign pirate-merchants.

> Our people from Suzhou and Hangzhou are engaged in smuggling. They voluntarily provide the illicit merchants with wine and food. They also send their children on board pirate ships to work for them … People from Hangzhou have made a fortune by harbouring pirate cargoes and supplying them with copper coins to make gun-barrels, lead to make bullets, saltpetre to make gunpowder, iron to make knives, leather to make shields and grain, cooking oil, linen and wine for their daily use.[776]

Others noted how merchants, peddlers and shop owners on the coast could easily make big money through a quick exchange of goods. A small investment could generate considerable profit, thus the temptations were great.[777] Tang Shu emphasized that trade was the key factor in resolving these issues: "Relieving social grievances will result from an improved maritime trade policy. Trade activities can engage all, rich and poor, and quench the aspiration for discord."[778]

Trade as a Source of Strength vis-à-vis Foreign Powers

Without the ability to dominate militarily, trade became the greatest political asset for the administration to safeguard its interests and security. The increase in border conflicts and domestic problems during the early sixteenth century shattered the illusion that the prohibition on trade, in conjunction with the tribute mission system, would guarantee security. The pro-trade camp pointed out that a good foreign trade policy would end all the humiliation, and return the dynasty to its golden days of privilege and domination. Yang Yiqing emphasized the importance of the tea trade for national security: "The tea trade with the 'barbarians' will enable us to control and deter them, because they will get sick and die without tea. Trade is more powerful than tens of thousands of armed soldiers."[779] According to such arguments, trade was a source of power, the means to overpower the Ming government's two main adversaries, the Mongols and the Japanese.

---

775 *MJSWB*, vol. 362, *j.* 1, p. 3a.

776 Hu Zongxian, *Chouhai tubian*, *j.* 11, p. 8a.

777 Zhen Lüchun, *Zheng Jiangong nianpu*, in *Siku cunmu* 史, fasc. 83, *j.* 4, p. 6a.

778 *MJSWB*, vol. 270, *j.* 1, p. 5a. .

779 "Wei xiu fu cai-ma jiuzhi yi fuyu fanyi anqing defang shi 為修復茶馬舊制以撫馭番夷安靖地方事" (My View on Re-establishing the Old Tea and Horse Trade System to Control the Barbarians and Secure Local Stability), in *Yang Shicong wenji* 楊石淙文集 (*Collected Literary Works of Yang Yiqing, Named After his Birth Place – Shicong*) by Yang Yiqing 楊一清 (1454–1530), in *MJSWB*, vol. 115, *j.* 2, p. 2b.

Li Hualong 李化龍 (*jinshi* 1574, Assistant Censor-in-Chief and Grand Coordinator of Liaodong) understood from personal experience the power of trade over the Mongols. "The Mongols attach primary importance to trade. Once they are involved in trade they will not loot. If they are engaged in trade today there won't be any looting. Whenever there is trade there is no fighting; wherever there is trade there is no pillaging."[780] His analysis also supported his assertion about the security situation in Kaiyuan 開原:

> Kaiyuan is at the extremity of our empire, surrounded on three sides by barbarians who are poor and militant. It is the most vulnerable place to defend … The horse trade became an institution for us to control the Mongols. The horse fair is the place where the Mongols can get what they need, hence they regard it as a source of wealth. Since they gain less from looting than that from trade, the Mongols are always afraid of losing trade. Kaiyuan is a different place from others. We can control the enemy by trade and still enjoy peace without military operations.[781]

He Dongxu reported to the emperor on the immediate repercussion of resuming the trade agreement with the Mongols. The Mongol *Jinong* 濟農 (also 吉囊), or Viceroy, promised to follow Anta and pay tribute: "It is the will of God when the Chinese and the Mongols are at peace, like those in the same family … and we will follow Anta to send all abducted people back to the Ming."[782] On the Chinese side, Zhang Siwei firmly believed in the power of trade, telling his uncle, the Supreme Commander Wang Chonggu: "Since establishing the tribute trade the Mongols have not harassed us, and the Mongol chief has abided by his promises. He strictly holds his men back from attacking us. I ask you, my uncle, to strictly order our soldiers not to lose their trust just for some trivial interest."[783] Similarly, He Dongxu was impressed by the quick impact that permission to trade had on the Mongols, reporting to the court: "After the tribute and trade endorsement, Jinong and his tribesmen finally settled down in different regions, which were managed by the respective regional leaders, and the Jinong forbade them from robbing Chinese. He is to punish anyone violating the rule by fining the perpetrator a horse, a cow and a lamb. Any Mongol who kills a Chinese has to pay with his own life."[784]

The power of trade over the Japanese was as significant as that over the Mongols. The 36th year of the Jiajing reign (1557) saw the security situation along the coast become very serious. A big pirate fleet, with some 2,000 military men on board each of the colossal ships, approached the coast of China. When their peti-

---

780 "Yi Yizhou mushi shu 議義州木市疏" (A Memorial about the Yizhou Timber Fair) by Li Hualong 李化龍 (1554–1611), in *MJSWB*, vol. 422, *j.* 1, p. 19b.

781 Ibid., *j.* 1, pp. 13a–b.

782 *MJSWB*, vol. 382, *j.* 1, pp. 7a–b.

783 "Yu Wang Jianchuan lun fenggong 輿王鑑川論封貢" (A Consultation with Wang Jianchuan about the Title and Tribute Status Conferred on the Mongols), in *Zhang Fengpan ji* 张鳳盤集 (*Collected Works of Zhang Siwei, Hao Fengpan*) by Zhang Siwei 張四維 (1526–1585), *MJSWB*, vol. 373, *j.* 1, p. 8b.

784 *MJSWB*, vol. 382, *j.* 1, p. 8b.

tion for the uplifting of the trade prohibition was declined, a 100,000 strong force, including an army led by most either two, but most probably four Japanese, namely Montarō 門多郎, Jirō 次郎, Yosuke 四助 and Shirō 四郎[785], looted Songjiang 松江 and Jiaxing 嘉興, and threatened to take Hangzhou and Nanjing. The government forces were too weak to check them. The pirate leader Wang Zhi made the point crystal clear that all that was required to prevent this occurring was the lifting of the maritime prohibition. And he promised to clear the sea of piracy once permission to trade was granted.[786] Qian Wei was convinced that this was the case: "The best policy to control foreigners lies in how we understand their needs … in this way the turmoil on the border will consequently disappear."[787] Xu Guangqi reinforced this point: "Only by trade can we pacify the Japanese … the Japanese need our products so they make great efforts to gain permission to trade, which grants us leverage to control them. If we institute a tribute trade system the Japanese will follow our orders and peace can be obtained."[788]

Tang Shu was one of those who emphasized the virtues of the pirate leader Wang Zhi, noting that he was a "great leader; the Japanese worship him and our own merchants rely on him for their living. In order to prove his loyalty to the court, he captured and executed Chen Sipan 陳思泮, a real pirate."[789] Hu Zongxian had tested Wang Zhi's loyalty by ordering him to capture another pirate, Ye Zongman 葉宗满, and to combat the pirates in Zhoushan 舟山. Hu noted that Wang Zhi did a great job.[790] Tang Shu was also convinced about Wang Zhi's influence in Japan:

> I am sure he can dominate the Japanese who are from various islands … the Japanese authorities are too weak to control the scattered archipelago. The Japanese rely on trade but this is controlled by our own people, as the Japanese themselves do not build ships, most of which are built in Fujian and Guangdong. We have a Chinatown in Japan and Chinese goods always get ashore first, from where the goods are traded to the rest of the islands. The Japanese are loyal to Wang Zhi.[791]

Tang argued that it was important to grant Wang Zhi's petition for trade, noting that the economic benefits of this would be far-reaching:

785 In China, this group of Japanese is mostly considered to have consisted of two persons, Montarō Jirō 門多郎次郎 and Yosuke Shirō 四助四郎. Cf. for example Wang Gang 王鋼, *Xu Wei* 徐渭. (Taibei: Zhishufang chubanshe, 1993), p. 113. Most probably, however, they were rather four than two persons. I am very grateful to Dr. Oláh Csaba who provided me with this information and with his thoughts about the identity of these Japanese. The famous pirat Wang Zhi 汪直 (?– 1559) is said to have enticed these pirates from the Gōtō Islands to China (傾貲勾引倭奴、門多郎次郎四助四郎等、為之部落, see *Chouhai tubian*, *j.* 9).

786 *Haikou yi*, pp. 1b, 2a, and 5a (no *juan*). See also *MJSWB*, vol. 270, *j.* 1, p. 7a.

787 MJSWB, vol. 214, *j.* 1, p. 24b.

788 *MJSWB*, vol. 491, *j.* 1, pp. 44b–45b.

789 *MJSWB*, vol. 270, *j.* 1, p. 7a.

790 Hu Zongxian, *Chouhai tubian*, *j.* 9, p. 33b.

791 *MJSWB*, vol. 270, *j.* 1, pp. 5b–6a.

> We have not had an effective policy to check piracy for the past four to five years, and it has exhausted the state revenue. Wang Zhi is now voluntarily requesting to organise an army from Japan to clear piracy and restore the political stability at sea. It is critical to restore normal economic life in the south-eastern part of the country as this is where the main source of our revenue is generated. It will no doubt serve our biggest interest.[792]

Through memorials such as these, it became more and more obvious that the stereotype opinion of 'barbarians' was wrong. The lack of understanding of foreigners and their needs was one of the pretexts for the failure of the prohibition on trade. Mao Yuanyi argued that the trade prohibition policy was a failure because it was against people's will, both Chinese and foreigners:

> Heaven cannot operate against the desires of humanity and an emperor cannot manage a country by ignoring the desires of its people. Though the products from Japan, such as knives and paper-fans, are not important to us, our silk, needles and porcelain provide the necessities of life [for the Japanese]. The prohibition on trade induces looting and smuggling ... Why do not we satisfy their needs by allowing them to trade while putting them under supervision and imposing a 10 per cent custom duty on it?[793]

Others argued that it was unreasonable to believe that prohibition on trade would prevent the pirates from coming. The prohibition did not mean that people could not sail abroad, or that the Japanese would no longer use Chinese silks, cottons, porcelain and medicine.[794] Tang Shu suggested that, in fact, "The more the prohibition is strengthened, the more rampant that piracy will grow ... It is easier to manage merchants than fight pirates; it is easier to manage people by meeting their desire for trade than going against their will and force them into smuggling and looting. We should not intentionally make trouble for ourselves."[795] Similarly, Xu Guangqi argued that "if our officials can realise this reality and reform the old policy, [if they can] understand our needs but also those of the other parties, [if they can] fight pirates but not merchants and prohibit smuggling while allowing the official trade, then the sea will be made peaceful without the need to shoot a single bow or harm anybody."[796] Xu was convinced that the Japanese would abide by Chinese regulations only when their desire for trade was satisfied: "The Japanese want nothing but trade from us ... they want our products but are unable to get them. [If] we open up trade with them and they know that they can get what they want ... [then] peace will be guaranteed.'[797]

792 Ibid., *j.* 1, p. 3a.
793 Mao Yuanyi, *Wubei zhi*, *j.* 230, pp. 12b–13b.
794 *Gujin tushu jicheng*, *j.* 40, p. 18a.
795 *MJSWB*, vol. 270, *j.* 1, p.4a.
796 *MJSWB*, vol. 491, *j.* 1, p. 31a.
797 Ibid., *j.* 1, p. 44.

Trade as a Means to Restore a China-Centred World Order

The mentality of the China-centred world order was shared by most Ming officials, reaching across factional lines. It was a way of understanding the world that provided a sense of identity as well as psychological comfort.[798] But the officials were divided over how to maintain such a desired status. And when the conservatives' policies, focused on moral conviction and military campaigns, had failed to conserve the designed political landscape, the pro-trade officials gained the opportunity to advance a new approach. Crisis legitimised different approaches.

The pro-trade officials contended that China's dominance in international relations in the past had been gained neither by superior moral conviction nor powerful military operations. On the contrary, the era when the China-centred world order was well preserved was the period when China was most actively engaged in international trade. Li Sancai 李三才 (*jinshi*, 1574) pointed this out, arguing that China must rely on trade.[799] Pro-trade officials invoked historical precedent to argue that a trade-orientated foreign policy generated enormous political benefits. The 21st year of the Yongle reign (1423) witnessed the arrival of 1,200 foreign envoys from sixteen countries, all of whom came to the Forbidden City to pay tribute and conduct trade.[800] The political impact of the Yongle maritime policy was equally significant. Tu Zhonglü noted that "the new trade policy made the Yongle emperor so powerful that he simply issued decrees to the Japanese government to follow. When a few groups of Japanese pirates were found harassing the Zhejiang coast, the Yongle emperor instructed the Japanese government to deal with them. The Japanese government captured twenty Japanese pirates immediately and extradited them to the court for execution. The emperor ordered the prisoners to be sent back to Japan for punishment. The Japanese mission did not hesitate to put the prisoners to death.[801] The following year the Japanese waged war on pirates in the Tsushima Strait 對馬 (基岐) and the Yongle emperor rewarded the Japanese ruler with the title of *Shou'an zhenguo zhi shan* 壽安鎮國之山 (The mountain that fortifies the kingdom).[802] The Yongle administration attached great importance to the role of trade in politics. The emperor himself is reported as emphasising this: "It is not because we need their horses but because we must trade with them because everything they need comes from China. Therefore, the prohibition on trade will result in their hatred, while allowing them to trade will show that we care and will help win their obedience."[803] When representatives from Brunei and Malacca came

---

798 For a collection of papers that explore these issues, see John K. Fairbank (ed.), *The Chinese World Order: Traditional China's Foreign Relations.* (Cambridge, Mass.: Harvard University Press, 1968).

799 *Zuiwei lu* 罪惟錄 (*A Record of the Contemplation of Crimes*) by Cha Jizuo 查繼佐 (1601–1676), in *Siku xuxiu*, fasc. 323, *liezhuan* 13, *xia*, p. 46b.

800 Tan Qian, *Guoque*, p. 188.

801 Hu Zongxian, *Chouhai tubian*, *j.* 12, p. 90a.

802 Tan Qian, *Guoque*, pp. 20 and 22.

803 Cao Renhu, *Qinding xu wenxian tongkao*, *j.* 26, p. 31a.

to trade spices, the customs officials requested that the court allow the department to charge duties, but this was refused. The imperial response indicated why: "How much can we get from the customs duties? Is it not better not to set obstacles in the way of foreigners who wish to show their admiration for our country?"[804] This openness to trade relieved the empire from the stress of conflict with foreign powers and created a supportive international context. This enabled the Yongle administration to pursue consolidation of the state and social and economic development, which underlay the great maritime expeditions led by Zheng He.

Looking back beyond the Ming, into the more distant past, the pro-trade officials maintained that commerce had played an important role in international politics. The Song dynasty provided a clear illustration of this. Wang Shizhen contrasted the power of military muscle with that of trade during the two Song eras.

> During the Taizong 太宗 reign (976–997), the Song dynasty suffered constant harassment from the Qidan nomads, and the emperor was even taken prisoner. Ironically, this was at the very time when the Song was more powerful militarily than the Qidan. However, during the Zhenzong 真宗 reign (998–1022), when the Song was militarily feeble and the Qidan much stronger, the Song enjoyed peace and prosperity. This was because of the availability of commodities obtained through the tribute agreement, which cost the Song no more than a prefecture's revenue. The emperor, the officials from the north and the south, and the people from both sides were happy about the peace that was guaranteed by the frequent visits of the envoys.[805]

He Qiaoyuan 何喬遠 (*jinshi* 1586, Deputy Minister of Works in Nanjing) related international trade to political stability during the Southern Song: "Since ancient times there has always been trade between China and foreign countries, among which the Song enjoyed the most prosperous time. The peace agreement produced three *boyi* 博易 (trade fairs) yearly and generated an annual revenue amounting to a million strings (*min*) of copper coins."[806] Qian Wei noted that this was the same for the situation along the coast. He noted that the reason why piracy had never been as ruinous as during the Jiajing years was that trade had always worked to neutralise conflict.

> China maintained a successful tribute trade during the Song era and enjoyed a prosperous private trade during the Yuan period when the official tribute trade was abolished. There had been no troubles for hundreds of years in foreign relations. Though the Hongwu Emperor occasionally exterminated the Japanese tribute missions, he still allowed them to trade.[807]

But the Jiajing years witnessed the disastrous days when the trade prohibition was intensified. With the empire in such distress, the late Ming administrators looked

---

804 Ibid., *j.* 26, p. 30a.

805 *MJSWB*, vol. 332, *j.* 4, p. 3b.

806 "Haishang shibo si 海上市舶司" (The Maritime Trade Supervisorates) by He Qiaoyuan 何喬遠 (*jinshi* 1586), *Yehuo bian* 野獲編 (*Unofficial Anecdotes by a Retired Scholars*) edited by Shen Defu 沈德符 (1578–1642), in *Siku jinnhui* 史, fasc. 4, *j.* 12, pp. 19b–20a.

807 *MJSWB*, vol. 491, *j.* 4, pp. 29b–30a.

back nostalgically on more prosperous and peaceful periods in the past further justified their dispute over the prevailing policy.

The pro-trade officials tried to rectify a misconception that the 'barbarian' was a disturbing factor in maintaining the China-centred world order. He Qiaoyuan observed: "Our emperor is the master of the world so that every other nation respects us and becomes obedient; only the Mongols and Japanese still cause trouble and pose a threat to us."[808] He was wrong. In fact, the so-called enemies, the Mongols and the Japanese, were active participants in the system and showed no objection to China's world order. It was not the Mongols or Japanese themselves but rather the Ming trade prohibition policy that barred them from joining the system. Many officials argued that the government paid too high a price for trying to keep the Mongol and Japanese at bay. Weng Wanda observed the difference between before the termination of the tribute relationship and after: "The situation deteriorated only after the tribute trade mission was abolished following the battle of Yutailing 虞臺嶺 at Xuanfu [in 1499], where we lost our whole army. Then the Mongols became aggressive and uncontrollable. There were no tribute missions, and the border regions were subject to invasion and pillage. Our people have suffered for the last forty years as a consequence."[809]

Such a dramatic change also took place on the coast. The Japanese began to kill people, loot property and burn houses after the tribute relationship was ended in the second year of the Jiajing reign (1522).[810] What justified the pro-trade officials' protest was the government's deliberate refusal to use trade to defuse war. Wang Chonggu argued: "It was the Mongols who came to beg to stop the conflict and asked to trade textiles and iron cauldrons. We need to trade with them in order to maintain peace."[811] By the time the Mongols invaded Beijing in the 29th year (1550) they had already begged for tribute and trade in the 20th (1541), the 26th (1547) and the 27th (1548) years of the Jiajing reign.[812] Until the time when the Japanese looted Ningbo in the 27th year (1548), they had already begged for tribute in the 23rd (1544), the 25th (1546) and the 26th (1547) years of the Jiajing reign, but again in vain.[813] Moreover, both the Mongols and the Japanese were prepared to sacrifice anything in order to gain permission to trade. The Mongols promised to retreat from Beijing and the Japanese to retreat from Korea and the Ryūkyū Islands.[814] Unfortunately, the conservative-dominated government failed to realise the enemies' willingness to participate in the Chinese world order; instead, the government organised military

808 Zhang Xuan, *Xiyuan wenjian lu*, *j.* 56, p. 2a.
809 *MJSWB*, vol. 224, *j.* 2, p. 7b.
810 Gu Yingtai, *Mingmo jishi benmo*, *j.* 55, p. 8b.
811 *MJSWB*, vol. 316, *j.* 1, p. 23b.
812 Shen Yue, *Huang Ming Jia-Long liangchao jianwen ji*, *j.* 6, pp. 32b and 34a, *j.* 7, p. 44a. See also Gu Yingtai, *Mingmo jishi benmo*, *j.* 60, pp. 6b & 7b.
813 Zhu Wan, *Piyu zaji*, *j.* 2, pp. 37a–38a.
814 Gu Yingtai, *Mingmo jishi benmo*, *j.* 62, p. 11a.

campaigns to keep them away. The subsequent exhaustion of human and material resources brought about more invasion, looting, pirating and smuggling.

Foreign trade, the pro-trade officials advocated, was an efficient institution that would imbue the government with the power of control over these foreigners. It was a power that could make the military redundant. The senior Grand Secretary Yan Song was convinced that trade access would provide the Ming administration with the coercive capacity to control the Japanese.

> We stick to our principle that we never have a tribute relationship with any country which does not maintain *li* 禮 (rites) ... It has been seventeen years since the *Zong She* 宗設 (Sōsetsu) incident (1523)[815] for which our emperor ordered the termination of the tribute trade relationship with Japan ... now that they come to ask to pay tribute, we have no justification to decline them. Our principle guides us to punish those who do not submit to us, but declining their request for tribute is not a proper way of controlling them ... We should include anyone who joins in the tribute community and exclude only those who are against our rule.[816]

Gao Gong stressed the importance of a demonstration of political obedience before the granting of permission to trade: "We do not trade with those who do not pay tribute."[817] For Gao, political submission through the observance of proper ceremonial ritual was the prerequisite for permission to trade, yet he admitted that it was the permission to trade that would have most influence.

> We can never control the barbarians with morality and regulations. Our power lies in satisfying their needs ... they came to beg for trade in the 19th year of the reign (1540) but our officials on the border did not understand their desire for trade. Instead, our military executed their diplomat, which dragged us into a miserable thirty year-long war ... Heaven grants us the leverage to control the 'barbarians' and we should use it properly ... We should use it to maintain our privileged status, to prevent destructive wars and save unnecessary military spending.[818]

Foreign powers were actually in a weak position as they could not survive without the Ming commodities. Trade was actually an ideal vehicle to maintain the Chinese world order and guarantee peace.

---

815 On the Ningbo incident, cf. Olàh Csaba, „Debatten über den japanischen Tribut nach dem Zwischenfall in Ningbo (1523) und der chinesische Umgang mit der ersten darauf folgenden japanischen Gesandtschaft (1539–40)", in Angela Schottenhammer (ed.), *The East Asian Maritime World 1400–1800: Its Fabrics of Power and Dynamics of Exchanges*. (Wiesbaden: Otto Harrassowitz, 2007), pp. 169–218; „Problémák, incidensek a hivatalos japán-kínai kapcsolatok történetében a 15–16. században – a ningbói incidens (1523) és annak hatásai a kínai tengervédelmi politikára", *Függőkert. Orientalisztikai Tanulmányok 2*. (Piliscsaba: Mondat Kft., 2005), pp. 9–50.

816 *MJSWB*, vol. 219, *j.* 1, pp. 30b–31b. Sōsetsu was leader of a Japanese tribute mission to the Ming from the feudal Japanese Ouchi family (*daimyō*).

817 "Yu Wang Jiachuan lun lao badu si hou shiyi 與王鑑川論老把都死后事宜" (A Discussion with Wang Jianchuan about the Aftermath of the Senior Batu's Death), in *Gao wenxiang gong wenji* 高文襄公文集 (*The Collected Works of the Honourable Gao Wenxiang*) by Gao Gong 高拱 (*jinshi* 1542), in *MJSWB*, vol. 302, *j.* 2, p. 3b.

818 *MJSWB*, vol. 301, *j.* 1, pp. 1b–2b.

The Ming rulers had every reason to enjoy the privilege that came with a tribute relationship. Shi Dao conveyed this to the emperor: "It is the most significant event for the Son of Heaven to have 'barbarians' come to ask for tribute status and to be able to trade with us."[819] Similarly, Gao Gong notes: "The world works in this way: we have the power over those who beg [tribute status] from us. If we begged others we would hand the power to them … when the Mongols come to beg us, we have the power to administer them … our power originates from their fear of losing the opportunity for trade."[820] Wang Zaijin also remarked on the power of trade to generate submission from foreigners: "The barbarians admire China in the same way as we admire Paradise (*shizhou sandao* 十州三岛); they admire our products as we admire the stores of the Tang dynasty *Xialin daying* 夏林大盈 (the state warehouse). As long as there are sea routes and sailing guides available they will come to China to get our products."[821] It was the commercial dependency of foreigners that encouraged them to show political submission. Xu Guangqi noted that the Japanese 'invasion' was motivated neither by political or commercial reasons, but rather by their instinct of survival:

> They were crying out for a guaranteed avenue for trade in order to obtain the necessities for life. The trade prohibition may serve as a temporary means to make the lives of Japanese people difficult in order to pressurize them to obey the Ming government, but it is not an effective means to control them in the long-term. Without officially sanctioned trade, smuggling will never cease because they rely on us for their daily necessities. An open trade will benefit both sides. An open trade will serve as a long-term means to gain revenue, prevent the outflow of prohibited goods and maintain security. It is groundless to think that tribute trade will lead to piracy … If they are only motivated by profit, they would not come when the tribute trade was in process, but only when it was not in process [when their profit would be much greater]. If they come to invade, they would come no matter whether or not they were allowed to trade.[822]

However, the conservatives worried that trade might adulterate the principles underlying the moral world order. Yang Shouchen 楊守陳 (*jinshi* 1451, Minister of Personnel) expressed such a concern:

> It is wrong to believe that trade can change the barbarians' craving for invasion and trade can lead them to civilization. They will invade our country regardless of whatever their status in the eyes of the Ming court. Can we trade with such people? If they come to our doorstep in the name of paying tribute and we fight them, we will have to bear the bad reputation of killing guests; if we accept their tribute we will fall into their trap … What we should do is to drive them away, refuse to accept their tribute and strictly guard our borders … [In this way] we will demonstrate our stance that we are not interested in bribes from barbarians ... we do not want

---

819 *MJSWB*, vol. 166, *j.* 1, p. 8b.

820 *MJSWB*, vol. 302, *j.* 2, pp. 3a–4b.

821 "Jin tongfan yi 禁通番議" (A Comment on the Prohibition on Contact with Foreigners), in *Yue juan* 越鐫 (*Papers from a Zhejiang Official*) by Wang Zaijin 王在晋 (*jinshi* 1592), in *Siku jinhui* 集, fasc. 104, *j.* 20, p. 13b.

822 *MJSWB*, vol. 491, *j.* 4, pp. 43a–b.

> to take their alien products … Only when foreigners revere our high principles and morality, will they dare not to insult us.[823]

The pro-trade officials criticized this 'morality-defuses-war' argument. For instance, Gao Gong suggested: "It was the typical attitude of our literati officials, who are fussy and picky … under their pressure we do not allow the Mongols to pay tribute, although it's good for us to show our trust in them … [we refuse their tribute] in order to avoid criticism from our own conservative officials."[824] Such a self-proclaimed world order, without more effective arrangements for trade, was too vulnerable to maintain. Zhang Wei approached the issue in a more pragmatic way: "Our way to control the barbarians should take account of our understanding of their desires. The Japanese are not interested in either gaining an empty tribute status or in invading China. They pay tribute because they need the products which are only available from the tribute trade."[825] The Minister of War, Su You, believed that trade was the only form of leverage that would enable the Ming to control the powerful Mongol leaders. Referring to the *Gengshu* Incident 庚戌之變 (1550), he noted:

> It surprised the capital that the Mongols dared to violate the heavenly order by invading Beijing … but now they repented for what they had done and admitted that God had punished them with epidemics. Their leaders acknowledge that looting was not as rewarding as trade, as booty had to go to all the tribe members while the tribute trade can be controlled by chieftains … Anta envied the Eastern Mongols who pledged allegiance to the Ming court and were rewarded handsomely."[826]

The appeal of incorporation into China's tribute trade system was equally tempting to the Japanese. Li Yangong argued: "If our court allows the King Tianwen (Emperor Temmon 天文) to pay tribute, the Japanese government will rush to eradicate the pirates and smugglers … The income from official trade will then go only into the Japanese state coffers. Even if he is an idiot, the Japanese king will understand this."[827]

Trade was also more influential than military muscle in keeping the maritime countries incorporated within China's world order. Both Tan Lun and Hu Zongxian, the two Supreme Commanders on the coast, advocated implementing the Song political theory of *wuwei er zhizhi* 無為而治之 (control without control). Tan argued: "Though the distinction in status between China and barbarians has to be strictly maintained, trade with each other for mutually needed products can never be barricaded. I especially like the thought of the Song official Su Shi 蘇軾 (1037–1101), who advocated a policy based on the political theory of 'control without control'."[828] This implied a belief in the power of trade rather than military muscle in

823 Hu Zongxian, *Chouhai tubian*, *j.* 12, pp. 103a–104a.
824 *MJSWB*, vol. 302, *j.* 2, p. 3a–b.
825 *MJSWB*, vol. 408, *j.* 1, pp. 20a–b.
826 *MJSWB*, vol. 216, *j.* 1, pp. 7a–b.
827 Hu Zongxian, *Chouhai tubian*, *j.* 12, pp. 92b–93a.
828 Tan Lun, *Tan Xiangmin zouyi*, *j.* 2, p. 46b.

foreign relations. Hu Zongxian wanted to implement the same theory by leaving foreign relations in the hands of private merchants. He wanted to appoint some private merchants to manage trade with Japan in order to control piracy.[829] In this way, officials wanted to help the emperor realize the vulnerability of basing security solely on military preparations.[830]

A century of humiliation in war and conflict with the Mongols convinced the pro-trade officials that China's only leverage over them would come from the mechanism of trade. Li Hualong reminded the emperor that "the Mongols regard trade as their 'golden way' to make a living. Since a tribute mission is the precondition for trade they always worry about losing the tribute status."[831] Tribute status could not only bring the wealth that came from trade but it could also enhance the holder's political power within the Mongol community. For instance, when the Mongol chieftain Bushughtu 卜失(石)兔 (1565–1624) was allowed to pay tribute, he charged licence fees to anyone wanting to sell things on his tribute and trade mission. He used his tribute status to demand that other chieftains give him a share of the income from any of the horses which they traded.[832] Li Hualong was very positive about the way that tribute trade could help to rein in the enemy. "What I know is that since the winter and spring seasons [after tribute trade relations were established], 2,000 abducted Chinese people have been repatriated and there has been no harassment at any of our fortresses, though they may ask for rewards. They have never dared to disobey our decision or argue otherwise."[833] Trade relations drew the Mongols more closely into a political and economic system largely directed by the Ming court. For example, when, in 1571, Bushughtu and Anta led a 20,000 strong army to loot the Xifan, the Chinese official Zhu Fu 褚鈇 (*jinshi* 1565) noted that although the Mongols did not loot a single Chinese town, the Xifan region was where the Ming obtained 6,500 horses annually for the *Sanbian* 三邊 garrisons. He asked the court to order Anta to stop the military campaign in the Xifan region.[834] This incident indicated the kind of control that the Ming court could exert over its tribute nations. All the government needed to do was to issue an order to have the Mongols change their activities.

Foreign trade could play a significant role in maintaining China's world order. The pro-trade officials wanted to restore a fair and long-lasting system of trade in order to guarantee China's security. Gao Gong urged the need to make foreign trade available to all. "When our empire is at the peak of power they [the foreigners]

829 Hu Zongxian, *Chouhai tubian*, *j.* 12, pp. 113b–114a.

830 See also, for instance, the comments of Qian Wei, in *MJSWB*, vol. 214, *j.* 1, pp. 21b–23b.

831 *MJSWB*, vol. 422, *j.* 1, p. 13a.

832 *MJSWB*, vol. 450, *j.* 4, p. 10b.

833 Liu Tao, "Shang zhulao zu xianning Chou Luan fa duoyan sanwei rongshu 上諸老阻咸寧侯仇鸞伐朵顏三衛書" (A Request that the Duke of Xianjing, Chou Luan, be stopped from Pursuing the Mongols at the Three Garrisons of Duoyan), in *MJSWB*, vol. 305, *j.* 2, p. 6a. See also Gu Yingtai, *Mingshi jishi benmo*, *j.* 60, p. 26a.

834 "Tiaoyi chama shiyi shu" 條議茶馬市宜疏 (An Itemized Memorial on the Tea-Horse Trade Policy) by Chu Fu 褚鈇 (1533–1600), in *MJSWB*, vol. 386, *j.* 1, pp. 14a–18b.

willingly come to submit in order to get what they need. This is much better than when they come to take what they desperately need by coercion … As we are the centre of the world our moral power should be extended everywhere; no difference should be made among them."[835] Qian Wei pushed for a fair trade system. He protested on behalf of the Japanese: "Barbarians from Liaodong are allowed to pay tribute and trade once every three years, and we permit the people from Turfan to trade in the capital for ten days: why do we not give the Japanese the same treatment?"[836] Some officials argued to recognize the Portuguese in the same way, suggesting that "they have never had evil intentions; what they wanted from us was nothing but the benefit of trade."[837] Gao Gong criticized the discriminating treatment given to the different Mongol tribes. He confronted the Supreme Commander of the *Sanbian* defence region, who maintained the prohibition in the region after trade had been opened at the garrisons of Datong and Xuanfu. "Why do we open trade in Xuanfu and Datong while still keep the prohibition in Sanbian? It gives Mongols an excuse to loot where there is no trade … Opening trade on both sides will pacify the Mongols, while if one side is unfairly treated it will give rise to hostility and looting."[838]

Jiang Chenying 姜宸英 (1628–1699) suggested the need to be proactive: "If we do not allow the Japanese to come to our shores, we can sail to Japan to take their tribute back and trade with them there. In this way we will maintain control [of the relationship], but the Japanese will still get what they need."[839] Hu Zongxian believed the task should be entrusted to private traders.[840] Some officials suggested opening trade in a fortified seaport: "Dinghai 定海 is a strategic place. We should have open trade there so long as we can fortify it with enough troops. If the Japanese are assured to get what they need, they will not have to behave unlawfully … Guangzhou provides poof of this. There was no piracy there and people were happy when tribute trade was left in operation."[841] Pang Shangpeng also suggested a similar scheme for the Portuguese policy: "The best way to avoid danger is to ask them to leave the place [Macao] and return to their ships and then allow them to trade. This is the best policy for defence reasons; the foreigners can be tamed, their aggressive intentions quenched and the potential danger [they pose] will be terminated."[842]

The Senior Grand Secretary, Zhang Juzheng, outlined the policy debate between the two factions and emphasized the critical position of foreign trade in the

835 *MJSWB*, vol. 301, *j.* 1, pp. 2b–3a.

836 *MJSWB*, vol. 214, *j.* 1, p. 24b. See also *Da Ming huidian*, in *Siku xuxiu*, fasc. 791, *j.* 105, p. 1b.

837 Zhao Yi, *Ershi'er shi zhaji*, *j.* 34, p. 19b.

838 "Da sanbian Dai zongdu 答三邊戴總督" (My Reply to Supreme Commander Dai, of the Sanbian Defence Region) by Gao Gong, in *MJSWB*, vol. 302, *j.* 2, pp. 13b–14a.

839 *Zhanyuan ji* 湛園集 (*Collected Works of Jiang Chenying, Hao Zhanyuan*) by Jiang Chenying 姜宸英 (1628–1699) and Huang Shulin 黄叔琳 (*jinshi* 1691), in *Siku quanshu*, fasc. 1323, *j.* 4, p. 38b.

840 Hu Zongxian, *Chouhai tubian*, in *Siku quanshu*, fasc. 584, *j.* 12, pp. 113b–114a.

841 *Gujin tushu jicheng*, *j.* 40, p. 18a.

842 *MJSWB*, vol. 357, *j.* 1, pp. 9b–10b.

destiny of the dynasty. He argued that relief from the crisis generated by war and conflict and the consolidation of the Ming empire's status were dependent on a successful foreign trade policy.[843] For Zhang Juzheng, the crisis had not just been political and military in nature, to a large extent it was also financial. By the late Jiajing years the intensification of hostile foreign relations had exhausted the state coffers, which literally put financial pressure on every taxpayer, including the emperor himself and the grand dowager. When the Longqing Emperor requested 300,000 *taels* of silver for palace maintenance, the grand secretary was forced to decline the request. Similarly, when the emperor's mother asked for 100,000 *taels* for a princess's wedding (the dowager's third daughter), the Minister of Revenue, Zhang Xueyan (*jinshi* 1553), refused to grant this.[844] After a century of conflict along the inland and coastal borders, there was not much left in the state coffers. How to solve the financial difficulties was another aspect to the intense policy debates between the landed conservatives and the pro-trade faction.

The Debate on How to Relieve the Financial Crisis

The protracted war with the Mongols and the Japanese placed a great strain on imperial finances. The two main forms of income for the state, the land tax and labour service levy were drained in order to support the costs associated with the border conflicts. As Su Yan 蘇琰 reminded the court: "The Ministry of War has bled the Ministry of Finance and the Ministry of Works."[845] In the 28th year of the Jiajing reign (1549), when the *Neifu ku* (Palace Storehouse) was in the red, the government began to borrow from the *Taicang* (Imperial Graneries, National Silver Vault), leaving it overdrawn to the tune of 1.67 million *dan*.[846] The administration was living on debt. Looking back on this, Zhang Juzheng reported: "From the 29th year of the Jiajing reign (1550), when the Mongols invaded the capital, military expenditure soared … expenditure reached 4,000,000 *taels* a year, while our annual revenue remained at 2,500,000 *taels*, including the cash collected from the conversion of land tax to silver, the selling of salt licences and and judicial punishment."[847] Worse still, the debt kept soaring. Sun Yingkui 孫應奎 (*jinshi* 1521, Minister of Revenue) reported that state spending was approaching 5,950,000 *taels* in 1551, which was three times the state's annual income.[848] Miserably, Jin Xueyan 靳學顏 (*jinshi* 1535, Grand Coordinator of Shanxi) argued that the spending was indispensable. He told

---

843 Zhang Juzheng, "Da Ji-Liao zongdu Wang Jianchuan 答薊遼總督王鑑川" (My response to Wang Jianchuan, Supreme Commander of Ji-Liao), in *MJSWB*, vol. 326, *j.* 3, p. 26b.

844 *MJSWB*, vol. 324, *j.* 1, p. 14a. See also "Titing qu tangyin shu 題停取帑銀疏" (A Memorial Calling for No More Expenditure from the State Coffers), in *Jin Shaozai zoushu* 靳少宰奏疏 (*The Memorial Collection of Jin Xueyan, the Deputy Minister of Personnel*) by Zhang Xueyan 張學顏 (?–1598), *MJSWB*, vol. 363, *j.* 1, pp. 25a-b.

845 Zhang Xuan, *Xiyuan wenjian lu*, *j.* 32, p. 1b.

846 Shen Yue, *Huang Ming Jia-Long liangchao jianwen ji*, *.j.* 8, p. 15b.

847 *MJSWB*, vol. 324, *j.* 1, p. 14b.

848 *Ming shi*, *j.* 78, p. 12b.

the emperor: "It is the military that has exhausted most of the state's income but it is a necessary disbursement. Take Shanxi, for example, we placed less than 50,000 troops on the 800 *li* border, as there is not a single day we can afford to relax; there is nowhere on the frontier we can afford to abandon defences, because there is not a single year when we are not afraid of invasion by the Mongols."[849] Along the coast, the war on piracy was an on-going daily phenomenon, which cost 2,000,000 *taels* a year.[850]

The mounting financial pressure prompted the Jiajing Emperor to often call for grand court meetings to debate how to relieve the financial crisis.[851] With this also, officials were divided into two camps. On one side stood the conservatives, who insisted on increasing taxes, executing compulsory tax debt collection and reducing officials' pay in order to save government spending. On the other side was the pro-trade group, who campaigned to stop the war by engaging in trade with the enemy as a way to reduce the need for this expenditure. The debate on how to relieve this financial crisis was a concurrent phenomenon with the wider debates on the political and military crises.

As the on-going conflict drained most of the tax revenue, the government had no option but to shift the financial burden to the taxpayers. "We have to rely on the people to make a contribution, otherwise who can we rely on?"[852] Sun Yingkui suggested the court "impose 1,250,000 *taels* in surcharges on the southern capital area (Nanji 南畿) and the Zhejiang region in the form of *jiapai* 加派 (a compulsory surcharge). Such compulsory surcharges became an increasingly common way to raise funds.[853] Gu Yanwu remarked on the rapid tax inflation during the Jiajing years, noting that the tax on *guantian* 官田 (state land) had risen nearly 50–65 per cent, while the rate on *mintian* 民田 (private land) had risen between 30 and 50 per cent.[854] Hu Shining 胡世寧 (*jinshi* 1493, Bureau Director of the Ministry of Justice) admitted that the rising expenditure was destroying the early Ming tax system: "Maintaining the maritime interdiction used up the local revenue, but this was still not enough. Beside the land tax there is also the *tibian* 題編 (advanced assessment) … and if this is still not sufficient, the shortage will be made up by the compulsory *mubing gongshi yin* 民兵工食銀 (surcharge on taxpayers to pay for the accommodation of troops and local militia). The people have been driven mad in protesting."[855] Money was milked in different ways and under different names to meet the costs of the conflicts. In 1554, 4,907 *taels* of silver were collected from Wuxi

849 "Qing qiu cai yong shu 請求財用疏" (A Memorial Requesting Proper Use of Finances), by Jin Xueyan 靳學顏 (1514–1571), in *MJSWB*, vol. 299, *j.* 1, p. 1a. The Finance Minister complained about the shortage of funds to accommodate the inadequate military force along the border line; but, although border defence drained up all the revenue, it was still far from enough.

850 Tang Shunzhi, *Chongkan Jingchuan xiansheng wenji,* in *Sibu congkan*, *j.* 8, p. 57b.

851 *Ming shi*, *j.* 214, p. 9b.

852 Zhang Xuan, *Xiyuan wenjian lu*, *j.* 34, pp. 11b–12a.

853 *Ming shi*, *j.* 78, p. 12b.

854 Gu Yanwu, *Tianxia junguo libing shu*, p. 28b,

855 Hu Zongxian, *Chouhai tubian*, *j.* 11, p. 62b.

county alone under the *zuopai haifang-yin* 坐派海防銀 policy (a compulsory surcharge for emergencies in coastal defence).[856] And in 1558, a 400,000 *tael* surcharge was imposed on taxpayers in Zhe-jiang and Fujian to finance the coastal defences.[857] These tax increases were often quite substantial, sometimes as much as 100 per cent. The land autumn tax for Wujin county 武進縣 in the 26th year of the Hongwu reign (1393) was 533,515 *dan*, but this had increased to 1,503,500 *dan* in the Jiajing years, mostly in the form of surcharges.[858] Feng En 馮恩 (*jinshi* 1526, Censor-in-Chief) noted how it was the local population who usually had to meet military-related costs: "The locals have to pay the cost of warships, soldiers' pay, shields and weapons. All households are subject to the obligation without exception. Half of the 28,000 *taels* needed to reinforce the city wall in Songjiang came from the pockets of the local residents."[859]

However, some conservative officials, too, opposed the tax increases. As an alternative, Zhou Yi 周怡 (*jinshi* 1538, a Supervising Secretary in the Ministry of Personnel) suggested that the government cut the pay for officials. He stated: "Increasing tax on our people is the worst idea so that the government should never adopt it. Our people have been impoverished by drought for several years in a row and they are even unable to clear their land tax liabilities for the present year. The only option is to cut officials' pay."[860] Some officials suggested the Ministry of Finance should enforce debt collection to raise revenue. The emperor sanctioned the idea and dispatched high-ranking personnel to head the debt collection operation.[861]

The pro-trade officials opposed all such taxation schemes, and criticized them for being uncaring, impractical and unjust. Zhang Juzheng objected to the proposals to increase taxes. He noted that: "Since the 29th year of the Jaijing reign (1550) the increasingly military demands have depleted the wealth of the country, so that our people can no longer afford to pay their present taxes … let alone bear more tax increases and surcharges."[862] Zhao Zhenji 趙貞吉 (*jinshi* 1535, an Investigating Censor) denounced the advanced assessment, or *tibian*, policy: "We should never have applied the *tibian* policy, putting more burdens on our people."[863] Looking back to this period in the late Ming, Gu Yanwu was critical of the practice of demanding the labour service levy ahead of its due time.[864] People were driven into debt, especially in the years when there was flooding or a drought and when the harvest was

---

856 Gu Yanwu, *Tianxia junguo libing shu*, *ce* 7, p. 54a.

857 *Ming shi*, *j.* 78, p. 13a–b.

858 Gu Yanwu, *Tianxia junguo libing shu*, in *Siku xuxiu*, 596, *ce* 7, p. 28a.

859 "Shang shaohu da xueshi shu 上少湖大學士書" (A Letter Submitted to Hu, Secretary of the Grand Council), in *Feng shiyu churao lu* 馮侍御芻蕘錄 (*The Works of Investigating Censor Feng*) by Feng En 馮恩 (*jinshi* 1523), in *MJSWB*, vol. 200, *j.* 1, p. 7b.

860 *Nexi zoushu* 訥溪奏疏 (A Memorial from Nexi) by Zhou Yi 周怡 (1506–1569), in *Siku quanshu*, fasc. 429, p. 4a (no *juan*).

861 Shen Yue, *Huang Ming Jialong liangchao jianwen ji*, *j.* 8, p. 15a.

862 *MJSWB*, vol. 324, *j.* 1, pp. 14a–b.

863 Cha Jizuo, *Zuiwei lu*, in *Siku xuxiu*, fasc. 322, *j.* 11, *xia*, p. 7b.

864 Gu Yanwu, *Tainxia junguo libing shu*, *ce* 7, p. 15b.

reduced. The debt collection plan seemed even more irrational and inhumane: "People riot wherever the collector goes."[865] As for the proposition to cut payments to officials: this seemed thoughtless and unsympathetic. As I have pointed out in an earlier chapter, the pay rate for officials was already extremely low and the subject of much complaint. Chen Tai 陳泰 (*jinshi* 1427, an Investigating Censor) argued that the court should be increasing payments to officials, not reducing them.[866] Pro-trade officials argued that the only effective solution to these issues was a complete overhaul of the foreign trade policy, which would bring an end to the conflict and thus reduce the need for such expenditure. They argued that the government had neither the military power to enforce its current policy nor the resources to cope with the expenditure it required. Only by ending the prohibition on trade could the government stop the drain of so much revenue to the frontiers. Only by restoring normal finances would the government be able to implement all the policies necessary for the economic recovery.

Low state revenue and high expenditure combined to undermine the economic and financial regimes instituted at the beginning of the dynasty that were based on the principle of self-sufficiency. During the early years of the dynasty, the state finances were under little pressure, and administrative and military costs were easily met. There were few large-scale conflicts thanks to the favourable international environment, which was safeguarded by the tribute trade system. The Hongwu Emperor told the Ministry of Finance in 19th year of his reign (1386): "Our tax rate has been fixed. If we conserve our spending, we can balance the books, so long as our men keep farming and our women weaving … your department should never gather [extra] wealth from the people."[867] He argued that it was unacceptable "to increase state income, which was viewed as enriching the emperor at the people's expense."[868]

The commitment to self-sufficiency meant that the state maintained few reserves and there was little capacity to cope with any emergency. Ma Sen 馬森 (*jinshi* 1535, Minister of Revenue) said: "According to our ancestors' system, four million *dan* of taxed grain from the south of Huaihe 淮河 was allocated for the capital and eight million from the north of the Huaihe for the Mongol frontier. A year's income would meet a year's need. The frontier never constituted a problem and never required additional support from the capital."[869] But once military expenditure grew, this self-sufficient system could no longer cope, military finance relied on the cash assistance from the *Jingshi* 京師 (*Neifu ku, Taicang*). It rose from about 300,000–

865 Shen Yue, *Huang Ming Jia-Long liangchao jianwen*, *j.* 8, p. 15a.
866 *Ming shi*, *j.* 159, pp. 6b–7a.
867 Xu Xueju, *Guochao dianhui*, *j.* 101, p. 1b.
868 Ibid., pp. 1b–2a.
869 "Guo yong buzu qi jizhong huiyi shu 國用不足乞集中會議疏" (A Memorial to Call for a Court Debate over the Financial Deficit), in *Ma gongmin gong zouji* 馬恭敏公奏集 (*Collected Memorials of Ma Sen, Shihao Gongmin*) by Ma Sen 馬森 (1506–1580), in *MJSWB*, vol. 298, *j.* 1, p. 19a.

500,000 *taels* a year to more than 2,300,000 *taels* a year during the Jiajing administration.[870] The late Ming years saw more and more grain that was earmarked for local administrations appropriated for military purposes.[871]

A similar situation occurred along the coast. Tan Lun notified the court that "since the war with the pirates the revenue from Fujian has had little chance to go to the capital."[872] In the 33rd year of the Jiajing reign (1554) the emperor transferred the whole year's land tax from Suzhou, Zhenjiang, Changzhou and Songjiang to prepare for war against Japanese pirates.[873] The cost of confronting piracy was not only consuming the *cunliu* 存留 (tax collected locally and kept in the region to meet local costs) but it also began to swallow up the revenue going to the state treasury. When in 1556 the Grand Coordinator of Yingtian 應天 asked the emperor to allow the local government to keep the 440,000 *taels* of *qiyun yin* 起運銀 (land tax converted to silver and designated for the capital), the Ministry of Finance was irritated: "Liangzhe 两浙 has already deducted 200,000–300,000 *taels* from their *qiyun yin*, [and now] you too ask to keep more. Why do you not care about the needs of the capital and the costs of the war with the Mongols?"[874] The Ming financial situation was chaotic and on the verge of collapse.

The urgency of the demands of meeting the costs of the border conflicts was used to justify the irregularities in fundraising. Wang Shizhen pointed out: "We have deployed our entire army to check the Mongols in the north and the pirates in the south, which consequently exhausted our revenue."[875] There was no alternative. The auctioning of government office, the selling of judicial penalties, such things now became an acceptable expediency to generate extra income. For instance:

> The government sold a *xiucai* 秀才 (Cultivated Talent) degree for 100 *taels* of silver, which enabled the holder to sit an examination for a higher degree. The holder was allowed to keep the title and enjoy the associated privileges. Admission to an official school was sold for 20 *taels* of silver, while 5–6 *taels* would guarantee the recognition of the title *shengyuan* (government student). The title authorizes the holder to wear student robes and enjoy the same social privileges.[876]

Even a high office, such as a county magistrate, a position authorized only by the court, was sold for 1,600 bales of hay (fodder).[877] The financial emergency offset any worries about the political consequences of this. Yuan Zhi 袁袠 (1502–1547) expressed clearly the consequences of selling government posts.

870 *MJSWB*, vol. 298, *j.* 1, pp. 19a–b.

871 Chen Renxi, *Huang Ming shifa lu*, in *Siku jinhui* 史, fasc. 16, *j.* 65, p. 6a.

872 Tan Lun, "Shan hou liushi shu 善後六事疏" (A Memorial on How to Properly Handle the Six Problems), in *MJSWB*, vol. 322, *j.* 1, p. 2a.

873 Shen Yue, *Huang Ming liangchao jianwen ji*, *j.* 9, p. 32a.

874 Hu Zongxian, *Chouhai tubian*, *j.* 11, pp. 63a–b.

875 Wang Shizhen, *Fengzhou biji houji*, in *Siku cunmu* 集, fasc. 114, *j.* 3, p. 2a.

876 *Nanzhong jiwen* 南中紀文 (*Records of Nanzhong*) by Bao Ruji 包汝楫 (*jinshi* 1607). (Luxiang block printed edition 廬襄刻印, 1521–1571), in *Congshu jicheng chubian*, fasc. 3144, p. 12.

877 *Ming Xianzong shilu*, *j.* 171, pp. 1b–2a.

> They [the office buyers] know nothing about law, and little about literature, and may even be illiterate. They are of low quality, dodgy personality, and are unfamiliar with the rites and etiquette. Their employees will not respect them and they themselves have no wish to be promoted. They will think nothing but doing things for personal gain. While the government indeed gets a few *taels* of silver, it harms the people and society. Are there any cases more absurd than this?[878]

Disregarding the possible political risk, Wan Gong asked the emperor to allow the military to adopt an unprecedented approach towards horse supply. The emperor surprisingly endorsed it. In the 31st year of the Jiajing reign (1552) Wan Gong put judicial punishment for the convicted military personnel on sale. Those convicted who held the rank of Battalion or Company Commander (*qianhu* 千戶 or *baihu* 百戶) could be released from their conviction in return for four horses, while those who held the rank of Commander (*zhihui* 指挥) needed to pay six horses, and those who were Regional Military Commissioners (*duzhihui* 都指挥) needed to pay nine horses.[879] Upon the horses being handed over, the convicted officers could walk free.

When the selling of office and the conversion of judicial penalties was still not enough to balance the books, the government resorted to 'borrowing' from merchants. The Ministry of Finance passed its financial burden on to those who could afford it. It was a 'borrowing' on credit, but with no fixed day for reimbursement. Merchants protested fiercely about the compulsory 'loans'. For instance, Ke Feng 柯奉, a fodder merchant, complained to Yang Wei 杨巍 (Supervising Secretary of the Ministry of War):

> The Ministry of Finance borrowed 50,000 *taels* worth of fodder from merchants of the *Anren fang* 安仁坊 warehouse, 20,000 *taels* from the *Mingzhi fang* 明智坊 warehouse, 50,000 *taels* from the *Beixin chang* 北新場 warehouse, 20,000 *taels* from the *Tianshi an* 天師庵 warehouse, 30,000 from the *Xiyu fang* 西城坊 warehouse, 25,000 *taels* from the *Taiji chang* 臺基廠, 5,000 *taels* from the *Xisheng suo* 牺牲所, and another 100,000 odd *taels* from assorted other places. But the Ministry of Revenue has never repaid us.[880]

Yang Wei voiced his discontentment about the schemes: "The rich families are the energy source of the capital; we will have nowhere to borrow from again, if we have bankrupted them. Therefore we should not borrow from them too much or exhaust their resources."[881] He asserted: "The wealthy in the capital have been exhausted. We know the capital is the centre of the country and that merchants are the source of wealth in the capital. We should support and develop them rather than exhaust them."[882]

---

878 *Shiwei* 世緯 (*Putting the World Back to Order*) by Yuan Zhi 袁袠 (1502–1547), in *Siku quanshu*, fasc. 717, *j*. 1, pp. 7b–8a.

879 Wan gong, "Tiao chen san guan tongbian deng shu 條陳三關通變等疏" (The Listed Memorials on Lifting the Interdiction on Trade at the Three Strategic Passes), in *MJSWB*, vol. 352, *j*. 2, p. 15a.

880 Zhang Xuan, *Xiyuan wenjian lu*, *j*. 34, p. 11b.

881 Ibid., *j*. 34, p. 12a.

882 Ibid., *j*. 34, p. 11b.

These methods of fundraising were very controversial. Officials from both camps felt unprecedented pressure to develop better strategies to save the empire from financial collapse. The pro-trade camp attacked the foreign trade policy and blamed it for the difficulties. They did not try to avoid a head-on clash with the conservatives on urgent issues, such as how to stop the border wars, how to save spending and how to resuscitate the economy. They argued that change was long overdue and vital for the survival of the dynasty.

Funding the Defence Systems

The *tuntian* system was designed to guarantee the provisioning of troops: "Every garrison was assigned with farmland and their own production was sufficient to cover both the consumption of the troops and the officers' pay."[883] However, by the Jiajing reign, continued conflict along the border had undermined the system. Guan Huaili 管懷理 (*jinshi* 1541, Supervising Secretary of the Ministry of Revenue) reported to the court: "The Mongols were always on the offensive, so the *tuntian* land was under martial law most of the time …, farmers were scared off and there was nobody left to farm. When the Mongols occupied the Hetiao area, farmers were too scared to farm next to them."[884] Pang Shangpeng observed the situation in the garrison of Yansui 延绥: "Fifty percent of the *tuntian* land went wild … because frequent attacks by the Mongols on the border led to the mass exodus of the *tuntain* farmers."[885] *Tuntian* production dropped dramatically from the Hongwu and Yongle era until the Jiajing period. The *Tuntian* deficit reached 70–80 per cent.[886] Liaodong troops 遼東 used to produce 750,000 *dan* but this had dropped to only 170,000 *dan*; Gansu troops 甘肃 used to produce 600,000 *dan* but this plunged to 130,000 *dan*; and production by Ningxia troops 寧夏 plummeted from 180,000 to 149,000 *dan*.[887] The system on the coast was also crippled. Tang Shunzhi reported that half of the *tuntian* land allocated for the garrisons became wild.[888] Provisioning the military became a major problem. And with the institution of *minyun* 民運 (land tax transported to the frontier by the taxpayers themselves) the supply to the military became precarious. The troops were always short of provisions.[889]

How to restore the *tuntian* system constituted a pressing issue. Pro-trade officials wanted to change the trade policy to stop harassment along the borders. Gao Gong drew on lessons from the past to make his point clear: "The enemy wanted nothing but trade, and refusing to allow them to trade for their necessities resulted

883 *Mingshi*, *j.* 82, p. 22a.
884 *Ming Shizong shilu*, *j.* 162, p. 3a.
885 *MJSWB*, vol. 357, *j.* 3, pp. 11a–b.
886 *MJSWB*, vol. 298, *j.* 1 , pp. 19a–b.
887 Ye Xianggao, "Tun zheng kao 屯政考" (A Study of the Administration of Garrison Farming), in *Cangxia zheng xuji*, in *MJSWB*, vol. 461, *j.* 1, p. 23a.
888 *MJSWB*, vol. 260, *j.* 2, p. 10a.
889 *Ming Wuzong shilu*, *j.* 37, p. 1b.

in their hostility and the unwanted wars."[890] The Grand Secretary Zhang Juzheng realised how simple the solution could be: "As long as we conduct tribute trade, our army can be reduced to a smaller size. We can restore the *tuntian* system and allow our army to have a rest. Trade will render substantial military deployment unnecessary; it can save thousands or millions of *dan* of grain."[891] Abolishing the trade prohibition as a way to end the war came to be seen as crucial for restoring the system of making the army self-sufficient. Yang Yuanxiang 楊元祥 (*jinshi* 1583, Complier and Examiner) was convinced: "Trade relations with the Mongols will [enable us to] restore the *tuntian* production along the border. Before we reached a truce agreement by resuming trade with them, our soldiers along the border had depended on taxpayers with boats and carts for their provisioning, which cost thousands upon thousands of *taels*. Now the war is over, the *tuntian* will yield enough food for use, and the *Taicang* in the capital will become full."[892] Once again, the empire's trade policy was seen as fundamental to resolving the financial crisis of the empire.

Yet although the self-sufficient farmer-soldiers provided an 'economical' military force during times of peace, they were not powerful enough to confront the Mongol cavalry and were too weak to meet the challenges posed by pirates. The state was forced to rely on mercenaries to sustain its defences. Mercenaries were of two kinds: the *mubing* 募兵 (mercenary troops) and *kebing* 客兵 (guest troops). The former were employed throughout the empire on military service while the later were soldiers borrowed from other garrisons. Both were paid in cash for their services. The *Ming shi* records how: "In the early years the *zhubing* 主兵 (the self-sufficient local farmer-soldiers) of the garrisons were enough to guard the borders but soon they become insufficient, and had to be enhanced by *kebing*."[893] Following the *Tumu* debacle, when trade relations with the Mongols ceased and war became an ongoing occurrence, the *jiubian* 九邊 (the nine defence regions along the Mongol border) began to employ *mubing*. In September of the 14th year of the Zhengtong reign (1449), the Yingzong emperor ordered generals from the nine defence regions to employ 90,052 *mubing* and have them trained in Zhili, Shandong, Shanxi and Henan.[894] A similar demand also came from the coastal defence. After the 2nd year of the Jiajing reign the Maritime Trade Supervisorate was abolished and Japanese pirates and smugglers waged constant military campaigns to break the maritime interdiction.[895]

War drained state resources in two ways. It shifted the million-odd soldiers who were supposed to be self-sufficient onto the government pay-roll and also in-

890 *MJSWB*, vol. 301, *j.* 1, p. 1b.

891 Zhang Juzheng, "Da Wang Jianchuan ji gongshi lihai 答王鑑川計貢市利害" (A Reply to Wang Jianchuan about the Advantages and Disadvantages of the Mongols' Tribute and Trade), in *Zhang Wenzhong* gongji, in MJSWB, vol. 326, *j.* 3, pp. 22b–23a.

892 Zhang Xuan, *Xiyuan wenjian lu*, *j.* 34, p. 25b.

893 *Ming shi*, *j.* 82, p. 22b.

894 *Ming Yingzong shilu*, *j.* 189, p. 4b.

895 The "Japanese no longer respected China … [and] there has not been a single peaceful day." Gu Yingtai, *Mingmo jishi benmo*, *j.* 55, pp. 8a–b.

creased the state's disbursement to pay mercenaries. It was a great disruption and a significant burden. According to Hu Zongxian's budget application of 100,000 *taels* of silver to employ 10,000 heads of *mubing* for Fujian, it was logically an implication that the government self-sufficient troops was no longer capable to do the job of coastal defence, *mubing* as a more competent force became the urgent solution. But it was a very expensive deal the government had no option but to take, spending as much as ten *taels* of silver in cash on each head employed.[896] "The more *mubing* and *kebing* are employed, the more difficult the financial situation becomes."[897] Cash became essential to fund military preparations. But this monetized system was also inefficient. "Army recruitment to deal with piracy has become unpredictable … the mercenaries will stay if they are paid enough but leave as soon as their paid-service is over."[898] The cost to maintain the *mubing* and *kebing* was high. Whereas the main *tubing* were paid nothing, the *mubing* were paid in full, both in cash and kind, to the tune of around three *taels* of silver and two bolts of cloth per head yearly, with one *dan* of grain also paid monthly.[899] The costs associated with the *kebing* were even higher. Their *gongshi yin* 工食銀 (service allowance) was one *tael* of silver per month per person.[900] Tang Shunzhi was anxious about the excessive spending on *kebing* in the war against piracy.[901] However, Ye Chunji 葉春及 (a Bureau Director in the Ministry of Revenue) justified their high pay: "Those mercenaries have left their families thousand of miles away and risked their lives. They would never be satisfied unless they were paid handsomely."[902] And as mercenaries came to shoulder more and more of the burden of confronting the pirates, the associated costs grew larger and larger.[903] In the 34th year of the Jiajing reign (1555) spending on government troops reached 1,400,000 *taels*, while that on mercenaries reached around 2,200,400 *taels*.[904] Financial difficulties undermined the defences and the conflict came to be unaffordable. Feng Qi noted: "If we do not have sufficient money, the city and army are not ours."[905] The government was forced to squander its revenue on paying mercenaries.[906] In 1567, the Minister of Revenue admitted: "We are driving forward the collection of revenue urgently, exhausting our sources for more

896 *Chouhai tubian*, *j*. 4, p.35b.

897 *Ming shi*, *j*. 82, p. 22b.

898 *MJSWB*, vol. 260, *j*. 2, p. 6b.

899 *Ming Xiazong shilu*, *j*. 101, p. 6a.

900 Hu Zongxian, *Chouhai tubian*, *j*. 11, p. 101b.

901 Tang Shunzhi, "Tiao chen bu bing zu shi shiyi shu 條陳補兵足食事宜疏" (An Itemized Memorial on Making up Troop Shortages and Securing Military Supplies), in *MJSWB*, vol. 260, *j*. 1, p. 8a.

902 *Shidong ji* 石洞集 (*Rock Cave Collection*) by Ye Chunji 葉春及, in *Siku quanshu*, fasc. 1286, *j*. 8, p. 43a.

903 Tan Lun, *Tan xiangmin zouyi*, *j*. 5, pp. 27b–28a.

904 *Ming Shizong shilu*, *j*. 425, p. 3a.

905 "Dong sheng fang wo yi 東省防倭議" (My Views on Defence against Japanese Piracy in the Eastern Provinces) by Feng Qi, in *MJSWB*, vol. 441, *j*. 2, p. 3a.

906 "Cha li gexiang qian liang 查理各項錢糧" (An Audit of Assorted Spending Accounts in Cash and Grain) by Xu Xueju, in *Guochao dianhui*, *j*. 102, pp. 16a–b.

revenue, levying more tax with irregularity; our people are milked, our granaries are empty everywhere. Not even Heaven can help us now."[907]

The war had to be stopped and the unaffordable spending had to be discontinued. Many recognised that opening trade relations was the only effective way to remedy the urgent situation: "To control the foreigners and save defence expenditure we should reduce hostility with the barbarians by allowing them to pay tribute and trade their local products."[908] Wang Chonggu led the campaign to halt the war by initiating trade relations. He argued that: "Trade will replace harassment on the border, as commodities will meet the Mongol's urgent needs while also bringing benefit to our own traders. Sustained trade activities will eradicate the motivation for war and peace will be able to be sustained."[909] In the 5th year of the Longqing reign (1571) Wang Chonggu proudly claimed: "Since the tribute trade agreement [was made] 30,000 mercenaries that used to be employed in the Nanshan 南山 region of Xuanzhe 宣鎮 became unnecessary … 70,000 *taels* in military purchases were saved … as there was not a single mercenary required."[910] He asked the government to use the military fund to finance trade in order to strengthen a trade-based defence mechanism:

> The government spends 50 *taels* to reward anyone who kills a Mongol. Each garrison usually claims around 100 enemy casualties, which costs 30,000–50,000 a year in rewards. And for each soldier who dies in battle, the government pays 20–30 *taels* compensation to their family. Since trade relations were resumed the government spent not a single *tael* as no one died in battle. We used to station 200–300 soldiers in each post (*dun* 墩) and now we can save 3,000–5,000 *dan* of grain a year.[911]

He also noted: "We can save tens of thousands of *taels* from military expenditure so we should use the money saved to finance merchants to encourage them to conduct more trade on the border."[912] He notified the central administration that he intended to abolish all the sentry posts in order to save tens of thousands of *dan* of grain. Instead, he proposed paying three *taels* of silver to each soldier, allowing them to go deep into the steppe to engage in trade with the Mongols.[913]

Tang Shunzhi also wanted the same trade-based mechanism to be applied with the coastal defences. He argued: "For a hundred years during the early Ming period we did not have too much trouble from the sea … our good military supply system was engendered from an efficient military deployment which was maintained by a sound maritime trade system … It is important to restore maritime trade, which I

907 *Ming Muzong shilu*, *j.* 15, pp. 6b–7a.
908 *Ming shi*, *j.* 81, p. 27a.
909 *MJSWB*, vol. 316, *j.* 2, pp. 11b–12a.
910 "Wei zun feng ming zhi jinghua beilu fenggong weituo shiyi shu 為尊奉明旨經划北虜封貢未妥事宜疏" (My Memorial on the Emperor's Instruction on the Unfinished Tribute Trade Arrangement with the Mongols), in *MJSWB*, vol. 316, *j.* 2, p. 24b.
911 *MJSWB*, vol. 316, *j.* 2, pp. 12b–13a.
912 Ibid., *j.* 2, p. 26a,
913 *MJSWB*, vol. 316, *j.* 1. pp. 11b–13a.

believe will terminate all the troubles once and for all."[914] Zheng Xiao emphasized the need to reduce foreign hostilities by restoring trade and saving on military spending: "The aim in reinstating trade is to exchange each party's needs, communicate and thus develop better understanding, ease the people's tax burden and alleviate financial pressure on defence."[915] Tang Shu regarded maritime trade not only as a strategy to quench the enemy's war drive but also as a profitable industry: "Maritime trade will generate a good annual income for the state coffers, money which unfortunately has been intercepted by the smugglers during the maritime prohibition. Establishing the shipping office [in Zhejiang] will generate customs duties many times more than those from Fujian and Guangdong."[916] Xu Fuyuan wanted to restore the peace that came with trade and to develop a trade-financed defence system. He noticed the significance of customs revenue from maritime trade.[917]

The maritime prohibition policy was denounced for not only increasing military spending but also for the associated ban on offshore maritime transportation. The interdiction blocked the most economical and efficient way of moving goods and people. For nearly two centuries the productive land in the south and the political and military centre in the north were connected only by the shallow and narrow *Jing-Hang* canal 京杭大運河. The shipment of millions of *dan* of land revenue collected in kind from the south and the transportation of numerous people and commodities across such a large landmass had to be managed by riverboats and wheelbarrows. The *caoyun* system was also extremely costly. Xie Zhaozhe noted that the provisioning of tens of thousands of soldiers in the nine defence regions depended on the thousand *li* long canal.[918] It cost four *dan* of rice to transport every *dan* of revenue to the capital or the frontier.[919] Overland transport was even more expensive.[920] It cost 60 *dan* to transport every *dan* of revenue to the northern border.[921] Worse still, the *caoyun* system was dreadfully precarious. In the 3rd year of the Longqing reign (1569), the canal burst its banks in Pei county 沛縣, where 2,000 grain-loaded ships had jammed. Two years later, it burst in ten places and 400,000 *dan* of rice was lost in the flood.[922] Zheng Xiao also complained of the difficult fi-

---

914 *MJSWB*, vol. 260, *j.* 2, pp. 9a–11a.

915 Hu Zongxian, *Chouhai tubian*, *j.* 12, p. 112b.

916 *MJSWB*, vol. 270, *j.* 1, p. 4b.

917 He suggested that the port of Zhangzhou 漳州 alone could contribute 20,000 *taels* per year, which was more than one third of the 58,000 *tael* military budget for the region. See *MJSWB*, vol. 400, *j.* 1, p. 3a.

918 Xie Zhaozhe, *Wu zazu*, in *Siku xiuxiu*, fasc. 1130, *j.* 3, p. 12a.

919 Tan Lun, *Tang Jinchuan wenji*, in *Siku quanshu*, fasc. 1276, *j.* 5, pp. 24a–b; see also Zheng Tianting 鄭天廷, *Zhongguo lishi da cidian* 中國歷史大辭典 (*The Great Dictionary of Chinese History*). (Shanghai: Shanghai cishu chubanshe, 2000), p. 810.

920 See, for instance, "Yi lu yun shu 議陸運疏" (Comment on Land Transportation), in *Zhang Yimin ji* 張毅敏集 (*Collected Works of Zhang Yangmeng, Shihao Yimin*) by Zhang Yangmeng 張養蒙 (*jinshi* 1577), in *MJSWB*, vol. 427, *j.* 1, p. 21a.

921 *Ming Renzong shilu*, *j.* 7, p. 7b.

922 *Ming shi*, *j.* 85, pp. 17b–19a.

nancial circumstances in organizing the river transportation. Between 20 and 30 per cent of the boats were usually damaged on its shallow bed. It was always difficult to get the funds necessary to build 1,500 riverboats to transport the 460,000 *dan* of rice.[923] Wang Zongmu 王宗沐 (*jinshi* 1544, Deputy Censor-in-Chief and Director General of the Grain Transport) reported to the court: "Freighting by river boats in the canal is much more awkward than transport by sea; it is hard to keep two ships abreast. If one boat is wrecked the rest of them have to stop. Fire on one boat will soon spread to another … but maritime shipping will make the supply much easier … Maritime freighting involves little risk … we cannot deny the difficulties of *caoyun* and the benefits of maritime transportation."[924]

The pro-trade officials condemned the maritime prohibition policy for not only draining the state's revenue but also for creating unnecessary strain for the coastal people. The interdiction banned people from sailing out into the coastal waters. Landless people were banned from making a living from the sea. But Tang Shunzhi noted how in Dinghai 定海 and Fenghua 奉化, where there was a lack of arable land, no fewer than ten thousand people were making a living from the sea by fishing or collecting seaweed.[925] Wang Zaijin noted how people in Fujian were forced to rely unaffordable grain transported from Guangdong in the south or Wenzhou in the north. Instead of paying a shipping fee at 3 cents for each 100 *dan* by a coastal route they had to pay 20 times more for transportation by a land route. And it was because of these restrictions that people were driven to violate the maritime interdiction.[926] Tan Lun reinforced this view, stating in a memorial: "We must put the end to the maritime prohibition because the coastal people cannot survive without making a living from the sea. They are becoming rebellious because they have been dispossessed of their basic way of survival."[927]

Gu Yanwu held the maritime interdiction responsible for causing the Liaodong famine in the 21st year of the Jiajing reign (1542). He painted a terrible picture:

> The grain price fetched as much as 6–7 *qian* per *dou* in the market [10 times more than the normal price]. Cannibalism became common. Heart-rendingly, the starvation did not result from the shortage of relief but from the cost of land transportation. Shandong peninsula had a bumper harvest in the same year, which was only an overnight sail away across Liaohai Bay. [The maritime interdiction made this impossible] Land transportation cost 10 times more.[928]

Guo Zaoqing 郭造卿 (an advisor to the Supreme Commander Qi Jiguang 戚繼光) argued that "overnight shipping by sea could save thousands of miles on land."[929]

923 Zheng Lüchun, *Zheng duanjian gong nianpu*, in *Siku cunmu* 史, fasc. 83., *j.* 4, pp. 12a–b.
924 "Qi guang xiang dao yi bei bu yu shu 乞廣餉道以備不虞疏" (My Memorial on Increasing Fundraising for Soldiers' Pay to Prepare for Emergency) by Wang Zongmu 王宗沐 (1523–1591), in *MJSWB*, vol. 343, *j.* 1, pp. 19a–20a.
925 Tang Shunzhi, *Jiangnan jinglue*, in *Siku quanshu*, fasc. 728, *j.* 8, *shang*, p. 35b.
926 Mao Yuanyi, *Wubei zhi*, in *Siku jinhui* 子 26, *j.* 214, pp. 19b–20a and 25a–b.
927 *MJSWB*, vol. 322, *j.* 1, p. 2a.
928 Gu Yanwu, *Tianxia junguo libing shu*, in *Siku xuxiu*, fasc. 596, *yuanbian*, *ce* 34, p. 20a.
929 Ibid., p. 22a.

And Shen Defu 沈德符 (1578–1642) argued that "maritime freight is the solution to alleviate the financial strain of transportation. Since ancient times there has never been a maritime prohibition. The 3,300 *li* from Huaian 淮安 to Tianjin 天津 only takes twenty days with favourable winds … maritime shipping can save 15,000 *taels* of silver for the transportation of 120,000 *tan* of grain from Huaihai 淮海 to the capital."[930]

Pang Shangpeng also blamed the maritime prohibition for suffocating business networks in Liaodong 遼東:

> The starvation is caused by the maritime interdiction which outlawed shipping and fended off merchants … Without merchants who import and trade foodstuffs the rich cannot do business and the poor have nowhere to borrow. If we lift the maritime prohibition Shandong can support Liaodong and Liaodong can support Shandong in time of need. It is only a matter of overnight shipping.[931]

Many officials argued the case to alter this policy. In the 37th year of the Jiajing reign (1558), the Supreme Commander of Jiliao 薊遼, Wang Yu 王忬 (*jinshi* 1541), sent an urgent memorial to the emperor to ask the court to lift the maritime ban in order to transport grain to Liaoyang 遼阳 for emergency relief.[932] Chen Wan 陳綰, a director from Liaozhen 遼鎮 wrote to the grand coordinators in Liaodong to question the legal grounds for the maritime prohibition. The maritime prohibition made it difficult to transport grain from Shangdong to Liaodong. He asked:

> Which is more important, to have 100,000 people starving to death or to maintain the maritime interdiction? There was no interdiction between Shandong and Liaodong before the Chenghua years [1458–1465], when commodities of all kinds were transported by the convenient and economic sea route … The only grounds for establishing it is to prevent the attacks from Japanese pirates … should we refuse to eat any food cooked by fire if our house burnt down? It is preposterous![933]

The Senior Grand Secretary Li Chunfang 李春芳 (*jinshi* 1547) confronted the policy straight on: "Why did we imitate the Yuan dynasty by relocating the capital to Beijing but then refuse to adopt their way of feeding the capital by shipping grain from the south by sea? How difficult is it to transport so much grain to the north from the south on these shallow boats, which always block the river on their trip?"[934]

The two factions, despite their different stances on relations with the Mongols, shared a common view that the Mongols were always a threat. The government had no option but to put another financial burden on taxpayers in order to raise horses

930 Shen Defu, *Ye huo bian*, in *Siku jinhui* 史, fasc. 4, *j.* 12, pp. 28a–b.

931 *MJSWB*, vol. 357, *j.* 2, p. 27a.

932 *Huang Ming dazheng ji* 皇明大政記 (*Primary Notes on Ming Administration*) by Zhu Guozhen 朱國禎 (*jinshi* 1589), in *Siku cunmu* 史, fasc. 16, *j.* 33, p. 3b.

933 Gu Yanwu, *Tianxia junguo libing shu*, in *Siku xuxiu*, fasc. 596, *yuanbian*, *ce* 34, pp. 19a–b.

934 *MJSWB*, vol. 281, *j.* 1, pp. 3b–4a.

for the military. This was the notorious and much hated *biaoma* 俵馬 policy.[935] Feng Shike 馮時可 (*jinshi* 1571, Administrative Vice Commissioner of Huguang) observed the ruthlessness of the *baioma* policy and the consequent exasperation: "Horse raising is assigned by toll and the area of land owned … we have 100,000 stud horses assigned to the population and 25,000 foals are contracted to be produced … many families became debt-ridden."[936] Individuals or families had to pay 16–20 *taels* if a horse died or went missing, and some had to sell all their family properties to pay the resulting debt while others simply fled their home.[937] When the *biaoma* system still could not cope with the demand, the government shifted part of the burden to the cavalrymen themselves: each rider was given 12 *taels* to buy a horse. If the horse died the riders had to fund the replacement themselves; consequently, the death of horse often led to desertion.[938]

However, China did not produce good war horses and domesticated horses were not useful for military purposes. Thus the pro-trade faction wanted to overhaul the *biaoma* policy by lifting the prohibition policy so that it would be possible to trade with the Mongols in order to obtain war-horses directly from them. It was seen as a stone that could kill two birds at once: trade would dissolve the enemy's war aspirations while allowing China to also obtain good war horses. Wang Chonggu eagerly promoted the benefit of the Mongol trade, noting that from the money saved in trying to raise horses domestically it would be possible to purchase three good Mongol horses, and, in the process, the levy imposed on those required to provide the horses could be lifted.[939] Shi Dao emphasized the financial and political advantages of horse trade:

> The horse fair is especially beneficial to us. We can pay a very low price to get great horses and the profit can be as much as three times. Trade can play a political role too: since horses are the Mongols' most powerful weapons in war, thus exchanging their horses with our cheaply-made materials can weaken the enemy while reinforcing ourselves. Let us think about the future when more and more horses will have come to our side. So long as the Mongols are engaged in trade they will not wage war on us. Our soldiers can be demobilized, military supplies spared and a lot of money saved.[940]

---

935 "Biao ma san 俵馬三" (Stallion Raising, section 3), in *Mazheng ji* 馬政記 (*Record on Horse-raising and Horse-supply Administration*) by Yang Shiqiao 楊時喬 (1531–1609), in *Siku quanshu*, fasc. 663, *j.* 3, pp. 6a–7a.

936 "Qing bianmai zhongma shu 請變賣種馬疏" (A Memorial Requesting the Selling of Stallions), in *Feng Yuancheng wenji* 馮元成文集 (*The Collected Works of Feng Yuancheng*) by Feng Shike 馮時可 (*jinshi* 1571), in *MJSWB*, vol. 434, *j.* 1, pp. 1a–2b.

937 Hou Xianchun, "Qing mazheng yi pi bianjiang zhong wu shu 清馬政以裨邊疆重務事" (Rectify the Horse Management to Benefit the Grand Task along the Frontier), in *MJSWB*, vol. 428, *j.* 2, pp. 8a–b. See also Gu Yanwu, *Tianxia junguo li bing shu*, in *Siku xuxiu*, fasc. 596, *yuanbian*, *ce* 18, p. 83a.

938 *MJSWB*, vol. 316, *j.* 3, p. 12b.

939 Ibid., *j.* 3, pp. 2a–b, p. 12a.

940 Shi Dao, *Shi Dufu zouyi*, *j.* 1, p. 11a.

Trade as a Means to Import the Silver

The late Ming financial crisis resulted not only from excessive military spending and the collapse of the self-sufficient economic system but also from the stagnant economy caused by the lack of a reliable currency. Ming China had few silver and copper reserves.[941] And without the secure backing in precious metal the Ming paper notes, the *Da Ming tongbao*, soon became virtually worthless.[942] In addition, the insufficiency of copper resources and the high demand for the coins led to their debasement and devaluation.[943] Since the self-sufficient economy was undermined to a greater and greater extent by increasing commercialization, the need for a stable and efficient currency became even more pronounced. This need was exacerbated by the *yitiao bianfa* (single whip reform), gradually implemented during the sixteenth century, which transferred the land tax and labour service levy into a single payment in silver. Demand for silver was high but little was produced domestically.[944]

Hao Jing 郝敬 (*jinshi* 1589, a Supervising Secretary in the Ministry of Revenue) described the craving for silver:

> The whole country is using the rarest metal for money. The military has consumed most of the silver, little of which was circulated back to society. Moreover, rich families hoard a lot of silver and stop it from circulating. Silver is neither rain from the heavens nor a kind of product that can be manufactured, so how can it not be exhausted? We know there is not much silver in circulation, but we still demand that everything be paid for in silver; how can we not harm our people's interests? Without revenue being collectable in silver, how can we not harm our state?[945]

The pro-trade officials attacked the maritime prohibition policy for causing such financial stress. Silver was in plentiful supply elsewhere, but because of the prohibition it was not being imported to China, where it was most sought for. Smuggling became the only way to get silver into the empire and help relieve some of the pressure caused by shortage of the metal. Merchants sailed to Japan where "there were no goods but silver."[946] People went to Luzon where "silver was as common as copper. The locals paid for everything in silver which is plentiful."[947] The pro-trade officials were justified in challenging the maritime prohibition policy. It was the government itself that deliberately blocked the silver inflow by fending off the foreign ships which were loaded with silver and were lining up along the coast and waiting for exchange. Lifting the maritime interdiction would in fact be the most effective solution for the crisis caused by the shortage of silver. If this occurred

941 See Chapter Two.

942 Cao Renhu, *Xu wenxian tongkao*, *j.* 10, p. 26b.

943 *Ming shi*, *j.* 81, pp. 7a–8a.

944 On this situation see Brian Moloughney and Xia Weizhong, "Silver and the Fall of the Ming – a Reassessment", *Papers in Far Eastern History* 40 (1989), pp. 51–78.

945 Sun Chengze, *Chunming mengyu lu*, *j.* 47, p. 9b.

946 Gu Yanwu, *Tianxia junguo libing shu*, in *Siku xuxiu*, fasc. 596, *yuanbian*, *ce* 26, p. 100.

947 Sun Chengze, *Chunming menyu lu*, *j.* 42, pp. 41a–b.

then a great deal of silver would flow into the country through official channels and the state would benefit.

Pro-trade officials attacked the maritime prohibition policy for leading to smuggling and the loss of state revenue. The late Ming years saw the economy become increasingly dependent on smuggled silver. Silver's high value in the Ming economy and its accessibility in foreign lands powered the collaboration between the foreign merchants and Ming smugglers. A large-scale illicit trade developed: "In the early years smuggling was limited to the Japanese, but the abundance of silver lured our people to join them. The shortage of the metal enabled the Japanese to find ready collaborators within the empire."[948] The pro-trade officials called for the government's direct management of the silver-orientated trade. Qian Wei pointed out that the "Japanese need our products and we want their goods [silver]. The trade prohibition creates conflict between the two peoples and the harassment will not end."[949] Zhang Han 張瀚 (1511–1593, Vice Censor in Chief) asserted the necessity for the government to monopolise foreign trade in order to increase state income. "Our Maritime Trade Supervisorate is supposed to have a monopoly. We should manage the maritime trade to generate revenue for the state by suppressing smuggling."[950]

Once the value of lifting the maritime prohibition was acknowledged, it did not take long before the empire's officials were devising means to profit from trade. Zhang Xie 張燮 describes the custom duty system that was soon put in place after the lifiting of the prohibitions. There were three duties: the *yinshui* 引税 (the licence fee); the *shuixiang* 水餉 (a tax on ship size); and the *luxiang* 陸餉(a duty on cargo). *Yinshui* were sold for six *taels* each. The *shuixiang* was levied at a rate of five *taels* for a ship 15 feet in length and half a *tael* more for every extra foot. The *luxiang* on cargo was 2 per cent. Ships from Luzon were also required to pay an extra levy, the *jiazheng* 加徵, a payment of 150 *taels* per ship, because they were usually loaded with nothing but silver bullion.[951] The lifting of the maritime interdiction meant that a substantial silver income could be generated from the fishing industry. A boat licence fee could fetch as much as five *taels* per ship, 20 *taels* per catch, and 10 *taels* for the *yeyin* 業银 (commercial fees). There was no trouble getting fishermen to pay such levies.[952]

Silver was a metal on which the Ming economic prosperity and political stability hinged. On one hand, the increased flow of silver into the empire would help relieve the monetary deflation, facilitate more rapid commercialisation of the economy and on the other, foreign trade defused the hostile relationships between the government with its neighbour states and its own people for providing a basic subsistence. A debate on whether or not the government should end the foreign

948 *MJSWB*, vol. 214, *j.* 1, p. 13a.

949 Ibid., pp. 15b–16a.

950 Zhang Han, *Songchuang mengyu*, *j.* 3, p. 10b.

951 Zhang Xie, *Dongxi yangkao*, *j.* 7, pp. 2b–3b.

952 Zheng Ruozheng, *Jiangnan jinglüe*, in *Siku quanshu*, fasc. 728, *j.* 8, *shang*, p. 22b.

trade prohibition to save its economy from bankruptcy and relieve the empire from the war-ridden national security crisis became the primary phenomenon in the late Ming politics. A grand lobbying campaign led by the pro-trade officials mounted a fierce and head-on confrontation with the 200 years long stronghold of the conservatives. Pang Shangpeng faced up to the policy frankly in his memorial: "As far as I understand, prohibiting our people from going to Japan for smuggling is impossible. Why don't we go with the desire of the people to abolish the interdiction? We can levy heavy duties on the traded goods and also prevent [our people] from collaborating with foreign pirates and trading prohibited goods. By doing so we can get good income for the state while also eliminate smuggling and piracy."[953] The late Ming economic crisis and political catastrophe and the helplessness of the government made the pro-trade officials the upper hand on a number of fronts – financial, economic, social, political and military. It consequently led to the formation of a new trade policy, which involved reshaping, successively, the maritime prohibition on the coast, the tea trade in the west and the horse trade in the north. When the business-like pro-trade group became a leading force in the government the Ming entered a new era, in which government policy was more closely aligned to the actualities of the society and the economy.

953 Jiang Chenying and Huang Shulin, *Zhanyuan ji*, *j.* 4, pp. 38b–39a.

CHAPTER VI

Conclusion

The lifting of the 200 year-old maritime prohibition in 1567, initiated by the Fujian Grand Coordinator Tu Zemin, meant that private merchants were free to apply for licences to embark on business trips to both the Eastern and the Western seas for the first time since the founding of the dynasty.[954] Although trade in Japan was still theoretically restricted, many merchants who were licenced to sail to the Eastern and Western seas actually travelled to Japan.[955] The huge profits from this trade attracted the rich to finance shipbuilding and the poor to work on board the ships.[956] The Japanese got what they wanted via the direct trade (still officially 'smuggling' but not prevented) and through indirect trade via other places. The relaxed trade policy gave rise to an expansive international commodity exchange and led to sustained stability along China's coast. As a result, "Japanese piracy disappeared, the fleet of tribute embassies vanished, and there was no more shortage of fabrics and utensils that come from China."[957]

The change to a maritime policy was not an isolated event. The late sixteenth century witnessed a general overhaul of foreign trade policy. Soon after the lifting of the maritime prohibition, Wang Chonggu initiated substantial changes in the policy governing trade with the Mongols. Horse fairs were officially opened in the 5th year of the Longqing administration (1571) and trade promptly surged up to a volume that saw 1,370 horses and 6,900 lambs, donkeys and cows change hands in the short period between 28 May and 14 June at the Dating garrison alone.[958] Although Anta's application for free tea trade in the 5th year of the Shenzong reign (1578) was declined, the tea-horse trade on the western border underwent a profound transformation. The official *chama* (tea-horse) trade went into disarray. Instead of observing the *jinpai* (golden trade) system, by which forty-one permits were fixed for 14,051 horses once every three years, the Wanli administration overhauled the policy in 1576 by allowing the exchange of tea and horses for three months, from May to July, every year.[959] Even so, the official trade was still declining. "The Xifan barbarians were reluctant to trade at the *chama si*, because tea from private traders was much cheaper."[960] The trade in smuggling eventually overtook the official trade to become the main channel for the Xifan to obtain tea.[961] Gu Yanwu observed that "the leverage to control the barbarians has shifted to the private merchants."[962]

---

954 Zhang Xie, *Dongxiyang kao*, *j.* 7, p. 2a.
955 Gu Yanwu, *Tianxia junguo libing shu*, in *Siku xuxiu*, fasc. 597, *j.* 26, p. 104b.
956 Ibid., p. 103b.
957 Jiang Chenying and Huang Shulin, *Zhanyuan ji*, *j.* 4, pp. 37b–38a.
958 Wang Shizhen, *Yanshan tang bieji*, fasc. 409–410, *j.* 89, pp. 23b–24a.
959 Cao Renhu, *Qingding xu wenjian tongkao*, *j.* 22, p. 41a and p. 48a.
960 Ibid., *j.* 22, p. 49b.
961 Gu Yanwu, *Tianxia junguo libing shu*, in *Siku xuxiu*, fasc. 597, *j.* 19, p. 104b.
962 Ibid., p. 104b.

In this thesis I have investigated the 'internal' dynamics underlying these policy changes, and in this my argument differs from those scholars who have based their explanations for the change in maritime policy on the modification of 'Japanese piracy'. Through the application of a structural approach, my analysis has dealt with maritime policy as one aspect of Ming foreign policy, which in turn is seen as having its foundation in the social and economic circumstances prevalent during the dynasty. By approaching this issue from the 'bottom up', I have explored the mechanism for the transformation of the social and economic landscape in order to trace the dynamics driving forward the process of policy alteration.

I have argued that the prohibition on foreign trade reflected the early Ming political culture of state domination over the economy. The economic destitution inherited by the early Ming years, a result of decades of war, combined with the political vulnerability of the new administration, compounded by the continued presence of the still powerful Mongol forces along the northern border, helped legitimise the government's commitment to a *tongzhi jingji* 統治經濟 (literally, a command economy). Chih-yu Shih has argued that "throughout China's economic history the central government has invariably played a leading role ... the government has significant influence over the course of development (or stagnation, for that matter)."[963] But no other administration in Chinese dynastic history equalled the early Ming in terms of state control of society. The Ming command economy involved comprehensive state control, from ideology to social organisation and from the mode of production to the means of exchange. The maritime prohibition policy was one part of this much larger system of control.

The Ming *tongzhi jingji* system was established on the basis of a steadfast ideological framework. The quick overthrow of the Yuan convinced the early Ming policymakers of the authority of China's traditional political ideology. As John Dardess has argued, after 125 years of alien rule, 'Confucian autocracy' emerged to an unprecedented degree under the early Ming.[964] Moral authority became the foundation of political authority. Political power was thus based on the implementation of the Confucian principles. The commitment to *jun* 均 (the equal distribution of social wealth) served the early Ming *tongzhi jingji* system well. It guided the re-distribution of social wealth that was achieved by nationalising farmland and allocating it on a per capita basis. This commitment to *jun* also justified the low level of pay given to the ruling group, and authorised the maintenance of a self-sufficient economy, which was believed to secure an egalitarian and just society. Commerce was vilified as a factor leading to exploitation and social injustice, as it was believed that a peasant economy was too vulnerable to stand up to the impact of free commercial competition.

A self-sufficient economy under government surveillance was devised to avoid social conflict. Peasants were required to produce their own necessities, from food

963 Chih-yu Shih, *State and Society in China's Political Economy: the Cultural Dynamics of Socialist Reform* (Boulder: Lynne Rienner Publishers, 1995), p. 33.

964 John W. Dardess, *Confucian Autocracy* (1983).

to utensils, while the state would rely on the state-run industries, from stationery to war supplies. The commitment to *zhongnong yishang* (promotion of farming and suppression of commerce) became the primary means to implement the Ming form of *tongzhi jingji*. Foreign trade for purely commercial purposes was incompatible with such a system and therefore was prohibited. The Confucian creed of *ren* 仁 (humanity or humaneness) also debarred the exchange of products with the 'barbarians', as it implied dealing with them on an equal footing and engaging in trade for reasons of profit. According to this belief, the world was strictly ordered, with China at the centre, and gaining its authority by providing a moral model for the 'uncivilized'. Trade was organized primarily as an adjunct to tribute, and thus was subsumed into a system that was designed to symbolise China's ceremonial control. Rewards, such as the benefits that came from trade, were used for political rather than commercial purposes. Similarly, it was feared that private foreign trade would weaken the legitimacy of the Ming dynasty in the morality-based system and therefore it was prohibited.

The early Ming *tongzhi jingji* system destroyed the infrastructure for commerce. As discussed in Chapter 2, the *lijia* system bound people to the land and made them subject to surveillance by administrators, commissioned village leaders and even their neighbours. The *luyin* system prohibited people from travelling out of their residential domain. The government regulated the market, fixed prices and had a monopoly on commodities such as tea and salt. In order to further enhance government control, the use of silver ingots in transactions was forbidden, with people required to use the politically imposed unconvertible paper notes, which had no intrinsic value at all. The long-term shortage of a reliable medium curbed the growth of trade. But what really led to the stagnation of commerce under the early Ming was the systematic and intensive suppression of social consumption. Luxury spending became a synonym for moral debasement. The Hongwu Emperor personally endorsed a puritan social model and the Ming government legitimized strict compulsory benchmarks for consumption. Any violation of the standards would result in judicial penalties. These things served to hollow out from the society the very drive needed to develop the economy. The result of trying to maintain political stability in this way was a society with few wealthy people, little capital accumulation and a dead market in terms of demand and supply. And without a domestic infrastructure there was no foundation on which to build foreign trade. The prohibition on foreign trade was a product of the early Ming commitment to a stability-orientated self-sufficient society in which commerce was strictly regulated, rather than a consequence of Japanese piracy or Mongol harassment.

The commitment to a *tongzhi jingji* system brought about a long period of enforced 'stability'. Shih argues that, "Dynastic regimes faced no external competition and were perfectly comfortable preaching the norm of harmony as opposed to competition in virtually all fields, including economic activity."[965] This is far too sweep-

965 Ibid., p. 49.

ing a statement, and does not apply to all dynastic regimes, but it does hold true for the early Ming period. However, there was a price to pay for this enforced stability. Such a 'man-made economic order' could be maintained only through coercive political enforcement. The *tongzhi jingji* system was bound to weaken as the daily surveillance of people and the rigid command of the economy generated not only financial complications but also dreadful social conflict, and this put the government's political resources under considerable stress. Worse still, the decline in political competence was made worse by the intensifying border clashes inflicted by the frustrated Mongols and Japanese, who relied on the Chinese products for daily consumption. Political and financial crises plagued the administration during the mid- to late Ming years. By the sixteenth century, the government had no option but to allow 'irregularities' to happen.

As the command economy began to fracture and weaken, the long repressed commercial industries re-emerged, and they showed great vigour. The century-long trade vacuum created a colossal market demand as people throughout the empire demanded consumer goods in order to improve their long restricted lives. Commerce soon came to occupy the centre of the new economic trend. Big landlords tended to invest more and more into the most profitable non-farming businesses and tenants swarmed to non-farming industries to generate cash income. Attracted by the high returns, members of the ruling élite also got involved in trade; they were no longer content with the low and slow dividends from land ownership and the poor remuneration they received for government work. Commercialisation was further stimulated by the mushrooming of private manufacturing industries after the decline and collapse of state-run industries. Tens of thousands of *taels* -worth of orders went to the private businesses instead of the state-run industries. Furthermore, commerce was also driven by overseas demand for Chinese fabrics, tea, ironwork and porcelain. Foreign trade generated the highest profits, as foreign merchants arrived with ships loaded with silver bullion and bought anything and everything. The demand for silver in China meant that it was of much greater value in the empire than in overseas markets. The massive inflow of silver bullion enriched everyone who participated in every phase of the commercial economy, from the production of raw materials to manufacturing and transportation. But those who benefited most from these changes were the merchants.

By the sixteenth century merchants had emerged as a very wealthy and powerful social group. The collapse of the *tongzhi jingji* system created an economic environment in which money played a leading role. Money generated social influence, as well as the ability to provide timely relief for the community in a disastrous year. Money also gave access to education and thus the chance of success in the imperial examinations. By the late Ming years, money also meant the ability to buy government positions, which were put on sale when the government desperately wanted to raise income to help it support the border conflicts. The rise in influence of a monied élite saw the emergence of a new political grouping, as the number of merchants with a merchant background snowballed. From the mid- Jiajing period onwards, the new faction found itself capable of influencing the decision-making process within the government in a significant way. Two different political groups, each with a distinct ideological position, were locked in a duel for domination; pragmatism engaged doctrinism and utilitarianism engaged conservatism at every phase in the policymaking process. The former campaigned for change while the later strove to maintain their vested interests in the old institutions.

By the Jiajing years the mounting political and financial pressure from continuous border conflicts with the Mongols and Japanese had reached a critical level. These circumstances combined to generate conflict among the political factions. The new political actors, empowered by their efforts to save the empire, confronted every policy that they believed contributed to bringing about the current situation – they even confronted the unchallengeable status of Confucianism. The new faction passionately opposed blindly following doctrine and advocated a more pragmatic and businesslike outlook. Deviating from Confucian principles, members of the new faction asserted that people should be guided by their own desire and rationality rather than inherited dogma. They took issue with many conventional principles. For example, they regarded selfishness as a part of human nature and thus deemed unavoidable. They also held that the long-promoted virtue of frugality was actually detrimental to social prosperity, while the much condemned practice of consumption was necessary for the economy of the society as a whole. They argued that the government should follow its own guidelines in administration and adopt changes when needed. With regard to foreign relations, they viewed foreigners as of equivalent status and believed that border incursions were most often directed at achieving commercial aims rather than conquest. Reversing the deep-seated prejudice about foreigners as inherently bellicose, they argued that it was the different social and economic development of foreign states and their unique geographical condition that made their people reliant on Chinese products. On this basis, they argued that it was in fact the Ming dynasty's trade prohibition that caused their aggression, and that this was driven by legitimate grievances.

Equipped with a new philosophy about foreign relations, the pro-trade officials re-defined the trade prohibition policy and the conflict with the Mongols and Japanese. They bravely acknowledged the unjustness of maintaining the trade prohibition. Pro-trade officials argued that the prohibition policy was responsible for the conflicts with foreigners who came for trade, not invasion; that it was fundamentally mistaken to pursue Chinese people simply for trying to make a living; and that it was almost impossible to defeat the foreigners when the Chinese troops were low in morale and when they had much sympathy for their enemies. They argued that it was foolish to believe that coastal patrols and peasant foot soldiers could prohibit foreign trade when the Japanese pirates were driven by such desperation, and when the Mongol cavalry, the local merchants and the landless peasantry were prepared to challenge the prohibition at any cost. The pro-trade officials demonstrated their great concern over the situation by submitting hundreds of memorials to the court, all arguing that the trade prohibition policy was politically destructive, generating animosity both at home and abroad. They believed that maintenance of such a policy would exhaust the state's financial resources and that a change of policy could turn an enemy into a business partner. Only by understanding the frustration of the 'enemies', altering preconceived ideas and lifting the detrimental prohibition could political stability be protected, national security guaranteed and China's 'master' status preserved. It was, they argued, high time to bring an end to the policy.

At the frontline of the debate over the financial crisis, the pro-trade officials organised a systematic attack against the trade prohibition policy. Their pragmatic and utilitarian approach led them to a head-on clash with the landed conservatives. They held the trade prohibition policy accountable for the border conflicts and blamed these 'invited' conflicts for the state's increasing financial burden. Instead of following the conservatives' format, to increase taxes and cut spending, they campaigned to abolish the prohibition on trade as a means to end the conflicts. Their position is summed up by the claim that, "The enemy wanted nothing but trade and refusing them the opportunity [to exchange their goods] for what they desperately need results in their hostility and the unwanted wars."[966]

Prosecuting these conflicts had put the economy in disarray. They had led to the collapse of the *tuntian* system along the northern and western borders and as a consequence the state had to take on the burden of feeding and equipping around half a million troops. The state's revenue was further depleted by having to fund highly paid mercenaries in order to strengthen the shaky defences. Worse still, the maritime prohibition resulted in a big drain on the state's revenue through the *caoyun* system, by which the transport of a significant volume of cargo from the south to the north of the empire was channelled into shallow canals and along the bumpy land route, instead of being transported more economically along the coast. This self-imposed system consumed ten or more times the resources that it would cost to use the sea route. The *bioama* institution was equally problematic, requiring taxpayers to raise horses at high expense because the state refused to buy much better quality Mongol horses at much less cost. The border conflicts had to be stopped and the *sine qua non* for this was lifting the ban on trade. Proponents of this argued that trade was not only the magic wand that would halt the conflicts but it was also a ready source of state revenue. Allowing maritime trade would not only save the two million *taels* spent on defence but it would also lead to an inflow of badly needed silver bullion, which would provide a timely 'blood transfusion' for a commercialising but deflated economy.

The policy debate remained heated until the lifting of the maritime prohibition in 1567, the opening of horse fairs with the Mongols in 1571 and the revival of the private tea trade along the western border. The late Ming policy overhaul marked the culmination of a political struggle between the landed conservatives and the pro-trade camp. The collapse of the self-sufficient economy undermined the very foundation of the early Ming institutional structure, while the new commercialised

966 *MJSWB*, vol. 301, *j.* 1, p. 1b.

economy ushered in a new ideology, new forms of social power and a new political landscape. The shift in power to the pro-trade camp determined the government's new direction, distinguished by its new foreign relations. The 200 year-long process of the Ming policy change provides the historian with a case study which confirms the argument that a coerced society with a command economy is bound to crumble, thus its superstructure policies based on such a society and economy is bound to alter with the framework transformation. The change to a centuries-old institution such as the maritime prohibition could neither simply result from the change of the external pressure, such as the situation of Japanese piracy, nor the changed political behaviour of an emperor or his courtiers. Rather, it reflected a grand reconfiguration of state, society and economy.

BIBLIOGRAPHY

Primary Sources

Source Collections

Congshu jicheng chubian 叢書集成初編 (*First Edition of the Collected Collectanea*) edited by Wang Yunwu 王雲五. (Beijing, Shangwu yinshuguan, 1937).

Gujin tushu jicheng 古今圖書集成 (*Collection of Historical Books throughout the Ages*) edited by Chen Menglei 陳夢雷 (1651–1723), Jiang Tingxi 蔣廷錫 (1669–1732) *et al.* (Beijing: Zhonghua shuju, 1934).

Guochao dianzhang 國朝典章 (*Imperial Statutes*), in *Siku cunmu* 史, fasc. 268, pp. 1–227.

Huang Ming zhaoling 皇明詔令 (*Imperial Edicts*), in *Siku cunmu* 史, fasc. 58, pp. 1–447.

Ming huiyao 明會要 (*Ming Political and Social Institutions*) edited by Long Wenbin 龍文彬 (1821–1893). (1887-edition), in *Siku xuxiu*, fasc. 793.

Ming jingshi wenbian 明經世文編 (*Collected Writings on Statecraft of the Ming Dynasty*) by Chen Zilong 陳子龍 (1608–1647) (ed.). (Beijing: Zhonghua shuju, 1997).

Ming shilu 明實錄 (*The Veritable Records of the Ming*) by Yao Guangxiao 姚廣孝 (1334–1418), Xia Yuanji 夏元吉 (1366–1430) *et. al.*, edited by the Taibei Zhongyang yanjiuyuan lishi yuyan yanjiusuo 臺北中央研究院歷史語言研究所. (Taibei: Zhongyang yanjiuyuan lishi yuyan yanjusuo, 1965).

Siku quanshu cunmu congshu 四庫全書存目叢書 (*The Complete Corpus of the Four Treasuries*) compiled by the Siku quanshu cunmu congshu bianzuan weiyuanhui 四庫全書存目叢書編纂委員會. (Jinan: Qilu shushe, 1997).

Siku jinhui congkan 四庫禁燬叢刊 (*Forbidden Books from the Complete Corpus of the Four Treasuries*) compiled by Siku jinhui congkan bianzuan weiyuanhui 四庫禁燬叢刊編纂委員會. (Beijing: Beijing chubanshe, 1998).

Wenyuange Siku quanshu 文淵閣四庫全書 (*Wenyuange: Complete Corpus of the Four Treasuries*) edited by Ji Yun 紀昀 (1724–1805) *et. al.* (Taibei: Taiwan Shangwu yinshu guan, 1986).

Xuxiu Siku quanshu 續修四庫全書 (*The Complete Corpus of the Four Treasuries: Continued and Revised*). (Shanghai: Shanghai guji chubanshe, 2002).

Individual Works

Ao Ying 敖英 (*jinshi* 1521), *Donggu zhuiyan* 東谷贅言 (*Superfluous Words from Donggu*), in *Siku cunmu* 子, fasc. 102, pp. 411–437.

Ban Gu 班固 (BCE 32–92), *Qian Han shu* 前漢書 (*The History of the Western Han Dynasty*), in *Siku quanshu*, fasc. 249–251, pp. 1–429.

Bao Ruji 包汝楫 (*jinshi* 1607), *Nanzhong jiwen* 南中紀文 (*Records of Nanzhong*). (Luxiang Block print edition, 1521–1571), in *Congshu jicheng chubian*, fasc. 3144.

Cai Jiude 采九德 (Ming), *Wobian shilüe* 倭變事略 (*Selected Biographies of Japanese Piracy*), in *Congshu jicheng chubian*, fasc. 3975.

Cai Sheng 蔡昇 (Ming), *Zhenze bian* 震澤編 (*A Collection on Zhenze*), in *Siku cunmu* 史, fasc. 228, pp. 666–776.

Cao Jiaju 曹家駒 (Qing), "Shuomeng yi 说梦一" (The Interpretation of Dreams, part one), in Fu Jin 富瑾 (ed.), *Qingren shuohui* 清人說薈 (*Collected Statements of Qing People*). (Caoye shanfang 掃業山房 edition, 1913–1917).

Cao Renhu 曹仁虎 (1730–1786), *Qinding xu wenxian tongkao* 欽定續文獻通考 (*Imperial Commissioned Encyclopeadia of Historical Records, Continued*), in *Siku quanshu*, fasc. 62, pp. 6–631.

Cha Jizuo 查繼佐 (1601–1676), *Zuiwei lu* 罪惟錄 (*A Record of the Contemplation of Crimes*), in *Siku xuxiu*, fasc. 321–323, pp. 1–688.

Chen Maoren 陳懋仁 (1573–1619), *Quannan zazhi* 泉南雜志 (*Random Notes about Quannan*). (Baoyan Tang, Shen's block print edition 沈氏刻寶顏堂秘笈, 1573–1620).

Chen Menglei 陳夢雷 (1651–1723), "Za shui bu 杂税部" (The Miscellaneous Levies), in *Gujin tushu jicheng* 古今圖書集成, *Jingji huibian shihuodian* 經濟彙編食貨典, *j.* 223. (Beijing: Zhonghua shuju, 1934), pp. 84381–84389.

Chen Menglei, "Kaogong dian 考工典", in *Gujin tushu jicheng, Jingji huibian kaogongdian* 經濟彙編考工典 *j.* 3. (Beijing: Zhonghua shuju, 1934), pp. 95296–95308.

Chen Menglei, "Yanzhou fubu fengsu kao 弇州府部風俗考", in *Gujin tushu jicheng, Fangyu huibian zhifangdian* 方輿彙編職方典, *j.* 230. (Beijing: Zhonghua shuju, 1934), pp. 9820–9835.

Chen Menglei, "Riben bu, bianyi dian 日本部, 邊裔典" (Collected Regulations on Neighbouring States: Japanese Section), in *Gujin tushu jicheng, Fangyu huibian bianyi dian* 方輿彙編邊裔典, *j.* 35. (Beijing: Zhonghua shuju, 1934), pp. 25152–25166.

Chen Qixiang 陳其纕 (Wujiang county magistrate, 1747) and Ni Shimeng 倪師孟 (*juren* 1727), *Wujiang xianzhi* 吳江縣志 (*The Gazetteer of Wujiang county*) (Qianlong edition), in *Zhongguo difangzhi jicheng* 中國地方志集成 (*The Collected Chinese Gazetteers*). (Nanjing: Jiangsu Ancient Books Publication, 1991).

Chen Renxi 陳仁錫 (1581–1636), *Huang Ming shifa lu* 皇明世法录 (*Rituals, Laws and Regulations of the State Administration of the Ming Dynasty*), in *Siku jinhui* 史, fasc. 13–16.

Cheng Kaigu 程開祜 (Ming), *Chou Liao shuohua* 筹遼碩画 (*Memorials about the Liaodong Defence*). (Beijing: reprinted from Wanli edition by the Commercial Press, 1936).

Chu Dawen 儲大文 (1665–1743) (ed.), *Shanxi tongzhi* 山西通志 (*Gazetteer of Shanxi Province*), in *Siku quanshu*, fasc. 542–550.

Chu Fu 褚鈇 (1533–1600), *Chu sinong wenji* 褚司農文集 (*The Collected Works of Chu Fu, the Mnister of Revenue*), in *MJSWB*, vol. 386, pp. 4179–4187.

Dong Gao 董誥 (1740–1818) *Quan Tang wen* 全唐文 (*Complete Documents of the Tang*). (Shanghai: Shanghai guji chuban she, 1990).

Dong Zhongshu 董仲舒 (BCE 179–104), *Chunqiu fanlu* 春秋繁露 (*Expositions on the Spring and Autumn Annals*), in *Siku quanshu*, fasc. 181, pp. 697–808.

Fan Lian 范濂 (b. 1540), *Yunjian jumu chao* 雲間據目抄 (*Happenings on Songjiang Observed through my Eyes*). (Shanghai: reprinted from the Zhe Family block print edition of Fengxian county 丰賢褚氏刻, 1928).

Fan Shouji 范守己 (*jinshi* 1574), "Quwei xinwen 曲洧新闻", (*News from Quwei*), in *Yu zilong ji* 禦子龍集 (*The Collected works of Yu Zilong*), in *Siku cunmu* 集, fasc. 162, pp. 495–731.

Fei Xin 費信 (1388–?), *Xingcha shenglan* 星槎勝覽 (*Overall Survey of the Star Raft*). (1599-edition), in *Siku xuxiu*, fasc. 742, pp. 407–427.

Feng En 馮恩 (*jinshi* 1523) *Feng shiyu churao lu* 馮侍御芻蕘錄 (*The Works of Investigating Censor Feng*), in *MJSWB*, vol. 200, pp. 2087–2094.

Feng Qi 馮琦 (1558–1603), *Feng beihai wenji* 馮北海文集 (*The Collected Works of Feng Beihai*), in *MJSWB*, vol. 442, pp. 4814–4857.

Feng Shike 馮時可 (*jinshi* 1571), *Feng Yuancheng wenji* 馮元成文集 (*The Collected Works of Feng Yuancheng*), in *MJSWB*, vol. 434, pp. 4735–4751.

Feng Zhang 馮璋 (*jinshi* 1538), *Feng Yangxu ji* 馮養虛集 (*The Collected Works of Feng Yangxu*), in *MJSWB*, vol. 280, pp. 2958–2967.

Fu Weilin 傅维麟 (?–1667), *Ming shu* 明書 (*Biographies, Annals, Records, and Monographs of the Ming Dynasty*), in *Siku cunmu* 史, fasc. 38–40, pp. 1–512.
Gao Gong 高拱 (*jinshi* 1542), *Gao wenxiang gong wenji* 高文襄公文集 (*The Collected Works of the Honourable Gao Wenxiang*), in *MJSWB*, vol. 301, pp. 3165–3197.
Gu Gongxie 顧公燮 (*juren* 1730), *Xiaoxia xianji zhaichao* 消夏闲記摘抄 (*Extracts from a Summer Resort Diary*). (Shanghai: Shanghai Commerical Publications, 1924.)
Gu Qiyuan 顧啓元 (1565–1628), *Kezuo zhuiyu*, 客座贅語 (*Superfluous Words to Entertain my Guests*), in *Siku cunmu* 子, fasc. 243, pp. 250–460.
Gu Yanwu 顧炎武 (1613–1682), *Tianxia junguo libing shu* 天下郡國利病書 (*Strengths and Weaknesses of the Various Regions of the Realm*). (Erlin zhaicang edition 二霖齋藏, 1901).
Gu Yanwu, *Tianxia junguo libing shu* 天下郡國利病書, in *Siku xuxiu*, fasc. 595–597, pp. 1–708.
Gu Yanwu & Huang Rucheng 黄汝成 (1799–1837), *Rizhi lu jishi* 日知錄集釋 (*Record of Knowledge Daily Acquired, with Commentaries*), in *Siku xuxiu*, fasc. 1143–1144, pp. 584–611.
Gu Yingtai 谷應泰 (Qing), *Ming jishi benmo* 明史記事本末 (*An Explanation of Important State Events and Policies of the Ming Dynasty*), in *Siku quanshu*, fasc. 364, pp. 117–1043.
Gui E 桂萼 (*jinshi* 1511), *Gui Wenxiang gong zouyi* 桂文襄公奏議 (*The Memorials of the Honourable Gui Wenxiang*), in *MJSWB*, vols. 179–182, pp. 1824–1867.
Gui Youguang 歸有光 (1506–1571), *Gui xiansheng ji* 歸先生文集 (*The Collected Works of Mr. Gui*), in *Siku cunmu* 集, fasc. 138, pp. 519–829.
Guo Tingxun 過廳訓 (*jinshi* 1604), *Benchao fensheng renwu kao* 本朝分省人物考 (*Biography of the Learned, Virtuous, and Good Officials Classified by Prefectures*), in *Siku jinhui* 史, fasc. 60–63, pp. 183–647.
Guo Zaoqing 郭造卿 (1532–1593), "Liaozhen tonghai yi 遼鎮通海議" (*Debate on the Lifting of the Maritime Trade Proscription in Liaohai*), in *Jiubian siyi* 九邊四夷 (*The Nine Borders and Four Kinds of Barbarians*), in *Tianxia junguo libing shu* 天下郡國利病書 by Gu Yanwu 顧炎武 (1613–1682), in *Siku xuxiu*, fasc. 597, pp. 601–602.
Han Bangqi 韓邦奇 (1479–1555), *Han Yuanluo quanji* 韩苑洛全集 (*The Complete Works of Han Bangqi, hao Yuanluo*), in *Siku quanshu*, fasc. 1269, pp. 331–710.
Han Dazhang 韓大章 (*jinshi* 1493), *Han* [*xx*] [967] *zoushu* 韓 xx 奏疏 (*The Memorials of Han* [*xx*]), in *MJSWB*, *j.* 2, pp. 5552–5556.
Han Yong 韓雍 (1422–1478), *Xiangyi wenji* 襄毅文集 (*The Collected Works of HanYong*), in *Siku quanshu*, fasc. 1245, pp. 603–809.
He Dongxu 何東序 (*jinshi* 1553), *He zhongcheng jiuyu shanfang ji* 何中丞九愚山房集 (*The Collected Works of He Dongxu, the Censor*), in *MJSWB*, vol. 382, pp. 4140–4148.
He Liangjun 何良浚 (1506–1573), *Siyou zhai congshuo* 四友齋叢說 (*Miscellaneous Notes from the Four-Friends-Hall*), in *Siku cunmu* 子, fasc. 103, pp. 281–560.
He Mingchun 何孟春 (1474–1636), *Yudong xulu* 餘冬序錄 (*Outline of my Works Written during the Winter Days of my Life*), in *Siku cunmu* 子, fasc. 101, pp. 556–780.
He Qiaoyuan 何喬遠 (1558–1632), *Min shu* 閩書 (*The Book of Min*), in *Siku cunmu* 史, fasc. 204–207.
He Qiaoyuan 何喬遠 (1558–1632), *Mingshan cang* 名山藏 (*Collection Hidden in Jingshan*), in *Siku jinhui* 史, fasc. 46, pp. 125–726.
He Sanwei 何三畏 (Prefecture Judge, 1583), *Yunjian zhilüe* 雲閒志略 (*A Brief Survey of Songjiang*), in *Siku jinhui* 子, fasc. 8, pp. 161–672.

967 These characters are missing.

He Tang 何瑭 (1474–1543), *Baizhai ji* 柏齋集 (*The Baizhai Collection*), in *Siku quanshu*, fasc. 1266, pp. 465–643.

Hou Xianchun 侯先春 (1545–1611), *Hou geijian zoushu* 侯给谏奏疏 (*The Memorials of Hou Xianchun, the Supervising Secretary*), in *MJSWB*, vol. 428–429, pp. 4674–4697.

Hu Zongxian 胡宗憲 (1511–1565), *Hu Shaobao zoushu* 胡少保奏疏 (*The Memorials of Hu Zongxian, the Tutor of the Heir Apparent*), in *MJSWB*, vols. 265–267, pp. 2796–2829.

Hu Zongxian, *Chouhai tubian* 籌海圖編 (*Illustrated Compendium on Maritime Security*), in *Siku quanshu*, fasc. 584, pp. 1–442.

Huang Pulu 皇甫錄 (1470–1540), *Huang Ming jiluo* 皇明紀略 (*A Brief Account of the Imperial Ming Dynasty*), in *Lidai xiaoshi* 歷代小史 (*The Mini Histories of the Former Dynasties*) edited by Li Shi 李栻 (*jinshi* 1562), in *Siku cunmu* 子, fasc. 24, pp. 71–87.

Huang Ren 黄任 (*juren* 1702) and Huai Yinbu 懷蔭布 (*jinshi* 1736), *Quanzhou fuzhi* 泉州府志 (*Gazetteer of Quanzhou Prefecture*), in *Zhongguo defang zhijicheng* 中國地方志集成福建府縣志集. (Shanghai, Shanghai shudian chubanshe, 2000), vol. 22, pp. 1–722.

Huang Shengzeng 黄省曾 (1490–1540), *Wuyue Shanren ji* 五岳山人集 (*Collection of the Huang Shengzeng, Hao Wuyue, the Hermit*), in *Siku cunmu* 集, fasc. 94, pp. 529–852.

Huang Yizhou 黄以周 (1828–1899), and Chen Zhongwei 陳重威, *Dinghai tingzhi* 定海廳誌 (*Gazetteer of Dinghai Prefecture*), in *Zhongguo difang zhi jicheng* 中國地方誌集成, vol. 38, (Nanjing: Jiangsu guji chubanshe, 1991), pp. 1–591.

Huang Yuangong 黄元恭 (*jinshi* 1547), "Lun tongshi 論通市" (*On Allowing Trade with Japan*), in *Gujin tushu jicheng*, vol. 40, *Riben bu zonglu Fangyu huibian yidian* 日本部總論，方輿彙編邊裔典, pp. 25202–25218.

Huang Yu 黄瑜 (*juren* 1456), *Xuanghuai suichao* 雙槐歲抄 (*Colletion of Annually Studying Notes from the Two Pagoda Trees Pavillion*), in *Siku cunmu* 子, fasc. 239, pp. 419–559.

Huang Zongxi 黄宗羲 (1610–1695), *Mingyi daifang lu* 明夷待訪錄 (*Waiting for the Dawn: A Plan For the Prince*), in *Siku xuxiu*, fasc. 945, pp. 465–492.

Huang Zongxi, *Mingwen hai* 明文海 (*Grand Collection of Ming Biographies*), in *Siku quanshu*, fasc. 1453–1458.

Huang Zuo 黄佐 (1490–1566), *Taiquan xiangli* 泰泉鄉禮 (*Community Decency,Ritual and Village Convants by Huang Zuo, Hao Taiquan*), in *Siku quanshu*, fasc. 142, pp. 591–662.

Huang Zuo, *Nanyong zhi* 南雍志 (*Annals of the Imperial Academy in Nanjing*), in *Siku cunmu* 史, fasc. 257, pp. 28–476.

Huo Tao 霍韜 (1487–1540), *Huo Wenmin gongwen ji* 霍文敏公文集 (*The Collected Works of Huo Wenmin*), in *MJSWB*, vols. 185–188, pp. 1883–1946.

Huo Yuxia 霍與瑕 (*jinshi* 1559), *Huo Mianzhong ji* 霍勉衷集 (*The Collected Works of Huo Yuxia, Hao Mianzhong*), in *MJSWB*, vol. 368, pp. 3974–3989.

Ji Shan 佶山 (Censor in salt administration, 1804), *Lianghuai yanfa zhi* 兩淮鹽法志 (*A Record of Salt Regulations for the Liang-Huai Region*). (Yangzhou: Yangzhou shuju, 1870).

Jiajing Woluan beichao 嘉靖倭亂備抄 (*A Back-up Copy of Records of the Unrest Caused by Japanese Pirates*), in *Siku cunmu* 史, fasc. 49, pp. 552–645.

Jiang Bao 姜寶 (1514–1593), *Jiang Feng'a ji* 姜鳳阿集 (*The Collected Works of Jiang Feng'a*), in *MJSWB*, vol. 383, pp. 4150–4162.

Jiang Chenying 姜宸英 (1628–1699) and Huang Shulin 黄叔琳 (*jinshi* 1691), *Zhanyuan ji* 湛園集 (*Collected Works of Jiang Chenying, Hao Zhanyuan*), in *Siku quanshu*, fasc. 1323, pp. 593–860.

Jiang Yihua 蔣以化 (*juren* between 1567 and 1573), *Xitai manji* 西臺漫記 (*Sketches by a Retired Censor*), in *Siku cunmu* 子, fasc. 242, pp. 61–160.

Jiao Hong 焦竑 (1541–1620), *Guochao xianzheng lu* 國朝獻徵錄 (*Ming Biographies up to the Wanli Reign Compiled by Jiao Hong, The Hanlin Academician*), in *Siku cunmu* 史, fasc. 100–107.

Jin Sheng 金聲 (1598–1645), *Jin Zhongjie gongwen ji* 金忠節公文集 (*Collection of Jin Sheng, Shihao Zhongjie*). (明末邵鵬程刻本, Late Ming Edition printed by Shao Pengcheng, 1889).

Jin Xueyan 靳學顏 (1514–1571), *Jin Shaozai zoushu* 靳少宰奏疏 (*The Memorial Collection of Jin Xueyan, the Deputy Minister of Personnel*), in *MJSWB*, vol. 299, pp. 3140–3149.

Kong Qi 孔齊 (Yuan), *Jingzhai zhizheng zhiji* 静齋至正直記 (*An Unbiased Observation of the Zhizheng Reign* (1341–1368) *by Kong Qi, Hao Jingzhai*), in *Siku xuxiu*, fasc. 239, pp. 199–285.`

Lan Dingyuan 藍鼎元 (1680–1733), *Luzhou chuji* 鹿洲初集 (*First Edition of the Collected Works of Lan Dingyuan, Hao Luzhou*), in *Siku quanshu*, fasc. 1327, pp. 567–870.

Li Chunfang 李春芳 (1510–1584), *Yi'antang ji* 貽安堂集 (*Collection from the Yi'antang Ancestry Hall*), in *Siku cunmu* 集, fasc. 113, pp. 1–323.

Li Chunfang, *Li Shilu ji* 李石麓集 (*Collected Works of Li Chunfang, Hao Shilu*), in *MJSWB*, vol. 281, pp. 2969–2977.

Li Fang 李昉 (925–996), *Wenyuan yinghua* 文苑英華 (*The best selected works by the scholars in history*), *j.* 422, in *Siku quanshu*, fasc. 1333–1342.

Li Guangjin 李光縉 (Ming), *Jingbi ji* 景壁集 (*The Scenic Wall Collection*). (Quanzhou: no publisher, 1637).

Li Hualong 李化龍 (1554–1611), *Li Xiangyi gong fuliao zougao* 李襄毅公抚辽奏稿 (*Collected Memorials on Liaodong by Li Hualong, Shihao Xiangyi, the Grand Coordinator*), in *MJSWB*, vol. 422, pp. 4592–4602.

Li Mengyang 李夢陽 (1473–1529), *Kong tong ji* 空同集 (*Collected Works with Nothing in Common with the Fashionable Style*), in *Siku quanshu*, fasc. 1262, pp. 1–612.

Li Weizhen 李維禎 (1547–1626), *Taimi shanfang ji* 太泌山房集 (*Collection of Works from Taimishan*), in *Siku xuxiu* 集, fasc. 150–153, pp. 276–746.

Li Xi 李熙 (Zhenghe county magistrate, 1911), *Zhenghe xianzhi*, 政和縣志 (*Gazetteer of Zhenghe County*), in *Zhongguo difangzhi jicheng* 中國地方志集成 (*Collected Chinese Gazetteers*), vol. 8. (Shanghai: Shanghai shudian chubanshe, 2000), pp. 407–733.

Li Xian 李賢 (1408–1466), *Gurang ji* 古穰集 (*Collected Works Named after my Home Town in Gurang County*), in *Siku quanshu*, fasc. 1244, pp. 481–798.

Li Xinchuan 李心傳 (1167–1244), *Jianyan yilai xinian yaolu* 建炎以來繫年要錄 (*Important Eventes Chronologically Arranged since the Jianyan Reign Period* (1127–1130), in *Siku quanshu*, fasc. 325–327.

Li Yangong 李言恭 (*jinshi* 1556) & Hao Jie 郝杰 (1530–1600), *Riben kao* 日本考 (*A Study of Japan*), in *Siku xuxiu*, fasc. 744, pp. 713–797.

Li Zhi 李贄 (1527–1602), *Cang shu* 藏書 (*A Book to Conceal*). (Beijing: Zhonghua shuju, 1974).

Li Zhi, *Cang shu* 藏書 (*A Book to Conceal*), in *Siku cunmu* 史, fasc. 23, pp. 266–790.

Li Zhi, *Lishi zupu* 李氏族譜 (*Clan Genealogy of the Li Family*). (Fuzhou: Hand-written copy from the Fujian Shifan University).

Li Zhi, *Li Wenling ji* 李温陵集 (*Collected Works of Li Zhi, Literary and Buddhist Name by Wenling, the Monk at Residence*), in *Siku xuxiu*, fasc. 1352, pp. 1–298.

Liang Cai 梁材 (*jinshi* 1505), *Liang Duansu gong zongji* 梁端肅公奏議 (*Collection of Memorials of Liang Cai, Shihao Duanxiao*), in *MJSWB*, vols. 102–103, pp. 909–931.

Lin Lian 林燫 (*jinshi* 1547), *Lin xueshi wenji* 林學士文集 (*Collected Works of Scholar Lin Lian, the Chancellor of the Hanlin Academy*), in *MJSWB*, vol. 313, pp. 3311–3321.

Lin Shiyi 林時益 (1618–1678), *Ningdu san-Wei ji* 寧都三魏全集 (*Complete Collection of the Three Wei Brothers from Ningdu*), in *Siku jinhui* 集, fasc. 4–6.

Lin Xiyuan 林希元 (*jinshi* 1517), *Lin Ciya xiansheng wenji* 林次崖先生文集 (*Collected Works of Lin Xiyuan, Hao Ciya*), in *Siku cunmu* 集, fasc. 75, pp. 409–761.

Liu Ruoyu 劉若愚 (eunuch, 1622–1627), *Zhuozhong zhi* 酌中志 (*A Eunuch's Unbiased Description and Observation of the Court Institutions, Events, and Policy Processes*). (The Qing edition of the Collected Unofficial Histories of the Ming), in *Siku xuxiu* 史, fasc. 437, pp. 433–585.

Liu Tao 劉燾 (*jinshi* 1538), *Liu Daichuan shugao* 劉帶川書稿 (*Policy Statements of Liu Tao, Hao Daichuan*), in *MJSWB*, vol. 308, pp. 3248–3254.

Liu Weiqian 劉惟謙 (Minister of justice, 1373), *Da Ming lü* 大明律 (*The Grand Ming Code*). (Fanyong luan keben, 1522–1573), in *Siku cunmu* 史, fasc. 276, pp. 469–730.

Liu Xu 劉昫 (888–947), *Jiu Tang shu* 舊唐書 (*Old History of the Tang Dynasty*), in *Siku quanshu*, fasc. 268–271.

Liu Zongzhou 劉宗周 (1578–1645), *Chengren sheyue yan* 澄人社約言 (*Moral Standards and Community Regulations to Become an Ideal Community Member*), in *Siku cunmu* 子, fasc. 15, pp. 298–307.

Long Yongbin 龍永彬 (1821–1893), *Ming huiyao* 明會要 (*Ming Political and Social Institutions*), in *Siku xuxiu*, fasc. 793, pp. 1–719.

Lou Xing 婁性 (*jinshi* 1481), *Huang Ming zhengyao* 皇明政要 (*Personal Statements on Government Administration by Five Ming Emperors – from Hongwu to Yingzong*), in *Siku cunmu*, 史, fasc. 46, pp. 191–344.

Lü Ben 呂本 (ed.), *HuangMing baoxun* 皇明寶訓 (*Imperial Ancestral Instructions of the Hongwu and Yongle Emperors*), in *Siku cunmu* 史, fasc. 53, pp. 655–890.

Lu Ji 陸楫 (1515–1552), *Jianxiatang gao* 兼葭堂稿 (*Writings from my 'Reeds House'*), in *Siku xuxiu*, fasc. 1354, pp. 591–652.

Lü Kun 呂坤 (1436–1518), *Lügong Shizheng lu* 呂公實政錄 (*Rules and Regulations for Practical Administration by Lü Kun*), in *Siku xuxiu* 子 fasc. 164, pp. 337–577.

Ma Sen 馬森 (1506–1580), *Ma gongmin gong zouji* 馬恭敏公奏集 (*Collected Memorials of Ma Sen, Shihao Gongmin*), in *MJSWB*, vol. 298, pp. 3129–3139.

Ma Wensheng 馬文升 (1426–1510), *Ma Duansu gong zoushu* 馬端肅公奏疏 (*Collected Memorials of Ma Wensheng, Shihao Duansu*), in *MJSWB*, vol. 62, pp. 503–549.

Mao Kun 茅坤 (1512–1601), *Mao Lumen wenji* 茅鹿門文集 (*Collected Works of Mao Kun, Hao Lumen*), in *MJSWB*, vol. 256, pp. 2700–27165.

Mao Kun, *Xuhai benmo* 徐海本末 (*Topically Arranged Histories on Xu Hai, the Pirate Chief*), in *Siku cunmu* 史, fasc. 128, pp. 745–752.

Mao Yuanyi 茅元儀 (*Chongzhen* period Hanlin official), *Wubei zhi* 武備誌 (*Coastal Defence Annals*), in *Siku jinhui* 子, fasc. 23–26.

Mao Yuanyi, *Wubei zhi* 武備志 (*Coastal Defence Annals*), in *Gugong zhenben congkan* 故宮珍本叢刊 (*The Imperial Palace Collection*). (Hainan: Hainan publication House, 2001), vols. 353–358.

Mingdai dengke lu huibian 明代登科錄彙編 (*Compendium of Files on the Successful Candidates in Imperial Examinations of the Ming Dynasty*). (Taibei: Taiwan xuesheng shuju, 1969).

Ouyang Xiu 歐陽修 (1007–1072) and Shen Deqian 沈德潛 (1673–1769), *Xin Tang shu* 新唐書 (*New History of the Tang Dynasty*), in *Siku quanshu*, fasc. 272–276.

Pang Shangpeng 龐尚鵬 (*jinshi* 1553), *Pang zhongcheng zhaigao* 龐中丞摘稿 (*Excerpts from the Writings of Pang Shangpeng, the Grand Coordinator*), in *MJSWB*, vols. 357–360, pp. 3832–3895.

Qian Wei 錢薇 (1502–1554), *Chengqitang ji* 承啓堂集 (*Collected Works from the Chengqi Hall*), in *MJSWB*, vol.s 214–215, pp. 2231–2253.

Qian Wei, *Haishi xiansheng wenji* 海石先生文集 (*Collected Works of Qian Wei, Hao Haishi*), in *Siku cunmu* 集, fasc. 97, pp. 1–442.

Qian Yong 錢泳 (1759–1844), *Luyuan conghua* 履園叢話 (*Collection of Stories Named After my Residence, the Luyuan House*), in *Siku xuxiu*, fasc. 1139, pp. 1–370.
Qiu Jun 丘濬 (1418–1495), *Daxue yanyi bu* 大学衍義補 (*Supplement to the Elucidation of the Great Learning*), in *Siku quanshu*, fasc. 712, pp. 1–370.
Qu Dajun 屈大均 (1630–1696), *Guangdong xinyu* 廣東新語 (*New Stories of Guangdong*). (Beijing: Zhonghua shuju, 1700–edition, 1983).
Rao Zongyi 饒宗頤 (1917–), *Chaozhou zhi* 潮州志 (*Gazetteer of Chaozhou Prefecture*). (Guangdong: 1522-edition, reprinted 1949).
Shen Chaoxuan 沈朝宣 (Jiangling county magistrate, *jiajing* reign), *Renhe xianzhi* 仁和縣志 (*Gazetteer of Renhe County*). (Ding's Jiahui tang edition 丁氏嘉惠堂, 1875–1907).
Shen Defu 沈德符 (1578–1642), *Yehuo bian* 野獲編 (*Unofficial Anecdotes by a Retired Scholars*), in *Siku jinhui* 史, fasc. 4, pp. 1–702.
Shen Hong 沈彤 (1688–1752) and Ni Shimeng 倪師孟 (*jinshi* 1723), *Wujiang xianzhi* 吳江縣志 (*Gazetteer of Wujiang County*), in *Zhongguo difangzhi jicheng* 中國地方志集成 (*Collected Chinese Gazetteers*). (Nanjing: Jiangsu Ancient Books Publication, 1991), vol. 19–20, pp. 343–571.
Shen Jia 沈佳 (*jinshi* 1690), *Mingru yanxing lu* 明儒言行錄 (*Statements and Implementations of the Confucian Principle by the Ming Literati*), in *Siku quanshu*, fasc. 458, pp. 591–1071.
Shen Jiefu 沈節甫 (1533–1601), *Jilu huibian* 紀錄匯编 (*Collections of Essays, Stories,Comments, and Quotations before the Ming Jiajing Reign*). (Chen Yuting 陳于廷 Publication, 1617).
Shen Shixing 申時行 (1535–1614) and Zhao Yongxian 趙用賢 (1535–1596), *Da Ming huidan* 大明會典 (*Collected Statutes of the Ming Dynasty*), in *Siku xuxiu*, fasc. 791, pp. 789–792.
Shen Yao 沈垚 (1790–1840), *Luofanlou wenji* 落帆楼文集 (*Collected Works from the Luofan Mansion*), in *Siku xuxiu*, fasc. 1525, pp. 353–673.
Shen Yiguan 沈一貫 (1531–1615), *Shen jiaomen wenji* 沈蛟門文集 (*Collected Works of Shen Yiguan, Hao Jiaomen*), in *MJSWB*, vol. 435, pp. 4759–4770.
Shen Yue 沈越 (*jinshi* 1532), *Huang Ming Jia-Long liangchao wenjian ji* 嘉隆兩朝聞見紀 (*Minutes of Jiajing and Longqing Administrations*), in *Siku cunmu* 史, fasc. 7, pp. 253–555.
Shi Dao 史道 (1485–1554), *Shi dufu zouyi* 史督撫奏議 (*Memorials of Shi Dao, the Supreme Commander and Grand Coordinator*), in *MJSWB*, vol. 166, pp. 1687–1695.
Sima Guang 司馬光 (1019–1086) and Hu Sanxing 胡三省 (1230–1302) (comment.), *Zizhi tongjian* 資治通鑒 (*Comprehensive Mirror for Aid in Government*). (Shanghai: Shanghai guji chubanshe, 1986).
Sima Guang, *Zizhi tongjian* 資治通鑒 (*Comprehensive Mirror for Aid in Government*), in *Siku quanshu*, fasc. 304–310.
Sima Qian 司馬遷 (BC 145–?), *Shi ji* 史記 (*Records of the Grand Historian*), in *Siku quanshu*, fasc. 243–244.
Sima Qian, *Shi ji* 史記. (Beijing: Zhonghua shuju, 1956).
Song Lian 宋濂 (1310–1381), *Yuan shi* 元史 (*History of the Yuan Dynasty*), in *Siku quanshu*, fasc. 29, pp. 2–295.
Song Yiwang 宋儀望 (*jinshi* 1547), *Song dufu zoushu* 宋督撫奏疏 (*Memorials of Song Yiwang, Governor and Inspector General*), in *MJSWB*, vol. 362, pp. 3900–3905.
Su You 蘇祐 (1492–1571), *Su sima zouyi* 蘇司馬奏議 (*Memorials of Su You, Minister of War*), in *MJSWB*, vol. 216, pp. 2254–2259.
Sun Chengze 孫承澤 (1592–1676), *Chunming meng yu lu* 春明夢餘錄 (*Writings After a Bright Spring Dream*), in *Siku quanshu*, fasc. 868–869.

Sun Erzhun 孫爾准 (1770–1832) & Chen Shouqi 陳壽祺 (1771–1834), (*Chongzuan*) *Fujian tongzhi* 重纂福建通志 (*Newly Compiled Gazetteer of Fujian Province*). (Zhengyi Academy 正誼書院, 1868).

Sun Zhiwei 孫枝蔚 (1620–1687), *Gaitang qianhou xuji* 溉堂前後續集 (*Collected Writings Consisting of the Former, the Later and its Continuation Parts, Named After my Dwelling House, the Gaitang*), in *Siku cunmu* 集, fasc. 206, pp. 469–848.

Tan Lun 譚倫 (1520–1577), *Tan Xiangmin zouyi* 潭襄敏奏議 (*Memorials for Court Debate by Tan Lun, Shihao* 謚號 *Xiangmin*), in *Siku quanshu*, fasc. 429, pp. 587–824.

Tan Lun, *Tan Xiangmin gong zoushu* 譚襄敏公奏疏 (*Personal Memorials by Tan Lun, Shihao Xiangmin*), in *MJSWB*, vol. 322, pp. 3432–3439.

Tan Qian 談遷 (1595–1658), *Guoque* 國榷 (*Annalistic Deliberations on State Affairs*), in *Siku xuxiu*, fasc. 35, pp. 8–359.

Tang Shunzhi 唐順之 (1507–1560), *Jinchuan ji* 荊川集 (*Collected Works of Tang Shuzhi, Hao Jingchuan*), in *Siku quanshu*, fasc. 1276, pp. 183–490.

Tang Shunzhi, *Chongkan Jingchuan xiansheng wenji* 重刊荊川先生文集 (*Newly Printed Collected Literary Works of Tang Shuzhi, Hao Jingchuan*). (Hanfen lou 涵芬樓, Wanli-edition). (Beijing: Commercial Press, 1919).

Tang Shunzhi, *Tang jingchuan jia cang ji* 唐荆川家藏集 (*The Family Collection of Tang Shuzhi, Hao Jingchuan*), in *MJSWB*, vols. 259–260, pp. 2735–2766.

Tang Shunzhi), *Tang jingchuan wenji* 唐荊川文集 (*Collected Literary Works of Tang Shunzhi, Hao Jingchuan*). (Jiangnan: Jiangnan shuju, 1549).

Tang Shu 唐樞 (1497–1574), *Yu Wo zazhu* 禦倭雜著 (*Assorted Works on Defence against Japanese Piracy*), in *MJSWB*, vol. 270, pp. 2849–2859.

Tang Zhen 唐甄 (1630–1704), *Qian shu* 潛書 [衡書] (*Undisclosed Analysis of Political Matters*), in *Siku cunmu* 子, fasc. 95, pp. 370–513.

Toghto 托克托 (1314–1355), *Song shi* 宋史 (*History of the Song Dynasty*), in *Siku quanshu*, fasc. 280–288.

Tu Shan 涂山 (Ming), *Xinke Ming zhengtong zong* 新刻明政統宗 (*Newly Printed Unoffical Veritable Records of the Ming Dynasty*), in *Siku jinhui* 史, fasc. 2–3, pp. 89–185.

Tu Zemin 涂澤民 (?–1569), *Tu zhongcheng junwu jilu* 涂中丞軍務集錄 (*Collected Works on Military Affairs by Tu Zemin, the Grand Coordinator*), in *MJSWB*, vol. 355, pp. 3816–3828.

Tu Zhonglü 屠仲律 (*jinshi* 1550), *Tu shiyu zoushu* 屠侍御奏疏 (*Memorials of Tu Zhonglü, the Censor*), in *MJSWB*, vol. 282, pp. 2978–2982.

Tu Zongjun 涂宗濬 (*jinshi* 1583), *Tu sima beilu fenggong shimo shu* 涂司馬北虜封貢始末疏 (*Itemised Memorials about Title Conferring and Tribute Status Grants to the Mongols by Tu Zongjun, the Minister of War*), in *MJSWB*, vol. 450, pp. 4946–4954.

Wan Biao 萬表 (1498–1556), *Haikou yi* 海寇議 (*Discussion on Piracy*), in *Siku cunmu* 子, fasc. 31, pp. 36–44.

Wan Gong 萬恭 (1515–1591), *Wan sima zouyi* 萬司馬奏議 (*Memorials for Court Debate by Wan Gong, the Minister of War*), in *MJSWB*, vol. 352, pp. 3772–3795.

Wang Chonggu 王崇古 (1515–1588), *Wang Jianchuan wenji* 王鑑川文集 (*Collected Works of Wang Chonggu, Hao Jianchuan*), in *MJSWB*, vols. 316–318, pp. 3343–3389.

Wang Daokun 汪道昆 (1525–1593), *Taihan ji* 太函集 (*Collected Works of Wang Daokun, Hao Taihan*), in *Siku cunmu* 集, fasc. 117–118.

Wang Dewan 王德完 (1554–1621), *Wang Dujian zoushu* 王都諫奏疏 (*Personal Memorials of Wang Dewan, the Supervising Secretary*), in *MJSWB*, vol. 444, pp. 4874–4888.

Wang Fu 王符 (85–162), *Qianfu lun* 潛夫論 (*Discussion [on Political Matters] by Wang Fu, the Hermit, Hao Qianfu*), in *Siku quanshu*, fasc. 696, pp. 355–432.

Wang Jiabin 王嘉賓 (*jinshi* 1562), "*Kai yan lu du jian meng yi quan shengde shu* 開言路杜姦萌以全聖德疏 (*A Memorial to Provide More and Better Means for Officials to Air their Views to Nip the Treacherous Bud to Safe-guard the Virtue of the Emperor*), in *Huang Ming liutai zouyi* 皇明留臺奏議 (*Memorials for Court Discussion from the Ming Censors*) edited by Zhu Wubi 朱吾弼 (*jinshi* 1589), in *Siku xuxiu*, fasc. 467, pp. 269–778.

Wang Mingqing 王明清 (1127–?), *Huicheng yuhua* 揮塵餘話 (*Remaining Words from my Conversations*), in *Siku quanshu*, fasc. 1038, pp. 566–616.

Wang Qi 王圻 (*jinshi* 1566), Xi Huang 嵇璜 (1711–1794) *et al.*, *Xu wenxian tongkao* 續文獻通考 (*Compilation of Dynastic Government Administration Documents, Continued*), in *Siku xuxiu*, fasc. 761–767.

Wang Qi 王琦 (*juren* Yongle reign), *Yupu zaji* 寓圃雜記 (*Miscellaneous Writings from my Garden*), in *Siku cunmu* 子, fasc. 239, pp. 685–729.

Wang Shixing 王士性 (1546–1598) *Guangzhi yi* 廣志繹 (*Extensive Interpretation of my Travel Diaries*), in *Siku cunmu* 史, fasc. 251, pp. 685–804.

Wang Shizhen 王世貞 (1526–1590), *Yanzhou sibu gao* 弇州四部稿 (*Notes in Four Sections by Wang Shizhen, Hao Yanzhou*), in *Siku quanshu*, fasc. 1279–1281.

Wang Shizhen, *Yanshantang bieji* 弇山堂別集 (*Collected Works from Yanshantang, Wang Shizhen's Ancestry Hall*), in *Siku quanshu*, fasc. 409–410, pp. 1–528.

Wang Shizhen, *Yanzhou shiliao qianji* 弇州史料前集 (*Historical Materials by Wang Shizhen, Hao Yanzhou; Former Part*), in *Siku cunmu* 史, fasc. 1279–1281.

Wang Shizhen, *Gubugu lu* 觚不觚錄 (*Nostalgia, Recalled from the Grand and Trivial Matters of Past Days*), in *Siku quanshu*, fasc. 1041, pp. 425–440.

Wang Shizhen, *Wang Yanzhou wenji* 王弇州文集 (*Collected Literary Works of Wang Shizhen, Hao Yanzhou*), in *MJSWB*, vols. 332–335, pp. 3543–3599.

Wang Shizhen, *Fengzhou biji houji* 鳳洲筆記後集 (*Random Notes from Fengzhou by Wang Shizhen; Supplement*), in *Siku cunmu* 集, fasc. 114, pp. 518–806.

Wang Shouren 王守仁 (1472–1528), *Wang Yangming xiansheng quanji* 王陽明先生全集 (*Complete Collected Works of Wang Shouren, LiteraryName by Yangming*), in *Siku cunmu* 集, fasc. 50–51, pp. 235–350.

Wang Tingxiang 王廷相 (1474–1544), *Wang shi jiacang ji* 王氏家藏集 (*Family Collection of Wang Tingxian*), in *MJSWB*, vol. 149, pp. 1479–1493.

Wang Weide 王维德 (1669–1749), *Lin wu minfeng* 林屋民風 (*Folk Ways from the Countryside*), in *Siku cunmu* 史, fasc. 239, pp. 341–540.

Wang Yingkui 王應奎 (1686–1767), *Liunan suibi* 柳南随笔 (*Random Notes by Wang Yingkui, Hao Liunan*), in *Congshu jicheng chubian*, fasc. 2961–2963.

Wang Yu 王忬 (1507–1560), *Wang sima zoushu* 王司馬奏疏 (*Personal Memorials by Wang Yu, Minister of War*), in *MJSWB*, vol. 283, pp. 2983–2998.

Wang Zaijin 王在晉 (*jinshi* 1592), *Haifang zuanyao* 海防纂要 (*Essentials of Writings on Coastal Defence*), in *Siku jinhui* 史, fasc. 17, pp. 445–710.

Wang Zaijin 王在晉 (*jinshi* 1592), *Yue juan* 越镌 (*Papers from a Zhejiang Official*), in *Siku jinhui* 集, fasc. 104, pp. 257–502.

Wang Zhuo 王晫 (b. 1636) and Zhang Chao 張潮 (Qing), *Tanji congshu* 檀幾叢書 (*Collection of Important Books Worth to be Offered on a Sandlewood Table*). (Shexian county, Bookmaker Zhang's Publication Hall, 歙縣張氏霞舉堂, 1695).

Wang Yuezhen 王曰楨 (1812–1881), *Nanxunzhen zhi* 南潯鎮誌 (*Annals of Nanxun Township*) (1858), in *Siku xuxiu*, fasc. 717, pp. 131–168.

Wang Zongmu 王宗沐 (1523–1591), *Wang Jingsuo ji* 王敬所集 (*Collected Works of Wang Zongmu, Hao Jingsuo*), in *MJSWB*, vols. 343–345, pp. 3674–3736.

Wanli sanshiwu nian dingwei ke jinshi luli bianlan 萬曆三十五年丁未科進士履歷便覽 (*A Brief Guide on the Jinshi Degree Holders of the 35th year of the Wanli reign*). (Shanghai: Shanghai Library digital copy).

Wei Shixiao 魏世效 (1655–?), *Wei Zhaoshi wenji* 魏昭士文集 (*Collected Literary Works of Wei Shixiao, Hao Zhaoshi*), in *Siku jinhui*, 集, fasc. 6, pp. 236–403.

Wei Su 危素 (1303–1372), *Wei xueshi quanji* 危學士全集 (*Complete Collected Works of Wei Su, the Hanlin Academician*), in *Siku cunmu* 集, fasc. 24, pp. 617–845.

Wei Yuan 魏源 (1794–1857), *Yuan shi xinbian* 元史新編 (*Newly Edited History of the Yuan Dynasty*). (1905-edition), in *Siku xuxiu*, fasc. 314–3115, pp. 1–494.

Wen Baozhong 温寶忠 (Ming), *Wen Baozhong yigao* 温寶忠遺稿 (*Posthumous Works of Wen Baozhong*), in *Qiankun zhengqi ji* 乾坤正氣集 (*Collected Works to Demonstrate the Spirit of Universal Integration*). (Jingxian County, 潘氏刻本, Pan family printing, 1849).

Weng Wanda 翁萬達 (1498–1552), *Weng Dongya wenji* 翁東涯文集 (*Collected Literary Works of Weng Wanda, Hao Dongya*), in *MJSWB*, vols. 223–224, pp. 2346–2362.

Wu Guifang 吳桂芳 (1521–1578), *Wu sima zouyi* 吳司馬奏議 (*Memorials for Court Debate by Wu Guifang, Minister of War*), in *MJSWB*, vol. 342, pp. 3662–3673.

Wu Shilai 吳時來 (*jinshi* 1553), *Wuzhai wenji* 悟齋文集 (*Collected Literary Works of Wu Shilai, Hao Wuzhai*), in *MJSWB*, vol. 385, pp. 4173–4178.

Wu Shoufu 吳受福 (Qing) & Shi Zhongyu 石中玉 (Qing), *Jiaxing xianzhi* 嘉興縣誌 (*Gazetteer of Jiaxing County*), in *Zhongguo difangzhi jicheng*, vol. 15. (Shanghai, Shanghai shudian chubanshe, 1993).

Wu Kuan 吳寬 (*jinshi* 1472), *Pao Wengjia cangji* 匏翁家藏集 (*Family Collection of Wu Kuan, Old Master Pao*). (Shanghai: Sibu congkan, 1506–1520).

Wu Yangxian 吳仰賢 (1821–1887), *Jiading fuzhi* 嘉興府誌 (*Gazetteer of Jiading Prefecture*), in *Zhongguo difangzhi jicheng*, vols. 12–14. (Shanghai: Shanghai shudian chubanshe, 1993).

Wu Yingqi 吳應箕 (1594–1645), *Loushantang ji* 楼山堂集 (*Collection from the Loushantang Hall*), in *Siku xuxiu*, fasc. 1388 and *Siku jinhui* 集, fasc. 11, pp. 321–561.

Wu Yuancui 伍袁萃 (*jinshi* 1580), *Linju manlu* 林居漫錄 (*Random Notes from my Retirement Days in the Countryside*), in *Siku cunmu* 子, fasc. 242, pp. 422-597.

Xia Xie 夏燮 (1800–1875), *Ming tongjian* 明通鑒 (*Ming Comprehensive Mirror for Administration*), in *Siku xuxiu*, fasc. 364–366.

Xie Jie 謝傑 (1536–1604), *Qiantai Wo zuan* 虔臺倭纂 (*A Record of Qiantai Piracy*), in *Xuanlantang congshu xuji* 玄覽堂叢書續集. (Nanjing: Guoli zhongyang tushuguan, 1947), fasc. 17–18.

Xie Zhaozhi 謝肇淛 (1567–1642), *Wu zazu* 五雜俎 (*Five Mixed Platters*), *Siku jinhui* 子, fasc. 37, pp. 347–703, and *Siku xiuxiu*, fasc. 1130, pp. 337–685.

Xu Fuyuan 許孚遠 (1535–1604), *Jinghetang ji* 敬和堂集 (*Collected Works by Xu Fuyuan, from the Jinghe Ancestral Hall*), in *MJSWB*, vol. 400, pp. 4332–4342.

Xu Guangqi 徐光啓 (1562–1633), *Xu Wendinggong ji* 徐文定公集 (*Collected Works of Xu Guangqi, Shihao Wending*), in *MJSWB*, vols. 488–493, pp. 5422–5471.

Xu Guangqi, *Nongzhen quanshu* 農政全書 (*Complete Handbook on Agricultural Administration*), in *Siku quanshu*, fasc. 731, pp. 1–930.

Xu Jie 徐階 (1503–1583), *Shijingtang ji* 世經堂集 (*The Shijingtang Collection*), in *Siku cunmu* 集, fasc. 79–80.

Xu Jie, *Xu Wenzhen gong ji* 徐文貞公集 (*Collected Works of Xu Jie, Shihao Wenzhen*), in *MJSWB*, vols. 244–245, pp. 2559–2577.

Xu Sanchong 徐三重 (*jinshi* 1577), *Caiqin lu* 採芹錄 (*Collection of Scholars' Academic Pursue*), in *Siku quanshu*, fasc. 867, pp. 357–418.

Xu Song 徐松 (1781–1848) *et al.* (comp.), *Song huiyao jigao* 宋會要輯稿 (*A Draft of Documents Pertaining to Matters of State in the Song Dynasty*). (Beijing: Zhonghua shuju, 1957).

Xu Wei 徐渭 (1521–1593), *Xu Wenchang ji* 徐文長文集 (*Collected Literary Works of Xu Wei, Hao Wenchang*), in *Siku cunmu* 集, fasc. 145, pp. 1–338.

Xu Xianzhong 徐獻忠 (1483–1559), *Wuxing zhanggu ji* 吳興掌故集 (*Collected Anecdotes of Wuxing*), in *Siku cunmu* 史, fasc. 188, pp. 660–885.

Xu Xueju 徐学聚 (*jinshi* 1583), *Guochao dianhui* 國朝典匯 (*Imperial Decrees and Regulations*), in *Siku cunmu* 史, fasc. 264–266.

Xu Yan 許琰 (Qing), *Putoushan zhi* 普陀山志 (*Annals of Putuoshan*), in *Siku xuxiu*, fasc. 723, pp. 237–440.

Xu Youzhen 徐有貞 (*jinshi* 1433), *Wugong ji* 武功集 (*Collected Works of Xu Youzhen, Earl of Wugong*), in *Siku quanshu*, fasc. 1245, pp. 1–234.

Xue Yunsheng 薛允升 (1820–1901), *TangMing lü hebian* 唐明律合编 (*Comparative Analysis of Tang and Ming Law Codices*). (Xu Shichang's Degengtang Publishing House 徐世昌得耕堂刻本 1922).

Yan Congjian 嚴從簡 (*jinshi* 1535), *Shuyu zhouzi lu* 殊域周咨錄 (*A Comprehensive Record on Foreign Countries*), in *Siku xuxiu*, fasc. 735–736.

Yan Song 嚴嵩 (1480–1565), *Nangong zouyi* 南宮奏議 (*Memorials for Court Discussion from the Secretariat*), in *MJSWB*, vol. 219, pp. 2284–2302.

Yang Jisheng 楊繼勝 (1516–1555), *Yang Jiaoshan ji* 楊椒山集 (*Collected Works of Yang Jisheng, Hao Jiaoshan*), in *MJSWB*, vol. 293, pp. 3082–3096.

Yang Shicong 杨士聪 (1597–1648), *Yutanghui ji* 玉堂薈記 (*Assorted Unoffical Materials and Casual Commentaries to Supplement the Official History by a Hanlin Scholar*), in *Siku xuxiu*, fasc. 1175, pp. 167–221.

Yang Shiqiao 楊時喬 (1531–1609), *Mazheng ji* 馬政記 (*Record on Horse-raising and Horse-supply Administration*), in *Siku quanshu*, fasc. 663, pp. 503–634.

Yang Yiqing 楊一清 (1454–1530), *Yang Shicong wenji* 楊石淙文集 (*Collected Literary Works of Yang Yiqing, Named After his Birth Place – Shicong*), *MJSWB*, vols. 114–118, pp. 1057–1131.

Ye Chunji 葉春及 (1532–1595), *Shidong ji wenxuan* 石洞集文選 (*Literary Extracts from Ye Chunji's Collected Works, Named Shidong, Where he Studied*), in *Siku quanshu*, fasc. 1286, pp. 229–762.

Ye Mengzhu 業梦珠 (Qing), *Yueshi bian* 閱世编 (*Collected Writings Examining the World*), in *Shanghai zhanggu congshu* 上海掌故叢書 (*Collected Anecdotes of Shanghai*) edited by Chen Tao 陳陶 (1881–1946). (Beijing: Zhonghua shuju, 1935), fasc. 1–10.

Ye Sheng 葉盛 (1420–1474), *Shuidong riji* 水東日記 (*Daily Recorded Notes from East of the Songjiang River*), in *Siku quanshu*, fasc. 1041, pp. 1–230.

Ye Xianggao 葉向高 (1559–1627), *Lun Wenyi jin hecang liangshu* 論文邑禁糴倉糧書 (*On the Prohibtion of Purchasing Grain for Granaries in Wenyi*), *Shihuo dian* 食貨典, *Huangzheng bu* 荒政部, in *Gujin tushu jicheng chubian*, *j.* 101, pp. 83231–83241.

Ye Xianggao 葉向高 (1559–1627), *Cangxia zheng xuji* 蒼霞正續集 (*Continuation of Collected Works of Ye Xianggao, Named After the Village Pavillion of my Hometown, Cangxia*), in *MJSWB*, vol. 461, pp. 5049–5069.

Yin Geng 尹畊 (*jinshi* 1532), *Sai yu* 塞語 (*Words About the Frontier*), in *Siku cunmu* 子, fasc. 31, pp. 45–78.

Yu Bian 俞弁 (Ming), *Shanqiao xiayu* 山樵暇語 (*Leasure Talk by a Firewood-Gatherer-Style Scholar*), in *Siku cunmu* 子, fasc. 152, pp. 1–81.

Yu Ji 虞集 (1272–1348), *Daoyuan ji* 道園集 (*Collected Works of Yu Ji, Hao Daoyuan*), in *Siku cunmu* 集, fasc. 22, pp. 19–413.

Yu Jideng 余繼登 (*jinshi* 1577), *Huang Ming diangu jiwen* 皇明典故紀聞 (*Record of Ming Emperor's Sayings and Deeds as Statutory Precedents*), in *Siku cunmu* 史, fasc. 52, pp. 518–792.

Yu Ruji 俞汝楫 (17th century) *et al.*, *Libu zhigao* 禮部志稿 (*Draft Monograph of the Ministry of Rites Containing Administrative and Ceremonial Regulations, Imperial Edicts, Memorials, etc.*), in *Siku quanshu*, fasc. 597–598.

Yu Shenxing 于慎行 (1545–1607) *Gushan bichen* 穀山筆塵 (*My Undertanding of Ming History from a Mountain Valley at Gucheng*), in *Siku xuxiu*, fasc. 1128, pp. 699–857.

Yuan Zhi 袁袠 (1502–1547), *Shiwei* 世緯 (*Putting the World Back to Order*), in *Siku quanshu*, fasc. 717, pp. 1–25.

Yuan Zhi, *Yuan Yongzhi ji* 袁永之集 (*Collected Works of Yuan Zhi, Zi Yongzhi*), in *MJSWB*, vol. 271, pp. 2860–2865.

Zeng Jiagao 曾嘉誥 (*juren* 1537) and Wang Xin 汪心 (Ming), *Weishi xianzhi* 尉氏縣志 (*Gazetteer of Weishi County*). (Tianyige Library 天一阁藏書, 1548).

Zeng Xian 曾铣 (?–1548), *Zeng Xiangmin gong futao tiaoyi* 曾襄愍公復套條議 (*Ordered Proposals for Regaining the Ordos Region by Zeng Xian, Shihao Xiangmin*), in *MJSWB*, vols. 237–240, pp. 2483–2514.

Zhang Chong 張翀 (*jinshi* 1553), *Zhang dujian zoushu* 張都諫奏疏 (*Personal Memorials of Zhang Chong, the Supervising Secretary*), in *MJSWB*, vol. 292, pp. 3074–3081.

Zhang Dai 张岱 (1597–1667), *Tao'an mengyi* 陶庵夢憶 (*Travel Notes of Zhang Dai, Zi Tao'an*), in *Siku xuxiu*, fasc. 1260, pp. 315–387.

Zhang Han 張瀚 (1511–1593), *Songchuang mengyu* 松窗夢語 (*Collected Works Recalling the Dream-like Old Days at my Window under a Pinetree*), in *Wulin wangzhe yizhu* 武林往哲遺著 (*Surviving Works from Great Men in Hangzhou History*) edited by Ding Bing 丁丙 (1832–1899). (Qiantang: Ding Family, Jiahui Publishing House block-print edition 錢塘丁氏, 嘉惠堂, 1898).

Zhang Junheng 張均衡 (1872–1927), *Huacun tanwang* 花村談往 (*Recalling the Past from Huacun, the Blossom Village*). (Zhang's Block Print in the Shiyuan Collection 張氏刻本適園叢書第十一輯, Part 11, 1912–1949).

Zhang Juzheng 張居正 (1525–1582), *Zhang Wenzhong gongji* 張文忠公集 (*Collected Works of Zhang Juzheng, Shihao Wenzhong*), in *MJSWB*, vols. 324–328, pp. 3450–3521.

Zhang Juzheng, *Xinke Zhang Taiyue wenji* 新刻张太岳文集 (*Newly Printed Collected Literary Works of Zhang Juzheng, Hao Taiyue*), in *Siku xuxiu*, fasc. 1345–1346.

Zhang Ruyu 章如愚 (*jinshi* 1196), *Qunshu kaosuo houji* 群書考索後集 (*Postscript to the Investigation and Scrutiny of Assorted Documents*), in *Siku quanshu*, fasc. 936–938.

Zhang Siwei 張四維 (1526–1585), *Zhang Fengpan ji* 张鳳盤集 (*Collected Works of Zhang Siwei, Hao Fengpan*), in *MJSWB*, vol. 373, pp. 4035–4051.

Zhang Siwei, *Tiaolutang ji* 條麓堂集 (*Collected Works from my Study at the Foot of Tiaoshan Mountain*), in *Siku xuxiu*, fasc. 1351, pp. 221–836.

Zhang Tingyu 張廷玉 (1672–1755) *et. al.*, *Ming shi* 明史 (*History of the Ming Dynasty*), in *Siku quanshu*, fasc. 297–302.

Zhang Wei 張位 (*jinshi* 1568), *Zhang Hongyang wenji* 張洪陽文集 (*Collected Works of Zhang Wei, Hao Hongyang*), in *MJSWB*, vol. 408, pp. 4430–4441.

Zhang Xie 張燮 (1574–1640), *Dongxiyang kao* 東西洋考 (*A Study on the Eastern and Western Oceans*), in *Siku quanshu*, fasc. 594, pp. 137–277.

Zhang Xuan 張萱 (1459–1527), *Xiyuan wenjian lu* 西園聞見錄 (*Record of Things Observed by Zhang Xuan, Hao Xiyuan*). (Cambridge, Mass.: Harvard Yanjing Library edition, 1940).

Zhang Xueyan 張學顏 (?–1598), *Zhang Xinzhai zouyi* 張心齋奏議 (*Memorials for Court Debate by Zhang Xueyan, Hao Xinzhai*), in *MJSWB*, vol. 363, pp. 3906–3923.

Zhang Yanghao 張養浩 (1270–1329), *Guitian leigao* 歸田類稿 (*Assorted Writings in Retirement*), in *Siku quanshu*, fasc. 1192, pp. 471–661.

Zhang Yangmeng 張養蒙 (*jinshi* 1577), *Zhang Yimin ji* 張毅敏集 (*Collected Works of Zhang Yangmeng, Shihao Yimin*), in *MJSWB*, vol. 427, pp. 4661–4673.

Zhao Bingran 趙炳然 (?–1569), *Zhao Gongxiang wenji* 趙恭襄文集 (*Collected Literary Works of Zhao Bingran, Posthumus Title by Gongxiang*), in *MJSWB*, vol. 252, pp. 2644–2699.

Zhao Jishi 趙吉士 (1628–1706), *Jiyuan ji suo ji* 寄園寄所寄 (*Collection of Accumulated Materials from the Jiyuan Garden by Zhao Jishi, Hao Jiyuan*), in *Siku cunmu* 子, fasc. 155, pp. 1–492.

Zhao Yi 趙翼 (1729–1814), *Ershi'er shi zhaji* 二十二史札記 (*Reading Notes on the Twenty-two Dynastic Histories*), in *Siku xuxiu*, fasc. 453, pp. 191–640.

Zheng Lüchun 鄭履淳 (*jinshi* 1562), *Zheng Duanjian gong nianpu* 鄭端簡公年譜 (*A Chronological Biography of Zheng Xiao, Shihao Duanjian*), in *Siku cunmu* 史, fasc. 83, pp. 505–703.

Zheng Luo 鄭洛 (*jinshi* 1556), *Zheng jinglue zoushu* 鄭經略奏疏 (*Personal Memorials from Zheng Luo, the Imperial Commisioner*), in *MJSWB*, vols. 404–405, pp. 4372–4409.

Zheng Ruozeng 鄭若曾 (1503–1570), *Jiangnan jingluo* 江南經略 (*Strategies for Jiangnan*), *in Siku quanshu*, fasc. 728, pp. 1–485.

Zheng Xiao 鄭曉 (1499–1566), *Jinyan* 今言 (*Historical Notes Collection on the Reigning Dynasty*), in *Congshu jicheng chubian*, fasc. 2803–2805.

Zheng Xiao, *Zheng Duanjian gong wenji* 鄭端简公文集 (*Collected Literary Works of Zheng Xiao, Shihao Duanjian)*, in *MJSWB*, vol. 218, pp. 2273–2283.

Zhou Chen 周忱 (1381–1453), *Zhou Wenxiang gong zoushu* 周文襄公奏疏 (*Personal Memorials of Zhou Chen, Shihao Wenxiang*), in *MJSWB*, vol. 22, pp. 170–176.

Zhou Shunchang 周顺昌 (1584–1626), *Zhongjie gong jinyu ji* 忠介公燼餘集 (*The Remains of the Burnt Works of Zhou Shunchang, Shihao Zhongjie*), in *Siku quanshu*, fasc. 1295, pp. 411–438.

Zhou Yi 周怡 (1506–1569), *Nexi zoushu* 訥谿奏疏 (*Personal Memorials of Zhou Yi, Hao Nexi*), in *Siku quanshu*, fasc. 429, pp. 557–586.

Zhu Guozhen 朱国禎 (*jinshi* 1589), *Yongzhuang xiaopin* 涌幢小品 (*Small Essays on Ming Matters*), in *Siku cunmu* 子, fasc. 106, pp. 165–770.

Zhu Guozhen 朱國禎 (*jinshi* 1589), *HuangMing dazheng ji* 皇明大政記 (*Notes on Great Matters of Ming Administration*), *Siku cunmu* 史, fasc. 16, pp. 1–543.

Zhu Wan 朱紈 (1494–1549), *Piyu zaji* 甓餘雜集 (*Ritual of Brick-carrying to Sharpen my Will; Miscellanous Writings to Demonstrate my Zeal*), in *Siku cunmu* 集, fasc. 78.

Zhu Wan, *Zhu Zhongcheng piyu ji* 朱中丞甓餘集 (*Collected Works of Zhu Wan, the Chief Censor*), in *MJSWB*, vols. 205–206, pp. 2155–2177.

Zhu Xi 朱熹 (1130–1200), *Sishu zhangju jizhu* 四書章句集注 (*Annotations on the Four Books in Paragraphs and Sentences*), in *Siku quanshu*, fasc. 197, pp. 1–214.

Zhu Xi, *Zhuzi yulei* 朱子語類 (*Sayings of Zhu Xi*), in *Siku quanshu*, fasc. 700–702.

Zhu Xi, *Er Cheng yishu* 二程遺書 (*Surviving Books by the Cheng Brothers*), in *Siku quanshu*, fasc. 698, pp. 1–279.

Zhu Yuangzhang 朱元璋 (r. 1368–1396), *Huang Ming zuxun* 皇明祖訓 (*Imperially Ming [Zhu Yianzhang's] Ancestral Injunctions*), in *Siku cunmu* 史, fasc. 264, pp. 165–189.

Zhu Yuanzhang, "Dagao xubian 大誥續編" (Imperial Pronouncement, Continued), *Zhaodai wangzhang* 昭代王章 (*The Great Law Code of the Venerated Dynasty*) by Xiong Mingqi 熊鳴岐

(*jinshi* 1607), in *Xuanliantang congshu xuji* 玄覽堂叢書續集. (Nanjing: Guoli zhongyan tushu guan, 1947), fasc. 73–82.

Zhu Yunming 祝允明 (1460–1527), *Huaixingtang quanji* 怀星堂全集 (*Complete Collection of Zhu Yunming, Named After the HuaixingAncestral Hall*), in *Siku quanshu*, fasc. 1260, pp. 363–785.

Zhu Zhe 朱淛 (1486–1552), *Tianma shanfang yigao* 天馬山房遺稿 (*Surviving Works of Zhi Zhe, Named After the Tianmashan Mountain of his Home Town*), in *Siku quanshu*, fasc. 1273, pp. 439–559.

Zou Yinglong 邹應龍 (*jinshi* 1556), *Zou zhongcheng zoushu* 鄒中丞奏疏 (*Personal Memorials of Zou Yinglong, the Grand Coordinator*), in *MJSWB*, vol. 329, pp. 3523–3529.

Secondary Literature

Adshead, Samuel Adrian M., *China in World History*. (New York: St. Martin's Press, 1988).

Braudel, Fernand, *On History*, (London, Weidenfeld and Nicholson, 1980).

Brook, Timothy, *The Confusions of Pleasure: Commerce and Culture in Ming China*. (Berkeley: University of Californai Press, 1998).

Breisach, Ernst. *Historiography: Ancient, Medieval and Modern*. (Chicago, University of Chicago Press, 1983).

Cai Meibiao 蔡美彪, Li Xun 李洵, Nan Bingwen 南炳文, Tang Gang 湯綱, *Zhonguuo tongshi* 中國通史 (*A General History of China*). (Beijing: Renmin chuban she, 1993).

Cai Meibiao 蔡美彪, *Zhonguuo tongshi* 中國通史 (*A General History of China*). (Hongkong: Sanlian Publication, 1995).

Chen Wutong, 陈梧桐, *Zhu Yuanzhang zhuan* 朱元璋傳 (*A Biography of Zhu Yuanzhang*). (Tianjin: Tianjin renmin chubanshe, 1986).

Chen Xuewen 陳學文, "Mingdai haijin yu wokou 明代海禁與倭寇" (*The Maritime Prohibition and Japanese Pirates in the Ming Dynasty*), in Yang Guozhen 楊國禎 (ed.), *Zhongguo shehui jingjishi yanjiu* 中國社會經濟史研究 (*Studies in the Socio-economic History of China*), 1st issue. (Xiamen: Xiamen University Press, 1983), pp. 30–38.

Chen Yan 陳炎, *Haishang sichou zhi lu yu zhongwai wenhua jiaoliu* 海上絲綢之路與中外文化交流 (*The Maritime Silk Route and Cultural Exchanges between China and Forein Countried*), in *Zhongguo yu haishang sichou zhi lu* 中國與海上絲綢之路 (*China and the Oceanic Silk Route*). (Quanzhou: Fujian Publishing House, 1991.

Dardess, John W., *Confucianism and Autocracy: Professional Elites in the Founding of the Ming Dynasty* (Berkeley: University of California Press, 1983).

Dawson, R. *The Chinese Experiences* (London: Weidenfeld and Nicholson, 1978).

Duo Luoken 多洛肯, *Mingdai fujian jinshi yanju* 明代福建進士研究 (*A Study on the Ming jinshi degree holders from Fujian*). (Shanghai: Shanghai cishu chubanshe, 2004).

Elison, George and Smith, Bardwell L., *Japan in the Sixteenth Century*. (Honolulu, University of Hawaii Press, 1981).

Fairbank, John K. & Reischauer, Edwin, O. *China, Tradition and Transformation*. (London: Allen & Unwin, 1989).

Fan Jinmin 范金民, "Mingqing liangdai guan ying si zao ye shengchan guimo de bijiao yanjiu 明清两代官营织造业生产规模的比较研究" (The Comparative Study of the Magnitude of the State Run Silk Manufacturing Industry between the Ming and Qing), *Shilin* 史林 4 (1990), pp. 59–62.

Frank, Andre G., *Reorient: Global Economy in the Asian Age*. (Berkeley: University of California Press, 1998).

Geiss, James "The Chia-ching reign, 1522–1566", in Frederick F. Mote & Denis Twtichett (eds.), *The Cambridge History of China,* Volume 7*: The Ming Dynsaty*, 1368–1633, Part One. (Cambridge: Cambridge University Press, 1988), pp. 403–439.

Gernet, Jacques, *A History of Chinese Civilization.* (Cambridge: Canbridge University Press, 1982).

Gu Cheng 顧誠, "Tan mingdai de weiji 談明代的衛籍" (A Discussion of Garrion Registration in the Ming Dynasty), in *Beijing Normal University Journal* 北京師範大學學報 5 (1989), pp. 56–65.

Hamilton, Earl J., *American Treasure and the Price Revulution in Spain*, 1501–1650. (Cambridge: Cambridge University Press, 1934).

Huang, Ray, *Taxation and Governmental Finance in Sixteenth-Century Ming China.* (Cambridge: Cambridge University Press, 1974).

Hucker, Charles O. (ed.), *Chinese Government Studies in Ming Times.* (New York: Columbia University Press, 1969).

Levack, Brian P., *Witch Hunt in Early Modern Europe.* (London: Longman, 1995).

Li Longqian 李龍潛, *Mingqing jingji shi* 明清經濟史 (*The Economic History of the Ming and Qing*) (Guangzhou: Guangdong Tertiary Eduction Publication, 1988).

Lin Renchuan 林仁川, *Mingmo Qingchu haishang siren maoyi* 明末清初海上私人貿易 (*Private Maritime Trade during the End of the Ming and Beginning of the Qing Dynasties*). (Shanghai: Huadong Shifan daxue chubanshe, 1987).

Lu Wei 蘆葦, "Songdai haiwai maoyi he dongnanya geguo guanxi 宋代海外貿易和東南亞各國關係" (Song Maritime Trade and its Relation with Southeast Asia), in *Haijiaoshi yanjiu* 海交史研究 1 (1985), pp. 12–20.

Lu Wei, *Zhongwei guanxi shi* 中外關係史 (*A history of China's foreign relations*). (Lanzhou: Lanzhou University Press, 1996).

Midelfort, Erik, H.C., "Heartland of the Witch Craze: Central and Northern Europe," *History Today*, No. 31 (1981), pp. 27–36.

Moloughney, Brian and Xia Weizhong, "Silver and the Fall of the Ming: A Reassessment," *Papers on Far Eastern History* 40 (1989), pp. 51–78.

Parry, J. H., "Transport and Trade Routes", in E. E. Rich (ed.), *The Cambridge Economic History of Europe.* (Cambridge: Cambridge University Press, 1941), pp. 155–219.

Peng Xinwei 彭信威, *Zhongguo huobishi* 中國貨幣史 (*A Montary History of China*). (Shanghai: Shanghai renmin chubanshe, 1988).

Polo, Marco, *The Travels of Marco Polo.* (New York: Liveright Publication Corporation, 1953).

Qian Maowei 錢茂偉, G*uojia, keju yu shehui: yi mingdai wei zhongxin de kaocha* 國家，科舉與社會：以明代為中心的考察 (*State, Society and the Civil Examination System: A study foused on the Ming dynasty*). (Beijing: Beijing Library Publication, 2004).

Qian Mu 錢穆 (1895–1990), *Guoshi dagang* 國史大綱 (*An Outline History of China*). (Taibei: Guoli chubanshe, 1977).

Qin Peiheng 秦佩珩, *Mingdai luncong jingji shi chugao* 明代經濟史述論叢稿 (*Explorations in Ming Economic History*). (Zhengzhou: Henan People's Publishing House, 1959).

Quan Hansheng 全漢升 (1913–2001), *Zhongguo jingji shi yanjiu* 中國經濟史研究 (*Studies in Chinese Economic History*). (Taibei: New Asia Institute, 1987).

Quan Hansheng, "MingQing Meizhou de baiyin de shuru Zhongguo 明清美洲白銀的輸入中國" (The Import of American Silver to China during the Ming and Qing Eras), in *Zhongguo Jingjishi luncong* 中国經濟史論叢 (*Expositions on Chinese Economic History*). (Hong Kong: Xinya chubanshe, 1972), pp. 435–350.

Quan Hansheng, *Mingqing jingji shi yanjiu* 明清經濟史研究 (*The Study of Ming and Qing Economic History*). (Taibei: Lianjing Publication House, 1987).

Robinson, James H., *The New History*. (New York: 1913).

Rossabi, Morris, "The Ming and Inner Asia", in Frederick W. Motes and Denis Twitchett (eds.), *The Cambridge History of China*, Volume 8: *The Ming Dynasty*, 1368–1633, Part Two. (Cambridge: Cambridge University Press, 1998), pp. 221–271.

Samson, George, *A History of Japan*, 1615–1867. (Stanford: Stanford University Press, 1963).

Samson, George, *A History of Japan*, 1334–1615. (Stanford: Stanford University Press, 1961).

Schottenhammer, Angela, "The Role of Metals and the Impact of the Introduction of Huizi Paper Notes in Quanzhou on the Development of Maritime Trade in the Song Period", in Angela Schottenhammer (ed.), *The Emporium of the World: Maritime Quanzhou*, 1000–1400. (Leiden, Boston, Köln: E. J. Brill, 2001), pp. 95–176.

Schottenhammer, Angela, *The East Asian Maritime World, 1400-1800. Its Fabrics of Power and Dynamics of Exchanges*. (Wiesbaden: Otto Harrassowitz, 2007).

Stavriaos, L. S., *A Global History: from prehistory to the present*. (Eaglewood: Prentice Hall, Cliffs, N.J. 1991).

Tang Lixing 唐力行, *Shangren yu zhongguo jinshi shehui* 商人與中國近世社會(*Merchants and China's Modern Society*). (Beijing: Commercial Press, 2003).

Terada Takanobu 寺田隆信 *Shanxi Shangren yanjiu* 山西商人研究 (*A Study of Shanxi Merchants*), translated by Zhang Zhengming 張正明, Dao Feng 道丰, Sun Yao 孫燿 and Yan Shoucheng 閻守誠 (Xi'an: Shanxi renmin, 1986).

Tetsuo Kamiki and Kozo Yamamura "Silver mines and Sung Coins – A Monetary History of Medieval and Modern Japan in International perspective," in John F, Richards, ed. *Precious Metals in the Later Medieval and Early Modern World*. (Durham, University of North Carolina Press, 1983).

Tian Changwu 田昌五 *Zhongguo fengjian shehui jingji shi* 中國封建社會經濟 (*The Economic Hisory of Traditional China*). (Jinan: Qilu Wenjin Publication, 1994).

Wang Gungwu, "Ming Foreign Relations: Southeast Asia", in Frederick W. Motes and Denis Twitchett (eds.), *The Cambridge History of China*, Volume 8: *The Ming Dynasty*, 136 8–1633, Part Two. (Cambridge: Cambridge University Press, 1998), pp. 301–332.

Wang Rigen 王日根, "Mingqing keju zhidu dui minying jiaoyu de cujin 明清科舉制度對民營教育的促進" (The Promotion to Private Education by the Civil Examination System during the Ming and Qing eras), *Xiamen University Journal* 廈門大學學報 4 (2001), pp. 98–104.

Wang Youye 王有夜, "Lun Mingchu zi gengnong daliang cinzai ji dui shihui fazhan de yingxiang 论明初自耕农大量存在及对社会发展的影响" (The Impact of the Great Magnitude of Self- Sufficient Farmers on the Early Ming Social Development), *Liaoning Daxue xuebao* 遼寧大學學報 6 (1981), pp. 60–65.

Warwick, Arthur, *The Nature of History*. (London: Macmillan, 1970).

Wills, John F., "Relations with Maritime Europeans," in *The Cambridge History of China*, Volume 8: *The Ming Dynsaty*, 136 8–1633, Part Two. (Cambridge: Cambridge University Press, 1998) , pp. 333–375.

Wu Chengming 吳承明, *Shichang, jindai hua, jingji shilun* 市場, 近代化, 經濟史論 (*Market, Early Modernization, the Economic History*). (Yunnan University Press, 雲南大學出版社, 1996).

Wu Renan 吳仁安, *Mingqing jiangnan wangzu yu shehui jingji wenhua* 明清江南望族明清江南望族與社會經濟文化 (*The Relation between the Ming and Qing Prominent Families from Jiangnan and the Social and Economic Cultures*), (Shanghai: Shanghai Remin Publication House, 2001).

Ye Xianen 葉顯恩, *MingQing huizhou nongcun shehui yu dianpu zhi* 明清徽州農村社會與佃仆制 (*The tenant and servant systems of Huizhou during the Ming and Qing dynasties*). (Hefei: Anhui renmin, 1983).

Yu Siwei 余思偉, "Guangzhou shibo si de lishi yan ge jiqi zai duiwai maoyi zhong de zuoyong he yingxiang 廣州市舶司的歷史沿革及其在對外貿易中的作用和影響" (The Evolution of the Guangzhou Superintedency of Maritime Shipping and its Role and Impact on Foreign Trade), *Haijiaoshi yanjiu* 5 (1983), pp. 71–85.

Zheng Tianting 郑天廷, *Zhongguo lishi da cidian* 中国历史大辞典 (*The Grand Dictionary of Chinese History*). (Shanghai: Shanghai cishu chubanshe, 2000).

INDEX

A

An Guo 安國 (1481–1534), 63
engaged in smuggling, 86
smuggling trade protected by local officials, 125
An Rushan 安如山 (*jinshi* 1529), 86
An Xifan 安希范 (*jinshi* 1586), 86
Analects, 26, 38
Ancestral Injunctions (*Huang Ming zuxun* 皇明祖訓), 4
ancha si 按察司 (Provincial Surveillance Commission), 80
Anta 俺答 (1507–1582), 132, 147, 155, 156
Beijing massacre, 98
horse fair, 112,
to free war captured for trade, 117
trade as a epidemic relief policy, 121
tea-horse trade appeal, 176
arbitrary limitation on trade missions, 111
Ashikaga Yoshimitsu 足利義滿 (1358–1408), 15
Ashikaga Yoshimochi 足利義持 (1386–1408), 15
Ashikaga Yoshiharu 足利義晴 (1511–1550),118

B

baiguan tingyi 百官廷議 (court policy discussions), 101
baihu 百戶 (Company Commander), 37, 163
baojia system 保甲 (the neighbours of anyone who violated the interdiction were to be equally guilty and subjected to the same punishments), 104
Batu Möngke 巴圖蒙克 (d. 1520), 112
beilu nanwo 北虜南倭 (Mongols in the north and Japanese pirates in the south), 4, 97
boyi 博易 (trade fairs), 151
Braudel, Fernand, 19
Brunei, 25, 150
Buddhist, suffering from oppression, 30
Hongwu Emperor as a novice, 23
landholder/ target of land reform, 30
Bushughtu 卜失(石)兔 (1565–1624), 156

C

Cai Jing 蔡京 (1046–1126), 8
Cao Fu 曹傅, 91
Cao Tai 曹泰 (Investigating Censor of Shandong), 32
caoyun system 漕運 (transportation by the military paid for by the taxpayers), 67, 168
Ceylonese, 16
Cha Bingyi 查秉彝 (1504–1561, Supervising Secretary at the Ministry of Revenue), 78
Chama shi 茶馬市 (tea-horse trade), 49, 53,57
Chama si 茶馬司 (Tea and Horse Trading Office),113, 178
Champa, 25, 52
Changde 常德, 12
Chen Jiude 陳九德, (Censor), 105
Chen Tai 陳泰 (*jinshi* 1427, an Investigating Censor), 161
Chen Xuewen 陳學文, 12
Chenghua 成化 reign (1465–1487), 44
chengxinlang 承信郎 (Gentleman of Trust/Master of Ceremonies for Foreign Trade), 8
China-Centred World Order, 150
Chong'an 崇安, 28
Chou Luan 仇鑾 (?–1552), 98
Choufen policy 抽分, (a fee for transportation licences be collected, in kind as a percentage of the total goods at road and river checkpoints), 47
Choufen jiu 抽分局 (Collection Bureau), 47
Chouhai tubian 籌海圖編 (*Illustrated Compendium on Maritime Security*)
on Japanese grievance, 111
Commerce 商
incompatible with Confucianism, 24–26
under suppression, 33–38
incentives, 113
in compulsory price controls, 111
and Confucian ideology, 24
Confucianism, 24, 26, 38, 76, 88, 182
Commercialisation of the Economy, 62–67
corvée, 58
corvée-free, 59
cunliu 存留 (tax collected locally and kept in the region to meet local costs), 162
Currency Control, 42–45

D

Da Ming tongbao 大明通寶 (Great Ming Circulating Currency), 43, 44, 69, 172
Dadu 大都, 6, 12, 23
dan 石 (= 1 hectolitre), 31
Da Ming lü 大明律 (Great Ming Code)
on land nationalization, 28–29
challenged by the Yongle trade policy, 140
Daoist, suffering from oppression, 30
Dashi fanke 大食番客 (a guest from an Arab country), 8
Datong 大同, 68, 109, 112, 119, 129,130, 142, 144, 157
de 德 (morality/virtue/ethics), 110

Ding Yan 丁炎 (a Supervising Secretary), 43
ding 錠 (silver ingot), 6
Dong Fen 董份 (*jinshi* 1541, a Minister of Rites), 60, 63
Dong Zhongshu 董仲舒 (BCE 179–104), 26, 39
dongyi 東夷 (eastern barbarians), 13
dou 斗, 32
Du Luzhen 杜汝禎 (*jinshi* 1538, Supervising Secretary at the Ministry of War), 105
duzhihui 都指揮 (Regional Military Commissioner), 163

E

eban 額辦, 47
Empress Ma 馬皇后, 39
export of copper of the Song, 71
export of silver of the Yuan, 72
external pressure, 97–100

F

Fairbank, J.K, 11
Fang Guozhen 方國珍 (1319–1374), 14
Febvre, Lucien, 18
fen 分 (hundredth of a *tael*), 66
Feng En 馮恩 (*jinshi* 1526, Censor-in-Chief), 160
Feng Qi 馮琦 (*jinshi* 1577, Minister of Personnel), 110
Feng Shike 馮時可 (*jinshi* 1571, Administrative Vice Commissioner of Huguang), 170
Feng Zhang 馮璋 (*jinshi* 1538),
oppose foriegn contact, 106,
on the destructveness of trade with foreigners, 143
Fengyang 鳳陽, 23, 104
Foreign trade, 3, 4,
of the Tang, 7–8
of the Song, 8—9
of the Yuan, 9
and the early Ming socio-economic institutions, 24—48
and collapse of the late Ming institutions, 54—80
Frugality,
as a garantee of maintaining people's social wellbeing, 33
as example set by the imperial family, 39,
as example set by officials, 41–42
incompatible to trade, 42
detrimental to economic growth, 78—79
fu 賦 (land tax), 58
Fujian, 6, 8, 9, 10, 16, 17, 25, 28, 61, 64, 65, 71, 85, 86, 103, 104, 107, 123, 124, 125, 126, 128, 132, 148, 160, 168, 169, 176

G

gangshou 綱首 (leader of a transport mission), 8
Gao Gong 高拱 (*jinshi* 1541, a Grand Secretary),
as a leading member of the pro-trade faction, 103
on Mongls grievance, 108, 109, 154,157
sympathy on coastal 'pirates', 127
on political strategy by trade, 153, 157, 164
criticize dogmatic pro-interdiction literati, 155
GDP,
about the percentage of the maritiem trade revenue in the Southern Song, 5
increase of the Hongwu reign, 32
Geiss, James, 11
gong lan shu zheng 躬覽庶政 (govern the empire diligently and personally), 24
gong 貢 (tribute), 25
gongbo 貢舶
tribute trade, 6
tribute ship, 116
gongshi yin 工食銀 (service allowance), 166
Gu Qingyu 顧青宇, 34
Gu Qiyuan 顧起元 (1565–1628, Vice Minister of Personnel), 79
Gu Yanwu 顧炎武 (1613–1682),
on land centralization 61
on officials's disaccounted income paid in kind, 70
on peasant's lack of silver to pay tax, 72
on peasant's smuggling for survival 125
on *guantian* 官田 (state land), 159
on labour service, 160
on maritime prohibition for causing famine, 169
on merchant's increased role in international politic, 176, 170, 171, 172, 185
guan 貫 (a string of cash/in paper currency), 9, 34, 40, 44, 112, 129
Guan Huaili 管懷理 (*jinshi* 1541, Supervising Secretary of the Ministry of Revenue), 164
Guangdong, 4, 6, 8, 10, 16, 35, 63, 65, 71, 75, 86, 103, 115, 124, 128, 143, 144, 145, 148, 168, 169
Guangzhou, 5, 8, 9, 52, 66, 107, 126, 157
guanjun 官軍 (government troops), 100
guanmai 官買 (government purchase/procurement), 7, 52
guantian 官田 (state land), 28, 159
guiguan daxing 貴官大姓, powerful families with a strong social background, 64
guiji 詭寄 (false registration commendation), 60

H

Haicheng county 海澄, 99

hajin 海禁 (maritime prohibition), 3, 4
Han 漢 dynasty (206 BC–220 AD), 26, 31
Han Wenluo 韓文洛 (1479–1555), 91
Han Wudi 漢武帝 (r. BCE 140–87), 25
Hao Jing 郝敬 (*jinshi* 1589, a Supervising Secretary in the Ministry of Revenue), 172
He Dongxu 何東序 (*jinshi* 1553, Prefect of Huizhou and Grand Coordinator of Yulin), 144
He Liangjun 何良浚 (1506–1573),
  on land discentralization, 31
  complaining of tax surcharge, 60
He Mengchun 何孟春 (1474–1536), 25
He Qiaoyuan 何喬遠 (*jinshi* 1586, Deputy Minister of Works in Nanjing),
  on the Song *boyi* policy, 151,
  about the bellicose Japanese and Mongls, 152
heqin 和親 (marrying a princess to the nomad chieftains), 139
Hezhou 河州, 52
Hongwu Emperor 洪武 (r. 1368–1398)
  on maritime interdiction, 3, 9, 10
  strategy for border security, 11
  politicalvulnerability under Mongol threat, 12
  pressure on Japanese emperor, 13
  on political rivals, 14
  on political stability, 23
  on Confucianism, 24
  on tribute trade, 25
  on *zhongnong yishang zhongnong yishang* 重農抑商 (support for farming and suppression of commerce), 26
  on world order, 27, 48
  on land reform, 27, 28, 45
  on dispossession of the rich, 29
  on dispossession of the privileged, 29–30
  on fish scale policy(*yulin ce* 魚鱗冊) (arable land reclaimed was cut into "fish scale" strips and distributed by the government to peasants on a per capita basis), 33
  on political institutional reform, 36
  on frugality, 39–40, 42
  ban on using silver currency, 43
  ban on tea and horse trade, 50
  on corvee exemption for scholars, 58
  on memorial system, 100-101
  on power of virtue in international politics, 110
Hongzhi 弘治, 32, 69, 73, 113, 121
Hongzhi reign 弘治 (r. 1488–1505), 7, 32
Hu Shining 胡世寧 (*jinshi* 1493, Bureau Director of the Ministry of Justice), 159
Hu Weiyong 胡惟庸 (Prime Minister, 1377–1380), 29
Hu Zongxian 胡宗憲 (*jinshi* 1538, Right Assistant Censor-in-Chief and Supreme Commander in Zhejiang),
  on identifing pirates, 17
  debate for lifting the maritime prohibition, 104, 115, 135, 155
  on the leverage over the Mongols by trade rather than culture, 109
  on tribute trade restrictions, 111
  on Japanese 'pirates' grievance, 118
  on Chinese eager assistance to Japanese pirates, 126, 127, 134
  on timely trade policy change, 139
  on the role of private merchants, 157
hu 胡 (Mongols from the north), 12
hu 斛 (weight unit), 31, 88
Huang Zongxi 黄宗羲 (1610–1695)
  on traditional barter economy, 43
  on literati officials' prejudice against commerce, 79
Huangce 黃冊 (Yellow Registers), 35
Huangchao uprising (*huangchao qiyi* 黄巢起義, 875–883), 5
huipiao 匯票 (a quasi-bank draft), 66
Huizhou 徽州, 62, 66, 86
Hunan, 13
Huo Tao 霍韜 (1487–1540, Minister of Rites), 83

I

Institutions, social and economic
  established in the early Ming, 24–48
  debated and changed in the late of Ming, 57–80
Insurgency, 123–127
Internal Pressure, struggle between political factions, 100–105
investment of merchant in official candidate, 89

J

Japanese piracy, 11, 15, 19, 127, 134, 140, 176, 177, 178
jia 甲 (11 households), 59
jiahao 加耗 (levy was introduced, which involved an extra amount of tax allocated on top of the fixed amount in order to make up for any loss during transportation and storage), 60
Jiajing Emperor 嘉靖 (r. 1522–1567), 34, 83, 87, 100, 101, 124, 159
Jiang Bao 姜寶 (*jinshi* 1553, a Minister of Rites), 115
Jiang Chenying 姜宸英 (1628–1699), 157
Jiangnan, 29, 35, 42, 60, 61, 62, 63, 66, 71
jiang 匠 (artisan), 82

Jianwen reign 建文 (1399-1401), 36
Jiaozhi, 交趾 (in present-day Vietnam), 10, 25
jiapai 加派 (a compulsory surcharge), 159
jiashou 甲首 (head of every ten households), 35
Jiaxing 嘉興, 148, 192
jiazheng 加徵 (a duty payment of 150 *taels* per ship), 173
Jigu ge 汲古閣, 91
Jiliao 薊遼, 170
Jin Xueyan 靳學顏 (*jinshi* 1535, Grand Co-ordinator of Shanxi), 158
jin 斤 (weigh unit), 32
Jing-Hang canal 京杭大運河, 168
JingHang canal 京杭運河, 67
jingtian zhi 井田制, 28
jinhuayin 金花銀 (grain and cloth tax collected in silver), 59
Jinong 濟農 (also 吉囊), 147
jinpai xinfu 金牌信符 (a golden trade permit plate), 52
jinshen 縉紳 (the landed gentry with an official title), 81, 92
jiubian 九邊 (the nine defence regions along the Mongol border), 165
jiuqing 九卿 (the nine government ministers), 101
joint ventures, 90
jun 均 (equality), 26, 177
jun 軍 (military), 82
junji 軍籍 (military occupation), 83
junguan 捐官 (office by purchase), 80

K

Kang Hai 康海 (*jinshi* 1502), 88
kanhe, 勘合 (permission to tribute trade), 15, 52
kebing 客兵 (guest troops transferred from other garrison and paid with cash), 100, 165

L

Land centralization, 57–62
landholding, 28, 29, 30, 33, 34, 45, 57, 58, 60, 62, 72, 73, 77, 89
landlordism, 62
lanmian 濫免 (abuse of the exemption quotas), 60
Lavack, Brian, P, 18
Li Chengxun 李承勳 (*jinshi*, 1493, Deputy Censor-in-Chief and Grand Co-ordinator of Liaodong, 115
Li Chongji 李崇極 (Censor-in-Chief), 103
Li Chunfang 李春芳 (1510–1584, a Grand Secretary), 67, 170
Li Dongyang 李東陽 (1447–1516), 32, 40
Li Hualong 李化龍 (*jinshi* 1574, Assistant Censor-in-Chief and Grand Coordinator of Liaodong, 147
Li Mengyang 李夢陽 (1473–1529), 81, 88
Li Tianchong 李天寵 (*jinshi* 1538, Grand Coordinator of Zhejiang, 105
Li Xian 李顯 (1408–1466), 34
Li Zhi 李贄 (1527–1602), 76, 77, 88
Liang Cai 梁材 (*jinshi* 1505, Minister of Revenue), 113
Lianghuai 兩淮, 81, 83, 84
Liaodong, 12, 71, 115, 129, 147, 157, 164, 169, 170
lijia 里甲-system (unit of 110 households), 35
lijia zhengyi 里甲正役 (the *corvée* and service levy imposed on *lijia* members), 58
Lin Xiyuan 林希元 (*jinshi* 1517, a Director of the Grand Court of Review)
about the Portugueses traders, 116-117, 118, 123
on the impracticality of trade interdiction, 124
on the military's involment with smuggling, 130
lingzhi jihu 領織機戶 (government commissioned silk manufacturers, 74
Liu Tao 劉燾 (*jinshi* 1538, Supreme Commander in Huguang and Grand Coordinator of Fujian),103, 108
lixu 吏胥 (government petty officials who are engaged in money-making matters), 36
lizhang 里長 (the head of a 11-household community), 35
Lo, Jung-pang, 102
Lu Ji 陸楫 (1515–1552)
on the economic unproductiveness of the culture of frugality, 78
luxiang 陸餉 (a duty on cargo), 173

M

Ma Sen 馬森 (1506–1580, Minister of Revenue), on state financial crisis, 99
on difficulty to finance the military, 161
Ma Wensheng 馬文升 (*jinshi* 1451, Vice Censor-in-Chief and Grand Coordinator of Shanxi),
on the power of virtue in foreign politics, 110
on the destructive impact of illicit trade by the military on border security, 131
Ma Ziqiang 馬自強 (*jinshi* 1553), 87
Maidiribala 買的里八剌, 12
make 馬課 (horse tax), 52
manyi 蠻夷, 25
Mao Kun 茅坤 (*jinshi* 1538, Assistant Surveillance Commissioner of Guangxi),
on the unavoidability of war with the Mongols, 114
on the misidentifing of Chinese illicit merchants as Japanese pirates, 125
on the incapability to fight piracy, 134
on justification of social insurgency, 139

maoji 冒籍 (assuming another person's registration in the civil examination), 83
Marco Polo, 6
maritime prohibition, 3, 4, 5, 11, 12, 13, 14, 16, 17, 18, 19, 42, 45, 67, 72, 93, 103, 108, 111, 114, 115, 116, 123, 125, 126, 143, 144, 145, 148, 168, 169, 170, 172, 173, 176, 177, 181
mashi 馬市 (horse trade fairs), 49
memorial system, 100-105
military supply, 69, 70, 71, 167
military's involvement in the illicit trade, 127–131
min 民 (farmer), 82
min 緡 (strings of cash), 6
Ming Shizong shilu 明世宗實錄, 61
mintun 民屯 (organized peasant farming), 67
minyun 民運 (land tax transported to the frontier by the taxpayers themselves), 164
minyun 民運-system, 68
Monopoly system of the state,
of the shipping trade of the Yuan, 9
of manufacturing industry, 46—47
of tea and salt, 47—48
collaspe, 74—75
of state maritime trade, 173
Montaro 門多郎 (Japanese soldier), 148
mu 亩, 28
mubing gongshi yin 民兵工食銀 (surcharge on taxpayers to pay for the accommodation of troops and local militia), 159
mubing 募兵 (mercenary troops), 100, 166

N

Nanjing 南京, 29, 42, 105, 125, 142, 148, 151,
Nanjing *Guozijian* 南京國子監 National University in Nanjing, 88
Neifu ku 内府庫 (The Palace Storehouse), 158
Neige 内閣 (Grand Sectretariat), 101
Ningbo zhi luan 寧波之亂 (Ningbo Incident), 98

O

outflow of copper coins, during Yuan, 71–72

P

Pan Dan 潘旦 (*jinshi* 1505), 86
Pan Huang 潘潢 (*jinshi* 1521), 83, 86
Pan Jian 潘鑒 (*jinshi* 1508), 86
Pan Yu 潘鈺 (*jinshi* 1483, Assistant Surveillance Commissioner of Fujian), 86
Paralysis of the state-run manufacturing industries, 73-75
politically correct clichés, 102
price control system, 113
Putuoshan 普陀山, 10

Q

Qi Jiguang 戚繼光 (1528–1587, Commander-in-Chief of Fujian), on the weakness of the Ming military vis-a-vis the Mongols, 132
Qian Wei 錢薇 (*jinshi* 1532, Supervising Secretary in the Ministry of Rites)
on the inevitability of illicit trade, 111
on Japan's dependence on China trade, 114, 120, 122
on Japan's grievance, 122
on Japan in China's maritime trade history, 133
on a fair foreign trade system, 157
Qin dynasty 秦 (BCE 246 to 206), 23, 28
Qin Shihuang 秦始皇 (259–210 B.C.), 23, 76
qing 頃 (area unit), 30
Qiu Jun 丘濬 (1418–1495), on the unprofitability of the tribute trade, 7
qiyun yin 起運銀 (land tax converted to silver and designated for the capital), 162
Qu Dajun 屈大均 (1630–1696),
on late Ming trade craze, 35
on the late Ming magnitude of private manufacturings, 75
Quanzhou 泉州, 52, 66, 92, 123
Qubilai Qan, 6, 9, 23

R

ren 仁 (humanity or humaneness), 24
Robinson, James Harvey, 19
rong 戎 (peoples from the west), 12
Rossabi, Morris, 49, 98, 117
Ryūkyū 琉球, 10, 35, 52, 66, 113, 152

S

san fasi 三法司 (the Ministry of Justice, the Censorate and the Court of Judicial Review), 105
Sanbian garrisons 三邊, 156
Sanwei 三衛: i.e. Duoyan 垜顏, Fuyu 福餘 and Taining 泰宁, 141
se 瑟 (harp), 139
self-sufficiency, economic, 45–48
semu ren 色目人 (Central and Western Asians), 57
Shandong, 4, 16, 30, 32, 43, 65, 68, 72, 126, 165, 169, 170
Shang Yang bianfa 商秧變法 (Shang Yang reforms), 28
shang 賞 (reward), 52
shangji 商籍 (merchant registration), 82
Shen Defu 沈德符 (1578–1642), 169
shengyuan 生員 (government students), 59, 162

Shenzong 神宗, Song Emperor (r. 1067–1085), 6, 25,
Shenzong 神宗, Ming Emperor (r. 1573–1619), 178
shi 食 (foodstuffs), 40
shibo (maritime tribute trade), 10, 49, 52, 57
Shigu zhai 師古齋 (publication house), 91
shi-nong-gong-shang ideology 士農工商 (scholar, peasant, artisan and merchant), 35
Shirō 四郎 (Japanese soldier), 148
shizhou sandao 十州三岛 (reference to paradise), 154
Shou'an zhenguo zhi shan 壽安鎮國之山 (Mountain that fortifies the kingdom), 150
shuixiang 水餉 (tax on ship size), 173
Silver,
  export of the Yuan, 6,
  increased value in the late Ming, 42, 44, 62,
  increased intrinsic value in the world market, 44, 72,
  banned from circulation, 43,
  threat to political stability, 44–45
  land tax converted, 59–60
  as a primary money, 66
  poor minings of the Ming, 71, 72
  scarcity and official's pay, 128–129
  rich deposit in Japan, 72
  attraction for foreign trade, 111
  import by trade, 172–174
  silver commander, 88
Sima Qian 司馬遷 (BC 145–c. 86), 26, 33
Singhalese, 16
sishu wujing 四書五經 (Four Books and Five Classics), 24
Social injustice,
  and insurgency, 123–127
  caused by exploitation, 179
social power of merchants, 92
Social status,
  from corvee exemption, 58
  lowered for scholars against economic commercialization, 77
  protected by degree and official's title, 81–82
  increased for merchants, 90, 91
Song Ne 宋訥 (1311–1390), 24
Song Xiaozong (r. 1163–1189), 10
Songjiang 松江, 24, 34, 42, 59, 81, 148, 160, 162
Southern Song 南宋, 5, 151
sufeng 素封 (princely status in wealth), 85
Sun Yingkui 孫應奎 (*jinshi* 1521, Minister of Revenue), 158
Su You 蘇祐 (1492–1571, Surveillance Commissioner for Xuanfu and Datong, and Minister of War), 143, 155
Suzhou 蘇州, 30, 60, 65, 74, 91, 124, 129, 131, 146, 162

T

Taicang 太倉 (Imperial Granaries, National Silver Vault for the administration of the capital) 99, 158, 161, 165
Tan Lun 譚倫 (*jinshi* 1544, Vice Commissioner in charge of Coastal Military Defence, Supreme Commander of Jiliao and Minister of War) piracy cuased by trade interdiction, 124
on *wuwei er zhizhi* (control without control), 155,
revenue exhausted to maintain maritime prohibition, 162
cause of possiblee rebellion, 169
Tang dynasty 唐, 5, 154
Tang Shu 唐樞 (*jinshi* 1526, Bureau Director at the Ministry of Justice),
  on "pirates and traders are the same people", 17
  on the failure of restricted tribute trade, 111
  geographical advantage for Japanese traders, 114
  mass participation of piracy, 124, 145
  the military's sympathy for the 'pirates'127
  on government's military vulnerability, 133
  open violation of trade prohibition leads to peace, 141, 146, 149
  pirates can be counted on, 148
  the profitability of maritime trade, 168
Tang Shunzhi 唐順之 (*jinshi* 1529)
  military weakness vis-a-vis pirates, 49
  land tax silver conversion, 69
  merchants' critical role in military supply, 71
  unaffordability of maintaining trade prohibition, 100, 127, 128, 166
  as a member of pro-trade faction, 103–104
  trade pacify pirates, 118, 169
  interdiction policy leads to social rebellion, 131
  the collapse of the *tuntian* system, 164
  trade relieves financial crisis, 167
Taizong 太宗 (r. 627–650), 7
Taozhou 洮州, 52, 113
tax reform, 67–73
Tian Qianqiu 田千秋 (BCE ? –77), 25
tianchao shangguo. 天朝上國 (the heavenly endorsed empire), 25, 106, 107
tianli 天理, 76
Tianshun 天順 reign (1458–1464), 113, 140
tianzi,天子 (Son of Heaven) 25
tibian 題編 (advanced assessment), 159, 160
Toghōn Temür 妥權貼睦爾 (r. 1333–1368) (r. 1333–1368), 23

tongzhi jingji 統治經濟 (literally, a command economy), 177
Toyotomo Hideyoshi 豊臣秀吉 (1536–1598), 72
trade diminishes conflict, 141-146
tributary mission, 7, 111
tribute trade, see (*gongbo* 貢舶), 6, 110
Tsushima Strait 對馬 (基岐), 150
Tu Zemin 涂澤民 (Censor-in-Chief in charge of military affairs)
on desperation to curb piracy, 134
memorial on lifting the maritime trade prohibition, 178
Tu Zhonglu 屠仲律 (*jinshi* 1550), 125
tudi geming,土地革命 (land revolution), 27
tugong 土貢 (local products tributed from each county to the court on an annual basis), 47
Tumu zhibian 土木之變 (Tumu debacle), 98
tuntain 屯田-system (military colonies), 67

W

Wan Biao 萬表(*jinshi* 1520, Assistant Commander of Ningbo garrison and Vice Secretary in the Central Military Commission in Nanjing), 125, 127, 130, 146
Wang Anshi 王安石 (1021–1086), 25
Wang Chonggu 王崇古 (*jinshi* 1541, Supreme Commander of the three defence regions of Shaanxi, Yanning and Gansu),
as a member of a merchant related family nextwork, 87
on Mongols high demand of Chinese products, 116, 120
Mongols grievance out of trade prohibition, 121
on the low morale in fighting but high spirit in trading with the Mongols, 130
Mongols as a tough opponent in war, 132
trade instead of war policy, 143
on suspected Mongols weaponery upgrading from trade with China , 144
political leverage over the Mongols by trade, 152
advocator of lifting trade prohibition in court debate, 167, 178
economic benefit from trade with the Mongols, 171
Wang Daokun 汪道昆 (*jinshi* 1547), 83, 84, 87, 90
Wang Gungwu, 11, 12
Wang Shixing 王士性 (1546–1598, Supervising Secretary in the Ministry of Rites), 79
Wang Shizhen 王世貞 (*jinshi* 1547),
on silver as the best currency, 42
from a merchant background, 87, 89
on vulnerability of national security, 98
on scholar officials' unpractical mentality, 102
pirate and merchant are one prople, 116
on Mongol's and Japanese commercial rather than territorial interests, 117, 120
as a champion of lifting trade prohibition, 140, 151
financial crisis caused by preventable war, 162
Wang Shuying 王叔英 (Hanlin compiler 1387), 35
Wang Tingxiang 王廷相 (*jinshi* 1502, Minister of War), 113, 120
Wang Yangming 王陽明 (1472–1529), 76
Wang Yu 王忬 (*jinshi* 1541), 170
Wang Yuanmei 王元美 (who served as an Assistant Minister of War during the Jiajing reign and whose father was a Chief Censor of the Surveillance Office), 60
Wang Zaijin 王在晋 (*jinshi* 1592), 93, 126, 127, 154, 169
Wang Zhi 王直, 17, 63, 117, 125, 130, 148, 149
Wei Shaoshi 魏昭士 (1628–1693), 78
wei 威 (force), 110
Wenzong 文宗, Tang Emperor (r. 827–835), 7
Wenzong 文宗, Yuan Emperor (r. 1328–1329), 9
Weng Wanda 翁萬達 (*jinshi* 1526, Right Assistant Censor-in-Chief and Supreme Commander of Xuanfu, Datong, Shanxi and Baoding),
on Mongol's war aim, 119
on trade prohibition results in war and suffering for the people, 152
Wills, John, 11
Wu Guifang 吳桂芳(*jinshi* 1544, a Magistrate of Yangzhou 揚州 and a Deputy Minister of War, 122
Wu Ji 吳季, 92
Wu Shilai 吳使來 (*jinshi* 1553, a supervising secretary of the Ministry of Justice), 130
Wu Yi 吳義 (county magistrate of Zhenghe 政和), 32
Wu zazu 五雜俎 (*Fire Mixed Platters*), 28
wuwei er zhizhi 無為而治之 (control without control), 155
Wuzong 武宗, Ming Emperor (r. 1506–1521), 25

X

Xizong 僖宗, Tang Emperor (r. 874–888), 5
Xia Yan 夏言(*jinshi* 1517, Senior Grand Secretary), 104
Xialin daying 夏林大盈 (State Warehouse), 154
xiangshi 鄉試 (provincial civil examination), 83
xiangyin 鄉飲 (a cumminitiy's ritual ceremony), 58
Xianzong 憲宗 Emperor, Ming Emperor (r. 1466–1486), 113
xiaqiu liangshui 夏秋兩稅 (summer and autumn land taxes), 5
Xie Zhaozhe 謝肇浙 (1567–1642), 28, 68

xing 行 (transport), 41
Xining 西寧, 52
xinwai wuwu, xinwai wushi 心外無物, 心外無事 (there is nothing beyond our heart and nothing beyond our senses), 76
xiucai 秀才 (Cultivated Talent), 162
Xu Er 許二, 125
Xu Fuyuan 許孚遠 (1535–1604, the Grand Coordinator of Fujian)
  on trade prohibition and social grievance, 125
  refutes the allegation that trade with Japan will increase its arsenal, 145
  on lucrative financial return from trade, 168
Xu Guangqi 徐光啟 (*jinshi* 1604, Minister of Rites), 103
Xu Wenbi 徐文壁 (Duke of Dingguo 定国公), 103
Xu Yanyang 徐晏陽 (*jinshi* 1574), 86
Xu Zhi 徐陟 (*jinshi* 1547), 86
Xu Zongkui 徐宗夔 (a Regional Inspector), 105
Xuanfu 宣府, 68, 104
xun'an yushi 巡按禦史 (Touring Censor), 80

Y

Yan Song 嚴嵩 (*jinshi* 1505, a Senior Grand Secretary for 20 years), 87
Yang Jisheng 楊繼勝 (1516–1555)
  trading with barbarians tarnish the heavenly ordained empire, 102, 107
Yang Shouchen 楊守陳 (*jinshi* 1451, Minister of Personnel), 154
Yang Wei 楊巍 (1514–1605, Minster of Revenue), 79
Yang Yuanxiang 楊元祥 (*jinshi* 1583, Compiler and Examiner), 165
Yangzhou 揚州, 13, 87, 99, 122, 134
Yanzhou 兗州, 64
yaoyi 徭役" liability (service levy), 58
Ye Tang 葉鏜 (*jinshi* 1541, Supervising Secretary at the Ministry of War), 104
yeyin 業银 (commercial fees), 173
yi shi zhu xing 衣食住行 (basic categories of life), 40
yi 衣 (clothing), 40
Yingzong 英宗, Ming Emperor (r. 1436–1449), 98
yinshui 引稅 (the licence fee), 173
Yongle 永樂, Ming Emperor (r. 1403–1424),
  it is shameful to make tribute trade profitable 7
  relax tribute trade prohibition with the *Kanhe* system, 15
  dispossess land of the rich and relocate them to cities, 29
  set example in frugal life style, 39
  establish trade fairs for the Mongols and trade with them with exceptional facourable conditions, 140
  the Ming power over Japan reached a new high, 141
Yongxi 雍熙, Song reign period (984–987), 8
Yosuke 四助 (Japanese soldier), 148
Yu Xizhi 魚希直 (magistrate of Kaifeng 開封), 32
Yuan dynasty (1206–1368), 6, 9, 23, 26, 27, 28, 30, 32, 57, 72, 170
Yuan Zhi 袁袠 (1502–1547), 135, 162, 163, 194
yuanxing dingyin 遠行丁引 (permit for long distance travel), 37
yulin 魚鱗 (fish scale), 30
Yutailing 虞臺嶺, 152
Yu Cong 於琮 (?–881, Prime Minister at the court of Tang Xizong 唐僖宗 (r. 874–888)), 5

Z

zaban 雜辦 (unfixed amount of taxes in local produce demanded randomly according to circumstances), 47
zafan 雜泛 (miscellaneous service levies), 58
Zeng Xian 曾銑 (*jinshi* 1529, Supreme Commander of the three defence regions in Shanxi), 104, 106
Zhang Chong 張翀 (*jinshi* 1553, a Bureau Secretary in the Ministry of Justice during the Jiajing reign, and Deputy Minister in the Ministry of Justice during the Longqing reign), 107
張瀚 (1511–1593, Vice Censor in Chief), 173
Zhang Jing 張經 (*jinshi* 1517, Minister of War and Censor-in-Chief), 103, 105
Zhang Juzheng 張居正 (1525–1582, Senior Grand Secretary),
  emphasizes the principal role of commerce in economy, 79
  accentuates the vital role of foreign trade in national security, 158
  opposes tax increase to relieve financial difficulties, 161
  backs trade rather than war to pacify enemy to avoid military overspending , 165
Zhang Luo 張羅 (Deputy Minister of Personnel), 103
Zhang Rong 張溶, 英國公 (Duke of Yingguo), 103
Zhang Shiche 張時徹 (*jinshi* 1523, Minister of War in Nanjin), 142
Zhang Shicheng, 14
Zhang Shouzhi 張守直 (Minister of Revenue), 103
Zhang Siwei 張四維 (*jinshi* 1553), 87

Zhang Wei 張位 (*jinshi* 1568, Minister of Personnel and a Grand Secretary), 109
Zhao Shixun 趙世勛 (*jinshi* 1571, Supervising Secretary in the Ministry of War), 74
Zhao Wenhua 趙文華 (*jinshi* 1529, Minister of Works), 104
zhaoshang maiban 召商買辦 (government purchase from private merchants), 74
Zhaozong emperor 元昭宗 (r. 1371–1378), 12
Zheng He 鄭和 (1375–1435), 7, 15, 16, 151
Zheng Xiao 鄭曉 (*jinshi* 1523, minister of Justice and acting minister of War), 4, 16, 41, 116, 167, 168, 195
Zhengde reign 正德 (1507–1520), 59
zhezhi 折支(payment commuted in paper notes or other items rather than in foodstuffs or cloth), 31
zhihui 指挥(commander), 163
zhongjun dudu fu 中軍都督府 (Chief Military Commission), 101
zhongnong yimo 重農抑末 (emphasising agriculture, the principal, while suppressing commerce, the marginal), 35
zhongnong yishang 重農抑商 (support for farming and suppression of commerce), 26, 36, 178
zhongshu sheng 中書省 (the prime minister's office), 36
Zhongtong baochao 中統寶鈔 (Yuan paper currency), 6
Zhou Chen 周忱 (1381–1453, Grand Coordinator of Jiangnan), 41,
Zhu Fu 褚鈇 (*jinshi* 1565), 156
Zhu Heng 朱衡 (Minister of Works), 103
Zhu Wan 朱紈 (*jinshi* 1521, Supreme Commander of the coastguard in Zhejiang and Fujian, and Grand Coordinator of Zhejiang),
as a main adversary of maritime merchant, 64, 127
accuses the powerful families of engaging in illicit trade, 64, 129
exposes officials as smuggler's collaborators, 102
lobbied against and condemned by the pro-trade faction, 104, 122
on prejudice-based foreign policy orientation, 107
avow capital punishment for those who violate the trade prohibition, 108
Zhu Xi 朱熹 (1130–1200), 26, 38, 195
Zhu Yuanzhang 朱元璋 (r. 1368–1395), 10, 12, 14, 23, 24
Zhu Yunming 祝允明 (1461–1527), 37
zhu 住 (housing), 41
zuopai haifang-yin 坐派海防銀 (a compulsory surcharge for emergencies in coastal defence), 160
zuzong chengfa 祖宗成法 (established practices of the ancestors), 4

FSC
www.fsc.org
MIX
Papier | Fördert gute Waldnutzung
FSC® C083411

Kolibri 360 GmbH
Ferdinand-Jühlke-Straße 7
99095 Erfurt, Deutschland
produktsicherheit@kolibri360.de